GROUP PROCEDURES: PURPOSES, PROCESSES, AND OUTCOMES

HOUGHTON MIFFLIN COMPANY
BOSTON

New York
Atlanta
Geneva, Illinois
Dallas
Palo Alto

GROUP PROCEDURES: PURPOSES, PROCESSES, AND OUTCOMES

Selected Readings for the Counselor

Edited by

RICHARD C. DIEDRICH
Rohrer, Hibler & Replogle, Boston

and

H. ALLAN DYE
Purdue University

Printed in the U.S.A.

Library of Congress Catalog Card Number: 71–176374

ISBN: 0–395–04364–6

Foreword

The use of groups to increase self-understanding and to improve the quality of interpersonal relationships is a sweeping social movement affecting psychology, medicine, education, social work, even business and industrial leadership. Not only is the group movement popular and extensive, it is also highly polarized. In any discussion of the use of groups—encounter groups, group counseling, sensitivity training, group psychotherapy—its defenders and its detractors are quickly identified. Few are neutral in their opinion of the group movement —chiefly those who are unfamiliar with it! It may be significant that individuals who praise the use of groups for the release of feelings and for a greater sense of personal reality are likely to be those who have experienced such groups, while the critics are likely to be those who have had no such personal experience. (They "wouldn't be caught dead in a group.")

Some critics, to be sure, are persons who have had bad experiences in a group, often because of poor leadership. Having been hurt by the experience, they shy away from any further group contact, as the once-burned cat avoids all stoves whether they are hot or cold. I would hazard a guess, however, that the great majority of persons familiar with group experiences view its benefits as greater than its liabilities. Carl Rogers, for instance, whose life is now dedicated to encounter group research and practice, believes that the group movement represents a major therapeutic step forward.

Work with groups has a long and honorable history in the field of social work. Then, historically, came the enormously innovative thinking of Kurt Lewin, and group dynamics was born. This use of groups was research-oriented, analytical, and specific in its findings. After World War II the practice of group psychotherapy came into widespread use in hospitals. The NTL Institute, which conducts programs at Bethel, Maine, and at regional laboratories throughout the country, has made sensitivity training a household word. Esalen, located in Big Sur, California, has become famous for its Gestalt therapy and sometimes "far-out" encounter groups.

Finally, group counseling emerged in schools and colleges. The mainstay of the school's instructional efforts, of course, has always been learning in groups. Group counseling is different, however, in both purpose and procedure. The purpose of group counseling is to learn about oneself, and the procedure is to involve other members of the group in the learning achievement. Some "group guidance classes" of earlier years had done this also, although much of group guidance differed but slightly from traditional classroom learning.

In group counseling, feelings become as important as cognition, often more so. The purpose is to help each participant express his feelings without fear, feelings about others as well as about himself. This involves some risk. Sometimes feelings get out of control and become too severely punishing to handle—without help. The leadership of a group is all-important. Some encounter groups and marathon groups (lasting 24 hours or a full weekend) in colleges or in community situations have proved very damaging to an individual in the group. The cause most often was the leader, who was too unskilled to sense the damage and to help contain it or repair it.

The readings of this book cover the several dimensions of the group phenomenon: purpose and process, leadership and membership, evaluation and ethics. The articles were selected from a very extensive literature, both professional and popular. Reading the selections as a group under each heading should do much to simplify understanding of a particular dimension of the group experience, even though the group process as a whole is far from simple.

The editors have their own rationale for their sequence of topics, but I would like to make a personal suggestion: After reading the selections under "Purposes: An Overview" go directly to the last section on "Ethics." So important are the issues in determining what is professionally and personally ethical that I would hope you could have these questions in mind as you read about processes and applications. Often, in group counseling, the interaction of group members with each other may release strong but hitherto repressed feelings. On the other hand, group counseling opens up delightful vistas, as a person senses that "I am real after all," and "people like me *as I am*"—new feelings which may need reinforcement to be accepted. Care is needed when feelings come to the surface. Group experiences can represent some of the most significant experiences in one's life, and yet in too many instances the facilitator (or leader) is not sensitive enough to offer help where it is most needed. There is an ethics of *counselor competence* as well as the ethics of client-counselor relationships. With respect to the latter, what happens, for example, to confidences expressed within the confines of a group;

is every member of the group expected to respond to a sense of professional ethics that is similar to that of the leader? How does the group leader handle the expression of a feeling that is of great personal significance to a person—are all members of the group to take an oath of confidentiality? Or should the group be warned at the outset that confidences cannot be guaranteed, and that each person is solely responsible for himself? Either of these approaches will certainly tend to inhibit group progress, although they are honest and straightforward. If these approaches are not satisfactory, then what guidelines should be followed by the group leader?

The American Psychological Association has a committee at work on an updated version of its present set of "Ethical Standards." One of the major areas of consideration is the recent burgeoning of counseling and therapy through groups. The issues raised by the seven writers in the last section of this book undoubtedly are being carefully studied by the APA ethics revision committee.

Group counseling—encounter, sensitivity, what have you—presents a significant set of opportunities for helping people become more *real*. I hope you will be excited, as I am, by what Diedrich and Dye have given us to read. It may open a new chapter in your life. It may teach you how to share yourself. It may make more transparent what is now opaque with regard to yourself and others.

C. Gilbert Wrenn

Preface

This book of readings represents a cross section of current thinking as to "what's happening" with groups. Although not an exhaustive survey of the field, the book includes both practical and theoretical selections from the social and behavioral sciences. The collection of readings has been prepared primarily for introductory courses in group procedures—group counseling, dynamics, or therapy—which may use the book either as supplementary material or as the basic text. Because of the wide range of topics and settings represented in the selections, the book may also be useful in intermediate and advanced courses concerning groups and group processes.

The majority of these readings have appeared since 1965; twenty-one of the forty selections were published during 1968 to 1971. Only useful and readable articles have been included, rather than philosophical or highly complex essays. Some of the selections are conceptual, while others deal with procedures or describe research. In spite of the range of disciplines and the variety of settings represented, the "common thread" of all the readings is a phenomenon or procedure which might be found in any group. Variety alone was not a selection criterion; rather, we feel it necessary for the student to examine many fields and approaches in order to develop a true understanding of the counselor's role in group processes.

The forty readings are organized to represent the major focuses of the field: purposes, processes, applications, outcomes, and ethical issues. Sixteen of the selections come from *Personnel and Guidance Journal, School Counselor,* or *Journal of Counseling Psychology.* The remaining selections are drawn largely from other major journals. In all, a total of thirteen journals is represented in the book. Three selections are being published for the first time. Readings from two books, one monograph, and two nationally popular magazines also are included. All levels of education and several noneducational settings are represented. Many of the selections are from sources which would not ordinarily be readily available to the counselors and students for whom this book is designed.

The major credit for this book belongs to the authors of the original articles. As the editors, we are grateful to each author and publisher for granting permission to reprint the selections. We express deep appreciation to Bruce Shertzer and Shelley Stone for providing the impetus and the constant encouragement which made it possible to prepare this collection. We also thank our production editor, Evelyn LaBan, and three other colleagues—Robert Conyne, Harold Hackney, and Gerald Osborne—for their contributions. The many graduate students who have participated in our group courses and group encounters deserve special thanks as a never-ending source of new ideas about groups and ourselves. Finally, the assistance provided by Diana Booher, Judy Floyd, Margie Sorrentino, and Judy Whaley was invaluable.

Richard C. Diedrich

H. Allan Dye

Contents

Part One

PURPOSES:
AN OVERVIEW
OF CONCEPTS
AND PROCEDURES

Perhaps people are coming together in small groups to escape feelings of emptiness so common in an increasingly technological and dehumanizing society. In group encounters people talk about their concerns and problems in an attempt to discover new ways of thinking, feeling, doing, or simply being, which will make life better for them in some way. Beyond this common but broadly defined motive there is great variation in the purpose, setting, and method employed in group work.

The "group phenomenon," or group movement, has occurred within a relatively short period of time. Both theory and practice have changed and evolved rapidly. Our initial objective in Part One is to illustrate the breadth of the field by presenting articles we think represent the best literature devoted to group work in education, psychology, and human relations training. The development of group procedures in the school setting is traced through descriptions of concepts and procedures which have been used for several

1

years. To illustrate the current status of group work in education we have included examples of contemporary thinking and practice.

A variety of contemporary applications of the group experience are described in "The Group: Joy on Thursday." This *Newsweek* article (1969) is a good introduction because it accurately describes the impact of the group phenomenon on life in America—without the sensationalism often evident in lay publications. Both the excitement and viability of this new human experience are documented as the article explains how group procedures have gone beyond the domains of professional educators and psychologists to become an important dimension of contemporary society.

In Part One we have attempted to document our belief that the popularity of the group experience in today's society is a function of the discovery and development of experiential learning about subjective phenomena—feelings, behavioral styles, motivation, and interpersonal relationships.

The use of group methods by counselors to achieve a variety of goals—increased personal awareness, improved interpersonal relations, educational and vocational counseling—has increased during the past two decades. In the late 1950's and early 1960's the literature devoted to group guidance and group counseling was largely cognitive and stylistic. The emphasis was on trait-centered learning about oneself and others in relation to a common topic, problem, or task. Success depended heavily on the counselor's skill in group composition and in the use of democratic leadership techniques. In comparison with counseling and personnel programs today, relatively little was known of group methods, and very few counselor training programs offered more than an elective, didactic course prior to the mid-1960's. An especially valuable contribution to the literature during this time was Thelen's brief article, "Purpose and Process in Groups" (1963), which calls attention to the crucial dimension of process in the group experience and provides a useful criterion for distinguishing between types of groups.

The use of group experiences to discover persons who might be in need of individual counseling has been cited by some authors as a justification for group work. Gradually the idea has gained popularity that a successful group experience is a valuable end in itself —that several necessary and desirable conditions for counseling are inherent in the group setting. Recent illustrations of this use of group procedures are included in the articles by Anderson and Johnson, "Using Group Procedures to Improve Human Relations in the School Social System" (1968), and Kinnick, "Group Discussion and Group Counseling Applied to Student Problem Solving" (1968).

Anderson and Johnson describe a new concept and purpose in the field: the improvement of human relations in the school. Their article appeared at a time when the need in our society for improved relationships between people of different races, generations, and professional groups was reaching crisis proportions. It was becoming clear that group methods are relevant in responding to this issue within the unique social system of the school.

The article by Kinnick deserves merit on three counts. First, it is a careful re-examination of the cognitive, topic-oriented group work of the preceding decade. The author substantiates his contention that this type of group experience can be useful, though less compelling, than a group which focuses on emotional processes. Second, a contemporary view of the differences between task groups and process groups is provided. Finally, the role of the counselor in each of these similar yet quite different types of groups is well articulated.

The articles by Thelen, Anderson and Johnson, and Kinnick were selected to give the reader a brief perspective of the purposes for which counselors have used group procedures in the past and in recent years. Eddy and Lubin, in "Laboratory Training and Encounter Groups" (1971), review developments and concepts in the field of small group training. They provide a brief historical perspective on group training and supply working definitions for some of the more frequently mentioned types of small groups—T-group, encounter group, marathon, and therapy group. The authors also introduce the reader to some of the research dealing with the effects of group training as well as professional and ethical issues.

A significant source of currently popular group methodology and theory is the NTL Institute for Applied Behavioral Science—the first and perhaps the largest organization devoted to sensitivity and human relations training. In our contacts with graduate students in education and psychology, practicing counselors, and trainers of counselors, we have observed that the emphasis of the NTL Institute on self, interpersonal awareness, process, and "here-and-now" learning is highly compatible with counseling theory and practice. In one of NTL's publications, "What is Sensitivity Training?" (1968), Seashore describes the assumptions, goals, and outcomes of sensitivity training—broadly defined—and enumerates the characteristics of the basic component, the T-group.

Osborne, Diedrich, and Dye's article "On Being in a Group: Another Step in Becoming" (1969), presenting a woman's account of her experience as a group member, concludes Part One's overview of concepts and purposes in group counseling.

Part One offers a contemporary view of several ways in which group techniques are applied by counselors. The scope and length of the book limits the variety of concepts and procedures which could be included. The selections represent our judgment of what is most relevant to the training of school and college counselors who wish to work with groups. We have attempted to avoid emphasizing any particular theory or methodology by presenting a variety of approaches.

Some of the doubt and confusion evident in virtually all thought and practice pertaining to groups is also present here. It is our hope that the following pages will assist the reader in knowing why people come together in groups and what happens once they get there. The nature of the readings should encourage the novice as well as the experienced counselor to identify specific questions and issues in group procedures, and to weigh carefully some of the current generalizations about groups. Essentially, these selections set the stage for additional study, training, and practice in the area of group procedures.

1/ THE GROUP:
JOY ON THURSDAY

"All right," bellowed the baldish, bearded leader to some 200 men and women sitting cross-legged and shoeless on the wooden floor. "Let's everybody begin by screaming as long and as loud as possible." A wild, raggedy, piercing shriek rose from the crowd. When it subsided, the participants dispersed into smaller groups, where they arm wrestled, fell backward into each other's arms, occasionally hugged each other warmly and kept pouring out to whoever was in earshot the most intimate emotions. By the end of the three-hour session, the participants were euphoric; one matronly woman wept softly. "Why can't it always be like this?" she asked.

Bedlam? Bellevue Hospital? No, just the auditorium of San Francisco's First Unitarian Church where 200 middle-class participants had paid $5 each for a one-night introduction to an encounter group—a relatively leaderless, structureless, agendaless "be-in" intended to express human feelings and to cultivate close emotional ties between people. The San Franciscans had come for a variety of reasons; some were just curious, others were looking for a short cut out of an increasingly urban, technologically complex, bureaucratic society and others were lonely and isolated. Whatever their motives, they are all part of the so-called human-potentiality (or sensitivity-training) movement that is involving Americans in their biggest emotional binge since V-J Day. "These groups are the most rapidly spreading social phenomenon in the country," observes psychologist Carl R. Rogers approvingly. "They are helping break through the alienation and dehumanization of our culture." But some behaviorists worry that the human-potentiality movement is faddism at best and just plain psychological dynamite at worst. "Encounter groups are like a new religious cult," complains Berkeley psychologist Edward Sampson. "They have uniforms and ceremonies and cult leaders. It's a religion in the worst sense: you do it on Sunday and then forget it for the rest of the week."

Growth

Encounter groups come in a wide variety of shapes and sizes. There are weekly four-hour "microlabs" involving as many as 100 people, weekend marathons of almost continuous emotional involvement for groups of fifteen people, five-day retreats at luxurious resorts in rural settings for large groups at costs up to $1,000 a person, and sometimes nude groups whose participants shed their clothes as well as their inhibitions. By most recent estimates, there are between 60 and 70 encounter-group "growth centers" in the U.S., including Chicago's Oasis, Washington's Orizon Institute and Laos House in Austin, Texas. Business also has gone into the field: Detroit's American Behavioral Science Training Laboratories are owned by the former rent-a-car magnate Warren Avis; Atlanta's Human Development Institute, a 45-man organization which grosses $1.5 million a year by conducting group sessions for businessmen, educators and interracial groups throughout the South, is a subsidiary of Bell & Howell.

Encounter groups are mainly aimed at the so-called "normal neurotic," the average adjusted citizen who psychologists say could presumably gain from greater emotional openness and experience, although people with more serious psychological problems often enlist as well. Group leaders draw on a mixed bag of psychological theories and techniques to accomplish this aim, including the experiences of group-psychotherapy and group-dynamics laboratories, the erotic theories of the late Dr. Wilhelm Reich, the psychodrama techniques of J. L. Moreno and the peak-experience psychologies of Carl Rogers and Abraham Maslow. All these elements (and others) are combined in an effort to help group participants work out their problems in dramatic—and often physical—confrontations with other people.

Adult

But at the same time, most group leaders insist they are not practicing psychotherapy. Participants, they say, are assumed to be mentally healthy rather than sick; little effort is made to delve into case histories. "We're not practicing medicine," says New York psychologist Harold Streitfeld. "It's adult education. We're teaching people about emotions in the same way we teach them about mathematics."

The classic form is the "T [for training] -group," developed shortly after World War II by three social psychologists working for Washington's National Training Laboratories and now popular on the East Coast. The focus is on the "here-and-now"—the immediate, common experience of the group. Participants come together—much like an assortment of people in an airport waiting room who begin to evolve into a group on the spot—and start talking, but on no assigned basis. There is no structure or organization and the group "leader" declines to direct the discussion. The task of the participants is to fill the vacuum left by the absence of a dominant leader and of an assigned topic for discussion. The T-group, explains one of NTL's directors, Charles N. Seashore, is designed to sharpen participants' perceptions of themselves and others and of group dynamics.

Personal

Encounter groups, in contrast to T-groups, are far less concerned with group dynamics. Instead, they focus on the individual, on getting each group participant to talk about and express his feelings as deeply and spontaneously as possible. And although group members talk mainly about the present, they sometimes try to work out their personal problems and past traumas in the groups. Not surprisingly, perhaps, encounter groups developed originally and now flourish in California, the birthplace of the hippies and other hedonistic movements; they have only recently begun to spread across the U.S.

The mecca for encounter groups in California is the Esalen Institute, which holds forth on the side of a verdant mountain in Big Sur, rising above the rugged Pacific Coast. Last year, Esalen, which has received extensive publicity for its nude encounter groups, attracted 10,000 participants; this year it expects some 25,000. Founded in the late 1950s by Michael Murphy, a Stanford philosophy and psychology graduate who inherited the Big Sur site from his grandmother, Esalen initially focused on meditation and talk of possibilities for human potential. Now, it tries to promote growth by whatever means show promise.

Body

In all the programs, heavy emphasis is placed on the body. Dr. William Schutz, one of Esalen's leading figures, has pioneered in developing physical techniques for encounter groups, drawing on psychodrama. Gestalt therapy and the "somatopsychic" techniques of psychologist Alexander Lowen. "The body is really being brought back into psychology," the 43-year-old psychologist notes with pleasure. In his five-day marathon "More Joy" workshops at Esalen, which are subscribed to months in advance, Schutz tries to bridge the gap between body and mind. The first day is spent talking rather generally about what people want and expect to get out of the sessions. In the evening, the participants take part in a microlab, where they may pound pillows and scream, look into each other's eyes and scream or just close their eyes and go inside themselves. Another technique Schutz uses is a high-school dance exercise in which all the women line up on one side of the room and all the men on the other. One by one the men go over and ask a girl to dance, either by touching her face or some other nonverbal method. She may accept or decline by pushing him away or merely failing to respond. "Hopefully, by the end of the evening, you are open to the feeling that anything goes," says Schutz.

During the remainder of the workshop, participants try to work out the feelings that have been generated and to attain "joy," which, says Schutz, means "realizing your potential." Encounter sessions are held every day from 10 a.m. until lunch and from 9 p.m. till midnight or later. The afternoons are filled with lectures, large-group fantasy (in which people let their thoughts wander together), massage, yoga or bathing in Esalen's hot sulphur springs. "On Monday and Tuesday, the second and third days of the workshop, we begin to dig down and get at the feelings," explains Schutz. "At first, you dig up all the negative feelings and look at them. Usually by Wednesday the positive feelings start to come and they're often more difficult to deal with than the negative feelings. And on Thursday comes joy."

Nudism

Los Angeles psychologist Paul Bindrim, 48, conducted the first nude sensitivity group in June 1967, after participating in encounters for seven years. He had observed then a growing tendency among group members to disrobe as emotional intimacy and transparency developed. Finally, after listening to a paper on nudism at a psychology conference, Bindrim saw the connection: "If a participant disrobed physically," Bindrim mused, "he might, by this gesture, gain the freedom to also disrobe emotionally. If this were true, it might be desirable to first disrobe and then interact, thus shortening the process and intensifying the beneficial results."

Bindrim first tested his ideas on a group of twenty middle-class people who gathered for a weekend at a nudist camp in Escondido, Calif. To avoid the possibilities of embarrassment or even an orgy, Bindrim required the participants to stay together throughout the session and to eschew any sexual expression that would be offensive in a conventional social setting. He opened the almost continuous program—participants got only six hours' sleep a night—by asking the group members to discuss their feelings about the prospect of nudity. After an hour's discussion, the group moved to a Jacuzzi bath, where they could bathe either nude or in swimming suits and where the water was at body temperature. "In the bath you don't know where the water really ends and the body begins," says Bindrim. "Touching becomes more casual and relaxed." In less than half an hour, all the participants were nude. Bindrim considered his initial experiment a success and has since conducted about 30 other nude marathons.

Elite

College students, naturally more open to experience than their elders, have been active participants in the human-potentiality movement, getting their sensitivity training from a wide variety of psychology courses, freshman-orientation programs and free universities. At the University of California's Berkeley campus, encounter groups have been around for several years. When sensitivity sessions were first introduced on campus, says 20-year-old Charles Webel, a former group leader, "they were somewhat clandestine, with only an elite group of trainers and initiates participating. In the second stage, starting last year, they were considerably popularized and it was the thing to do. Now, there is a growing demythologization of groups as people realize that all they can really do is show you what you are in the eyes of others."

Berkeley psychologist Sampson, one of the first to use sensitivity groups on the campus, doubts that students' expectations have become more realistic. In 1962, Sampson included T-groups in his course on "small group structure and process" to teach students about group processes. As the popularity of the groups increased, Sampson found students taking the class mainly to participate in the groups rather than to learn about them. "They came in wanting psychotherapy, wanting to touch somebody or have an experience," he says. "The participants are people who epitomize the trouble with society. They come for an emotional jolt, for the week's pill."

Dr. Clifford J. Sager, president of the 2,000-member American Group Psychotherapy Association, has expressed concern about the proliferation of sensitivity groups, both on and off the campus. For one thing, he says, many group leaders are untrained and are unable to recognize danger signs among the participants in the sessions. Sager cites the example of a girl who has recently received sensitivity training at a New York growth center and now plans to lead her own groups. "She is very sick. This is murder. It's like stopping somebody on the street who has always wanted to be a doctor and giving him a prescription pad with his name on it." Moreover, Sager says, the new techniques are being picked up indiscriminately, "even by better, established practitioners," although their effects have scarcely been studied. But there is little Sager's AGPA can do about the situation; no laws regulate the use of therapeutic techniques because states have been unable to define psychotherapy satisfactorily. At most, the AGPA can only try to educate the public and investigate its members for unethical practices.

Strength

Most group leaders contend that there is not much danger in sensitivity training. California psychologist Frederick Stoller, who pioneered in developing marathon sessions, says that everyone has the strength to deal with the encounter experience. In some groups that he has led, Stoller recalls, psychotics have broken down and become disorganized. But, he advises, "if the leader doesn't become frightened, these people will often go through the experience and come well out of it." Adds University of Michigan psychologist Richard Mann: "The thing a really inefficient trainer does is produce a really boring group. That's much more likely than that people will go crazy."

Actually, for all the dramatic examples of success or failure, no one really knows how effective these groups are. (The same problem, of course, besets orthodox psychiatry and psychoanalysis.) What is needed is large-scale, objective research on what happens to participants after they've left the groups and returned to their normal environments. So far, the main methods psychologists have devised to do this are through personal feedback from a client and the psychologist's own personal observation. And these techniques, observes Notre Dame psychologist Thomas L. Whitman, have grave weaknesses. For one thing, people may say good things about the experience either because they actually feel better or because they don't want to seem ungrateful to the group leader. "And besides," Whitman adds, "therapists are biased observers because to say that they are failing is to negate everything that they are doing."

Dr. Abraham Maslow, a former president of the American Psychological Association, who has studied many psychological experiments to help people achieve their highest potential, has provided one of the best evaluations of sensitivity groups to date. Five years ago, Maslow "reluctantly" took a look at the groups run by the National Training Laboratories in Bethel, Maine. "I was brought up in psychoanalysis," says Maslow, "and I expected a lot of crap." Instead, he was fascinated by what he saw: "These people behaved and talked in a spontaneous and free way that I have ordinarily associated with people who have been under psychoanalysis for a year or two at least." As a result, Maslow revised his psychoanalytic view that changing one's character is a very long-term process. "Apparently, it can happen a lot faster," he says, "very much faster in this kind of social situation."

Frontier

Since that time, Maslow has taken a closer look at the entire human-potential movement. Although he has found "an awful lot of charlatanism" in the movement, Maslow says that "there is much careful, very promising, even revolutionary work going on. If we take the best of it, it's of the utmost importance. It's the great frontier in social psychology now."

Whether they're a fad or a new frontier, sensitivity groups are likely to be around for a long time. Notre Dame psychologist Whitman suggests that American society is developing into a "therapy culture," in which people are convinced by all the talk about psychological problems that they themselves are suffering and need professional help. In such a culture, the sensitivity groups, properly supervised, could serve a valuable function. The psychiatrist, notes Chicago psychologist Eugene Gendlin, often acts as a "paid friend" for his patient, and this role could just as well be performed by encounter groups. "You shouldn't have to plead sick in order to have personal relationships," says Gendlin. "I think these groups will eventually become an institution in our social fabric, like friendship is."

2/ PURPOSE AND PROCESS IN GROUPS

Herbert A. Thelen

What may or may not be accomplished in and by a group? This depends on two kinds of congruence: between what actually happens and what must happen if the convening purposes of the groups are to be met; and between the way of life expected by the group for itself and the way of life already being lived by each person. The actual happenings in the group stand between two sets of demands: the logical demands inherent in purposes and the demands inherent in the life styles of members.

The meeting of the group confronts these two sets of demands with each other; the leadership determines to what extent and how these confrontations will occur; the processes of the group are negotiations to reconcile the two kinds of demands. Self-training and "learning" by members depend on the way the members are involved in these processes, on the relationship between this reality experience and past experience, and on the change potentials and adaptive viability of their life styles. The outcome of the group's work is the changed actual or prospective performances of the members with respect to the problem, each other, and future instances of similar confrontation.

It seems to me that discussions on the nature, care and feeding of groups can be insightfully compared by asking what is assumed and advocated or implied about the kinds of congruence—member to group, and group to purpose. In short, there are those who would

Herbert A. Thelen, "Purpose and Process in Groups," EDUCATIONAL LEADERSHIP 21 (3): 143–45; December 1963. Copyright © 1963 by the Association for Supervision and Curriculum Development. Reprinted with permission of the Association for Supervision and Curriculum Development and Herbert A. Thelen.

start their thinking with the personalities and backgrounds of the members; and this results in discussion of need to "understand" children, in one kind of rationale for "sensitivity" training, in emphasis on expression of feeling, and, in aggravated cases, the doctrine of withdrawn leader permissiveness no matter what.

Those who start with the group-task congruence make a thing of "communication," inquiry, cognitive process, and organizational policies. In the one case the group is seen as the milieu for each individual's comfort and need-meeting; in the other case the group is seen as a small producing society responsible for certain functions within an interlocking network of functioning groups.

The great trick, of course, is to assign appropriate weights to both orientations. What makes this a trick is that thinking about the milieu requires an interpersonal, psychological frame of reference and thinking about the society requires an objective, logical, legalistic frame of reference. Conflicts arise because the evaluations of any given behavior may be different from the two points of view and because from the two points of view one sees and responds to different behaviors.

To pull off the trick requires one or both of the following: the development of a third, "larger" frame of reference to which the other two are instrumental parts; or the development of techniques of group operations through which one can tell in the immediate situation which frame of reference (and its associated concerns) to pay attention to. The former theoretical development is being approached in modern systems theory; the latter practical, empirical approach is the distinctive contribution of the "laboratory" method. We need a lot more development of both.

But developments of theory and practice only put instruments into our hands. The outcome depends on how we use these instruments, and that depends on what we are committed to as the purpose of group endeavor. The two partial views discussed here have inherent purposes: the group, responded to as a milieu for each person, is there to facilitate individual self-realization and "personality growth"; the group, responded to as a producing society, is there "to get the job done." The tricky aspect is recognized when one sees that the group always has both facets, and that the outcome depends on whether these aspects reinforce and enrich each other or oppose and inhibit each other.

Further examination of the two purposes shows that without severe qualification, neither is valid. Thus the group as milieu for "personal growth" of each individual is a sound concept only if:

(a) the individuals are identical; or (b) the individuals are different but all are effectively able to adapt themselves and the group to each other; or (c) the group can somehow be a pluralistic set of milieux, and each sub-milieu be appropriate for each person. These qualifications are recognized respectively in: (a) efforts to control the composition of the group; (b) encouragement of psyche-group and out-of-group interactions among members; and (c) various efforts to utilize both formal and informal organizational structures of the group.

The other view, that the group exists "to get the job done," needs considerable clarification with respect to "the job." Is "the job" defined by institutional expectation, leader fiat, majority vote, or personal wish—or all together? In the schools, for example, the alleged need-meeting activities of students are actually for the most part directed to meet the needs of teachers. There is no "*the* job to be done"; there is instead activity to be participated in and carried out to a conclusion satisfactory to the teacher. The concept of "the job" only indexes a more fundamental concept, that of the authority which governs decisions and policies under and through which the group works. The authority may be the capricious wish or explicit goal of an individual who has recognized power; it may be requirednesses interpreted from the pooled experiences of members; it may be a publicly stated purpose which brought the members together voluntarily in the first place; it may be the expectations of the various offices or role-positions of the members *vis-à-vis* each other within the organization or community. In addition to any of these, there is the authority, usually not recognized and often resisted or resented, of the group's need to deal with its own hidden agendas or focal conflicts.

I think the purpose of the group, in whose service the theoretical and practical instruments are to be developed and utilized, is "to move toward the fulfillment of implicit and explicit purposes held for the group and for themselves by each individual in his capacity as a member of the group." This definition is cast to call our attention to several facts about groups: (a) members have different purposes, hopes, expectations and wishes, depending on their different ways of life—identifications, loyalties and values; (b) the purposes, wishes, etc., exist in different degrees of awareness in the minds of the members; (c) the purposes of a member respect both the changes he would like to make in himself but also those he thinks others ought to make; (d) within the life-style of each person, only certain of the purposes (or only certain ways of achieving the purposes) are legitimate ingredients in the negotiations of the group; and (*e*) each person must accept responsibility for defining what being a member or developing membership in the group is to mean to him.

The kind of significance a group will have to its members and to society depends, I think, on the adequacy of the processes instrumental to the understandings just listed. Making wishes known, being encouraged to become aware of what one really seeks, defining one's own place and function *vis-à-vis* others in the action system, recognizing and accepting the parts of one's life involved in the group and subject (in some way) to its jurisdiction, and, finally, reflecting on and assimilating the concerns, insights and purposes of the group within his own style of thought and life—these are the processes on which the creativity, adaptiveness, and significance of group life depend.

3/ USING GROUP PROCEDURES
TO IMPROVE HUMAN RELATIONS
IN THE SCHOOL SOCIAL SYSTEM

Alan R. Anderson and Donald L. Johnson

"You know, when I talk with you I come away having no idea about whether you like me or whether you don't, whether you agree or disagree with what I've said, or whether you have any intentions of doing anything as a result of our conversation, and it makes me damned uncomfortable." Several people nodded in agreement and the person to whom they were expressing their feelings pondered a moment, then wondered aloud if that were the kind of relationship he really wanted with these people. The setting was the second of nine weekly group counseling sessions in a Minnesota high school. The person being addressed was the district superintendent. The speaker was one of the counselors in the high school. The other group members were the assistant superintendent, the high school principal and assistant principal, the counselors in the school, and several teachers.

The high school was preparing to convert to modular scheduling and team teaching. They had discovered that much of the planning was bogging down because there was not sufficient trust among the staff to really share with each other. Many teachers were fearful of the "small group seminars" which were a prominent part of their new design; others were afraid of exposing weaknesses to colleagues and administrators. A human relations training laboratory was being planned and the group counseling was seen as a way of preparing a nucleus of key personnel for the kind of open, confrontive communication necessary for an effective laboratory. It was to con-

From SCHOOL COUNSELOR, *1968, Vol. 15, pp. 334–342. Copyright 1968, American Personnel and Guidance Association. Reprinted with permission of authors and publisher.*

sist of an intensive educational experience in a retreat setting, focusing mostly on group counseling or T-groups and on theory about small group process and organizational development. During the laboratory, people began testing the limits of honesty and openness which they could express to each other. In most cases they found they could get valuable help in examining their ideas, feelings and behavior, in finding out how they came across to others, and in modifying their behavior where it seemed appropriate.

More recently some of the teachers in the school have asked the counselors to organize a group of interested staff members for an on-going counseling experience. They feel they could profit from more self-examination, reflection, and possible modification. The counselors also have organized groups of students from a psychology class. Some of the groups are examining the subject matter of the course in relation to its implications for their individual growth and development. Others are examining their own growth and development in terms of career planning, family relations and school achievement. Counselors are leading some of the groups, the assistant superintendent is (with the help of the counselors) leader in two of them, and some of the groups have no appointed leader. Plans are now under way for the counselors to provide instruction for teachers in small group process and for the assistant principal in working with the student council and with groups of students whose behavior is posing a problem to the school.

These incidents reflect a number of trends in the field of guidance. One of these trends is the increase in the involvement of counselors in the total school program, as opposed to the ancillary role which has been typical of most guidance programs. As counselors demonstrate their interpersonal competence in a broader spectrum of the learning process, their role as facilitators of human growth and development will be accepted by students and staff alike. The second trend identifiable throughout the country is toward a more active, aggressive role for the counselor in reaching out beyond the confines of his office to people who may want or need the kind of help he can give, but who, for one reason or other, have not asked for it. A third trend is the tremendous increase in the use of group procedures by counselors. It is not, in our opinion, coincidental that these trends are occurring simultaneously.

The need for group programs was recognized early in the guidance movement. To begin with, school guidance programs were concerned primarily with vocational development and adjustment and were implemented through home room activities and units or courses called vocational guidance (Glanz & Hayes, 1967). Usually the responsibility for conducting these programs fell upon teachers who worked easily and effectively with classroom groups. Although in most cases these "guidance groups" were seen essentially as instructional and were conducted much like a regular class, many teachers came to feel that the subject matter of guidance could not be "taught" in the same way one would teach science or mathematics . . . *new* techniques were needed. Gradually many of the concepts of "group leadership" being developed by Kurt Lewin, Ron Lippitt and other social psychologists who were studying the dynamics of groups provided a framework for "teaching" guidance groups in a more personal and satisfying way. At the same time the guidance program was broadened to include more concerns related to personal adjustment, and group guidance activities began to deal with such things as dating habits, family relations, etc. (Wrenn, Hein, & Schwarzrock, 1961), usually as part of the homeroom program. For example, Metcalf (1946) reported a program in which the dean of students led several guidance groups with the idea of getting to know the students better and in turn to be seen by the students in a more personal way, to give students an opportunity to interact about personal concerns and to encourage students to see their counselor individually. They reported success on all counts. McFarland (1953) conducted homeroom groups in a rather permissive fashion encouraging students to share common problems. He felt that this program helped the students in their personal and vocational development and that it also stimulated the student activity program. Strang (1961) found that most students in her school disliked the homeroom classes chiefly because of their academic flavor. Homeroom activities were well received, however, when they were set up with a more permissive structure and had open-ended discussions dealing with the concerns of the students. Likewise Sherman (1963) found that students responded much more positively to homeroom groups where the subject matter emerged from the students than to those where it was imposed by the leader.

Although "failures" are seldom reported in the literature, it is our impression that reactions to homeroom activities have been more negative than positive and that other group guidance efforts have met with only moderate success. Goldman (1962) suggested that such inconsistent reactions to group guidance were in part due to lack of understanding of the roles of both content and process and that often either content was lacking entirely or the process used was inappropriate for the content.

Until Froehlich (1958) raised the question, "Must counseling be individual?" it was commonly accepted that when counselors worked in groups, that was guidance. Counseling had to be "one-to-one." Since that time there has been a proliferation of attempts at what generally is labelled group counseling. As acceptance of group work by counselors increases, and as the purposes and objectives for which groups are organized become more varied, the distinction between group "guidance" and group "counseling" becomes less clear. The preceding review of a few successful group "guidance" activities suggests that the oft-repeated assertion ". . . group guidance is instruction," (Hewer, 1967b)—and that that is what distinguishes it from counseling—is not only oversimplified but may be inappropriate. In several of the studies, deletion of the "instructional" aspects of the programs was seen as largely responsible for their success. Indeed, we wonder whether there is any real point to making such distinctions. In the schools, counseling is part of the guidance program. Each counselor must decide on the purposes for which he wishes to organize groups, and perhaps it is the goal or purpose for which a given group is set up which supplies the significant label.

Pioneer efforts in vocational group counseling followed Stone's (1958) query, "Are vocational orientation courses worth their salt?" Hoyt (1955), Hewer (1959) and Kemp (1962) attempted to compare the effects of group and individual counseling in this area. Both methods appeared to increase the realism of vocational choices made, and there were no measurable differences between the two methods in achieving these results. Volsky and Hewer (1960) used a "case conference" approach where groups of students shared and discussed their vocational goals in the light of available test data. They reported similarly favorable results. Hewer (1967a) followed up some of her student groups and found that the large majority of them had fulfilled their vocational choices and were presently involved in both the type of work and occupational level they had selected earlier. Wright (1963) compared the effects of individual and group counseling on students' ability to interpret test data accurately. Both methods proved successful and no differences were found between the group and individual approach. Gribbons (1960) reports that eighth graders significantly increased in awareness and accuracy in appraisal of their own abilities, values, and interests following group counseling.

Attempts to improve academic performance through group counseling have produced inconclusive evidence. Groups studied by Anderson (1956), Christensen (1963), and Northman (1964) showed no evidence of academic improvement, while Ross and Boyd (1936), Moroney (1963), and Ofman (1964) did find evidence of significant improvement in grade point averages following group counseling. Ofman's groups did not evidence their gains, however, until two semesters after their group experience. Spielberger, Weitz and Denny (1962) and Spielberger and Weitz (1964) found that by identifying potential dropouts and putting them through group counseling they could lower the dropout rate and increase grade point averages significantly, as compared with control groups of similar students. Some of these groups centered their discussions around topics pertinent to academic achievement, while others dealt with personal feelings, anxieties, etc. Both types of groups produced essentially the same positive results on the factors indicated. Chestnut (1965) and Gilbreath (1965) compared the effects of leader-structured groups, in which the leader presented information about the dynamics of poor achievement and asked the members to respond in terms of their own feelings and experiences, and group-structured groups, in which all content originated spontaneously within the group. Results indicated more productive results with the leader-structured groups.

Krumboltz and Thoresen (1964) successfully increased the amount of independent information-seeking behavior on the part of eleventh-grade students by selectively reinforcing statements related to this kind of behavior in the group. Ryan (1966) trained non-professional group leaders, such as residence hall counselors and undergraduate college students, to selectively reinforce certain types of behavior considered desirable in developing effective academic skills and to ignore "nonproductive" behavior. Systematic methods of introducing and discussing material within this framework were developed. These groups were highly successful in increasing the study skills and grade point averages of the group members.

There have been a number of attempts to use group procedures to orient students to a new school situation or to make the school situation more meaningful to them. Arbuckle (1949) and Rosenberg and Fuller (1955) found that small group discussions with new students significantly improved social and emotional adjustment as well as reducing attrition. These students also achieved better in core-curriculum classes than had previous groups of students. Smith (1963) also reported lower attrition among college freshmen who participated in small group discussion sessions. In a well-designed study, Williams (1959) demonstrated that a one semester orientation course significantly reduced reported problems on the Mooney Problem Check List. An attempt to compare permissive small group discussions and a reading improvement program in inducing a more positive attitude toward academic achievement showed advantages in favor of the small group discussions (Reiter, 1964). Scoresby (1966) successfully showed that students oriented to college in small groups (8 to 10 members) obtained higher GPA and higher levels of self-acceptance than comparable students oriented in medium sized (50) or large (100) groups or for control students receiving no orientation.

Reported attempts to facilitate personal adjustment and development through the use of group counseling have been largely positive. Clements (1965) found that participation of college-bound seniors in group sessions effectively reduced anxiety about themselves and their role in college. Broedel, Ohlsen, and Proff (1960) and Siegel (1965) used group counseling to effect positive academic and personality changes in gifted under-achievers. In a related study, Cohn, Ohlsen, and Proff (1960) were able to identify the various roles played by adolescents in both productive and unproductive group sessions.

A number of studies (Caplan, 1957; Brach, 1958; Davis, 1959; Gutsch & Bellamy, 1966; and Rappaport, 1966) have demonstrated the usefulness of group counseling with junior high and high school students having disciplinary and social adjustment problems in school. These studies were typically characterized by relatively unstructured sessions where few rules were established. In some cases the discussion content was introduced by the leader, but students were encouraged to express their views and feelings freely. Positive results included better citizenship in school, increased self-acceptance, improved academic achievement and better relations with peers and parents.

A "guidance club" organized in a fourth-grade class composed mostly of children with socially and economically deprived backgrounds may suggest a direction for elementary counselors. The class was given one hour per week to talk about almost anything they wanted to. Class officers were elected who helped lead the discussions, and a "suggestion box" provided an opportunity for students to indicate what they wanted to discuss. Family and social problems soon emerged as areas of most concern. Participation was general, even among normally non-verbal students, and it appeared to be productive in terms of self-understanding and social development (Berk, 1967).

A Look Ahead

It seems clear that group counseling has come of age. Counselors now tend to see group work less as a threat to their time-honored "one-to-one" relationships and more as an addition to their armamentarium of ways of helping people. The crucial question is no longer, "Shall I use group counseling?" but "Under what circumstances might I use group counseling to advantage?" and "What do I need to learn in order to do group counseling?" If this premise is accepted—that group counseling really is counseling, and not some threatening foreign intruder on the guidance scene—then it follows that the philosophy behind and methodology employed in group counseling will have to be consonant with what is done in individual counseling. A major difference would simply be that the group process is more complex because there are more people interacting at once; hence, more data have to be processed and communicated than in individual counseling. A second major difference might be that in addition to "doing counseling" the leader is also attempting to teach a group of people to "counsel each other." In any case an adequate counseling theory would have to be sufficiently comprehensive that it can account for what happens in both individual and group counseling.

Many of the uses of group counseling already have been alluded to. Given adequate knowledge and skills the counselor generally can achieve the same sorts of things in group counseling that he can in individual counseling. Under what circumstances and with what kinds of clients one is more efficient than the other are yet to be determined. But if it is accepted that because of his deep appreciation for and understanding of human development and behavior, and his expertise in the prediction and modification of behavior the counselor has a unique and essential role to play in building a dynamic educational program which remains attuned to the needs of students, then a counselor's clientele becomes the entire "group" (social system) which constitutes the school. Learning to work with this group and the many sub-groups which comprise it may become his major focus of attention.

Most schools have considerable data, which are relatively untouched and unheeded, about the needs and characteristics of students and staff. These data, effectively organized and summarized, might provide the basis for many small group discussions which lead to more realistic evaluation of policies, curriculum, and recruitment practices. The character of the school as a social system which is providing models for growing youngsters is probably one of the most significant aspects of the learning process, yet it is seldom systematically observed and made explicit. The nature and impact of change in a school is obviously an ever-present phenomenon which pleases and excites some but poses a real threat to others. If plans for change are based on accurate data and upon decisions made by the groups who are to be most directly affected by the plans, they are likely to have the continued support of those who must implement them (Bauer, 1966). The counselor who sees guidance as "a primary agent in the reconstruction of the school culture," (Shoben, 1962) and whose primary interest and task is facilitating communication and programs through which students and staff develop the kind of responsible freedom which reflects a truly liberal (liberating) education, will recognize other vistas for getting groups together in the interests of personal growth and development (Watson, 1967).

One such area, where our experience has shown group counseling to have distinct advantages over an individual approach, is that of improving the human relations within a system. Human relations training is an attempt to improve the efficiency and productivity of an organization (such as a business, school or family) through more open communication, increased self-understanding and greater sensitivity to the feelings of others. One of the most successful approaches to human relations training grew out of the field of group dynamics and is based on an understanding of group process and development (Bradford, Gibb, & Benne, 1965). We see great potential benefits to a school in getting together groups of students of different socioeconomic strata or of different levels of interest in the educational enterprise or of different races to learn to really communicate and try to understand each other. Experimental groups of parents, teachers, administrators, board members and a combination of all of these together *with* the students is proving to be both exciting and productive of more satisfying and viable working relationships (Union School Project, 1967).

Another area, still largely unexplored, which we see as particularly amenable to group counseling, is the involvement of teachers and parents as well as students in career development. Much work has been done in developing vocational guidance units, and it might well be that we are now ready to involve parents, teachers and students in small group discussions in which they talk about their own past or projected career development. Such discussions might well be the most realistic vocational guidance a student could receive, and we suspect that with a group leader who understands group processes as well as career development, the parents and teachers might well receive considerable help too.

There are undoubtedly many other areas of fruitful endeavor which the creative counselor already has considered. The concepts and research data from social psychology provide a rich source from which to draw in developing more effective ways of helping people in groups. The classic study of authoritarian, democratic and laissez faire leadership (Lewin, Lippitt, & White, 1939) helps to understand the effects of leadership roles and functions. The work of Sherif (1953) and Asch (1956) on the effects of suggestion and peer group pressure on perception indicates the potential power of a cohesive group. Translating these concepts and data into the practice of group counseling becomes the task of the counselor and the counselor educator. It represents another demand in the lives of busy professionals. It also represents a major avenue of growth in our capacity to be more productive in our own interpersonal relations and career development.

REFERENCES

Anderson, R. L. An experimental investigation of group counseling with freshmen in a women's college. *Dissertation Abstracts*, 1965, *16*, 1100–1101.

Arbuckle, D. S. A college experiment in orientation. *Occupations*, 1949, *28*, 112–117.

Asch, E. E. Studies of independence and submission to group pressure: I. A minority of one against a unanimous majority. *Psychological Monographs*, 1956, *70* (416).

Bauer, R. A. Social psychology and the study of policy formation. *American Psychologist*, 1966, *21*, 933–942.

Berk, P. A group guidance club in the elementary school. *The School Counselor*, 1967, *14*, 173–178.

Bradford, L. P., Gibb, J. R., & Benne, D. B. *T-group theory and laboratory method, innovation in re-education*. New York: Wiley, 1964.

Broedel, J., Ohlsen, M. M., & Proff, F. C. The effects of group counseling on gifted adolescent under-achievers. *Journal of Counseling Psychology*, 1960, *7*, 163–170.

Brach, A. M. Reaching young teens through group counseling. In H. E.

Drivers (Ed.), *Counseling, a learning through small group discussion.* Madison, Wisc.: Monona, 1958.

Caplan, S. W. The effect of group counseling on junior high school boys' concept of themselves in school. *Journal of Counseling Psychology,* 1957, *4,* 124–128.

Chestnut, W. J. The effects of structured and unstructured group counseling on male college students' under-achievement. *Journal of Counseling Psychology,* 1965, *12,* 388–394.

Christensen, E. W. Group counseling with selected scholarship students. *Dissertation Abstracts,* 1963, *24,* 619–620.

Clements, B. E. The effects of group counseling with college-bound high school seniors on their anxiety and parent-child empathy. *Dissertation Abstracts,* 1965, *25,* 3966–3967.

Cohn, B., Ohlsen, M. M., & Proff, F. C. Roles played by adolescents in an unproductive counseling group. *Personnel and Guidance Journal,* 1960, *38,* 724–731.

Davis, D. A. Effect of group guidance and individual counseling on citizenship behavior. *Personnel and Guidance Journal,* 1959, *38,* 142–145.

Froehlich, C. P. Must counseling be individual? *Educational and Psychological Measurement,* 1958, *18,* 681–690.

Gilbreath, S. H. The effects of structured and unstructured group counseling on certain personality dimensions of male college students who underachieve. *Dissertation Abstracts,* 1965, *26,* 199.

Glanz, E. C., & Hayes, R. W. *Groups in guidance.* Boston: Allyn & Bacon, 1967.

Goldman, L. Group guidance: content and process. *Personnel and Guidance Journal,* 1962, *40,* 518–522.

Gribbons, W. D. Evaluation of an eighth-grade group guidance program. *Personnel and Guidance Journal,* 1960, *38,* 740–745.

Gutsch, K. A., & Bellamy, W. D. Effectiveness of an attitudinal group approach as a behavior determinant. *The School Counselor,* 1966, *14,* 40–43.

Hewer, V. H. Evaluation of group and individual counseling: a follow-up. *The Journal of College Student Personnel,* 1967, *8,* 265–269.

Hewer, V. H. Group counseling. Paper presented at the APGA Convention, Dallas, Texas, April, 1967.

Hewer, V. H. Group counseling, individual counseling and a college class in vocations. *Personnel and Guidance Journal,* 1959, *37,* 660–665.

Hoyt, D. P. An evaluation of group and individual programs in vocational guidance. *The Journal of Applied Psychology,* 1955, *39,* 26–30.

Kemp, G. A. A comparative evaluation of the effectiveness of group guidance and individual counseling with freshmen. *Dissertation Abstracts,* 1962, *22,* 4270.

Krumboltz, J. D., & Thoresen, C. E. The effect of behavioral counseling in group and individual settings on information-seeking behavior. *Journal of Counseling Psychology,* 1964, *11,* 324–333.

Lewin, K. Group decision and social change. In G. E. Swanson, T. M. Newcomb, & E. L. Hartley (Eds.), *Readings in Social Psychology.* New York: Holt, Rinehart & Winston, 1947, 330–344.

Lewin, K., Lippitt, R., & White, R. K. Patterns of aggressive behavior—experimentally created social climates. *Journal of Social Psychology,* 1939, *10,* 271–299.

McFarland, J. W. Developing effective homerooms. *School Review,* 1953, *61,* 400–405.

Metcalf, H. H. Group counseling at the eleventh-grade level. *School Review,* 1946, *54,* 401–405.

Moroney, K. A. Effectiveness of short-term group guidance with a group of transfer students admitted on academic probation. *Dissertation Abstracts,* 1963, *23,* 3238.

Northman, F. H. The effect of three methods of group counseling with college students on probation. *American Psychologist,* 1964, *19,* 455.

Ofman, W. Evaluation of a group counseling procedure. *Journal of Counseling Psychology,* 1964, *11,* 152–159.

Rappaport, D. Small group counseling. *The School Counselor,* 1966, *14,* 119–121.

Reiter, H. H. The effect of orientation through small-group discussion on modification of certain attitudes. *Journal of Educational Research,* 1964, *58,* 65–68.

Rosenberg, P. P., & Fuller, M. Human relations seminar. *Mental Hygiene,* 1955, *39,* 406–432.

Ross, C. C., & Boyd, P. P. An experiment in group counseling for freshmen. *Kentucky Personnel Bulletin,* 1936, 16.

Ryan, T. A. Model-reinforcement group counseling to modify study behavior. Paper presented at the APGA Convention, Washington, D.C., April, 1966.

Scoresby, A. L. An experimental comparison of three methods of new student orientation at Brigham Young University. Unpublished Master's thesis, Brigham Young University, 1966.

Sherif, M., & Sherif, C. *Groups in harmony and tension.* New York: Harper, 1953.

Sherman, R. Exploratory experiences in group guidance. *The School Counselor,* 1963, *10,* 200–203.

Shoben, E. J. Guidance: remedial function or social reconstruction? In R. L. Mosher, R. F. Carle, & C. D. Kehas (Eds.), *Guidance, an examination.* New York: Harcourt, Brace & World, 1962, 110–126.

Siegel, M. Group psychotherapy with gifted under-achieving college students. *Community Mental Health Journal,* 1965, *1,* 188–194.

Smith, B. M. Small group meetings of college freshmen and frequency of withdrawals. *Journal of College Student Personnel,* 1963, *4,* 165–170.

Spielberger, C. D., & Weitz, H. Improving the academic performance of anxious college freshmen. *Psychological Monographs,* 1964 (78, Whole No. 590).

Spielberger, C. D., Weitz, H., & Denny, J. P. Group counseling and the academic performance of anxious college freshmen. *Journal of Counseling Psychology,* 1962, *9,* 195–204.

Stone, C. H. Are vocational orientation courses worth their salt? *Educational and Psychological Measurement,* 1958, *8,* 161–181.

Strang, R. Group guidance as students view it. *The School Counselor,* 1961, *8,* 142–145.

The Union School District of Jackson, Michigan. Strategy for planned educational change through in-service training. Unpublished manuscript, Operational Grant, January, 1967.

Volsky, T. C., & Hewer, V. H. A program of group counseling. *Journal of Counseling Psychology,* 1960, *7,* 7:–73.

Watson, G. (Ed.) *Change in school systems.* Washington, D.C.: National Training Laboratories, 1967.

Williams, C. An experimental study to determine the effectiveness of the freshmen orientation course at North Texas State College. *Dissertation Abstracts,* 1959, *19,* 3241–3242.

Wright, E. W. A comparison of individual and multiple counseling for test interpretation interviews. *Journal of Counseling Psychology,* 1963, *10,* 126–135.

4/ GROUP DISCUSSION AND GROUP COUNSELING APPLIED TO STUDENT PROBLEM SOLVING

Bernard C. Kinnick

The purpose of this article is to demonstrate the appropriateness of group discussion and group counseling to the field of group problem solving. On the surface, many would suggest that the two processes are quite dissimilar. However, this author posits that much of what is germane to group problem solving through discussion is likewise applicable to certain phases of group counseling. The paper is limited to a comparison between group discussion and group counseling as they may be utilized in junior and senior high schools, but implications may be seen for other areas as well.

Problem Solving Through Group Discussion

Group discussion has been described as the cooperative and constructive deliberation on a common problem by a group attempting to reach agreement on a solution to that problem. The term "problem" has been defined by Smith (1965, p. 23) as "any situation in which an individual or individuals seek a practical means by which to overcome a barrier or barriers to a worth-while goal." Logically then, an accepted definition of group problem solving (through discussion) would be an attempt by a group of people, through informal but orderly conversion, "to decide how to achieve a common goal by overcoming barriers to it, or to establish new goals in light of these barriers" (Smith, 1965, p. 30).

From SCHOOL COUNSELOR, *1968, Vol. 15, pp. 350–356. Copyright 1968, American Personnel and Guidance Association. Reprinted with permission of author and publisher.*

Problem-solving discussion can further be defined as an effort on the part of a small, face-to-face group to reach a solution to a problem through informal interchange of information, knowledge, and ideas. The primary purposes of group discussion in a democratic school setting would be that (1) it would provide a means of helping the student learn skills so widely recognized as necessary, improve his ability to solve his own problems, and work with others toward a common goal; and (2) it would enhance the student's understanding of, faith in, and skill to participate in democracy at all levels of society.

Discussion is both a critical and a creative process providing for a degree of order in one's thinking to avoid confusion. The necessary order is achieved through following the five-step pattern of constructive thinking suggested by John Dewey and summarized by Smith (1965): (1) identify the goal; (2) analyze the problem (i.e., the relationship between the common goal and barriers to it); (3) suggest all possible solutions to the difficulty; (4) select the most satisfactory solution or solutions; and (5) consider ways to implement the solution.

The pattern cited above should be followed closely enough to insure an orderly approach to the problem but modified by the group when an approach more appropriate for a given problem becomes evident. The discussion process attempts to achieve agreement by members of the group on a solution to the problem under consideration as well as providing participants with a deeper insight into the problem being discussed. At the same time, the process of discussion itself tends to unify the group and thus provides an equal opportunity for all to contribute. The control of the group results from self-direction and self-discipline and, because of this, discussion is considered by many as the most democratic of group methods in problem solving.

Group discussion is then a problem-solving process and, as in the case of individual problem solving, the methods used are the rather definite techniques of reasoning (Howell & Smith, 1956). It follows that an individual who would be a group leader or group participant in discussion should not only know about the reasoning activity but be skilled in the application of particular methods of reasoning to various kinds of problems for which the group seeks solutions through discussion.

A study conducted by Shaw (1932) demonstrated that results of group discussion warrant its continued use by groups in solving certain problems faced by the group as a whole. Shaw's conclusions were as follows: (1) groups gain a much larger proportion of correct solutions than individuals do as a result of the rejection of incorrect suggestions and checking of errors by the group; (2) more incorrect suggestions are rejected by other members of the group than by the individual who proposed the suggestion; and (3) in erroneous solutions, groups do not err so soon as the average individual.

Shaw's conclusions could be amplified to a considerable extent by citing additional studies which support the continued use of group discussion in problem solving (Thorndike, 1938; Lewin, 1947; Kelly & Thibaut, 1954). Not only is the group goal achieved sooner, with a more appropriate solution being adopted, but the process itself has a most worthwhile effect on the individuals participating in such problem-solving discussions. Strang (1960) indicated that, as an implement of democracy, group discussion has two main values: (1) increases the individual's sense of personal worth, giving him information and modifying his values or attitudes; and (2) provides a process of clarifying questions, solving problems, arriving at sound decisions, and developing plans of action important not only to the group but to the individual as well.

Students in junior and senior high schools will tend to have many similar problems or areas of concern, and group discussion will lend itself successfully in their attempts to question, evaluate, and solve problems that are present in or out of school. Such school-related topics as the world of work, choosing a college, and how to study are salient discussion topics for a large percentage of students. Even such out-of-school topics as parent-student relations may find fruitful examination in student group discussions. While the above approach may not be a precise replica of individual problem solving, such group discussions develop through stages not unlike those which characterize reflective thinking.

The values of group discussion are legion. And, as a method of group problem solving, discussion seems to have a composite of values unequalled by any other known method. Smith (1965) lists the salient values of group discussion as follows: (1) decisions are better; (2) decisions are better supported and accepted by the group making them; (3) morale is higher; (4) groups develop unity; (5) strengthens the individual; and (6) strengthens democracy as group discussion is consistent with democratic procedure. What better educational tool is available in the junior and senior high school than such group discussion techniques?

Problem Solving Through Group Counseling

Group counseling is not individual counseling applied to groups, although it is a group method designed to help individuals with problems—the normal emotional problems of everyday living as well as more serious problems (Warters, 1960). Group counseling is a planned, not an incidental process that includes, among other things, identification with, analysis by, and support from the group. It involves permissiveness, protection, and changes in personality and behavior that take place more rapidly in group counseling than in life in general. This author suggests that group counseling consists of processes occurring in formally organized groups which bring about moderate change in personality and behavior of individual members through specified and controlled group interaction.

Individual students, in pursuing daily needs, encounter frustrations of one sort or another. These may range from minor irritations growing out of their contacts with other people to cases of extreme anxiety. Nonetheless, each student believes that his problems are extremely different from those of his peers. In many instances, group counseling sessions may be warranted to assist the individual in a reassessment of his approach to the amelioration of existing problems. For a student to encounter others who have the same outlook is often just the reassurance necessary for progress in reorganizing one's own self-image.

Generally speaking, the term group counseling suggests assistance for normal but troubled (not severely disturbed) individuals. Group members may be individuals who are handicapped in achieving their goals because of strong feelings of anxiety, insecurity, or inferiority; they may be persons who have set too high or unrealistic goals for themselves and to some extent are aware of the discrepancy between themselves and their aspirations; or they may be concerned with lesser problems which still seem more appropriate to group discussion and solution than individual attention.

The purposes or objectives of group counseling differ only slightly from those in individual-centered counseling. They are, in general, to help counselees achieve increased maturity in terms of integration, acceptance of reality, sociality, realistic goals, adaptability, and responsibility for self (Warters, 1960). Even though many problems may lend thmselves to individual counseling, a significant number are also common problems faced by the individual and his peers in the social and cultural environment and thus fitting topics for group counseling.

Wright (1959) indicated that the objectives of group counseling are essentially to assist the individual in the following: (1) evaluation of himself, or gaining knowledge necessary for wise choices; (2) decision making and self-direction or growth in the ability to make decisions and be responsible; and (3) carrying through of learning to action, i.e., changed behavior. He also outlined the unique characteristics of group counseling as: (1) All members have a common problem; (2) All members identify with this common element; (3) The counselor functions as leader but functions from within the group; (4) A permissive, safe atmosphere favors free expression; (5) Interactions and mutual help among members are essential; (6) If group counseling is effective, participants are stimulated by group standards to accomplish the generally accepted goals of individual counseling.

The values of group counseling can be experienced in terms of (1) the life-like setting for making decisions and choices; (2) the influences of peers through group interaction and group norms; (3) the opportunity for free expression of opinions and emotions with less personal reference; and (4) the opportunity to give and receive support as a group member (Wright, 1959). It should be obvious that a person's very sense of identity is shaped by such group involvement.

Although research studies are few in number, the findings lend support to the suggestion that group counseling holds promise as an efficient and effective counseling technique which facilitates group problem solving (Broedel et al., 1960; Volsky & Hewer, 1960; Cohn & Sniffen, 1962; Clements, 1964). Group counseling does exhibit many characteristics similar to group discussion as a technique in problem solving, and these will now be examined.

Group Discussion—Group Counseling: A Comparison

It should be obvious from the above description of group discussion and group counseling that the solving of certain kinds of problems and greater understanding of individual concerns can be realized through such group processes. Nonetheless, the discerning individual could not help realizing that, even though certain similarities do exist, minor differences between group counseling and group discussion must also be noted.

Participants and Problems

Considering the involvement of students in the aforementioned group processes, one may conclude that participants in either process would meet with but few limitations. The most important factor, of course, would be the individual's interest in the problem under consideration by the group and whether he felt his involvement would realize for him some advancement in understanding reality situations, both in himself and in his outer environment. In group counseling, one may assume that more problems of a personal nature would be examined than in most group discussions. In group counseling, under ideal conditions, group members serve as "multiple counselors" for each other in that they assist one another in the expression of emotions, interpret meanings, clarify feelings, give support, and exert some influence on behavior. The above-enumerated characteristics of group counseling may well go beyond the normal interactions found in group discussion but there are similarities that allow adequate comparison. It is especially important to note that problems would be examined more from an affective approach in group counseling and primarily from a cognitive approach in group discussion. Finally, problems examined and solutions reached would be the sole responsibility of the group in group discussion—unlike group counseling, where similar problems may be examined but where each student in the final analysis would decide how appropriate a solution would be from his own perceptual field.

Goals

The goals (human desires toward which one is willing to work) of the group would be an expression and extension of individual members' own personal desires. In group discussion and counseling alike, participants in most instances would select the problem or problem area to be discussed and proceed then to examine them by reference to problem-solving techniques—that is, how the goal may or may not be obtained. In group discussion, a common goal is absolutely essential, for without it, acceptance of values and procedures may never reach a consensus. In problem solving through group discussion, one may find a slight tendency for the needs of individuals to become somewhat subservient to the goals of the group, whereas in group counseling individual needs merit prime importance. Even though there exists, for example, an over-all goal of self-improvement in group counseling, it may present different meanings to individuals depending on their level of self-perception and self-acceptance.

One may suspect that problems attacked through group discussion may tend to be more concerned with questions of fact and the diagnosis or interpretation of certain data collected, whereas problems in group counseling may tend more to reflect attitudes or feelings. In group counseling, members are often concerned not so much that something is, or why it is, or what objectively is likely to happen. Rather, they may be more concerned with how one ought to feel and what attitudes members should take toward the situation. Discrimination toward minority groups may provide one example. In group counseling, it may well be that members know a good deal about the reasons for discrimination, the means by which the pattern is perpetuated, and the likelihood of its continuation into the immediate future. But there still remains the question of how one feels and how one ought to feel and react toward acts of discrimination. Obviously, in group counseling, there may be more affective than cognitive interaction. In group counseling, individuals may be more concerned with the naked reality of their self-image than appropriate solutions to more general societal problems which discussion groups as a whole would find more rewarding.

Still, one must quickly state that group discussion as well is particularly conducive to fostering wholesome human relations, since it helps students gain genuine understanding of and respect for each other's feelings, needs, and viewpoints (McBurney & Hance, 1950). Perhaps in no other democratic group process will students gain more real understanding of their problems and the problems of others, as well as the appropriate means to remove the problem.

Nature of Problem Solving

The pattern of problem solving is generally quite similar in group discussion and group counseling. Perhaps the pattern is followed more closely in discussion as there may be greater concern for the time factor. Time limitations are not necessarily considered as important in group counseling. The five steps in constructive thinking may likewise be more appropriately used in group discussion. However, the earlier examination of this method would lead one to believe strongly in its usefulness in group counseling. It may be true that groups in counseling occasionally select truncated problems, solutions to which do not involve all the steps in a complete act of problem solving. In the end, however, the group will have to adapt procedures described earlier to meet specific requirements of the problem being discussed. Smith (1965) states that the problem-solving process is to facilitate rather than hamper decision making and that modifications in the process of problem solving may be quite acceptable in group discussions. Obviously, similar modifications are acceptable in group counseling.

LEADERSHIP ROLE

Democratic group-centered leadership in group discussion is an absolute necessity. Only with democratic group leadership can discussions occur which will allow for most interaction and the attainment of common goals in problem solving. So also in group counseling, even though an experienced counselor is present, his role is one of facilitating, not directing, the discussion. The status of the counselor may prove an initial barrier to the flow of communication in group counseling, but "when the counselor eventually becomes a background figure, it should be because he is an unobtrusive rather than an inactive member" (Warters, 1950, p. 200).

The chief function of the group counselor is to help the group establish a friendly atmosphere in which the members can explore problems and relationships. Through his calmness and consistency, impartial interest and objectivity, and permissiveness, he helps the members feel comfortable with one another and thereby strengthens members' relations. He shows confidence in the group's capacity to direct itself by relinquishing leadership responsibilities he may have exhibited prior to the formation of the counseling group. The group counseling process compares rather favorably with group discussion when one designates a similar leadership role for both group processes. The eventual leadership role in group discussion is that posited by Smith (1965, pp. 140–141) when he states that "the group centered approach to leadership is the only approach that is purely democratic; it is the only approach to leadership in which the authority for leadership rests completely with the group and the only approach to leadership in which the group maintains control over the leader of the group."

Perhaps the group leader's control is mainly over himself; that is, he tries to keep his natural tendencies—to play the role of authority—from interfering too much with the developing group process. The group leader in counseling sessions or in group discussions is no longer the sole decision maker. If group members are to shoulder the responsibilities that go with freedom, they must have sufficient authority to be able to make real decisions—even under conditions of incomplete information, and equally true in both group processes.

Conclusion

It should be relatively clear that group discussion and group counseling are more alike than dissimilar. In a world in which conditions change rapidly and in which individuals also are always in a state of change, it is essential that techniques are developed to maintain a balance between inner and outer forces. If education in the junior and senior high school is to help prepare individuals for the life-long adjustments they will be called upon to make, training in group problem-solving process must be a component of education.

Problem solving connotes a creative process by which individuals are able to evaluate changes in themselves and their environment and make new choices, decisions, or adjustments in harmony with life goals and values which may also be in a state of flux. As here described, problem solving must be considered a fundamental technique of living in a democratic social order, be it through group discussion or group counseling. Both can contribute to the furtherance of man's drive for excellence and self understanding in a democratic society.

REFERENCES

Bennett, M. E. *Guidance in groups.* New York: McGraw-Hill, 1955.

Broedel, J., et al. The effects of group counseling on gifted underachieving adolescents. *Journal of Counseling Psychology,* 1960, 7, 163–170.

Clements, B. E. The effects of group counseling with college-bound high school seniors on their anxiety and parent-child empathy. Unpublished doctoral dissertation, Arizona State University, 1964.

Cohn, B., & Sniffen, A. M. A school report on group counseling. *Personnel and Guidance Journal,* 1962, 41, 133–138.

Froehlich, C. P. Multiple counseling: A research proposal. Unpublished manuscript, University of California (Berkeley).

Howell, W. S., & Smith, D. K. *Discussion.* New York: Macmillan, 1956.

Kelley, H., & Thibaut, J. W. Experimental studies of group problem solving and process. In G. Lindzey (Ed.), *Handbook of social psychology.* Vol. 1. Reading, Mass.: Addison-Wesley, 1954, 735–785.

Lewin, K. Group decision and social change. In T. M. Newcomb, et al. (Eds.), *Readings in social psychology.* New York: Holt, 1947, 330–344.

McBurney, J. H., & Hance, K. G. *Discussion in human affairs.* New York: Harper, 1950.

Shaw, M. E. A comparison of individuals and small groups in the rational solution of complex problems. *American Journal of Psychology,* 1932, *44,* 491–504.

Smith, W. S. *Group problem-solving through discussion.* Indianapolis: Bobbs-Merrill, 1965.

Strang, R. *Group activities in colleges and secondary schools.* New York: McGraw-Hill, 1960.

Thorndike, R. L. The effect of discussion upon the correctness of group decisions, when the factor of majority influence is allowed for. *Journal of Social Psychology,* 1938, *9,* 343–362.

Volsky, T., & Hewer, V. H. A program of group counseling. *Journal of Counseling Psychology,* 1960, *7,* 71–73.

Warters, J. *Group guidance: principles and practices.* New York: McGraw-Hill, 1960.

Wright, E. W. Multiple counseling: Why? when? how? *American Personnel and Guidance Journal,* 1959, *37,* 551–557.

5 / LABORATORY TRAINING AND ENCOUNTER GROUPS

William B. Eddy and Bernard Lubin

Participation in some form of intensive group learning experience is becoming increasingly commonplace. In many schools, churches, business management groups, and social service agencies, involvement in a T-group, encounter group, or sensitivity training session is seen as a part of one's overall development. Such learning goals as getting to know oneself better, learning how one comes across to others, understanding more about human interaction, and getting a better feel for group operations are relevant to many vocational roles.

Two major factors seem to be accelerating the use of small face-to-face group experiences as learning vehicles: (a) the fast-changing, large, complex, and impersonal society in which we live; and (b) the increasing amount of organizational work-life that takes place in small face-to-face groups.

In regard to the former, Rogers (1968) states what he believes to be behind the rapid growth of the small group training phenomenon:

. . . one of the most rapidly growing social phenomena in the United States is the spread of the intensive group experience. . . . Why? I believe it is because people—ordinary people—have discovered that it alleviates their loneliness and permits them to grow, to risk, to change. It brings persons into real relationships with persons. (p. 269)

From PERSONNEL AND GUIDANCE JOURNAL, *1971, Vol. 49, pp. 625–635. Copyright 1971, American Personnel and Guidance Association. Reprinted with permission of authors and publisher.*

The second factor, equally compelling, is the increasing amount of the work in organizations that takes place in small, face-to-face groups (planning, decision-making, problem-solving, etc.). Organizations and individuals recognize the need for training methods that improve the functioning of these work groups. Another aspect of current organizational life is the growing regard for temporary structures—committees, project teams, task forces, conferences, consulting relationships, etc. (Bennis & Slater, 1968; Miles, 1964). It is becoming increasingly important for individuals to have the ability to move rapidly into team relationships in which there is mutual trust, adequate team spirit, and creative stimulation among members.

The counselor and personnel worker are often in a position to provide guidance and information to individuals who think they want to participate in a small group training experience. Also, an increasing number of counselors and personnel workers are attending small group training programs themselves in order to improve their group leadership skills. Because of this widespread participation, it is important to understand the differences among the various small group approaches—including their goals and methods. In this article, we will provide a brief historical perspective on small group training and working definitions for some of the more frequently mentioned types: the T-group, the encounter group, the marathon group, and the therapy group. We will also comment on some of the questions often raised regarding professional ethics in this field.

Historical Overview

Intensive small group training methods have their roots in the workshop method of the 1930's and 1940's, including the action-research methods of Kurt Lewin and the spontaneity training and role-playing methods of Moreno. The general approach did not begin with a primary focus on personality change or overcoming social and psychological isolation; rather, it started as a wedding between social action and scientific inquiry (Bunker, 1965). Its parent disciplines were adult education and the applied research interests of Lewin and some of his colleagues in social psychology—Ronald Lippitt, Leland Bradford, Kenneth Benne, and others. Their innovations were responsible for the first training workshops held, beginning in 1947, in isolated New England communities such as Bethel, Maine—"cultural islands" free from some of the usual situations in people's daily lives that pressure against change.

The National Training Laboratories (NTL), affiliated with the National Education Association, grew out of these efforts. It was found that participants learned and changed in their ability to deal with human relations problems, not only by listening to lectures and participating in role-playing but also by analyzing the here-and-now characteristics of their own conference groups. The social scientists discovered, partly by accident, that participants were very much interested in behavioral data that researchers who observed the groups collected about the group interaction. The analysis of this "process" data provided trainees a "laboratory" in which to deal more dynamically and personally with some of the human relationship issues they were studying.

Although NTL has played a major role in the evolution of group training, there have been other important influences. Group trainers with clinical and counseling backgrounds brought to NTL workshops and similar programs the skills and interests for dealing with personality variables within groups. Also, individuals with consulting and change agent skills (many of whom were members of the NTL consulting network) have applied their efforts to programs in which the goals are to effect change in the organization and the community.

In another direction, the existential-humanistic "human potential" approach has moved beyond the methods of traditional social science by employing various expressive, intrapsychic, and somatopsychologic techniques. Esalen Institute at Big Sur, California, has led in this development. (For a more comprehensive history of group training, see Benne, 1964, and Bradford, 1967.)

Some Definitions

It is impossible to deal with small group training and the issues and problems surrounding it as a single, general phenomenon. Widely different, experience-based training approaches are currently being conducted, and to lump them together confuses rather than simplifies. Further, the need to make decisions about the appropriateness of programs and qualifications of trainers requires the ability to differentiate between kinds of programs. It is even questionable whether the various types of small groups used for educational, training, or therapeutic purposes should be subsumed under one rubric; to do so implies more commonality than actually exists. Unfortunately, there are no generally accepted meanings for many of the terms often used. The following definitions are somewhat arbitrary but seem to mesh with the historical progression.

Sensitivity training is one of the first and most generic terms in the field. It originally referred to the small group training conducted by the National Training Laboratories. Currently, it is used by some to subsume all small group training approaches. However, most practitioners do not find it a useful term because it is frequently used so broadly (to include group therapy, for example) that it has lost its power to define. Also, training personnel whose methods are only peripherally related to the original sensitivity training approach have picked up the term and have applied it to their ventures.

We find the term *laboratory training* a more useful conceptualization; it is used to refer to an educational method that emphasizes experience-based learning activities. Participants are involved in a variety of experiences, usually including small group interaction, and their behavior provides the data for learning. Thus, laboratory training involves learning by doing. The subject matter of such programs deals with some aspect of human interaction, and the goal is to be more aware of and responsive to what is going on. A specific laboratory training program (human relations lab) may run from a few hours to two or more weeks and may contain a combination of elements designed to provide experiential learning. Although laboratory training is often used to refer to NTL-sponsored programs, we use it here to include experience-based learning approaches in general.

A basic element of most laboratories is the *T-group* (T for training). In the standard NTL-type of T-group, participants find themselves in a relatively unstructured environment in which their responsibility is to build out of their interaction a group that can help them meet their needs for support, feedback, learning, etc. The behaviors exhibited by members as they play out their roles provide the material for analysis and learning. Thus, T-group members have the opportunity of learning ways in which their behavior is seen by others in the group, the kinds of styles and roles they tend to take, their effectiveness in playing various kinds of roles, ways of being more sensitive to the feelings and behaviors of other group members, methods for understanding group behavior dynamics, etc. Time is usually provided for trainees to integrate what they have learned and plan to apply their new knowledge after the laboratory ends.

Some trainers within and outside the NTL network have evolved T-groups that provide a *personal growth* focus. Weschler, Massarik, and Tannenbaum (1962), who first described a laboratory with a "personal-interpersonal emphasis," provided the following explanation and rationale:

Our version of sensitivity training increasingly concerns itself with strengthening of the individual in his desires to experience people and events more accurately, to a process of individual growth toward ever-increasing personal adequacy.

Encounter groups, as we define the term, refer to intensive small group experiences in which the emphasis is upon personal growth through expanding awareness, exploration of intrapsychic as well as interpersonal issues, and release of dysfunctional inhibitions. There is relatively little focus on the group as a learning instrument; the trainer takes a more active and directive role; and physical interaction is utilized. Other modes of expression and sensory exploration such as dance, art, massage, and nudity are currently being tried as a part of the encounter experience.

Marathon groups are time-extended encounter groups that use the massed experience and the accompanying fatigue to break through participants' defenses. Many organizations have sprung up around the country to offer encounter groups and related continued education programs. They often call themselves *growth centers* and view their offerings as a part of the *human potential movement.*

COMPARISONS WITH PSYCHOTHERAPY GROUPS

Since all of the above groups, in one way or another, deal with emotional experience, the self-concept, and impressions of the behavior of others, and since they stress honest communication, the question is sometimes raised, "How do these groups differ from therapy groups?"

Lubin and Eddy (1970) have summarized the differences stated by Frank (1964):

Therapy group members are seen by themselves and others as having psychological problems and needing help, whereas T-Group members are seen as relatively well-functioning individuals interested in improving old skills and learning new ones; attitudes which therapy attempts to modify

are usually concerned with persons who are close to the patient and therefore more central and resistant to change, whereas the T-Group attempts
to modify more peripheral attitudes; the therapist is a much more central
person than the trainer and dependency upon him continues to be strong
throughout: and the T-Group, focusing less upon the individual, evokes
more moderate emotional responses.

Also, the group-focused T-group emphasizes the here-and-now of
group development and transactions among its members. By contrast, the therapy group sanctions the search for factors associated
with conflicts and problems in the patient's past life experiences.

Another conceptualization of the current group psychotherapy
scene would be helpful at this point. Parloff (1970) suggests that the
diversity of objectives among group psychotherapists can be reduced by sorting them into two broad categories: "headshrinking"
and "mind-expanding." "Headshrinking objectives" are similar to
the ones mentioned by Scheidlinger (1967), i.e., amelioration of
suffering and restoration or repair of functioning. "Mind-expanding
objectives" include heightened positive affective states, self-actualization, and self-fulfillment.

When encounter groups, marathon groups, and T-groups with a
personal-interpersonal focus are compared with therapy groups
which have mind-expanding objectives, fewer differences can be
specified. Major distinctions that remain are:

1. T-groups with a personal-interpersonal focus, encounter groups,
   and marathon groups are relatively brief in duration and are
   time-limited.

2. The T-group with a personal-interpersenal focus usually is em-
   bedded in a larger laboratory design.

3. In general, the T-group with a personal-interpersonal focus, the
   encounter group, and the marathon group define members as
   "participants" rather than patients.

The latter distinction holds true only for the T-group with a personal-interpersonal focus, as the NTL Institute discourages participation by people who have serious emotional problems; on the
other hand, psychotherapists occasionally refer patients to encounter groups and marathon groups in order to move past therapeutic
impasses.

Laboratory Training and T-Groups

A participant in an NTL training laboratory will find the T-group a major component of the design, in terms of both time and involvement. If the program is a week in length, he will spend perhaps 30 hours or more in intensive discussion with about 10 other people. The trainer assigned to the group probably will open with a statement somewhat similar to this:

> This group will meet for many hours and will serve as a kind of laboratory where each individual can increase his understanding of the forces which influence individual behavior and the performance of groups and organizations. The data for learning will be our own behavior, feelings, and reactions. We begin with no definite structure or organization, no agreed-upon procedures, and no specific agenda. It will be up to us to fill the vacuum created by the lack of these familiar elements and to study our group as we evolve. My role will be to help the group to learn from its own experiences, but not to act as a traditional chairman nor to suggest how we should organize, what our procedure should be, or exactly what our agenda will include. With these few comments, I think we are ready to begin in whatever way you feel will be most helpful. . . . (Seashore, 1968, p. 1)

In programs with a personal-interpersonal or "personal growth" focus, the trainer might emphasize the goal of "getting to know and understand ourselves better." If the laboratory is designed to train a specific vocational group such as managers, teachers, or ministers, the opening remarks might acknowledge the relevance that group learnings have to work "back home."

After his initial remarks, the trainer usually recedes from active leadership, and the group must proceed without the usual guidance of formal authority. As the group seeks to establish goals and procedures that are acceptable and useful to its members, to develop ways of making necessary decisions, to establish norms that support its needs and goals, and to deal with the conflicts that ensue, it experiences in "real life" many of the major dilemmas in social interaction. If members can learn, with the trainer's assistance, to examine the interaction process as it unfolds, and if they can develop a trust level that will allow them to express the emotions associated with group events, learning takes place. When the appropriate climate has developed, group members share feelings and perceptions ("feedback") regarding observed behavior in the group.

THEORY AND RATIONALE FOR THE T-GROUP

There is no single theory of T-groups. What is known or hypothesized is a combination of theories, some transplanted from other settings. There are, however, several major theoretical positions which most practitioners in the field find useful and which provide a theoretical base. These include Lewin's model of attitude change (unfreezing-changing-refreezing) (Schein & Bennis, 1965), experience-based learning as contrasted with the one-way lecture approach, and overcoming emotional barriers to social learning through trust development and feedback (Lubin & Eddy, 1970).

EFFECTIVENESS OF T-GROUPS

Do training laboratories emphasizing T-groups work? Do participants actually learn and change their real-life behavior? If so, in what ways and for how long?

In spite of the fact that there are no final answers to these questions, it is *not* true that outcome research on T-groups has been ignored. It seems safe to assert that there has been more research done on T-groups than on any other training approach. The authors of the American Psychiatric Association task force report, *Encounter Groups and Psychiatry* (1970), point out that:

T-Groups, springing from the field of social psychology, have behind them a long tradition of research in group dynamics. No comparable body of knowledge has been generated by group therapy, a field notoriously deficient in any systematic research. Thus, what is presently known of the basic science of group psychotherapy stems almost entirely from social-psychological research with task groups and T-Groups; psychotherapy owes to the T-Group much of its systematic understanding of such factors as group development, group pressure, group cohesiveness, leadership, and group norms and values. Furthermore, T-Group research has elaborated a wealth of sophisticated research techniques and tools of which the group therapy field is now slowly availing itself. (p. 19)

Bibliographies and analyses of research studies have been compiled by Stock (1964), House (1967), Campbell and Dunnette (1968), Durham, Gibb, and Knowles (1967), Buchanan (1965), and others. Undoubtedly there is disagreement about what the findings, taken together, mean. We offer the following generalization. A majority of participants (about 60 percent) reports strong to fairly strong positive feelings about their T-group experiences and believe they have have been helped to change and improve their behavior. A minority (20 to 30 percent) reports either mild positive or neutral response, and a smaller group (10 percent or less) feels negative about the experience. The question of what happens behaviorally after a T-group experience is a most difficult one to answer. One factor that has baffled research designers is that "desired" behavior outcomes cannot be specified for all participants. Each brings his own set of needs and interests which he pursues in his own way and which he may change or add to in the course of the program. In addition, comparable indices of performance-related behavior change in the work or family setting are extremely difficult to develop. A number of studies indicates that such changes do take place with significant frequency, although not all the studies are sufficiently well designed or controlled to satisfy the rigorous researcher completely.

One point seems fairly clear, however. Laboratory learnings are more likely to persist and to contribute to improvements in performance when they are supported and reinforced in the back-home situation. Employees from firms that support the general norms of laboratory training through organization development programs, or married couples who have both had successful T-group experiences, are most likely the ones who find lasting benefits.

Future trends in laboratory training will probably proceed in the direction of greater linkages between training and application. Laboratories will be augmented by further training experiences which deal with the real people, processes, and problems back home. Skills, norms, and approaches to problem-solving learned in training laboratories will be put into practice through programs at community or organizational levels.

Encounter Groups

The term *encounter group* has been used generically by some writers to refer to any group, regardless of methodology or objectives, that emphasizes intensive interaction, honest communication, and self-revelation. In this sense, all the groups described in this article can be called encounter groups. To use the term in this way, however, is to invite considerable conceptual confusion at a time when clarity is urgently needed. Part of the problem arises from the dearth of definitions about encounter groups. The literature in this area is mainly of an anecdotal nature; there has been no systematic attempt to specify methods, processes, or outcomes.

Burton (1969) states that "encounter groups have been so busy being expressive that they have had little time to look to their theories" (p. ix). After studying many different kinds of encounter groups, Lieberman, Yalom, and Miles (1970) conclude that "our analysis to date strongly suggests that a view of encounter groups as a uniform activity is incorrect. It thus appears that the generic title encounter groups covers a wide range of operations by leaders that lead to many kinds of group experiences, and perhaps to many types of learnings."

Despite the lack of stated theory and the diversity of leader styles, various types of encounter groups seem to share a general view of man that grows out of the existentialist-humanist tradition: "Encounter group practitioners believe that man functions at a small fraction of his potential and that methods which remove blockages and release this potential enable him to integrate at substantially higher levels of functioning" (Lubin & Eddy, 1970). Most encounter group leaders would agree with this statement by Gibb and Gibb (1968):

People can grow. Man's potential for growth is vast and, as yet, relatively unexplored. In his inner depth—in his *essential* reality—man is capable of giving and receiving warmth, love, and trust. He is moving toward interdependence and confrontation. Growth is a kind of freeing of this inner self of these internal processes—an emergence and fulfillment of an unguessed inner potential. Growth is a process of fulfilling, realizing, emerging, and becoming. (p. 101)

Encountering methods are designed to facilitate the freeing of growth processes in a rapid manner and to circumvent defenses. Some of the methods used by various leaders are deepening of sensory awareness, muscular tension and relaxation, guided fantasy, nonverbal games, physical contact, meditation, symbolic movement, etc. Any attempt to list the methods used will of necessity be incomplete because encounter group leaders are continuously trying out new methods.

In general, cognitive activity or conceptualization of experience in encounter groups is devalued. Departures from "experience" generally are viewed as intellectual defensive maneuvers. The major exception is reported by Ellis (1969) who champions both affect and cognition.

The encounter group leader occupies a very central position in the group's activities and experience. The leader's situation bears many resemblances to that of the psychodrama director, alternately suggesting activities, concentrating his and the group's attention on various members (Haigh, 1968), regulating the time spent in various activities, etc.

Encounter groups resemble the mind-expanding (Parloff, 1970) forms of group therapy in the depth and extent of personal change that is sought, the pressure toward total self-disclosure, and the leader's centrality. Many people attend encounter groups expecting to achieve peak experiences (Maslow, 1962); these expectations are aroused by promotional material and lay literature.

Research on the effectiveness of encounter groups is almost totally nonexistent. This lack is due only partly to the newness of the field; until very recently many practitioners took the position that the outcome of encounter groups was self-evident and did not need formal evaluation. Bach (1967, 1968a) reports two studies on his marathon groups, but the reports neither compare the effectiveness of the marathon technique against other techniques nor do they contain comparison with nontreated controls. Also, duration of effect is not studied. Even though data were collected at the end of the group experience, these seem to be process rather than outcome studies. Elsewhere, Bach (1968b) has indicated that he is planning long-term follow-ups on group members. Also, the previously cited study by Lieberman et al. should provide much needed data on the effectiveness of the various encounter group methods.

Professional and Ethical Issues

During its earlier years, the laboratory training field did not encounter many problems related to maintaining standards for trainer preparation and behavior. Summer internship programs followed by co-training assignments provided an avenue of induction for the modest number of newcomers to the field. Most entered with doctorates in applied psychology or education. This situation has changed dramatically. It is no overstatement to assert that the situation regarding standards for training is in complete disarray.

No one knows how many T-groups, encounter groups, marathons, therapy groups for normals, and other intensive group experiences are held weekly in the United States. Certainly the figure runs into hundreds. Some are conducted by qualified scientists who have acquired group training skills in special programs provided by NTL, universities, or other comparable organizations. Others are being conducted by behavioral scientists, including psychiatrists, clinical psychologists, counselors, and others without special training who assume that their therapeutic skills are sufficient. And many are being conducted by individuals whose background is peripheral to or outside behavioral science. In the eyes of many, laboratory training is no longer "owned" by professionals. T-groups and encounter groups—perhaps by slightly different names—are offered by a wide variety of individuals. Undoubtedly some of the "amateur" group trainers are competent and ethical and help provide participants in their groups a worthwhile experience. Others may not be competent and in conducting groups may be satisfying primarily their own needs for control, recognition, affection, etc., rather than the learning needs of participants.

One problem is that techniques of group training, like therapy, appear deceptively simple and easy to reproduce. The T-group trainer remains silent much of the time—injecting only an occasional observation or comment. Furthermore, superficial observation might suggest that the encounter group leader requires only an easily memorized catalogue of behavioral interventions. Cookbook-type manuals of exercises and encounter tapes and films have helped provide group leaders, including the marginally qualified ones, with additional tools.

The NTL Institute has never accredited or certified trainers. In granting Fellow or Associate status to behavioral scientists, it has included them in its "network" of trainers and change agents who are utilized in NTL laboratories and other programs. A new category, "Professional Membership," indicates demonstrated beginning competence but does not imply any commitment for use on the part of NTL. Recently, the matter of standards and trainer qualifications has come under increasing discussion.

As a partial measure to exert some control over training quality, the NTL Institute has developed and ratified a policy manual defining *Standards for the Use of the Laboratory Method in NTL Institute Programs* (NTL Institute for Applied Behavioral Science, 1969). It sets forth the organization's position on such matters as trainer qualifications, participant selection, goals of training, professional ethics and values, and applications of laboratory learnings. The thrust of the policy statement is in the direction of more rigorous standards. It endorses the American Psychological Association's ethical standards, sets forth a comprehensive list of requisite skills, experiences, and ethics for its trainer members, and specifically rejects the notion that participation in one or more "basic" laboratory experiences constitutes preparation to do training.[1]

Negative Effects of Training

A common criticism of laboratory training is that it is potentially psychologically harmful. Stories about someone who "cracked up" while attending a laboratory program are not uncommon, and the assumption is that the T-group experience was the cause of the problem. A few large sample studies and several anecdotal reports are available. NTL Institute records indicate that of 14,200 individuals who participated in its summer human relations programs and industrial training programs between 1947 and 1968, the experience was stressful enough for 33 (.2 percent) to require them to leave the program prior to its completion. Almost all of these individuals had a history of prior disturbances (*NTL Institute News and Reports,* 1969). The YMCA located four individuals who had "negative experiences" out of approximately 1,200 participants in its laboratory programs (.3 percent) (Batchelder & Hardy, 1968). Three of the four, upon follow-up, seem to have gained ultimately from the disruptive experience.

The majority of studies reports the incidence of difficulty at between .2 and .5 percent, although some have higher proportions of negative results reported. Most of these studies deal with only one or two groups, and many with situations that differ from the traditional one- or two-week "stranger" laboratory led by professionals, i.e., they refer to weekend encounter marathons, training programs for psychiatric residents, classroom-type settings, leaderless groups, etc. A summarization of the data seems to indicate that laboratory training should *not* be viewed as a benign and foolproof method. In residential programs run by professionals where purposes are advertised as clearly educational rather than therapeutic, the incidence of difficulty seems quite low. On the other hand, in situations in which there is doubt about the qualifications of the trainer, the expectations of the clients, the intensity and duration of the program, and other situational pressures, there may be reason for caution.

[1] A copy of the Standards Manual may be obtained by writing the NTL Institute, 1201 16th Street, N.W., Washington, D.C. 20036.

Conclusion

The small group training field finds itself in a curious paradox. Its value system advocates an open, accepting, nonjudgmental approach. Yet it is aware of the need to protect the public and itself by seeing to the competence and appropriateness of training offered. The challenge will be to find ways of setting and maintaining viable standards and of informing the public about them, without establishing exclusive and restrictive systems.

REFERENCES

American Psychiatric Association. *Encounter groups and phychiatry.* Report of Task Force on Recent Developments in the Use of Small Groups. Washington, D.C.: American Psychiatric Association, 1970.

Bach, G. R. Marathon group dynamics: II. Dimensions of helpfulness: Therapeutic aggression. *Psychological Reports,* 1967, *20,* 1147–1158.

Bach, G. R. Marathon group dynamics: III. Disjunctive contacts. *Psychological Reports,* 1968, *20,* 1163–1172. (a)

Bach, G. R. Discussion of paper "Accelerated interaction" by Frederick H. Stoller. *International Journal of Group Psychotherapy,* 1968, *18,* 244–249. (b)

Batchelder, R. L., & Hardy, J. M. *Using sensitivity training and the laboratory method: An organizational case study in the development of human resources.* New York: Association Press, 1968.

Benne, K. D. History of the T-group in the laboratory setting. In L. P. Bradford, J. R. Gibb, & K. D. Benne (Eds.), *T-group theory and laboratory method: Innovation in re-education.* New York: Wiley, 1964.

Bennis, W. G., & Slater, P. E. *The temporary society.* New York: Harper & Row, 1968.

Bradford, L. P. Biography of an institution. *Journal of Applied Behavioral Science,* 1967, *3,* 127–143.

Buchanan, P. C. Evaluating the effectiveness of laboratory training in industry. *Explorations in Human Relations Training and Research,* No. 1. Washington, D.C.: National Education Association, 1965.

Bunker, D. R. Individual applications of laboratory training. *Journal of Applied Behavioral Science,* 1965, *1,* 131–148.

Burton, A. (Ed.). *Encounter: The theory and practice of encounter groups.* San Francisco: Jossey-Bass, 1969.

Campbell, J. P., & Dunnette, M. D. Effectiveness of T-group experiences in managerial training and development. *Psychological Bulletin*, 1968, *70*, 73–104.

Durham, L. E., Gibb, J. R., & Knowles, E. S. A bibliography of research: 1947–1967. In *Explorations in applied behavioral science*. Washington, D.C.: NTL Institute, 1967.

Ellis, A. The rational-emotive encounter group. In S. Burton (Ed.), *The theory and practice of encounter groups*. San Francisco: Jossey-Bass, 1969.

Frank, J. D. Training and therapy. In L. P. Bradford et al. (Eds.), *T-group theory and laboratory method*. New York: Wiley, 1964.

Gibb, J. R., & Gibb, L. Leaderless groups: Growth-centered values and potentials. In H. A. Otto & J. Mann (Eds.), *Ways of growth: Approaches to expanding awareness*. New York: Grossman, 1968.

Haigh, G. Two residential basic encounter groups. In H. A. Otto & J. Mann (Eds.), *Ways of growth: Approaches to expanding awareness*. New York: Grossman, 1968.

House, R. J. T-group education and leadership effectiveness: A review of the empirical literature and a critical evaluation. *Personnel Psychology*, 1967, *20*, 1–32.

Lieberman, M. A., Yalom, I. D., & Miles, M. D. The group experience project: A comparison of ten encounter technologies. In L. Blank, G. G. Gottsegen, & M. Gottsegen (Eds.), *Encounter confrontations in self and interpersonal awareness*. New York: Macmillan, 1970.

Lubin, B., & Eddy, W. B. The laboratory training model: Rationale, method and some thoughts for the future. *International Journal of Group Psychotherapy*, 1970, *20* (3), 305–399.

Maslow, A. H. *Toward a psychology of being*. Princeton: Van Nostrand, 1962.

Miles, M. B. On temporary systems. In M. B. Miles (Ed.), *Innovation in education*. New York: Teachers College, Columbia University, 1964.

NTL Institute for Applied Behavioral Science. *Standards for the use of the laboratory method*. Washington, D.C.: NTL Institute for Applied Behavioral Science, 1969.

NTL Institute News and Reports, 1969, *3* (4), 1.

Parloff, M. B. Assessing the effects of head-shrinking and mind-expanding. *International Journal of Group Psychotherapy*, 1970, *20*, 14–24.

Rogers, C. R. Interpersonal relationships: Year 2000. *Journal of Applied Behavioral Science*, 1968, *4*, 265–280.

Scheidlinger, S. Current conceptual and methodological issues in group psychotherapy research: Introduction to panel—Part I. *International Journal of Group Psychotherapy*, 1967, *17*, 53–56.

Schein, E. H., & Bennis, W. G. *Personal and organizational change through group methods: The laboratory approach.* New York: Wiley, 1965.

Seashore, C. What is sensitivity training? *NTL Institute News and Reports*, 1968, *2*, 1–2.

Stock, D. A survey of research on T-groups. In L. P. Bradford et al. (Eds.), *T-group theory and laboratory method.* New York: Wiley, 1964.

Weschler, I. R., Massarik, F., & Tannenbaum, R. The self in process: A sensitivity training emphasis. In I. R. Weschler (Ed.), *Issues in training.* (NTL Selected Reading Series.) Washington, D.C.: National Education Association, 1962. Pp. 33–46.

6 / *WHAT IS SENSITIVITY TRAINING?*

Charles Seashore

Sensitivity training is one type of experience-based learning. Participants work together in a small group over an extended period of time, learning through anaysis of their own experiences, including feelings, reactions, perceptions, and behavior. The duration varies according to the specific design, but most groups meet for a total of 10–40 hours. This may be in a solid block, as in a marathon weekend program or two to six hours a day in a one- or two-week residential program or spread out over several weekends, a semester, or a year.

The sensitivity training group may stand by itself or be a part of a larger laboratory training design which might include role playing, case studies, theory presentations, and intergroup exercises. This paper focuses mainly on the T Group (the *T* stands for *training*) as the primary setting for sensitivity training. However, many of the comments here also apply to other components of laboratory training.

A Typical T-Group Starter

The staff member in a typical T Group, usually referred to as the trainer, might open the group in a variety of ways. The following statement is an example:

This group will meet for many hours and will serve as a kind of labora-tory where each individual can increase his understanding of the forces which influence individual behavior and the performance of groups and organizations. The data for learning will be our own behavior, feelings, and reactions. We begin with no definite structure or organization, no agreed-upon procedures, and no specific agenda. It will be up to us to fill the vacuum created by the lack of these familiar elements and to study our group as we evolve. My role will be to help the group to learn from its own experience, but not to act as a traditional chairman nor to suggest how we should organize, what our procedure should be, or exactly what our agenda will include. With these few comments, I think we are ready to begin in whatever way you feel will be most helpful.

Into this ambiguous situation members then proceed to inject themselves. Some may try to organize the group by promoting an election of a chairman or the selection of a topic for discussion. Others may withdraw and wait in silence until they get a clearer sense of the direction the group may take. It is not unusual for an individual to try to get the trainer to play a more directive role, like that of the typical chairman.

Whatever role a person chooses to play, he also is observing and reacting to the behavior of other members and in turn is having an impact on them. It is these perceptions and reactions that are the data for learning.

Underlying Assumptions of T-Group Training

Underlying T-Group training are the following assumptions about the nature of the learning process which distinguish T-Group train-ing from other more traditional models of learning:

1. *Learning responsibility.* Each participant is responsible for his own learning. What a person learns depends upon his own style, readiness, and the relationships he develops with other members of the group.
2. *Staff role.* The staff person's role is to facilitate the examination and understanding of the experiences in the group. He helps participants to focus on the way the group is working, the style of an individual's participation, or the issues that are facing the group.
3. *Experience and conceptualization.* Most learning is a combina-tion of experience and conceptualization. A major T-Group aim

is to provide a setting in which individuals are encouraged to examine their experiences together in enough detail so that valid generalizations can be drawn.

4. *Authentic relationships and learning.* A person is most free to learn when he establishes authentic relationships with other people and thereby increases his sense of self-esteem and decreases his defensiveness. In authentic relationships persons can be open, honest, and direct with one another so that they are communicating what they are actually feeling rather than masking their feelings.

5. *Skill acquisition and values.* The development of new skills in working with people is maximized as a person examines the basic values underlying his behavior as he acquires appropriate concepts and theory and as he is able to practice new behavior and obtain feedback on the degree to which his behavior produces the intended impact.

The Goals and Outcomes of Sensitivity Training

Goals and outcomes of sensitivity training can be classified in terms of potential learning concerning individuals, groups, and organizations.

1. *The individual point of view.* Most T-Group participants gain a picture of the impact that they make on other group members. A participant can assess the degree to which that impact corresponds with or deviates from his conscious intentions. He can also get a picture of the *range of perceptions* of any given act. It is as important to understand that different people may see the same piece of behavior differently—for example, as supportive or antagonistic, relevant or irrelevant, clear or ambiguous —as it is to understand the impact on any given individual. In fact, very rarely do all members of a group have even the same general perceptions of a given individual or a specific event.

   Some people report that they try out behavior in the T Group that they have never tried before. This experimentation can enlarge their view of their own potential and competence and provide the basis for continuing experimentation.

2. *The group point of view.* The T Group can focus on forces which affect the characteristics of the group such as the level of commitment and follow-through resulting from different methods of

making decisions, the norms controlling the amount of conflict and disagreement that is permitted, and the kinds of data that are gathered. Concepts such as cohesion, power, group maturity, climate, and structure can be examined using the experiences in the group to better understand how these same forces operate in the back-home situation.

3. *The organization point of view.* Status, influence, division of labor, and styles of managing conflict are among organizational concepts that may be highlighted by analyzing the events in the small group. Subgroups that form can be viewed as analogous to units within an organization. It is then possible to look at the relationships between groups, examining such factors as competitiveness, communications, stereotyping, and understanding.

One of the more important possibilities for a participant is that of examining the kinds of assumptions and values which underlie the behavior of people as they attempt to manage the work of the group. The opportunity to link up a philosophy of management with specific behaviors that are congruent with or antithetical to that philosophy makes the T Group particularly relevant to understanding the large organization.

Research on Sensitivity Training

Research evidence on the effectiveness of sensitivity training is rather scarce and often subject to serious methodological problems. The annotated bibliographies referred to in the suggested readings at the end of this paper are the best source for identifying available studies. The following generalizations do seem to be supported by the available data:

1. People who attend sensitivity training programs are more likely to improve their managerial skills than those who do not (as reported by their peers, superiors, and subordinates).

2. Everyone does not benefit equally. Roughly two-thirds of the participants are seen as increasing their skills after attendance at laboratories. This figure represents an average across a number of studies.

3. Many individuals report extremely significant changes and impact on their lives as workers, family members, and citizens. This kind of anecdotal report should be viewed cautiously in terms of direct application to job settings, but it is consistent enough that

it is clear that T-Group experiences can have a powerful and positive impact on individuals.

4. The incidence of serious stress and mental disturbance during training is difficult to measure, but it is estimated to be less than one per cent of participants and in almost all cases occurs in persons with a history of prior disturbances.

SELECTED REFERENCES

Bradford, L. P., Gibb, J. R. & Benne, K. D. (Eds.) *T-group theory and laboratory method: Innovation in re-education.* New York: Wiley, 1964.

Craig, R. L., & Bittel, L. R. *Training and development handbook.* New York: McGraw-Hill, 1967.

Durham, L., Gibb, J. R., & Knowles, E. S. A bibliography of research. In NTL series, *Explorations in Human Relations Training and Research,* 1967, No. 2.

Harrison, R. Problems in the design and interpretation of research on human relations training. In NTL series, *Explorations in Human Relations Training and Research,* 1967, No. 1.

Miles, M. B. *Learning to work in groups.* New York: Teachers College, Columbia University, 1959.

Schein, E. H., & Bennis, W. G. *Personal and organizational change through group methods.* New York: Wiley, 1965.

Tannenbaum, R., Weschler, I. R., & Massarik, F. *Leadership and organization: A behavioral science approach.* New York: McGraw-Hill, 1961.

The Journal of Applied Behavioral Science. Washington, D.C.: NTL Institute for Applied Behavioral Science.

7 / ON BEING IN A GROUP: ANOTHER STEP IN BECOMING

Gerald E. Osborne, Richard C. Diedrich, and H. Allan Dye

Those involved in working with groups are often asked to describe the process of the group. The interested individual asks: What are groups like? What do they do? Most attempts to respond helpfully are met with more questions, quizzical looks, and pleasant but questioning smiles. Probably the most frequent response to the query of the interested but uninitiated prospective group member is: "Really, you have to participate in a group before you will be able to understand them." Perhaps this need not be the case. If one who has participated in a group were able to share the experience in a very personal way, the experience of that one might be sufficient for the understanding of many. Someone has very graciously and generously offered to do just that. Though she will remain anonymous to the reader, she may become very real as a person reaching out to share with another human being.

Earlier this year, the State Department of Public Instruction, Division of Pupil Personnel Services, sponsored a residential workshop devoted to group work for a number of school counselors from throughout the State of Indiana. The program was conducted over a period of three days and two nights and involved all of the participants in a sensitivity and human relations laboratory training experience. Each participant was asked to complete some evaluation instruments both during and after the workshop which was conducted by staff from the Counseling and Personnel Services Section of Purdue University. A month after the program, the participants were again assembled for the purpose of extending the goals of

From INDIANA PERSONNEL AND GUIDANCE JOURNAL, *1969, Vol. 4, No. 1, pp. 2–5. Copyright 1969, Indiana Personnel and Guidance Association. Reprinted with permission of authors and publisher.*

the workshop. It was during this last meeting that our anonymous friend, now named Mary Pat, offered to share her impressions with you, the reader.

In the course of the original program, each member was involved in a T-group which met five times for sessions of approximately three hours each. At the close of each session, the members were asked to describe their feelings about that particular group experience on each of 17 variables by rating each adjective from 1 (not at all applicable) to 7 (very applicable). Mary Pat's responses appear in Table 1. An eighteenth and optional variable was included so that members might respond in any other way they chose by merely writing in a feeling or impression. Mary Pat's extemporaneous comments are a vivid documentary of the joys and torments inevitably experienced in the struggle of being one person among many persons: 1st session) "I felt as though our feet were set in blocks of concrete and we were unable to move or even mark time"; 2nd session) "Perhaps the increased feeling of worth is in some way tied

TABLE 1

Mary Pat's Responses to the Group Reaction Questionnaire

Adjective	Group Meeting				
	1	2	3	4	5
Rewarding	1[a]	5	5	6	5
(Not) [b] Boring	5	6	6	7	3
Open	5	6	5	7	7
(Not) Anxiety-provoking	6	4	3	6	7
(Not) Superficial	3	7	6	6	7
(Not) Frustrating	6	6	3	7	7
Exciting	1	6	6	6	4
Helpful (personally)	1	4	4	7	6
(Not) Hostile	7	6	6	7	7
(Not) Phoney	5	6	7	7	7
Anxiety-reducing	1	1	2	3	4
Meaningful	1	3	4	6	6
Comforting	3	1	3	6	6
Honest	3	4	6	7	7
Deep	1	4	5	6	6
Warm/close	2	3	6	6	7
Uninhibited	5	5	5	6	6
Mean Value	3.29	4.72	4.82	6.24	6.00

[a] 1—not at all applicable; 7—very applicable.
[b] The original Scale did not include the notation (Not); the directionality of the six scales now preceded by (Not) has been changed for this presentation to allow for the calculation of a mean value for each group meeting.

in with the active participation, whether it was accepted by the group as worthwhile or not"; 3rd session) "No one thing appropriate here—there are so many"; 4th session) "I'm glad for this morning. When I came in I was wishing I could be some place else because I felt the time would be wasted. How very fortunate the group was so responsive. I can leave with a better feeling about the value of T-groups"; 5th session) "I leave with a warm and fulfilled feeling. Thanks."

At the completion of the workshop, each member was given an open-ended questionnaire to be completed and returned before the follow-up meeting a month later. Mary Pat began by thanking the staff for an eventful and inspiring workshop. It seems that she is the one who should be thanked because she shared so much of herself, even though she is typically reticent: "This (completing the questionnaire) is contrary to my reluctance to put feelings on paper. Written comments can be damaging—you are responsible for them." Mary Pat shared her *reluctance* to initially trust the assigned leaders because "trust requires time and association"; her *frustration* because of "her lack of skills"; her *discovery* "that others see me differently than I see myself; I felt good to find that others see me as a warmer, more concerned person than I judged myself to be"; her *joy* that the group experience made her "feel better about working with (her) 7th and 8th grade students"; and her *escape* from a doubt born during a disturbing experience in her counselor training program: "I feel free of the doubt now and my natural self-confidence is strengthened. I'm sure I will be a better counselor because of this experience."

Mary Pat wrote of her newly found ease in accepting others since in the group she had "discovered that the leaders and other members had as much difficulty verbalizing feelings as I did. It was reassuring to find we were all in the same boat, so to speak." When asked about the changes that had occurred in her *behavior*, Mary Pat replied: "I can be more relaxed in my associations with others since they perceived me as warm and understanding. I can be more comfortable when receiving good feelings rather than slightly embarrassed or cautious." Many days after the completion of the workshop, Mary Pat described the intensity of her experience as follows: "Terribly intense. On the long drive home I thought over the experience—and almost every day since. I see the value in delaying the evaluation several days, since in retrospect many small things take on new meaning. It was such an intense experience that I still feel exhausted and drained."

At the follow-up meeting, the group members were again invited to meet and share with one another the meaning of the group experience for them. Mary Pat described how her ability to understand how other people saw her had helped her in teaching and counseling. She said that she was "more secure, more self-confident, and more aware of other people." Mary Pat viewed her experience as "an initial learning" that she believed was increasing through practice. She felt that she behaved differently because "two people can't meet for even five minutes and go away unchanged," and, when asked if she could be more specific, Mary Pat suggested that "each will have to evaluate (the change) for himself."

Can the meaning of the group experience be easily and quickly described? Our friend, Mary Pat, seemed to think so. She felt that the meaning of her experience could be summed in a single word: "FAITH—the strength to do." Mary Pat extended her summation with the following final comments:

> FAITH—the strength to do.
> Where do we get it?
> From others.
> Where do they get it?
> From others.

Part Two

PROCESSES: GROUP LEADERSHIP, MEMBERSHIP, AND DEVELOPMENT

Groups labeled as *sensitivity, encounter, process, training, human relations,* or *counseling*—all have achieved a prominent, if not somewhat faddish, position in our society. People who work with groups are asked with increasing frequency to describe the group experience. Most attempts to answer are met with more questions and quizzical looks. Yet constant questioning need not upset the group practitioner. Since the group phenomenon is based on research and rational observations, in addition to unique personal experience, some definitive answers exist about the nature of group leadership, membership, and development.

Leaders and members all join groups for many reasons. Each person selects the group in which he desires to participate as well as the role he wishes to play in the group. The individual member or leader must have a clear picture of his own role and function in the group. He should choose a personal style of participation and interaction which furthers the purposes of the group. A clear statement of the goals and expectations of a given group will largely determine the roles and responsibilities of leaders and members.

The leader and members are jointly responsible for the establishment of viable "ground rules"; together they guide and influence the interaction of the group. As each person fulfills his function, the group develops and matures organically. The individual is responsible not just for himself, but for the entire group. He learns the skills required to help change behavior in himself, in others, and in the group as a whole. Thus, the group has the capacity to develop the potential of its members.

The selections in Part Two have been included to help the group worker understand and make use of the forces within a group which contribute to or interfere with group effectiveness. The first eight articles focus on the various functions of leaders and members, while the last four describe group process and development.

How, when, and why the leader intervenes is but one critical aspect of group process and development. Content management typically serves only to differentiate one form of group experience from another. Various approaches to conducting a group experience are described in the section on *Group Leadership.*

Gordon, in "A Description of the Group-Centered Leader" (1955), writes about the kind of leadership most often provided in group experiences. The author identifies and discusses the differences between group-centered and leader-guided approaches to group leadership. Advocates of the group-centered approach consider the contribution of every member to be valuable, and Gordon suggests replacing the traditional role of leader with as many potential leaders as there are group members. The popularity of this approach is due in part to its foundation in democratic principles and the minimal emphasis on counselor intervention. In these respects it is similar to the client-centered approach to individual counseling favored by many counselors and educators. Proponents of group-centered leadership believe its appropriateness and effectiveness have been established empirically.

Williams' article, "Limitations, Fantasies, and Security Operations of Beginning Group Psychotherapists" (1966), is a fascinating firsthand account of the impact of role limitations, fearful fantasies, and security operations on the effectiveness of the beginning group therapist. Dyer, in "An Inventory of Trainer Interventions" (1963), discusses the leadership role from the perspective of kinds of intervention and approaches used by the leader. Finally, Dye's article,

"Some Considerations for School Counselors Who Work with Groups" (1968), provides a general description of the characteristics of group counselors, preparation for working with groups, and the challenges faced by the group practitioner.

The section on *Group Membership* opens with a previously unpublished paper by South, entitled "Observation Guide: On Seeing, Hearing, and Feeling." The student will find the observations of this process-oriented guide invaluable to his understanding of what influences group climate. Bonney, in "Pressures Toward Conformity in Group Counseling" (1965), explores the principles of group dynamics as applied to counseling groups and suggests that counselors use the phenomenon of conformity to examine the process of group counseling. In "Therapeutic Interaction in Adult Therapy Groups," previously unpublished, Andrews stresses the importance of six therapeutic dynamics in facilitating group therapy. Berzon and Solomon's article, "The Self-Directed Therapeutic Group: Three Studies" (1966), reviews research efforts and developments with self-directed groups and describes in detail a "program" of stimulus material. (This article could have appeared instead in the section on group leadership, but we considered its placement here to be the more appropriate location.)

What really goes on in a group? Specific trends or tendencies are evident in most groups. Some of these patterns or stages have been described by skilled researchers and group practitioners. The articles which appear in the *Group Process and Development* section of Part Two were chosen to clarify for the group leader and members the process patterns which develop in groups. The four articles in this section provide the reader with some functional observations which can be used to examine the developing and variable behavior of a group. Groups do not just "happen." The group counselor requires special knowledge and expertise which are not generally acquired through learning how to counsel individuals. The group practitioner must understand group dynamics as well as individual personality; he must have a feel for some of the common elements in the group experience. A sound theoretical frame of reference is far more crucial than precise techniques or exceptional creativity in developing new exercises.

Rogers' article, "The Process of the Basic Encounter Group" (1967), is a naturalistic, descriptive account of his various experiences with basic encounter groups and their process. He identifies and traces the unfolding development of a group. Gendlin and Beebe, in "An Experiential Approach to Group Therapy" (1968), offer a stimulating examination of the "propositions" for experiential group process and provide some safeguards for these ground rules. In "A Developmental Model for Counseling Groups" (1966), Foley and Bonney examine a theoretical model of group development and present a method for identifying developmental stages in a group. The final article by Tuckman, "Developmental Sequence in Small Groups" (1965), is a comprehensive analysis of fifty articles dealing with stages of group development. Articles were classified by settings and realms (interpersonal stages versus task behaviors) and in terms of how they fit a conceptual model of changes in group behavior proposed by Tuckman.

Until the group practitioner achieves a thorough understanding of the complex nature of group processes, he will remain less than totally effective in helping groups to develop, understand, and maintain themselves. The careful reader will discern that the twelve selections presented in Part Two have a broad scope and hardly scratch the surface of the many varied processes of group leadership, membership, and development.

Group Leadership

8 / A DESCRIPTION OF THE GROUP-CENTERED LEADER

Thomas Gordon

It is particularly at the behavioral level of leadership that fundamental differences between various approaches stand out most sharply. Most of the recent descriptions of "democratic" approaches to leadership share a common philosophical appreciation of the worth and potentiality of the individual, as well as a common theoretical belief in the value of "participation of group members," "a permissive group climate," "the distribution of leadership throughout the group," and other such concepts. But when one looks more closely at the different roles played by the leader as defined by these different "schools of thought," important and quite radical differences are apparent. It often takes a very close look, however, to discover these differences, in part because the same words are being used to describe all of these newer approaches to leadership. Different meanings emerge for these commonly used words when the specific behavior patterns of the leader are examined carefully.

An appropriate example is the word "permissiveness." Many theories emphasize that the leader must be permissive, yet some of the descriptions of the role of the "permissive" leader sanction such things as checking overaggressive participants, drawing in nonparticipants by skillful questions or reassurance, placing some members under personal attack in order to get emotional involvement, sidetracking irrelevancies, and so on. To other leadership theorists, and to us, these behaviors as part of the leader's role would seem

From GROUP-CENTERED LEADERSHIP by Thomas Gordon (Boston: Houghton Mifflin, 1955). Excerpts from Chapter 8, "A Description of the Group-Centered Leader," pp. 159–200. Copyright 1955, Houghton Mifflin. Reprinted with permission of author and publisher.

far from permissive—in fact, perhaps even manipulative. Another example is the term "nondirective," the original purport of which, as derived from a particular group of psychotherapists, was to convey that the therapist did not try to direct the verbal expressions of clients undergoing therapy. Recently in connection with "democratic leadership" one writer suggested the use of the technique of "nondirective leads"—questions designed to direct the thinking of the group in some direction desired by the leader. In the long run, these semantic paradoxes, such as "nondirective directing" and "permissive manipulation," will actually hide the real differences between points of view instead of bringing them out in the open as differences to be settled in time by experience and research.

The particular bias underlying the point of view here is that in many of the recent formulations of "democratic" leadership the actual behavior of the leader has not always been consistent with basic democratic values or with the proponent's expressed philosophical or theoretical orientation. In short, in some of the current descriptions of democratic leadership, the leader's behavior was not as "democratic" as his professed philosophy and theory. Theorists have not gone far enough in developing a coherent description of the leader's role which rather consistently implements their theoretical principles or their democratic values. It is the purpose of this chapter to describe a particular leader role which appears to us to be at variance with some of the existing conceptions of the role of a "democratic leader."

Our description will include a general statement of the group-centered leader's philosophy, particularly as it concerns the group and the persons who make up the group. In addition, we shall describe the group-centered leader in more objective terms. An attempt will be made then to describe certain aspects of the group-centered leader's behavior during his initial contact with a group. Finally, we shall try to analyze the group-centered leader's behavior as he carries out a changing role over a period of time with his group, for it has become clear that the role of the group-centered leader is a changing one. At first, when he is actually perceived by the group members as someone filling a position, having more status, and possessing more power, the group-centered leader finds it necessary to play a different role than later, when the group has become more self-directing and self-responsible and when the leader has actually lost his leadership position and is perceived as merely another group member. When the leader is successful in achieving this state of affairs, we can stop talking about *the* leader and begin talking only about group members. For in theory, group-centered leadership is an approach which aims at replacing a single leader with as many potential leaders as there are group members. As we have emphasized before, however, in most groups there will already be a perceived or designated leader. Our description is of a role which such a perceived leader can initially adopt, if he wishes to use his position to develop the leadership potential of his group members.

Attitudinal Foundations of the Group-Centered Leader's Role

Already some of the values and attitudes of the group-centered leader may have been inferred from the earlier discussion of the group-centered way of looking at the concept of leadership in groups. Nevertheless, some of the more specific values and attitudes of the group-centered leader need closer examination because of their significance as determiners of his actual approach to groups and of his behavior in interaction with group members. It should be emphasized again that these values and attitudes toward groups have come to be accepted by the group-centered leader as a result of his experiences in groups—they have not been drawn out of thin air or extracted from sterile philosophical and theoretical systems. Neither have these attitudes become crystallized all at once for him. Rather he has gradually learned to accept them over a period of time, while constantly experimenting with different approaches to groups. They have been continuously revised on the basis of this ongoing experience, and needless to say they are at present only hypotheses which await further testing.

A General Description of His Philosophy

To the group-centered leader, a group exists for the realization of the purposes and goals of its members. These purposes and goals will vary from group to group and will vary from time to time within a single group, yet always the group is simply the means by which the members are enhanced through the achievement of *their* purposes. It is incompatible with the values and attitudes of the group-centered leader that a group should exist for the realization of the purposes and goals of the leader, apart from the group. It is also inconsistent with his philosophy that a group should exist for the accomplishment of the aims and objectives of someone outside the group. The group-centered leader, therefore, believes that responsibility should reside with the total group. It is the group, not the leader, who has the responsibility for setting its goals and defining its purposes; and consequently it is inconsistent with the values he holds to deny the group such responsibility. It is the group that should have the responsibility for making decisions on matters that will affect its members; and consequently the group-centered leader finds it incompatible with his values to make such decisions *for* the group. Finally, the group-centered leader believes that it should be the responsibility of the total group to set its own rules, its standards of member behavior, its laws and regulations, within the limits dictated by the external situation in which the group is operating.

Believing as he does that the group exists for the fulfillment of certain of the needs of its members, the group-centered leader sees the procedures, forms, structure, or rituals of the group as having no value in and of themselves. Insofar as they contribute to the enhancement of the members of the group, however, they have definite value. The group-centered leader cannot accept the way some business or industrial executives worship "policy" to the extent that human values are often made secondary to the value of rigidly maintaining and sticking to "the company's age-old policy." Although the group-centered leader recognizes the need for a group to have policies, procedures, and rules of behavior, nevertheless it is his conviction that they should be merely the *products* of group functioning, the means by which the group may actualize itself, the instruments of the group. As such, they should serve the group rather than determine how the group always must function. For example, the writer has become increasingly aware of the extent to which strict adherence to the honored and universal "parliamentary procedures" can strait-jacket a group so effectively that its functioning is no longer appropriate to the problems it must solve. One wonders how such a set of standard group procedures, which might have been very appropriate for a particular legislative body operating in a different century, could have become accepted as the required mode of operation for so many diversified groups varying all the way from a board of directors of a large corporation to a boys' club organized for fun and recreation.

Just as the group-centered leader prefers to operate on the basis of a philosophy characterized by faith in the individual, so he has chosen to adopt an attitude that the group can be trusted. His philosophy is at variance with the underlying assumptions of such writers as LeBon and Freud, who stressed the notion of the ignorant masses and the competent leader. LeBon's point of view clearly made the crowd a mob of instinct-ridden, uncritical, and unstable individuals. The eminent sociologist, William Graham Sumner, championed this same conception that the masses were men who were on a basis of equality and who could never be anything but hopeless savages. Though one seldom hears such extreme attitudes expressed today, the influence of such writers on present-day thinking should not be minimized.

Nevertheless, the group-centered leader prefers to grant the group a good deal more potential. He has much more respect for the capacity of the group for self-direction, critical thinking, resistance to external influence, and appropriate problem-solving behavior. Although he recognizes that history can furnish many examples of groups which seem to fit Freud's or LeBon's description, he is not blind to the fact that other groups have demonstrated quite opposite characteristics. The group-centered leader recognizes the existence of both positive and negative characteristics within every group. However, his clinical experience in dealing with individuals in the process of therapy has sensitized him to the fact that much of their negative behavior is a consequence of earlier experiences in which they have been subjected to the authoritarian control of parents, teachers, employers, and other leaders. In other words, individuals, and likewise groups, *can* become reactive, hostile, aggressive, destructive, submissive, dependent, suggestible—or they *may*, in Freud's words, "want to be ruled and oppressed," "demand illusions," "submit instinctively to anyone who appoints himself as master." They can and do exhibit these tendencies, but to the group-centered leader these are the tendencies of sick individuals, these are the characteristics of a group that has not been given the opportunity to develop and express its more constructive modes of behavior. It is precisely at this point that Freud and others erred in their diagnosis. Their argument ran like this: groups need a powerful master and a forceful leader because the group possesses negative characteristics. The conviction of the group-centered leader, however, is that *groups develop these negative characteristics because they have already been controlled by powerful masters and authoritarian leaders.*

The group-centered leader has a respect for individual people. He tries to see each person as having a certain worth and significance quite unrelated to that person's social class, occupational status, personal traits, skills, abilities, appearance, race, religion, or other such characteristics. The significance of the person lies more in the fact that he is a complex, developing organism, a living demonstration of the miracle of life. Instead of respecting a group member because he happens to be very intelligent, comes from a prominent family, and occupies a high status position in his profession, the group-centered leader endeavors to respect this group member simply as a person—someone quite distinct from any other person. Even more important, the group-centered leader strives to develop an equal amount of respect for the person who possesses characteristics that in our culture are judged less desirable or who represents a class of people which has lower status and prestige in our cultural hierarchy. In short, the group-centered leader is constantly struggling to see the worth and significance of each person, divested of the traits, trappings, and symbols on which society ordinarily places some kind of value. He hopes to learn to respect the worker as much as the manager, the teacher as much as the principal, the dull and un-attractive student as much as the bright and handsome one, the aggressive and defensive "neurotic" as much as the more placid and secure "normal," the Jew as much as the Gentile, the child as much as the parent. The group-centered leader is attempting to break through the numerous cultural stereotypes by which we evaluate others, in order that he may learn to respect the person for being a person rather than merely a representative of a class of persons.

The group-centered leader prefers to adopt as his working hypothesis the belief that the individual has a vast store of untapped potential for positive, constructive, intelligent, and mature behavior. His is the positive, optimistic, and hopeful philosophy about the nature of man to which reference has already been made in an earlier chapter. The group-centered leader has grown to believe that the central core of man's personality, that which has been called his basic "animal nature" or his "organismic self," is something that can be trusted and relied upon, not something that has to be checked, inhibited, controlled, and feared. Thus, if the group-centered leader is successful in facilitating the release of the person's potential, he is confident that what is released will be positive, social, forward-moving, and creative.

These two values of the group-centered leader, his respect for the uniqueness of the person and his faith in the positive quality of man's basic nature, are closely related and in fact inseparable. For if as a leader he had no faith in man's potential for positive and constructive behavior, it is unlikely that he would have much respect for the unique potential of each individual, or would put his ener-gies into the task of releasing the individual's unique capacities. We will strive to release something only if we have faith in what comes out, and we will strive to control and bottle up that which we fear. This aspect of the group-centered leader's philosophy is difficult to communicate clearly. Perhaps because the opposite beliefs and attitudes have become so much a part of our thinking, it is not easy to find the words to express a belief in the positive nature of the human organism.

The First Contact with the Group

All leaders who have attempted a group-centered approach will agree that the first contact with the group is extremely important to the relationship subsequently established between the leader and the group. In the first contact the group members will be forming first impressions of the leader which may tend to persist, even though the leader's behavior might later change. Furthermore, with groups in which membership is completely voluntary it is important for the leader at the outset to establish the kind of relationship that does not discourage members from returning after the first meeting.

Experience teaches the group-centered leader that people are extremely sensitive to his initial behavior, often responding to subtle and seemingly insignificant aspects of it. Experienced public speakers, recognizing this same tendency in people, often recommend that a speaker should never say anything important for the first few minutes in order to allow the audience to look him over and size him up. From the psychotherapists we can learn how crucial the first interviews with a client can be in determining whether or not the client will continue beyond that point. Recently, for example, when the writer was conducting a follow-up interview with a client who had completed a successful series of interviews, the client made the following statement:

In coming here, I know, especially after the first or second interview, I considered you as definitely a supporting individual. When I was disturbed I was able to . . . there was . . . I mean, I was not overwhelmed because I knew I always had you to come to. This was quite a support during that period. And I was evidently extremely sensitive to everything you did. For instance, at one time you had to tell me that it was time to stop the interview. When you said this it was a rebuff to me. I noticed little things such as when you would come in the waiting room downstairs, what I felt your attitude to be—whether you overlooked me or if you were friendly and so forth. You were quite an important individual.

It is apparent that the impression the therapist made upon this client at the beginning of the interviews was of real significance to her. Consequently she was extremely sensitive to nuances of his behavior.

Leaders who have tried to be group-centered will also agree that the first contact provokes a great deal of anxiety in the leader himself. As he faces a group for the first time it is only natural for him to be apprehensive. He will be wondering: How will the group respond to this strange new role I am to play? Will they be hostile? What if they refuse to take responsibility themselves and demand it of me? What if no one speaks up? Will not the group simply wait for me to start things going? These and many other similar questions will be running through the mind of the leader as he makes his introduction to the group. At this point, while he feels uncertain and insecure, he will be most tempted to deviate from his earlier intention to allow the group to take full responsibility.

Perhaps this explains why current theories of leadership differ so greatly over the initial role of the leader, and particularly over his approach to the group at the first meeting. It is hard for leaders to approach the first meeting without feeling a strong need to take over, to start the ball rolling, to set the stage, or to direct the group in some way.

Should the Leader "Structure"?

If a leader is going to assume a new role with a group, should he not first explain this to the members and then define specifically how he is going to operate? In other words, should he not "structure" his role for the group so that the members will understand better what is going on? As carried out by leaders advocating this approach, structuring usually consists in telling the group members that their leader is not going to direct their activities; giving reasons why he is not; informing the group that it will be up to each member to take an active role; denying that the leader has any implicit goals for the group; and so on. In one sense, structuring may be an attempt to get prior acceptance from the group for the role to be played by the leader. The leader informs the members in advance what they should expect, in the hope that understanding on their part will reduce their confusion and hostility. He tells the group how he is going to act as its leader, and tries to justify this in some way or another. The underlying assumption is that an intellectual understanding on the part of the group will facilitate acceptance of the new role of the leader and will accelerate the process by which the group becomes self-responsible.

Experience with such structuring leads the writer to conclude that it is seldom effective. Intellectualized explanations usually fall on deaf ears, either because the members find this strange new leader role foreign to their previous experience, or because they do not really believe that the leader can honestly carry out this kind of role. Unsuccessful attempts to structure with groups run parallel to the experience of client-centered therapy. Although it was formerly customary for client-centered therapists to try to explain to clients how the therapist was going to behave and how they might behave, most therapists have dropped this practice. They found that it was seldom possible to communicate verbally the relationship that develops between the client-centered therapist and his client. Apparently it is so unlike other relationships that it can be understood only by actually *experiencing* it over a period of time, in contrast to merely *hearing about* it. For this reason, most client-centered therapists of the writer's acquaintance make no effort to explain this role they will play, but simply go ahead and play it. If they are consistently nondirective, nonintervening, and nonleading, the client gradually begins to believe in the sincerity of the therapist's intentions. In this case the therapist's actions speak louder than any number of words to explain the nature of his role.

Some Distinctive Functions Performed by the Group-Centered Leader

In addition to carrying out a different role during his first contact with a group, the group-centered leader continuously performs certain distinctive functions throughout the life of the group, but especially during the initial stages of the group's development. These functions gradually are taken over by other members of the group as the members lose their initial dependence upon the leader; but during the early stages of the group's development, these functions are often performed predominantly by the leader.

When we analyze a role as complex as that of a group leader, we do some injustice to its dynamic and personal nature. We need to keep in mind at all times that picking apart the leader's role tends to depersonalize him, making him appear as a collection of discrete and mechanical techniques rather than as a real person with attitudes and feelings, functioning in an integrated and purposeful manner. Nevertheless, it can be extremely helpful to isolate and identify some of the distinctive behaviors of the group-centered leader, in this way making it easier for others to understand how the group-centered leader differs from other kinds of leaders.

Social science can now help in making this kind of analysis, for we are now able through electrical recordings to reproduce group discussions accurately and we have systems of categorizing different kinds of verbal communication. In the present description of the role of the group-centered leader, use has been made of these methods of analyzing the verbal behavior of the leader.

LISTENING

Probably the most important single function performed by the group-centered leader is that of listening to the contributions of others in the group. This would hardly seem worth mentioning were it not for the fact that the group-centered leader practices a very special and distinctive kind of listening.

What We Mean by Listening. Psychotherapists have introduced us to a new kind of listening. They have shown that it can be a powerful agent for helping persons with emotional problems. Its therapeutic effect can be understood when we consider that the emotionally disturbed individual himself suffers from faulty communication, both within himself and with others, and listening by the therapist seems to improve his communication dramatically. Rogers (Rogers & Roethlisberger, 1952) expresses this idea clearly when he writes:

> The whole task of psychotherapy is the task of dealing with a failure in communications. The emotionally maladjusted person, the "neurotic," is in difficulty first because communication within himself has broken down, and second because as a result of this his communication with others has been damaged. If this sounds somewhat strange, then let me put it in other terms. In the "neurotic" individual, parts of himself which have been termed unconscious, or repressed, or denied to awareness, become blocked off so that they no longer communicate themselves to the conscious or managing part of himself. As long as this is true, there are distortions in the way he communicates himself to others, and so he suffers both within

himself, and in his interpersonal relations. The task of psychotherapy is to help the person achieve, through a special relationship with a therapist, good communication within himself. Once this is achieved he can communicate more freely and more effectively with others. (p. 46)

What the therapist has learned to do is to enter a relationship with another in which he consistently listens with understanding. He has discovered a way of getting into the thought processes of the other person, or we might say that he has learned how to enter into the person's own unique "frame of reference." To do this requires an intent to understand how the other person is looking at the world, how he is perceiving things. The therapist puts on the spectacles of the other person so that he may view reality in the same way. This requires putting aside one's own spectacles, suspending one's own ideas, shutting out as completely as possible one's own way of looking at things.

This is precisely what the group-centered leader tries to do as he listens attentively to the expressions of his group members. Having no need to get his own idea across, having no secret intentions, having no particular goals which he expects the group to reach, he is thus more able to listen to the contributions of others without being concerned about their ultimate effect upon the group. In a sense, he "permits" himself to listen with understanding because he has freed himself from the need to influence and direct the group's discussion.

This type of listening requires certain attitudes on the part of the leader. He must *want* to understand how the speaker is looking at the world. There must be an earnest intent to "be with the other person," with respect to *his* thoughts, feelings, and attitudes. Such an attitude is quite different from one that predisposes the listener to try to change the other person's way of looking at things. Instead of listening with the feeling, "You should be seeing things differently," the leader tries to maintain an attitude of, "Let me try to understand how you *are* seeing things." This attitude is different, too, from one which leads a listener to interpret or "go beyond" what the speaker is perceiving at the moment. It is common practice, for example, for some group leaders to listen for the deeper meanings, for "the unconscious aspects of communication," for that which is not intended by the speaker. This is a different kind of listening attitude from the one we are describing. The group-centered leader tries to hear only what is present in the speaker's awareness and to read nothing additional into the communication.

The Test of Listening. Because we can never be sure that we have completely understood another person, it is important to test the accuracy of our listening. Unfortunately, in most situations involving an attempt to communicate with others, we rarely put our understanding to a test. Consequently, we often misunderstand others or distort their meanings. One of the best ways of minimizing this misunderstanding and distortion is for the listener to try to restate in his own language the expression of the speaker and then to check to see if the restatement is acceptable to the speaker. This is essentially what the group-centered leader is continuously doing throughout the initial stages of the group's development. He calls it "reflection of feelings or meanings," to convey that he is trying to mirror the speaker's expressions so accurately that the speaker himself is satisfied that he has been understood.

This is an extremely difficult thing to do, even momentarily. The reader who is interested enough to test out the accuracy of his own listening will find the following experiment both interesting and revealing:

> Choose a situation in which you have become involved in a controversial discussion or argument with another person. Suggest to the other that you both adopt a ground rule and follow this strictly throughout the discussion. The rule: Before either participant can make a point or express an opinion of his own he must first reflect aloud the statement of the previous speaker; he must make a restatement that is accurate enough to satisfy the speaker before he is allowed to speak for himself.[1]

This little experiment if it is seriously carried out, will demonstrate, first, that it is very difficult to adopt another's frame of reference. Second, it will give the participants a new kind of experience in which they will find that emotions tend to drop out and differences become minimized. Furthermore, each participant will discover that his own views are changing and will admit that he has learned something new from the other.

The Element of Risk in Listening. Not only does listening with understanding require a firm intent to understand another and a kind of rapt attention that we seldom give to speakers; it also requires a certain amount of courage and personal security. This is because there is a real risk involved in this kind of listening. We run the risk of being changed ourselves, for when we really under-

---

[1] Suggested to the writer by S. I. Hayakawa, the semanticist.

stand another we may be exposing our own ideas and attitudes to opposing ones. To understand completely an opposing point of view means that we have at least momentarily looked at the world through our adversary's spectacles—in a sense, we have tried to become *him* for the moment. In the process we have suspended judgment and withheld evaluation. Consequently, we run the risk of actually adopting the other's point of view or of having our view altered by his. To expose ourselves to such a change requires courage, because each of us is organized to resist change. It is upsetting to discover we are wrong. Therefore it takes a good measure of personal security to enter into a relationship knowing that the stage is being set for a possible alteration of ourselves.

Perhaps it is fortunate that there is some compensation for the risk assumed by one who is willing to listen with understanding. Strangely enough, listening to another also facilitates change in him. This has been proved by the clinical experience of psychotherapists and is supported by a growing body of research findings in this area. Clients who successfully complete a series of interviews with client-centered therapists show measurable changes in their attitudes toward themselves and toward others. There is also evidence that changes may occur in their basic values and in their personal philosophy.

Listening facilitates change in the speaker in a very indirect way. If a person knows someone is listening carefully and is trying to understand, he may make more effort to express his attitudes and ideas more clearly. By so doing, he may obtain new understandings simply because he is expressing his own ideas more clearly. In trying to understand another person, then, a listener may actually encourage that person to express himself more understandably. This is suggestive of the old saying that "we never really know something unless we can explain it clearly to someone else."

Why the Group-Centered Leader Listens. We have mentioned several of the effects of listening with an intent to understand another. There are many by-products or expected results from this type of intensive listening. In subsequent chapters we shall present evidence for some of these effects, chiefly from the diaries, interviews, and follow-up reports of the delegates. It may be useful at this point, however, to summarize some of the effects the group-centered leader has come to expect from his listening to the contributions of his group members:

First, group members will feel that their contributions are of sufficient worth to merit being listened to and understood by the leader. This should greatly facilitate participation by the members through reduction of the threat of devaluation.

Second, group members will make a greater effort to express their ideas and opinions more clearly, knowing that someone in the group is listening attentively and is going to reflect their ideas back to them for confirmation.

Third, group members will begin to drop their defensiveness, open their minds to new understandings, think more flexibly, reason more effectively. This should not only improve the quality of contributions but increase the problem-solving ability of the group as a whole.

Fourth, when conflicts or controversies arise in the group, each member is more likely to alter his own point of view rather than defend it vigorously and stubbornly.

Fifth, group members observing that the leader is listening with understanding will themselves begin to listen to each other more attentively and with more understanding.

Sixth, the leader himself will learn far more from listening to others in the group than he would through giving lectures, presentations, and other leader-centered activities.

These, then, are some of the important results the group-centered leader expects to achieve through listening with understanding and through testing his understanding by reflecting the meaning of members' verbal contributions. Each of these results will contribute significantly to the group-centered leader's long-range objectives and goals—(a) creating a nonthreatening group atmosphere conducive to creative participation by the members, and (b) facilitating communication so that the various members' contributions will be understood by the others and utilized by the group.

Conveying Acceptance

One of the barriers to creative participation by group members is their fear of being changed, influenced, evaluated, or rejected. People are not as free to give of themselves and to express their uniqueness in an atmosphere that is threatening, judgmental, evaluative, critical, or moralizing. Consequently, an important function of the group-centered leader is to create an atmosphere that is nonthreatening, nonevaluative, and nonrejecting.

Such an atmosphere cannot be created at once. It may take many sessions before people will begin to feel accepted and free from the threat of change or evaluation. The process can be accelerated, however, if the leader consistently is able to avoid certain kinds of responses and relies heavily on certain other responses.

Responses That Convey Intent to Change Others.   There are ways of responding to others which most of us would agree show a fairly obvious intent to change others, to direct their behavior, or to influence them to behave in some particular way. Examples of such responses are:

Ordering, Commanding, Demanding, Requiring, Prohibiting

> You must do this.
> You cannot do this.
> You have to be careful.
> I expect you to do this.
> Calm down.
> Don't take these facts too seriously.

Obligating, Persuading, Warning, Cautioning

> You should do this.
> You ought not to say such things.
> You need to improve your vocabulary.
> You'd better not try that.

Appealing, Imploring, Wishing, Hoping

> I wish you would do this.
> Please do this.
> Can't you do this for me?
> I am counting on you to speak clearly.

Advising, Suggesting

> You might try this.
> Why not take another look?
> Perhaps you would like to talk about something else.
> You could do this, perhaps.

These four categories of responses frequently convey to the speaker that he is not accepted *as he is,* that he is being told to change in some way. What is being communicated to him is the other's desire for him to think, feel, or behave differently. He is likely to think, "I must change," "I ought to change," "It would be desirable to change," "It would please others for me to change."

Such attitudes are not conducive to the feeling of being accepted.

Consequently, the group-centered leader tries to avoid using these four types of responses. As we have emphasized earlier, he will be more successful in doing this if he has freed himself from the need to change others and if his genuine attitude is one of accepting others as they are. It is difficult for a leader to avoid giving orders, persuading, advising, and appealing, unless his basic attitude is one of accepting people as opposed to wanting to change them.

Indirect Attempts to Change Others. There are other ways of responding to people which convey somewhat less directly a desire for them to change, but which nonetheless can be quite as threatening to them as the four types listed above. Consider, for example, responses which convey:

Criticizing, Condemning, Devaluating, Moralizing, Judging
> That was a stupid thing to say.
> You are wrong.
> This is a ridiculous way to look at it.
> Your work is not up to par.
> You are not being cooperative.

To respond to another person with such statements frequently shows an intent to influence him to adopt new ways of behaving by "extinguishing" or "punishing" the old way of behaving. Unlike the four kinds of responses described previously, where the desired way of behaving is specified, this type of response relies upon getting rid of the undesired behavior. As opposed to saying, "You should do this," the person who makes evaluative statements is saying, "You should not do that." Both communicate an intent to change the other; both can convey lack of acceptance of the person as he is.

People can be threatened by evaluation more often than we generally suppose. This kind of threat can have an immediate and lasting effect on their behavior in a group, causing them to withdraw and avoid participating, or to expend their energies in persistent defense against such attacks on their ideas. Moreover, when the evaluation comes from the leader, who is frequently seen as an authority figure, they tend to place the locus of evaluation with him rather than with the group. This often results in an overdependence upon the leader for evaluating the ideas or behavior of the members. We have all observed groups in which the members rely heavily on the leader for evaluating the worth of contributions, because they are afraid to accept this responsibility themselves.

Does the group-centered leader also try to avoid making *positive* evaluations? It is easy to understand the potential threat contained in negative evaluations, but what is the effect of responses that convey:

Approving, Praising, Rewarding, Reassuring, Agreeing, Supporting

> That was a good idea.
> You did well.
> That was the right thing to say.
> I think you should have done what you did.

Such statements as these can also convey to another that you want him to change. The positive evaluation is often a means of rewarding past desirable behavior in order to "reinforce" it—that is, to insure that it will occur again in the future. On the other hand, it is probably true that people feel less threatened by positive evaluations than by negative ones. This does not always hold, because an approving remark sometimes embarrasses a person and may even mildly threaten him, if he himself does not share the positive evaluation of his idea or behavior. However, there are other possible effects of positive evaluations which should be considered. They, too, tend to shift the locus of evaluation away from the speaker, perhaps even more than negative evaluations. If a leader of a group tends to make frequent positive evaluations of the contributions of members, he runs the risk of encouraging members to rely on his judgment of the worth of the contributions. Furthermore, there is the risk of influencing members to make only those contributions which they feel will be approved by the leader. Finally, the leader who frequently praises others' contributions may build up such an expectation of approval that, should he fail to respond positively to some member's response, it might easily be perceived as lack of approval.

Giving Information. A leader may convey lack of acceptance simply by giving information. This is especially true when the information has not been asked for, but may also be true when the information has been openly requested. Much depends, of course, upon the leader's own attitude and his manner of giving information. As each of us knows, a person who gives us the impression of "knowing it all" or of being "positively correct" will make us bristle up and become for the moment defensive. By his own manner of informing others, he devaluates their worth. He conveys, "I know, but you do not; my way of thinking is correct, yours is not." Lack of acceptance may be conveyed, though to a lesser degree, even when a leader's manner of giving information is not so extremely dogmatic. People tend to resent "being told," even when the informer genuinely has their interest in mind.

Making Interpretations. Another type of response that often communicates lack of acceptance is that of making inferences or interpretations of the feelings, perceptions, motives, or values of the other person. All the following responses might be considered in this category:

> You are being cynical.
> I always thought you knew better.
> You are saying this because you are angry.
> You must want us to agree with you.
> You don't really mean what you say.

Although it is not possible to say that such responses as these always are perceived by people as indicating a lack of acceptance of them, nevertheless clinical experience as well as common sense tells us that people often react defensively, or even with hostility, to attempts to interpret their motives, their intentions, or their inner thoughts. This can be said regardless of whether the interpretation is "correct" or not. To interpret a statement of another often has the effect of conveying an evaluation, a disbelief in the validity of his spoken words, or even an intention to influence his thoughts or behavior (as in the statement, "You are being cynical," which might often convey, "You should not be cynical").

One research study has produced findings bearing on the effect of interpretations on the verbal behavior of the subjects. These findings strongly support the clinical observation that interpretations tend to discourage clients' further self-expression in therapy. In this study, Bergman (1951) analyzed the verbatim protocols of therapeutic interviews in an attempt to study the effect of different types of counselor-statements on the subsequent responses of the client. He discovered that interpretations by the counselors (trained in client-centered methods) were followed *more* often by "abandonment of self-exploration" than would be expected by chance, and were followed *less* often by "self-exploration and insight" than would be expected by chance.

In a significant paper by Porter (1952) on the nature of psychotherapeutic interpretation, an unpublished study by J. Rickard is described. Rickard obtained results similar to Bergman's on the effect of interpretation in Freudian, Adlerian, Horneyian, and Rogerian therapy interviews. This study indicated that counselors' interpretations were followed by "resistance" with greater than chance frequency.

While these studies do not present exhaustive or conclusive evidence, they do support the thesis that interpretation of a person's inner thoughts and feelings is an effective way to inhibit his self-expression and to produce resistance in him. It does not seem too great a generalization to suggest that these findings from individual therapy sessions would probably be duplicated in a similar study of the interaction of members of a group. At least this is the position taken by the group-centered leader, who tries always to avoid interpreting the statements of group members.

In summarizing these paragraphs, we might state that a leader conveys acceptance of the members of his group by avoiding statements which convey a direct attempt to change the members, statements which convey evaluation of their contributions, statements which convey an interpretation of members' inner thoughts and feelings, and statements which convey that the members are "being told" by the leader. We will conclude this summary by re-emphasizing the importance of the leader's attitudes in determining the impact of his verbal responses upon the members, and by pointing out that the members' own personalities will also influence their perception of the meaning of the leader's responses. To put it simply, a leader with evaluative and nonaccepting attitudes may communicate them to members regardless of the kind of verbal responses he uses. Similarly, some group members may be so insecure as to read evaluation and lack of acceptance into any response made by the leader.

THE "LINKING" FUNCTION

Another important function which the group-centered leader serves in the group is the "linking" function. In face-to-face discussion groups, it often happens that one person will say something, then a second person will add a new idea but without conveying the relationship of his idea to the first contribution. The thought of each member remains independent or unlinked to other thoughts. Occasionally, someone may enter in and relate his thought to that of another, but usually we can observe several currents of thought in a group, each going its own way. If, however, the group-centered leader makes an effort to perceive the linkage between the separate comments and then conveys this relationship to the group, the discussion then seems to flow in one current, building up force as each new contribution is linked to it.

The "linking" function of the group-centered leader is related closely to his function of reflecting the meanings of members' statements. This is because the meaning of a member's comment often *is* the link to the main stream of thought or to the previous comments. Its actual linkage is frequently hidden by the content of the comment. Thus, by clarifying the meaning of a comment, the group-centered leader makes clear to the group how the new contribution is related to the previous discussion. An illustration from a recorded group discussion may clarify this point. In the following excerpt the group is carrying on a discussion of how one of the members, a social worker, should approach a group of young married people to get them to take social action in their community:[2]

1. BILL: I would like to go on record with a very serious objection here. This was the implied assumption that somehow church socials or gatherings in communities for discussion are somewhat more valuable and better and people should do these rather than go bowling. I felt this implied assumption. Why shouldn't men rather go there than to church—

2. DON: I don't go along with that implied assumption.

3. BILL: Well, *I* certainly wouldn't. I would like to bring in a diagnosis that my wife has made from the feminine viewpoint of our society. She, perhaps not peculiarly, much prefers the company of a group of men to a group of women. And I don't think this is necessarily a sex factor. She says you can almost predict what a group of women are going to do.

4. JANE: I'll say.

5. BILL: They're forced into a mold somehow by our society. She doesn't understand what it is. But a group of women get together and one group is pretty much like another. And very often women join groups not because they want to but because of social pressures. Where men—they seem to live in a much freer and easier society where what they do and who they join with is a function of their own choice. In—

[2] Throughout the excerpt the number in parentheses in each note at the bottom of the page refers to the same numbered item in the group discussion. The writer has used this example in a previous publication (1951, pp. 359–362).

6. Frank: I think Mrs. Adams [Bill's wife] overestimates considerably both the interest and the variety of men's society.

7. Group: (Laughter.)

8. Leader: Bill, your point would be what? I'm not sure I understand what—

9. Bill: That much of the operation of women in these social groups is not a function of choice on their part. It's not satisfying their personal needs. It is a function of the role that society kinda forces them into.

10. Leader: You are using that as an illustration of your original objection to the effect that we should attach certain values, positive or negative, to these interests and you object strongly to doing that—saying that one interest is of more social value than another one?

11. Bill: It seemed to me that what we were essentially saying is that the things that the men wanted to do were not as good for them—were not satisfying their needs—as well as the things that men didn't want to do. And I just kinda don't—

12. Cathy: If women get together to clean up the alleys, after all it's the women who have to sit and look at the alleys all day. The men are out working all day. They are not as concerned about the alleys as their wives. They should be. The fact that there isn't a playground for the children, by and large the mothers would be more concerned with that than the fathers. Questions of this sort wouldn't necessarily hit home to her husband. It seems to me they would be much more interested than their husbands might, who also because of our culture would say, "Why, that's the mother's job."

13. Stu: Well, would you carry that further and say that social action interests in general are more natural to the women?

14. Cathy: They aren't more natural. I'd say that the culture sort of—

(8) The leader here is attempting to understand the meaning and intent behind Bill's last three comments. This is especially important here, since in number 2 Don interrupts to defend himself and in number 6 Frank humorously objects. The group responds to Frank with laughter, thus in a sense rejecting Bill. The leader does not understand the link between Bill's comments and the previous discussion.

(10) Here the leader is linking Bill's illustration to a previous objection of his, yet he does this in the tentative form of a question.

15. STU: Yeah, owing to our cultural situation, would you say in general that they are more politically active, and so forth?

16. LEADER: Are we really understanding Cathy? I'm not sure that I am. You see a basic difference here, Cathy, between the interests of men and the interests of women?

17. CATHY: I see a great deal of difference when it comes to a group discussion, yes. That it can be that there is more interest in a neighborhood group, particularly in the working class, that the wives and mothers would have a more neighborhood interest.

18. LEADER: In terms of leader behavior, this would—you are simply saying that this would be a better diagnosis of women's needs and that we have to be careful in diagnosing women's needs versus men's.

19. CATHY: I think we have to be very careful.

20. SAM: I would like to raise a kind of a point of order and wonder are we trying to be a sociology class in this emphasis upon diagnosing needs. To me we keep wandering from what our primary job is. I just sort of pull that out—

21. CATHY: You're right.

22. SAM: I'd be quite glad to pull back in my shell, but I'm wondering if we are not beyond ourselves. We have no resources in this area. We keep bringing up personal records which really don't count for much in our total assessment.

23. LEADER: Diagnosing individual needs is not pertinent to our problem, Sam?

(16) Again the leader is trying to understand Cathy and to link the meaning of her somewhat involved illustration to the previous comments. Stu, on the other hand, in numbers 13 and 15 is apparently trying to push Cathy to a broader generalization, which she does not accept in number 14.

(18) The leader here provides the linkage between the difference Cathy sees between the interests of the sexes and the role of the leader, which was the topic under discussion prior to Bill's comment in number 1.

(22) Apparently Sam has not perceived any linkage between the discussion of group members' needs and leadership. He feels dissociated from the original topic.

(23) Although Sam has not stated his feeling as such, the leader reflects tentatively Sam's meaning, thus even linking Sam's comments to the preceding topic of needs.

24. SAM: Well, I was about to jump in with all sorts of personal references. I work with these groups all the time and I can present some anecdotes on the other side but it occurred to me that that wouldn't be relevant.

25. STU: It seems to me we are analyzing here, or raising the question, about the function of leadership. If one attitude toward leadership is accepted—in general the community center's point of view on leadership, the social worker's point of view—well, then one must know—one must be able to diagnose the needs of the people in order to function as leader. If another concept of leadership wins the day here, then we can dispense with all of this diagnosis.

26. SAM: Then we should discuss the two aspects of leadership and not diagnosis.

27. LEADER: Stu, you are not willing to accept that that is the best way of leading—diagnosing the group and going out and fulfilling needs for—

28. SAM: Yes. That's the point I'd rather argue.

In a group there may be as many different channels of thought as there are members. This often can be seen in the early stages of group development, when each member has his particular axe to grind, when contributions are likely to be more ego-centered than group-centered, when members are responding to their own personal needs to the exclusion of what is going on outside of themselves. It is during this stage that the group-centered leader's linking function is so important. It might be said that the leader, by perceiving these linkages, helps the individual members to become aware of elements in the total perceptual field which previously were not perceived; that the leader helps the group members to enlarge the scope of the phenomenal field to which they respond,

(25) Stu, taking over the linking function, makes a successful attempt to tie together the ideas about needs and the earlier topic of leadership.

(26) Sam's comment is not accepting of the group's exploration of the problem of diagnosing needs. Stu's linkage in number 25 was much more useful, as well as accepting, to the group.

(27) The leader in trying to catch Stu's meaning went beyond him a little. He might better have said, "You see the problem of diagnosis in relation to one type of leadership but not necessary for another type."

thus increasing the chances that their contributions will be more appropriate to the existing situation.

Some Misunderstandings about the Leader's Role

Because the initial role played by the group-centered leader is so unlike that of traditional leaders, it is not surprising that some people have developed certain misunderstandings about it. It may be helpful to the reader to know what some of these misunderstandings are.

Does Listening Mean Agreeing?

One misunderstanding has to do with the function of "listening with understandng." It is often assumed that when the group-centered leader listens and reflects the meaning of a member's statement this necessarily conveys to the speaker that the leader is *agreeing with him*. It is understandable why this misapprehension arises, for we have become accustomed to the kind of communication which *does* convey either agreement or disagreement. When we talk to others, our responses invariably fall into a dichotomy of agreement or disagreement. We tend to convey to others that what they have expressed is either right or wrong, sound or unsound, logical or illogical, appropriate or inappropriate, and so on. We may even go farther and convey some sort of evaluation of the speaker himself —that "he is a sound thinker," "he has good ideas," or "he is one of those hide-bound conservatives." Furthermore, this tendency to respond to another by agreeing or disagreeing is heightened considerably when the conversation involves a subject about which the participants have strong feelings. The presence of emotion in a discussion almost insures that evaluative responses will be made by each of the discussants.

As an example, someone says to you, "I believe teachers with Communist leanings should be ousted from our schools." Your natural reaction will be to make a response that conveys either agreement or disagreement, such as, "I think so too," "You are absolutely right," or "That is a very dangerous philosophy in a democratic nation."

Somehow both our social experience and our educational experience reinforces this tendency to dichotomize everything—to categorize what people say as right or wrong, correct or incorrect. Perhaps even the nature of our language encourages the habit of having to express either agreement or disagreement with others. What is seldom learned is a way of responding to others that conveys *neither* agreement nor disagreement, but rather mere understanding. Why is it so uncommon to hear someone respond to another with a statement that simply conveys, "I hear what you are saying," or "I gather this is what you believe"?

So, because people are accustomed to being agreed with or disagreed with, they may *at first* misconstrue an understanding or reflecting response as an agreeing one. However, from the experience of psychotherapists who have discovered that accepting and understanding responses facilitate communication, we have learned that people very soon begin to feel the difference between a response that is accepting and one that is agreeing. Sometimes they only *feel* the difference, as they experience a sense of being understood and encouraged to express themselves. Often, however, they even *recognize intellectually* that the listener is responding to them in a unique way. As one client said to the writer, his therapist, "You neither agree nor disagree with me, it feels strange. You understand what I'm saying, I know, but you don't tell me your opinion. This gives me a chance to look at my own feelings further."

Is Group-Centered Leadership Simply "Laissez-Faire Leadership"?

Some writers have equated the role of the group-centered leader with the laissez-faire leader, the one who does nothing. By this they usually mean that the group-centered leader is passive, indifferent, and nonhelpful like the laissez-faire leader in the Iowa experiments in which this type of leader was contrasted with the "democratic" and the "authoritarian" leaders (Lippitt & White, 1947). The implication of this identification is that the group-centered leader (like the Iowa laissez-faire leader) will foster a kind of nonproductive, anarchic, and aggressive group.

Actually, the group-centered leader as we have tried to describe him is far from passive and indifferent, nor does he "do nothing." His role is a very active and intense one, as those who have tried it will testify. To listen attentively to all the contributions of members, to try earnestly to understand others from their frame of reference, and to test the accuracy of one's understanding by reflecting back the meaning of the speaker (to his satisfaction)—all this not only requires a great deal of energy but also results in an intense involvement of the leader in the process of communication going on in the group. The group-centered leader is not listening passively; he is listening attentively and is actively projecting himself into the stream of thought of the group. He cannot be disinterested, else he will find it impossible to understand others; he is not "leaving the group alone," for he is a dynamic influence on the effectiveness of the group's communication.

Is Reflecting Meanings a Mechanical "Technique"?

A frequent reaction to the group-centered leader's function of reflecting the meaning of members' statements is to denounce it as simply a mechanical and artificial technique, rigidly used in an unnatural or forced way by the leader. Viewed in this way, reflecting by the leader is perceived as a technique that group members will "see through" and dislike. The writer has heard the criticism, "Nobody wants to be responded to like a parrot." Then, too, there is the usual number of jokes, most of which are variations on the following theme:

If a group member asks where he can go to get a drink of water, the group-centered leader is certain to reply, "You want to know where you can get a drink of water." This leaves the member both frustrated and thirsty.

It is true that the reflecting function can be a rigid and mechanical technique and may at first seem strange and unnatural to group members, especially under any of the following conditions:

1. If the leader is just beginning to try out this way of responding and has not learned it well enough to practice it naturally and easily.
2. If the leader does not sincerely want to listen with understanding to the meaning of others' contributions.
3. If the leader simply parrots the content (the actual words) of the speaker's statements, instead of using his own language to reflect the speaker's real meaning.
4. If the leader does not understand the basic purpose of reflecting meanings.

Experience in leadership training leaves no doubt that, in the early stages of learning this new way of responding nonevaluatively to others, leaders often do sound mechanical and unnatural in their attempts to reflect. Like a novice at golf, whose swing will at first seem unnatural and mechanical, the leader's first attempts at reflecting will be self-conscious and "forced." Like the golfer, however, he will soon find that he becomes more natural and less mechanical with his new skill as he gains experience through practice.

The leader will find it hard to carry out this function effectively if he tries to reflect when he does not genuinely desire to understand another's point of view. It is difficult (and certainly not completely honest) to convey verbally an attitude of understanding if one's real attitude is something else. Usually under such conditions the responder's words do not hide his real attitudes or intentions. Without the intent to understand, there will seldom be real understanding, and an attempt to reflect another's meaning will end as a parroting of his words rather than a mirroring of the real meaning of the spoken words.

Practice in trying to understand and reflect the meaning of members' statements gradually reduces the tendency to parrot their actual words. As a leader gains experience in carrying out this important function, reflecting will become second nature to him and his responses will become more and more characteristic of his own unique manner of speaking. In order to satisfy himself that he has understood, the more experienced leader will want to rephrase in his own words what others say. This becomes his only real test of the accuracy of his understanding of the other person.

Finally, a leader will be more effective in carrying out this function if he understands the purpose of reflecting and the part it plays in facilitating communication. Reflecting is simply a means by which a listener tests out his understanding and communicates this understanding to the speaker. In much that is communicated, the meaning is perfectly clear to the listener. Hence no test of his understanding is required, for he is certain he understands and the speaker is certain that he has been understood. A statement such as, "I read a book last night," would seldom call for a special effort to convey to the speaker that you have understood him. In fact, reflection of such a statement might seem strange and unnatural to the speaker. On the other hand, there are many times when a speaker needs to feel that his listener has understood—for example, when he is expressing something that is difficult to put into words (a deep feeling), or when he is uncertain that the listener actually could be understanding and accepting of what he is saying. Statements such as, "I was really upset by what I read last night," "For the first time in two years I read a book last night," or "I read something last night which supports my argument and refutes yours," might more appropriately be reflected by the listener in order to assure both listener and speaker that real communication has occurred between them.

A Summarizing Statement of the Role of the Group-Centered Leader

To bring together all the various aspects of our description of the group-centered leader into a brief summary statement, we present below a list of highly condensed statements describing the philosophy and behavior of the group-centered leader. These statements represent only a current conception of this type of leadership, and it is recognized that such a description is bound to be modified by future experience and research.

In order to minimize the possibility of a misunderstanding of such highly condensed statements, we shall attempt to contrast the various components of the group-centered approach to leadership with similar components of a very different approach—one we have called for convenience a "leader-guided" approach. Our aim here is not to try to represent accurately another point of view, for this is risky business. Rather, we are using this device to highlight and clarify our own description of the group-centered leader.

Our list is not an exhaustive one, for it has been constructed to summarize and integrate the description in the present chapter, rather than to serve as a detailed and all-inclusive formulation.

Two Contrasting Approaches to Leadership in Small Groups

Basic Philosophy

GROUP-CENTERED	LEADER-GUIDED
1. Most effective group is one in which each member can contribute his maximum potential.	1. Most effective group is one in which each member can contribute his maximum potential.
2. Spontaneous and creative behavior of members will in the long run be of most help to the group.	2. Spontaneous and creative behavior of members will in the long run be of most help to the group.

3. Group has the capacity for making sound decisions and reaching effective solutions to its problems.
4. Group can best learn to utilize potential of each member when it is free from dependence on a formal leader or some other authority.
5. New group has the skills and capacities for self-determined, self-responsible behavior, but is afraid to use them.
6. Goals set by the group will in the long run be most beneficial to the group.

7. Change that is significant and enduring must be self-initiated change. Resistance to change will often result from bringing to bear outside forces and pressures.
8. Democratic ends do not justify undemocratic means. Democratic behavior cannot be taught by undemocratic methods but only by experiencing democracy in action.
9. Change that is self-initiated will take place most effectively in a nonthreatening, accepting psychological atmosphere.
10. Leadership of a group is not the property or the sole function of any one person, but is conferred by the group on that member who can

3. *Mature* groups have the capacity for making sound decisions and reaching effective solutions to their problems.
4. Group can best learn to utilize potential of each member by depending at first on guidance of its leader.
5. New group may not have the skills and capacities for self-determined, self-responsible behavior, so it must be taught them by the leader.
6. Goals set by the leader (of a new group) will be more beneficial in the long run, although eventually a group should be mature enough to set its own goals.

7. Change can be facilitated by bringing to bear influence of leader's ideas, insights, and knowledge.

8. Democratic ends justify use of manipulative and authoritarian means. Leader must retain his authority in order to influence group to reach desired goals.
9. In a nonthreatening, accepting atmosphere group members are not likely to change without direction of some kind from the leader.
10. Leadership of a group should be vested in the person who has the most experience, knowledge, maturity, skills, insights, and so on.

best meet its needs by leading it in a certain direction.

11. Structuring of a group situation to contain "a leader" simply provides the group with an additional task, namely, either to assimilate the limits imposed by the leader or to depose the leader (physically or psychologically).

11. A group situation should be always structured in such a way that it contains "a leader." Groups demand structure; without it they will be anxious.

Principal Behaviors

GROUP-CENTERED

1. Allows group to diagnose its own needs. Tries to facilitate communication in group during this process.

2. Allows group to plan its own experiences. Tries to facilitate communication during this process.

3. Avoids making decisions for group, except those which facilitate bringing members together initially.

4. Preparation involves doing things that will improve his own contributions to group.

5. Tries to lose his special status position so that he can participate in decision-making without having his contributions given special consideration by group.

6. Leaves responsibility with each member for participating. Tries to facilitate group's developing a permis-

LEADER-GUIDED

1. Finds out as much as possible about group's needs, in order to provide group with situation where it can get what it needs.

2. Plans specific learning situations and/or group experiences from which group may draw insights.

3. Makes decisions for group when group seems too immature to make correct decisions.

4. Preparation involves doing things that will improve his own contribution and things that he feels group needs.

5. Uses influence of his special status position in group to bring about decisions or to guide group in certain directions.

6. Facilitates participation by subtle or direct methods of involving each member in group activity.

9 / LIMITATIONS, FANTASIES, AND SECURITY OPERATIONS OF BEGINNING GROUP PSYCHOTHERAPISTS

Meyer Williams

Literature concerning the training of group psychotherapists and particularly focusing on the everyday problems of trainees attempting to master this highly complex and personally taxing treatment approach is sparse. Slavson (1943, 1964), Powdermaker and Frank (1953), and more recently Mullan and Rosenbaum (1962) have delineated and discussed some of the general problems from an educational and supervisory standpoint. Geller (1958) and Levin and Kanter (1964) have commented more specifically on actual training experiences and have suggested considerations from a supervisory standpoint. This paper is offered as an addition to the above contributions and will explore the effects of personal and social limitations, fantasies, and security operations of beginning group psychotherapists upon their group work.

The comments which follow are based on observations of fifty supervisees who have undergone training with the author in the last fifteen years. They are the product of direct contact in intensive supervisory sessions, cotherapist participation, and didactic group psychotherapy seminars occurring in both a neuropsychiatric and a general hospital setting, as well as in institutional outpatient settings in more recent years. The subjects of these observations were advanced psychology trainees, psychiatric residents, social workers, and staff members in these specialties, all of whom had had at least one year's previous training in individual psychotherapy and most of whom had been in group therapy training with the author for

From INTERNATIONAL JOURNAL OF GROUP PSYCHOTHERAPY, *1966, Vol. 16, pp. 150–162. Copyright 1966, American Group Psychotherapy Association. Reprinted with permission of author and publisher.*

at least one year. Most supervisees were involved in carrying out intensive group psychotherapy (three to five sessions per week, in-patient; one session per week, outpatient) for periods ranging from six months to two years. All were being trained along group-dynamically oriented lines.

Before presenting my observations and commentary, some framework should be provided regarding the general orientation for therapy given to these supervisees and its implications for group therapist characteristics and behavior. Briefly, the approach taught was that group psychotherapy is a small-group sociopsychological treatment procedure wherein the therapeutic power or agent lies not primarily in the therapist, but potentially in the collective capacities of a group of peers striving together for greater personal understanding and social maturity. It is the therapist's task to weld this group of suffering strangers into a strong cohesive social and therapeutic body by means of purposive catalytic activities and techniques. Such a collective entity, once genuinely established, provides both a vehicle for increasing and deepening examination of individual feelings and conflicts and an experimental ground for interpersonal development. To be effective, the group's transaction must occur in a relatively unstructured atmosphere in which free verbal and emotional expression is the cardinal rule, yet in which individual integrity and dignity are also safe-guarded.

Looking at group psychotherapy this way, the demands on the neophyte therapist can appear overwhelming, and for some they were so. All saw group psychotherapy as demanding much more of the therapist than individual therapy and as exposing them to the threat of more direct personal and professional evaluation than most other treatment activities. Needless to say, in the beginning, anxiety was always high and defensive reactions to it abundant. The problems which arose were multiple, but this paper will be confined to three related aspects, namely: (1) inability to assume an effective group-dynamically oriented therapist role, (2) fearful fantasies regarding group attitudes and behavior toward the therapist, and (3) adoption of special pseudotherapist roles as security operations against personal threat.

Therapist Role Limitations

The problem of assuming the role of a group-dynamically oriented group psychotherapist appeared on a number of levels. First, some rather socially immature and inexperienced supervisees were far from socially perceptive and verbally facile individuals. Their life history suggested little movement toward groups, little leadership experience, more comfort in one-to-one situations, and a lack of flexible communicating in common social situations. They were traumatized by the openness of feeling and unrestricted communications required in group situations, even by the lack of physical barriers, such as a desk between the patients and themselves. Moreover, the absence of opportunity to have a special relationship or privacy with each patient, as they might in individual therapy, caused them to become highly constricted and to feel exposed. They tended to fear constant scrutiny and evaluation by their patients, and all spontaneity was dampened by their need to be cautious and correct. Their groups tended to disintegrate or the therapist found some reason to withdraw from group therapy activities.

Second, other supervisees, less socially limited in the above manner, nevertheless were frequently insensitive to group process, despite much didactic preparation and supervision. They promoted multiple individual patient relationships with themselves but could not promote or allow interaction among group members, consequently blocking group development and movement. Without the necessary group-centered catalytic action on their part, which implies faith in and genuine commitment to group process, their groups tended to become a concurrent series of watered-down individual therapies. In reality, these supervisees feared a group-dynamic approach because they saw it as threatening their self-esteem and personal control by diminishing their authority. They could not relinquish authority or work at moderating their role as the focal person in the group. Consequently, their groups failed to develop or to feel their own strength and cohesiveness. Such supervisees could only operate as didactic group therapists.

Third, many supervisees, though sensitive to group process, varied in their ability to carry out the group therapist's requirement of being able to handle, as well as withstand, a number of intense transferences at one time, even though these were diluted by the presence of other group members. This was particularly true when multiple transferences involved the concurrent pressures of extreme hostility, dependency, and eroticism from different patients. It was also difficult for many of these supervisees to be faced with an intense collective group transference attitude, usually in the form of strong hostility or dependence. Reactions varied from highly restrictive dealing with transference material to total shift or regression from therapist-group-centered interactions to old, more comfortable, therapist-individual-centered interactions with group members. The therapist's reactions here were distinguished from specific countertransference problems in that they appeared to relate to unresolved problems regarding the assumption of parental roles as well as a lack of leadership experience. Sharing of transferences with cotherapists and intensive supervisory support tended to modify these problems.

Finally, there were a number of supervisees who, unlike these three subgroups, were indeed capable of developing a group with high morale and cohesiveness. Their difficulty appeared to be inability to utilize their groups as effective therapeutic instruments or media for therapeutic work with individual members' specific problems and conflicts. As long as their groups dealt with group feelings and common problems, these therapists were effective and restrained their activity, allowing the group to be interactive. However, they were negatively reactive to any sign of subgroup development or any demands by individual patients for group consideration of more specific personal problems or feelings. Such efforts were either blocked, rapidly compromised, or ignored, frequently with a spasm of activity on the therapist's part. Interestingly, these supervisees were generally socially active and popular individuals in their personal lives. They made contacts easily, talked well, intellectualized readily, and usually presented a fine veneer of social sophistication. Yet, virtually all had a common characteristic: a resistance to examination of their own inner conflicts and a need to see all problems as interpersonal only. Above all, most enjoyed such strong narcissistic gratification from their feelings of acceptance as group leaders that they perpetuated the stage of "group ego" formation, seeking only to enlarge this formation as if it were the sole goal of group therapy. Personal therapy, stressing character analysis, was helpful in allowing some of these supervisees to become more effective group psychotherapists.

Fearful Fantasies

As one works with many group therapy supervisees, certain common therapist fantasies come to light, which are quite helpful to an understanding of many facets of the therapists' ineffectiveness or early problems with their groups. I have dubbed these the "fearful fantasies" since they all have in common marked anxiety in regard to specific threatening therapy situations which conceivably could come to pass but which, in reality, infrequently do. Some of these fantasies are entrenched strongly and secretly in the minds of almost all beginning group psychotherapists, and must be brought to light and dealt with in supervision. Six of the most common fantasies observed by the author will be discussed.

Virtually all beginning therapists harbor a frightening fantasy of encountering unmanageable resistance during the early group sessions. Such fantasies are evident in statements or questions such as, "What if they don't talk?" or, "What if they just sit and look at me?" or, "What if they keep asking how talking to other patients as sick as they are can help them?" When the underlying fantasy comes to light, the therapist's feelings of social impotence and his personal doubts regarding the group approach become evident. Usually, he is so impressed by, and anxious over, the massed individual psychopathology confronting him in the group, that he loses sight of the underlying communality of human feelings and thought processes. Frequently, during supervision, it becomes apparent that the therapist himself is resistant to the notion of being treated in a group and projects this resistance upon the patients. Thus, while giving lip service to the rationale of group therapy, he finds himself trying to carry out a procedure which is ego-threatening to him and in which he does not, in actuality, have faith.

Related to the above, is the fantasy of losing control of the group. Here the supervisee often comments: "This patient talked for the whole session and no one could shut him up," or "They just ignored any comments I made," or, "I couldn't get them to stay with anything." In supervision, this beginning therapist reveals little leadership experience and often shows concern over his own aggressiveness, which he confuses with hostility. He is fearful of asserting himself and of group confrontation, and frequently rationalizes this in adherence to a theoretical therapy model stressing permissiveness. He interprets the catalytic activity of the therapist as one of relative inaction, so that his interventions with the group are weak, and aggressive patients step in to fill the vacuum. When, with increased experience, he begins to see that firm and frank dealing with shared group phenomena brings group cohesiveness and movement, he may begin to enjoy his role as therapist and, if he is characterologically able, he moves out from behind his passive defense.

Many budding group therapists raised in restrained middle-class environments with emphasis on suppression of hostile expression are much preoccupied with the fantasy of excessive hostility breaking out in their groups, particularly hospitalized groups. They raise questions such as, "What if they disagree and start a fight instead of talking?" or, they anxiously complain, "They all seem mad at me because I don't answer their questions," or, "I can just feel that something terrible is going to happen" (i.e., that the patients will harm him). As suggested, the therapist's own overconcern about, and oversensitivity to, hostile expression makes him unable to gauge the true level of hostile expression in his patients. Not infrequently, he projects his own ego-alien hostile feelings onto his patients. Moreover, it often becomes apparent that these therapists have the same unfounded fear as the public at large, namely, that psychiatric patients as a group are violent. The lack of communication which exists early in the group tends to reinforce this notion, since it is interpreted by the therapist as stemming from hostility rather than the patient's social fear. Strong supervisory efforts to get the supervisee to recognize the potential for group control which lies latent in his group, but which can easily be mustered, can reduce concern. Obviously, if such fantasies remain unaltered, group movement will be thoroughly impeded by suppression of hostile feelings in the group and by the therapist's failure to deal actively with negative transference.

Another fantasy which arouses immense anticipatory anxiety in new therapists is that of possible acting out by group members. The new therapist afflicted with such fantasies will frequently question: "What if a sexual affair develops between two of my patients?" or, "What if he threatens to leave treatment if the group criticizes him?" or, "Should I continue him in the group if I think he's potentially suicidal?" Reflected most frequently by fantasies of acting out are two underlying problems: (1) an unspoken concern about what colleagues and members of other disciplines might think about the therapist should the patient act out, and (2) an unfounded hope that therapeutic change can occur without mobilization of strong affects and their potential risks. Young therapists harboring these acting-out fantasies frequently do not yet understand the powerful influence of group members in stressing responsible behavior in order to maintain group integrity and continuity. In addition, they tend to neglect the extratherapeutic relations and arrangements necessary for good group therapy to proceed. Consequently, they look upon their colleagues, and particularly the administration, as critics rather than allies. Perhaps of greatest importance here is the necessity for neophyte group therapists to learn that change always involves risk and that it is only in an emotionally charged atmosphere where acting out is a possibility that new, more adaptive behavioral patterns can emerge and be tried out. In fact, for some patients, acting out may be a sign of progress. Only critical personal experiences, as well as long-term group experiences and a secure supervisor to lean on during initial, trying times, reduce the new therapist's anxiety.

Fearful fantasies of overwhelming dependency demands on the therapist are another variety of concern developing in new therapists. These are sometimes concealed in statements such as: "They're an awfully sick bunch of people," or, "They keep asking me why they are sick," or, "They tell me I should tell them what to talk about." In all these instances, the beginning therapist usually feels much burdened and put upon by his group. Sometimes, there is real basis for these feelings, particularly if he has done a poor job of composing his group and ended up with a majority of passive-dependent and verbally impoverished patients. Quite often his problems are the result of his own need to maintain authority and control. Thus, he unwittingly comports himself in such a manner as to discourage interaction among group members and to block the emergence of neurotic patient leaders. His group, consequently, continues in the traditional dependent medical model, namely, "You're the expert, so cure me." Also troubled by dependency fantasies are those young therapists who confuse responsibility for treatment with total responsibility for the patient. Such omnipotence sparks fantasies of overwhelming demand when the young therapist imagines or actually faces six to eight suffering souls in the cold light of the group situation. If he can foster real group development, he will learn that the group and many of its members also have a strong sense of mutual responsibility as well as personal assets to support one another, and that, while they may be able to live better with him, they can generally survive without him.

To complete this discussion of fantasies, comment will be made on perhaps the greatest fearful fantasy of all beginning group psychotherapists, that of the fantasy of group disintegration. Recently, listening to the beginning of a recording of an outpatient group therapy session, a fairly routine procedure in our training program, the author heard one cotherapist say half-jokingly to the other prior to the group's members arriving, "I wonder if anyone will show up today." More frequently, the author hears in supervision such depressive comments as, "I don't think I'll have a group left after this session." Themes of this nature are most commonly heard from therapists in the early sessions but may reappear at any time when the group's feelings have been running high, usually in opposition to group interpretation or during multiple transference struggles. In reality, the author has seen very few new groups disintegrate where adequate attention has been given to group composition and patient preparation and, of course, therapist preparation. The persistence of this fantasy is generally a function of the new therapist's underlying feelings of impotence being stimulated by his lack of experience and faith in the group process. Such feelings of impotence are readily mobilized by early group resistance and tend to break through the omnipotent fantasies many new therapists secretly maintain to bolster them through the initial group sessions. Close scrutiny of the therapist's comments at such times will reveal that he is usually struggling with a mixture of guilty and hostile feelings toward his patients. He generally speaks more easily of his guilty feelings (his felt inadequacy) than of his hostile feelings (his resentment over their resistance). In either case, the fantasies of group disintegration emerge—either patients will leave him because he is inept or, projecting his hostility, he feels they will leave him because they resent him for not being what they want him to be. Since one cannot do therapy or promote adequate group process without patients, the group's greatest threat to the therapist is not to come to the next session. Until sufficient group development has taken place to allow the new therapist to see that in the long run, group members do not come for the therapist alone but also for the emotional support and understanding of the group, he may have to proceed by borrowing faith and technical guidance from his supervisor.

Security Operations

Having commented on some of the built-in limitations in personal and social development which make some beginning therapists relatively ineffective and the fantasies which frighten most new therapists, consideration of the characteristic security operations of beginning therapists in carrying out group therapy will be discussed. These usually entail the unconscious adoption of specific roles to reduce personal threat and to satisfy primary personal needs. Powdermaker and Frank (1953) remarked on some of these tactics and, hopefully, this paper will elaborate on and add to their list. In the author's experience, these therapist roles can be classified according to three overriding needs which become apparent during supervision, namely, the need to control, the need to avoid self-exposure, and the need to be liked. Doubtless, the reader will see how much related to therapist personal characteristics and fearful fantasies these needs are.

First, the need to be in control as a response to the threat of the group will be examined. This need is satisfied by the adoption of a consistent authoritarian leadership position which may range from relative benignness to strict tyranny. Classic examples are found in the types best classified as "The Doctor" and the "Benign Authority." "The Doctor" is typically a psychiatric resident or staff man, one who not infrequently enters the therapy situation wearing a white coat with a rubber hammer protruding from his pocket. He typically is drawn into lectures by his group on physical symptoms, drug treatment, and psychiatric symptoms, all material with which he feels comfortable and which allows him to dominate the group since he is usually more knowledgeable than his patients in these areas. In supervision, he defends his approach by indicating that, after all, he is a doctor and it is not his fault that patients relate to him in this way. He rationalizes that he must establish a relationship to get therapy under way, and this way seems natural and to his patients' liking. If he is not too rigid and insecure, he soon begins to see the contradictions in his approach and takes off his armor (the white coat) and stops lecturing. Those who cannot give up this security operation end up denouncing group process or running psychiatric information programs under the rubric of group psychotherapy.

More difficult to detect is the security operation best named the "Benign Authority." The cardinal sign of his effect on his group is that his group members are active, businesslike, and noncontroversial, but they move very little and express little real affect. Study of the "Benign Authority's" interventions shows him to be most accepting and tolerant of group members' participation until they show affect. Here he is bound to step in, consistently minimizing or neutralizing all expressions of feeling by focusing on content and "reality." His patients soon appreciate that he regards expression of feeling as bad or sick and adopt a level of discussion based on fact or, even worse, banalities. In essence, the "Benign Authority" communicates to his patients, "If you want to be in my favor and get my help, don't make waves." In supervision, the "Benign Authority" is usually calm and sure and justifies his approach as one stressing the highest level of personal and social adjustment of his patients, specifically rational thinking and reality-consciousness. Only long and patient supervision and growing realization on the therapist's part that his group likes him but does not move, allows such therapists to begin to see how they are controlling the group situation to restrain the strong affective expression which basically is frightening to them.

A second need stimulating a whole gamut of related security maneuvers is the need for the therapist to remain unexposed. This need can be so severe that, on occasion, the author has encountered the new therapist whom he calls "The Sleeper." "The Sleeper" is so fearful that the group will see him as a limited human being and professional that he engages in total psychological withdrawal within the group, namely, dozing or actually falling asleep during group discussions. The presence of an active cotherapist facilitates this withdrawal. More commonly, one sees the type best termed "The Underactive One." This therapist busily gives the appearance of intense listening to his group members and may even step out from behind this facade from time to time when patient discussions lag to get the patients talking again. His rationale in supervision is that he is listening and refraining from interfering with group process. Of course, in time it becomes apparent that his group is not moving but is engaged in superficial bull sessions which he approvingly promotes. Then the real fear of truly interacting with his group emerges, and his doubts about himself, which he is sure the group will see, are voiced.

Related to the underactive one who fears personal exposure is the type easily recognized as "The Professor." "The Professor" is not infrequently a psychology trainee or full-fledged psychologist who sits in his group in a tweed jacket, calmly smoking a pipe, and acting primarily as a commentator on the group scene before him. The cardinal characteristics of his remarks are that they are highly intellectual, objective, textbooklike, and removed from the patients' level of communication. If the patients talk of being "pissed off," he speaks vaguely of hostility; if they speak of "screwing," he uses the term sexual intercourse. During supervision he justifies such language usage as "raising the group to a higher level of communication and teaching them objectivity." He is usually hard put to understand why his patients remain distant from him or even kid him on occasion (as one group did by all coming to a session smoking pipes), since he consciously is utterly sincere, avidly interested in group dynamics from a theoretical basis, and is highly permissive in allowing his group to talk about anything. With a supervisor who speaks basic English and placement in a group with the "cowboy" type of cotherapist who interacts affectively and freely with the ebb and flow of group process, some of the less defensive therapists of this variety slowly open themselves to their groups and to the satisfactions of real emotional exchange. Others are doomed to be intellectual commentators on the group scene but never participants in it.

Protective operations relating to the need to be liked are the most difficult of the three categories to alter. Therapists presenting this set of defenses give every outward evidence of friendliness, altruism, dedication, and tolerance. Their need for love and personal acceptance unconsciously supersedes all other needs. Their range of roles is from that of missionary to fellow patient. Two common types will be discussed. The first may be classified as "The YMCA Therapist." This supervisee interprets instruction in group techniques as methods of promoting good fellowship and friendliness. His groups exude positive feelings, and his patients somehow feel that improvement lies primarily in positive thinking and conformistic behavior. Therapists masquerading in this role minimize pathology in their groups, see good in all their patients' maneuvers, often refuse to believe in unconscious processes, and are quick to rationalize away acting out or the persistence of maladjustive behavioral patterns in their patients. In return, their group members frequently feel and comment on what a nice, understanding fellow their therapist is and how devoted he is to them. In essence, a private contract is made by this type of therapist with his group in which they conceal their pathology and negative feelings in the group in return for the therapist's love. The therapist, in turn, feels loved, valued, and, most importantly, unthreatened. Attempts to expose this unwritten contract in supervision frequently end up with the therapist feeling that his supervisor is hardhearted and prone to see only the badness in people. Since many dependent and suggestible patients will show transient symptom reduction and even pseudo personality change in such a group atmosphere, the therapist will be even more convinced of the correctness of his approach. Only long-term life experience with a few real personal traumata plus personal therapy tends to make some of these individuals aware of the basis of their therapeutic stance, which is more appropriate to religious leadership than to group psychotherapy.

Lastly, in this need to be liked by the group, there is the all too frequent "I-Am-One-of-You Type." This is a therapist whose need for personal acceptance is so great that he literally tends to reduce his position to that of just another patient in the group. Initially, he insists that everybody call everybody, including himself, by first names. Early he begins to share his own personal feelings with the group and to join in with personal material. At first, his group of patients, if not too heavily made up of patients with paranoid inclinations, tend to give him what he wants: acceptance and the feeling he is a nice guy, not distant or authoritative like many of his colleagues. In time, when they sense the absence of real direction and his overinvolvement in the treatment, they end up resenting him, just as they do themselves, as weak, insecure, and fearful of taking firm stands and making decisions. In supervision this therapist espouses theories about democratic approaches to patients and the need to feel like a patient in order to understand and gain rapport with his patients. After seemingly initial success, he commonly gets emotionally overinvolved with some of his patients, who begin making inappropriate and unwelcome demands upon him both in and out of the treatment. Unable to gratify them, he finds love changing to hate, and, in his impotence, he usually turns in a most dependent manner to his supervisor to be rescued or becomes quite emotionally disturbed. In more severe cases it has been necessary to substitute other therapists or to terminate the group, and, not infrequently, to refer these overinvolved therapists to personal therapy.

Training Recommendations

What to do about all these problems is obviously a topic which merits much thought, experimentation, and volumes of exposition. However, the writer cannot refrain from listing a number of general recommendations. In his experience these problems can be minimized by:

1. Group and social experience prior to group psychotherapy training, such as experiencing leadership in clubs and on committees in nonpsychiatric settings plus vigorous involvement in milieu therapy programs in psychiatric settings.

2. Personal psychotherapy, including, if possible, concurrent group psychotherapy, and if not possible, group process workshops.

3. Thorough didactic preparation emphasizing group dynamics and group process prior to undertaking group work, and formal group review concurrent with it during the first year.

4. Prior clinical experience in intimate, long-term patient contacts.

5. Undertaking group psychotherapy with a competent, experienced cotherapist before engaging in it independently.

6. Close supervision by an experienced supervisor, with supervision

starting well before group work so that a working relationship has already been established.

7. A successful group psychotherapy experience early in training. This experience will have the greatest possibility of taking place if the above recommendations are implemented and early experience occurs in a carefully composed group having maximal group-dynamic potential for cohesiveness and movement. Success for the beginning group therapist is no accident. It should be a carefully planned and prepared eventuality which in the long run will have great effect on moderating many of the problems discussed in this paper.

REFERENCES

Geller, J. J. Supervision in a hospital group psychotherapy program. *International Journal of Group Psychotherapy*, 1958, *8*, 313–322.

Levin, S., & Kanter, S. S. Some general considerations in the supervision of beginning group psychotherapists. *International Journal of Group Psychotherapy*, 1964, *14*, 318–331.

Mullan, H., & Rosenbaum, M. *Group psychotherapy*. New York: Free Press of Glencoe, 1962.

Powdermaker, F. B., & Frank, J. D. *Group psychotherapy*. Cambridge, Mass.: Harvard University Press, 1953.

Slavson, S. R. *A textbook in analytic group psychotherapy*. New York: International Universities Press, 1964.

Slavson, S. R. *Introduction to group psychotherapy*. New York: The Commonwealth Fund, 1943.

10 / *AN INVENTORY OF*

TRAINER INTERVENTIONS

William G. Dyer

Central to human relations training (and to an important degree to discussion groups, group-centered classrooms, and group counseling) is the role of the trainer. While some programs have eliminated the trainer, he is generally seen as important. Certain key questions concerning his behavior confront the trainer. This paper is concerned with the kinds of things the trainer should do when he intervenes and the many approaches the trainer can use.

Content Focus

If the group is discussing a topic such as "How should an effective supervisor behave?" a content intervention would be to share an experience, some research data, or an opinion. In a discussion group where the focus is on content, the content intervention may contribute to group goals, provided it is not a contribution a member might have made had the trainer encouraged wider sharing of member resources. However, a content intervention may give legitimacy to the topic and keep the group from looking at its own processes.

Process Focus

This intervention attempts to shift the focus to what is happening in the group. One of the most standard, almost to the point of becoming a cliché among trainers, is "I wonder what is really going on in the group now." Others would prefer, "Were you all aware that only two persons voiced an opinion, yet a decision was made?" (Argyris, 1962, p. 167, rejects "I wonder" interventions as not encouraging authentic relationships. "I believe I know why they are doing it. And perhaps more important I believe they feel that I know.") How a trainer helps the group focus on its own processes is probably determined by his own personal style or his training strategy.

Asking for Feelings

An intervention of this type would be, "Ed, how did you feel when the group rejected your idea?" Some trainers and many participants find the sharing of feelings the most interesting part of the training process. For some, it is the first time they have been able to find out how others feel about their behavior. Certainly this is an important learning goal. However, if the trainer concentrates on this he may neglect other important facets of group action.

Direction-Giving

The trainer may structure the group by having members write out name cards, use a tape recorder, or have them stop at some given time. Later he may provide observation forms or even suggest an exercise.

Some trainers offer directions only as suggestions while others arbitrarily impose certain actions, feeling that members should learn how to handle forced direction if they dislike it. It would appear that if a trainer has a high need to control he may satisfy this need by direction-giving, or he may recognize this need and overreact, not supplying direction when it might be helpful. The trainer has to decide whether to let the group try to work through its own impasse, at the possible cost of time wasted, or to supply some direction, at the risk of reinforcing dependency. Relevant factors include the length of the training program, the level of dependency, the resources available to the group, and the trainer's own tolerance of ambiguity.

Direct Feedback

The trainer may give direct feedback to a member or to the group. Some trainers give direct feedback early, as a model to legitimize the giving of feedback. Others prefer to wait until they have worked through some of the authority problem. Here again the trainer is faced with a dilemma. Group members are often anxious to know how the trainer sees them. However, the reactions of the trainer are often no more valid than those of other group members. The trainer must somehow share his reactions and, at the same time, get the group to use data from all members.

Cognitive Orientations

The trainer may provide relevant "theory" or information. He must determine whether the participants will learn more if they can glean the same insight from their own experience and whether he may really be satisfying his own need to be seen as an expert.

Performing Group Functions

The trainer may intervene by performing task-maintenance functions to help the group maintain itself as an effective system and accomplish its task of promoting learning. For example, the trainer may intervene with such task functions as seeking opinion or reactions to what has happened in the group. He may share his own opinion. He may initiate a new group goal, a definition of the problem, or a way of organizing for work. He may elaborate an idea; he may summarize; he may test consensus. To meet maintenance needs, the trainer may intervene by encouraging, harmonizing, "gate-keeping," standard-setting, or releasing tension.

To satisfy individual needs, group members sometimes act as aggressor, blocker, recognition seeker, self-confessor, playboy, dominator, and so on. Trainers may intervene at times in these ways, but it is questionable whether such interventions facilitate learning.

Some trainer strategy calls for intervening early along the task-maintenance dimensions, reducing such interventions as members develop greater ability to perform such functions themselves.

Diagnostic Intervention

The trainer may diagnose what he sees happening. For example, "There are a number of possibilities why the group is apathetic. One is that our goals are not clear. Another is that we are afraid if we start to work again, old conflicts may be reopened." He may then ask the group for other possibilities. The exploratory intervention is designed to suggest ways of looking at process and to encourage a diagnostic approach.

Protection Intervention

This type of intervention has been suggested by Blake (1963). The trainer may intervene to keep members from "overexposure," that is, sharing personal incidents or feelings that may not facilitate learnings appropriate to the training goals or that may create a situation neither the members nor the trainer is capable of dealing with.

A trainer may also protect a member if he feels that feedback is ill-timed or unnecessarily severe. Or the trainer may help a member maintain his identity despite group pressures to conform.

Some trainers prefer to focus on process and ask the group if a given behavior seems appropriate to their goals.

Intervention is only part of the total strategy of the trainer, the overall plan by which he proposes to bring about learning goals he has helped establish. It reflects the trainer's theories of individual and group behavior. It involves such factors as when and how often to intervene, around what concerns, how much of the trainer's own emotional reactions are funneled into the group, how much control he maintains, and whether he tries to become a group member, maintains his trainer status, or participates with group members outside the group.

In an interesting study, Reisel (1961) has pointed out some possible effects of the personality of the trainer on the interventions he makes. The trainer may intervene in terms of his own needs and his patterns of responding to anxiety, conflict, and ambiguity. He may not be aware of how these internal forces influence his behavior, nor of certain language and speech patterns or mannerisms that also become part of the intervention. One would hypothesize that the trainer with a high need to control might use more direction-giving, cognitive orientation, direct feedback, and summarizing interventions. The trainer who avoids conflicts and feelings may find it more comfortable to make content and direction interventions and to perform harmonizing functions.

It may be valuable to study the nature of trainer interventions and their effects more systematically. By use of an intervention inventory it may be possible to bring to light some of the personality factors affecting training. Such an inventory might note the type of intervention (content focus, process focus) frequency, timing, the focus (on individual or group dynamics), and the effect (ignored, used briefly then dropped).

While it may never be possible nor desirable to reduce training to standardized responses, if more trainers are to be developed and training improved, there must be more effort to ascertain what types of trainer style or strategy produce maximum learning. The approach suggested here is to observe and catalogue interventions to see what pattern maximizes certain measured learning goals.

REFERENCES

Argyris, C. *Interpersonal competence and organizational effectiveness,* Homewood, Ill.: Dorsey, 1962.

Blake, R. Studying group action. In L. P. Bradford, K. Benne, & J. Gibb (Eds.), *T-Group theory and laboratory method.* New York: Wiley, 1963.

Reisel, J. Observations on the trainer role: A case study. In *Leadership and organization.* New York: McGraw-Hill, 1961.

11 / SOME CONSIDERATIONS FOR SCHOOL COUNSELORS WHO WORK WITH GROUPS

H. Allan Dye

There is considerable evidence indicating great interest on the part of school counselors in the use of group procedures, but the reactions can best be described as mixed. One genuinely curious aspect of these mixed feelings is that counselors frequently wonder whether the group approach is a natural and therefore appropriate way of being helpful to young people.

The fact is that in several respects—background, preparation, values, interpersonal orientation—it would seem more natural to work with students in groups rather than individually. Virtually all counselors enter the field from a teaching background where their interest in students focused on social as well as academic development. As teachers they tended to emphasize the fact that success in life often depends upon being the right kind of person as much as upon grade average and rank in class. Personal and social development, along with self-understanding, are facilitated by experiences in which students interact with others in the examination of values, attitudes, and ambitions. The typical classroom situation, however, imposes severe limits upon the extent to which a teacher can respond to the students' personal and social needs.

The lack of opportunity to relate with students in the instructional setting and the frustrations created by these circumstances combine to form a common motive for entering the field of counsel-

From FUNDAMENTAL GROUP PROCEDURES FOR SCHOOL COUNSELORS by H. Allan Dye. Guidance Monograph Series, Series 2, No. 9 (Boston: Houghton Mifflin, 1968). Adapted from Chapter 4, "Counselor Characteristics, Evaluative and Administrative Considerations," pp. 44–55. Copyright 1968, Houghton Mifflin. Reprinted with permission of author and publisher.

ing. The necessary interpersonal demands of individual counseling, however, are found by many to be different from, even foreign to, their former orientation as teachers. Some of the original interest in students' social development may diminish during the acclimation to individual counseling relationships. This loss seems unfortunate. Group procedures thus provide a means of utilizing the counselor's innate interest in the social maturation process.

It might also be observed that counselor functions which are appropriate in a group—talking, observing, reflecting, generalizing—are naturally characteristic of many people who become counselors. At the same time a common trait among people in "helping" professions is shyness. Few regard themselves as *personally* and consistently able to produce significant change in the behavior of others. Rather than manifesting a predilection for individual remediation, treatment, and manipulation, counselors live and work within a framework of self-understanding, growth, and development. Upon considering these factors, along with the gregarious nature of adolescents, the case for group experiences assumes major proportions. On the bases of personal orientation, professional preparation, and experience, counselors appear to be more appropriately endowed for group rather than individual counseling.

In the final analysis it seems foolish to debate whether individual or group methods have squatter's rights on the manner in which counselors may be helpful. There is no valid justification for regarding the matter as an either/or proposition; the potential effectiveness of both individual and group approaches has been adequately demonstrated. Reservations about the appropriateness of group procedures are difficult to warrant except to the degree that they represent a departure from established patterns of preparation and practice.

Personal Preferences

Perhaps the only universal preference among counselors who work with students in groups is that of working with students in groups. Beyond this there appear to be only a few preferential characteristics associated with effectiveness in group work.

Counselors who employ group procedures prefer the dynamic, vital interaction which emanates from free, informal, minimally-structured situations. Reaction and behavior are less predictable in a group. The sheer mass of stimuli generated by multiple interpersonal relationships virtually precludes comprehensive anticipation. It becomes necessary to share responsibility, a process which group counselors find fascinating and meaningful to everyone involved.

A taste for variety and breadth of experience is also characteristic. The tedium-emotional fatigue-staleness syndrome is well known among those whose daily schedules consist entirely of individual personal interviews. The fresh contrast afforded by the setting, functions, and challenges of group work appeals to many.

Group counselors are likely to portray either an individually-centered or democratic orientation to their work. Preferences for expediency and efficiency which require relatively more control are frustrated by the lack of counselor autonomy in a group setting. Some counselors have experienced a sensation not unlike relief upon becoming able to relinquish the subtle, unintended restraints inherent in individual counseling.

Abilities

While not exclusive to counselors who work with groups, the following brief descriptions of attitudes and abilities are suggested as appropriate if not necessary for those who utilize group procedures:

1. a willingness to study and become knowledgeable about group procedures, counselor functions, and the ways in which people interact in groups;

2. tolerance for stress and discomfort—personally and on the part of members—and understanding of the parts these reactions play in the processes of learning and becoming aware;

3. a willingness to invest in and care in a non-possessive manner about each person in the group;

4. a willingness to be accessible, to sponsor a *reciprocal* investment for each member;

5. an ability to accept fully each of a variety of viewpoints, philosophies, and attitudes, some of which may be diametrically opposed to those of the counselor;

6. the ability to focus simultaneously on the underlying feelings and attitudes of each member, the counselors, and the group as a whole;

7. the ability to originate and nurture interaction between and among group members;

8. the ability to maintain consistent perspective both as a counselor and member of the group;

9. confidence in one's helping potential, the members, and the process;

10. the ability to find joy, humor, and satisfaction in the experiences of oneself and of others.

Preparation for Working with Groups

An optimal preparation pattern would include laboratory experiences as a group member during the first year of graduate study, followed by didactic work and supervised experience during the second year. However, instruction and laboratory experience in group work have only recently become a part of counselor preparation programs. Currently there is a need for information about the extent and nature of group-work curricular offerings throughout the country. A consensus among counselors and counselor-educators would probably reflect that a didactic experience is generally available during the first year of graduate study but is not required in a majority of institutions.

Advanced study including supervised practicum is regarded as desirable but is largely unavailable. Operating in the existing situation are several factors including lack of qualified counselor-education staff, limited student interest as a function of degree/certification restrictions, absence of needed on-campus facilities, and the logistics problems which arise in obtaining practicum clientele. While the latter two conditions can be partially resolved by making off-campus arrangements, the problems of staff and student availability tend to be aggravated as programs move away from the campus.

An assessment of preparation for group work leads to these conclusions: (1) a minimal amount of formal preparation is becoming increasingly common; (2) a small number of graduate students are able to include advanced study in their programs; and, (3) the majority of practicing counselors have had little or no preparation for group work. Based on the foregoing assessment, the need for post-degree study and a variety of in-service programs is abundantly clear. State departments of public instruction and local and regional professional groups are making important contributions by conducting workshops and conferences. It is interesting to note the increasing tendency of these programs to *involve* rather than merely address those who attend them.

Irrespective of formal circumstances, the following sequence of preparatory experience for counseling with groups is suggested:

1. Achieve a satisfactory degree of confidence in dealing effectively with personally vital issues and concerns on an individual basis. This prerequisite need not be met prior to sponsoring groups whose purposes are informational, attitudinal, or socially discussive. Along with individual counseling, prior experience in leading informal discussion groups is highly relevant.

2. Take advantage of the available information about group work by engaging in a study of the literature—theory, methodology, research. If possible, utilize the assistance of someone whose knowledge and experience can help in identifying relevant sources of information.

3. Obtain supervisory or consultive service for evaluation and assistance.

4. Begin by selecting a group whose concerns are well-suited to the amount of counselor experience and preparation and whose reactions to the group experience can be reasonably well anticipated. In a word, make maximum provision for a "successful" initial experience during which counselor learning can occur.

Challenges Encountered in Utilizing Group Procedures

A major challenge is represented by the fact that the counselor in a group is subject to close and constant scrutiny. This condition inherent in the situation can almost certainly be expected to expose any tendency of the counselor to play a role or portray an image *whether or not* the counselor is conscious of such behavior. A group affords no place to be inconspicuous, so that only two alternatives exist for counselor behavior. One course of action is to put on more defensive armor and become increasingly insulated from personal relationships. The other course of action in responding to this personal identity challenge is toward openness and spontaneity. The decision to respond and relate with students in a natural, unpretentious manner does not necessarily remove the need for making judgments concerning appropriate counselor behavior and participation. Those who work with groups find it necessary to achieve a consistent balance between participation both as a co-member and as one with additional responsibilities. Relinquishment of overall responsibility in favor of equal membership status deprives the group of valuable leadership and reference service. By the same token, restrained participation consisting only of formal, impersonal leadership functions contributes little to the establishment of a climate within which members are encouraged to deal effectively with their concerns. Upon recognizing restricted participation by members as a function of the counselor's inability or failure to provide personally meaningful dialogue and experience, the counselor must shed his anonymity and let himself be known as a person.

A second challenge is essentially the inverse of the first. Counselors who enjoy the company of young people, respect them as individuals, and take personal satisfaction in assisting with the problems and concerns they present can be sucked in and swallowed by the perceived emotional demands of a counseling group. A possible result is the group's subsequent preoccupation with the counselor's concerns! This challenge requires the counselor to retain a degree of personal autonomy and individuality necessary both for his own survival and for continuing to provide a stable, relatively objective personal resource for the members.

The essence of these two challenges, although they differ in degree and direction, is objectivity. The field of counseling has in the past attracted many who may be described as interpersonally delicate rather than truly sensitive. The delicate are handicapped by being able to perceive while simultaneously unable to evaluate and respond appropriately to the significant behavior of others. An important task facing counselor-educators is that of finding ways to utilize this natural talent of perceptivity, the raw form of which can have little or no helping value without implementation. Each person who undertakes to develop group competencies must face the necessity of determining what personal orientation is both effective and comfortable.

Group Membership

12 / OBSERVATION GUIDE:

ON SEEING, HEARING, AND FEELING

Oron P. South

As the rate of change increases in our society, much of what we know goes out of date; our knowledge begins to have a half-life of five or ten years. Similarly, many of our habits, practices, and feelings also become obsolete, although generally we do not conceptualize feelings from this point of view.

Since our educational and organizational concepts and practices have not been developed with the notion that feelings would have a limited time value, tremendous strains have developed both in our educational and organizational systems as well as between persons in these systems. There seem to be two reasons for this. One is that continuous efforts are made to add new knowledge to that already accumulated. This produces the sensation of being overwhelmed. The second reason is that our traditional educational approaches emphasize division and specialization of knowledge, rather than integration. As a result, graduates often do not know how to deal with their feelings. More specifically, they are not able to use feelings to see and to solve problems.

The human condition, in an age of specialization and the explosion of knowledge, has been commented on by a number of observers. Archibald MacLeish (1960), for example, says that the inability to "see feelingly" is the critical flaw of our age.

Our crisis is man, the new man in whom this new knowledge is carried—along with the old ignorance which was there before: the new scientific man who knows but does not know, who can but can't, who will but

Unpublished paper, December 1969. Copyright 1971 by Oron P. South. Printed with permission of author.

won't—and who is dangerous to himself and others because he has lost his relation to his own reality in losing his relation to a world he thought he knew (p. 29).

MacLeish continues by saying that it is now possible, for the first time in history, to know as a *mind* what you cannot comprehend as a *man*. The way out, in his opinion, is to regain the ability to see feelingly—to approach life as something to be felt and experienced, rather than manipulated (p. 30).

What MacLeish calls the "ability to see feelingly" is what I think many Blacks have in mind when they speak of "soul." That is, if one has soul, he "sees" problems and solutions that are not visible to those who lack the quality.

Given the difficulties with our educational systems, changes have been suggested by a number of observers. The American Association for the Advancement of Science, for instance, has been studying the feasibility of learning about science from the standpoint of *process* rather than *content*. That is, instead of spending classroom time in teaching people what scientists have learned, students are helped to learn and to apply the processes scientists use in their work. The basic processes used are observing, classifying, using space-time relationships, using numbers, communicating, measuring, inferring, and predicting. The more complicated processes involve formulating hypotheses, controlling variables, interpreting data, defining operationality, constructing models, and experimenting.

At the same time as the conviction has been growing that man needs to be able to see feelingly, and that our educational and organizational systems need to be changed, new views of the nature of man have been developing among physical and behavioral scientists (see Bugental, 1967). In general, the older view tends to conceptualize the psyche as a mechanical system subject to the operation of the laws of cause and effect. A major concern is with the individual's relation to the world outside and how he copes with it. Learning helps the individual to substitute "good" ways of relating to the world outside for "bad" ways.

The newer view tends to conceptualize the psyche as a *growth system*. The major concern is with the individual's inner world and his relation to it. Interest centers around intentions, choice, problem-solving, and decision-making as means for growth.[1]

[1] For a contrast between mechanism-centered and growth-centered approaches to learning, see Rossi, 1964.

In this paper I have tried to combine the three viewpoints described above—the notion of seeing feelingly, process learning, and the humanistic view of man—in preparing an observation guide. For those who have been accustomed to a content approach to learning, this guide may be difficult to use at first. One reason for this is that it calls for a different psychology on the part of the learner. A few words about this may be helpful.

The traditional approach to learning generally calls for the learner to be passive. His task is to *receive* from a book, teacher, article, film, or some other authoritative source, information which has been collected and organized by others. This approach contains the assumption that the learner is being prepared for known roles or functions. That is, the objective is to produce a "good" student, teacher, manager, economist, lawyer, engineer, and so forth, *within known dimensions.* The dimensions are known by the educator, who identifies relevant information for the learners and also directs their attention to known problems. As individuals grapple with problems, the educator directs their attention to known problem-solving methods. After they have arrived at their solutions, the educator compares these with known solutions to see if they have arrived at an appropriate or correct answer. As learners accumulate standardized bits of information and develop uniform techniques, the educator directs them to additional information and more complicated techniques. In its operation, this approach to education turns out people who are prepared to deal with problems already well defined and which can be approached by known standardized techniques.

The application of this approach, particularly as standardized bits of knowledge and techniques accumulate, produces the educator who worries about covering specified material and who is concerned about learners who "fall behind" (that is, who do not keep up with their quota). Grading serves to verify how much has been accumulated, and a diploma—if obtained from a "good" school that maintains "standards"—means a standard product, certified as to acquired information or techniques.

When learning is approached from a process orientation, quite different assumptions are made about the nature of the teaching and learning functions. One is that in a time of change it may be a disservice to try to educate people for known roles or functions. That is, since it is not clear what it will mean to be a student, manager, teacher, or psychologist next year or five years from now, it is not possible to prepare for a fixed future.

With this orientation, learners are prepared to be self-directed and autonomous in formulating their own problems, identifying relevant information, and seeking their own resources. Learning techniques as such are de-emphasized, and individuals are encouraged to develop their own methods. The ability to invent appropriate new problem-solving techniques is valued more than learning techniques developed by others. Similarly, learners are encouraged to develop their own standards for evaluating results—standards which are appropriate to their own needs and situation.

As individuals gain more familiarity with this approach, they begin to be more inventive and to integrate their learning faster. This produces an ability to apply learning in different situations, rather than only in the contexts in which the learning took place. In addition, learners tend to become more aware of their own learning processes and what they need to know. This reinforces their self-direction and autonomy.

One way to highlight some of the major differences between the two methods of learning is to indicate how they look in a brief comparison:

TRADITIONAL LEARNING	PROCESS LEARNING
1. Educator knows proper definition or function of manager, student, etc., and of a person.	1. Definition of manager, student, person, etc., is something to be worked on by both educator and learner.
2. Educator is authority and controls power; learning is enhanced when learners defer to authority.	2. Power is shared; learning is enhanced when all have access to equal power and influence.
3. Members are placed in a structure in which role is precisely defined, i.e., educators are "teachers," and learners are "students."	3. Members are placed in a network of relationships in which role becomes a function of interaction and involvement. Teachers can be learners, and learners, teachers.
4. Educator formulates problems and identifies relevant information and resources.	4. Learner formulates problems and identifies relevant information and resources. Educator can aid but does not control.
5. Educator provides technique for problem-solving and standards for solutions.	5. Learner develops technique for problem-solving and standards for solutions.

6. Learner works with what is external and abstract to him.

6. Learner works with what is external and internal, and distinctions between the two tend to disappear; what is immediate is the focus for learning.

7. Educator continuously defines what needs to be learned next; he tries to be aware of learner's process of learning.

7. Learner defines his own educational needs and develops ways to see his own learning process.

8. Individual seeks to know himself through measuring himself against an ideal type (i.e., man, woman, manager, teacher, etc.).

8. Individual seeks to know himself through the choices he makes, the relationships he enters into, and the knowledge he seeks.

9. Major learning problems are efficiency (standardized bits of information accumulated rapidly and in proper quantity) and motivation (keeping learners devoted to task).

9. Major learning problems are communication (increasing understanding), involvement (finding a satisfactory level of participation), and risk-taking (being self-directed).

While other dimensions could be given, I hope this outline, along with the previous discussion, will serve to indicate some of the differences between the two approaches to learning and provide a background for the following suggestions on observation.

The suggestions offered in the guide which follows are based on the assumption that the reader will be observing a group at work. He may be a part of the group, or he may be observing without participating. It also is assumed that the observer is interested in learning what influences group climate and process.

1. Pacing Signals

A. Nonverbal
1. Body configuration—position of head, arms, trunk, and legs.
2. Body state—muscle tone, alertness, attention, involvement.
3. Movements—nods, gestures, eye contacts, positioning with respect to others.

B. Verbal
   1. Voice tone, inflection, and pitch.
   2. Speaking speed.

When people work together, they pick up cues from one another as to the pace of work. By observing closely, it may be possible to see what these cues are and how people react to them. The objective is to be able to relate signals that people give, intentionally or unintentionally, to the pace at which a group is working.

Discussion. Body configuration often will give cues as to how people are reacting to others and to what is being done. If, for example, the observer sees someone who sits with his arms folded over his chest with his head positioned in such a way that he resembles a judge, he might try to discover if others react to him as a judge and listen to see if he offers judicious remarks.

When people feel uneasy or threatened by what is going on, they sometimes will cross their legs, fold their arms over their midsection, and hunch their shoulders. The effect communicated is that danger is sensed and an effort is being made to protect the vital organs. If the observer sees someone sitting in the position described, he might listen to discover how he is participating.

Frequently, when a person tunes out a discussion he moves his chair backward or turns his body away from others, as if to signal that he has pulled out physically. Conversely, a person may pull his chair up or lean forward when he anticipates getting into the discussion or making a point.

A member of the group may assume the "mugwump" position. That is, his "mug" is in the group, and his "wump" is out. This may mean that he wants to be heard but is unwilling to commit himself firmly to others—he wants to have his cake and eat it too.

Nods, gestures, eye contacts, and so forth can be used to support others and to urge them on, or they can be used to slow down proceedings or to convey to others: "Be careful—take it easy." Exactly what is communicated can be determined only by observing to see what effect is achieved with different actions. Some people, for example, will smile or nod so much that after awhile the smile loses its ability to have any effect. Likewise, a frown also may lose its effect. Or it may be noted that those who smile or frown all the time tend to be disregarded and that attention is concentrated on those whose expressions change.

Voice tone, inflection, pitch, and talking speed often can provide cues as to how a person wants the group to operate. An individual who speaks slowly and deliberately may be signalling that he wants the group to work slowly and deliberately. Someone who tries to banish emotion from his voice may be signalling that he will be uncomfortable with any show of emotion. Conversely, an individual whose voice changes pitch and who appears to speak without thinking may be signalling that he likes for people in a group to be spontaneous and to express their feelings.

In observing verbal and nonverbal cues, it is important to remember that the signals are not invariant. That is, if someone speaks slowly and deliberately, it does not always mean that he prefers for a group to operate slowly and deliberately. In fact, it may never mean that. What the meaning is in a particular group can be determined only by observing and verifying observations to see what effect is obtained.

2. Intentionality Signals

A. Influence wanted
   1. Type
   2. Spread or span

B. Influence accepted
   1. Type
   2. Point of origin

C. Relationships desired
   1. Type
   2. Spread

D. Membership structure
   1. Separateness—conformity
   2. Types of positions

E. Responsibility
   1. Apportionment
   2. Acceptance

We may assume that people have certain intentions when they work with others, although they may not in all instances recognize what they are or be able to state them. In many instances, intentions are habits developed over time. That is, people grow accustomed to certain kinds of behavior in themselves and others; from habit they come to expect the same kinds of behavior to be repeated in other situations.

When groups meet, members have some expectations of the type of influence they want or expect to have. This will vary among individuals, but the observer may note what kind of influence different individuals want. Some persons may want to influence major decisions; they wish to be able to say "yes" or "no" to important items but do not care about routine matters. Some may want to influence one or two people, while others want to influence everyone. The kind of influence a person wants to have can be observed by noticing when he comments in a discussion, the kinds of comments he makes, and whose points he comments on.

Accepted influence can be gauged by noting how much attention is paid to different members of the group. If only one or two persons are thought to be really important, comments from anyone else may be listened to politely but not accepted as really important. Or it may be that only certain kinds of statements will be noted. Some, for example, may listen only to short statements forcefully delivered, while others may tune out any statements that are not quiet and deliberate.

Relationships among members may be of many types. Some persons will signal, "If you can't say something mean and belligerent to me, don't say anything." Others may signal, "If you don't keep your voice down and quit using those strong words, I won't listen to you." Some will want people to express how they feel, desiring authentic relationships, while others will view expression of feelings as dangerous, preferring role relationships ("You act like a plant manager and I'll act like a plant manager"). Some individuals will prefer confrontation, while others will prefer to handle disagreements by taking a coffee break or by talking privately in the washroom. Some will want accepting, caring relationships, while others will prefer to remain distant. The kind of relationships desired by individuals can be observed by noting how they respond to one another. Are feelings toward others being expressed, or repressed? Do members accept the feelings of others, or do they try to argue others out of their feelings? Can members own the thoughts they have, or do they tend to say, "I don't really mean that"? Do members play games with each other?

Groups tend to develop different kinds of membership patterns. The observer should look for the degree of conformity enforced or encouraged and see if members encourage others to be themselves.

He should check also to see patterns which emerge around problem-solving and decision-making. That is, do certain members seem to make all the decisions? If a problem comes up around procedure, how does the problem get solved? Who seems to feel free to offer alternatives, and who does not?

Membership patterns also can be determined by observing the participation pattern. Who takes up most of the air time, and who the least? Is this pattern a continuing one? If all the members of the group were lined up in the order in which they have influence, would it be easy to determine who would be at the head of the line and who would be at the end? If members were lined up in terms of who feels free to express what he is thinking and feeling, what would the line look like? If members were arranged in terms of how well they listen to others, what would the arrangement look like?

Finally, how is responsibility for group operation and effectiveness apportioned? Do some expect others to take responsibility, or do all members feel equally responsible? Do some feel that they have no responsibility for handling problem members—those who talk too much, or too little, or in some way disrupt operations? Do some feel it is up to them, not others, to insure the efficient operation of the total group?

3. Environment-Relating Signals

    A. Reference to contexts
        1. Here-and-now
        2. There-and-then

    B. Provision of material
        1. Relationship to context
        2. Relationship to individual

When members of a group encounter difficulty in working together, they may examine their difficulties in terms of what they are experiencing at the moment (here-and-now), or they may talk about their problems in terms of abstractions (there-and-then). For example if a person thinks someone did not hear what he said, or ignored his suggestion, he might say: "I don't believe you heard what I said," or "My impression is that you ignored what I said to make a point of your own." Or, he could say: "I believe we will operate better if we will pay attention to what others are saying," or "In my experience, groups get into trouble when people don't take the trouble to listen to what others have to say."

As groups work together, individuals will signal whether they prefer to examine group issues in the context of here-and-now, or there-and-then.

If they are willing to work in a here-and-now context, they will describe how others are affecting them. They will tend to say things such as: "I feel this way about what you did"; "My impression is that you intended to cut off discussion"; and "I am pleased with the way we are moving." The material they provide will relate to the problem before the group in the here-and-now and will give some indication of where the individual is with respect to what is going on.

If the there-and-then context is preferred, people will tend to talk in terms of generalizations and abstractions. They will say such things as: "At our place we solve problems like that this way"; or "That was tried last year over at Podunk and it failed miserably"; or "What we need to do is to get organized." The material provided will not relate to the problem or issue before the group, except indirectly, and will not give much indication of where the individual is with respect to what is going on.

4. Goal-Setting Signals

A. Type
  1. Integrative and synergistic, or idealistic
  2. Reductionistic
  3. Individualistic
B. Relevance
  1. To group
  2. To task
  3. To individual

Groups can set goals, in terms of members working together, that are integrative and synergistic, or idealistic. By "integrative" and "synergistic" it is meant that the output represents the best possible outcome from the members working together and is based on an integration of inputs from each individual; and that the inputs from all individuals are combined in such a way that the output is better than any one member could have produced. The output represents the best the group is able to produce and thus is synergistic. An idealistic goal represents the assumption of an ideal solution to a problem or decision—the group works toward this ideal without regard to what the group as a whole is capable of producing. The type of goal a group sets for itself can be noted by observing whether members emphasize and pay attention to how they are working together, or whether they emphasize ideas and pay little attention to how they work.

Frequently, groups may settle for a reduced goal that is, the first solution that will work. This happens when members do not have much faith and trust in one another and feel that the group as a whole cannot get much done. As a result, they diagnose their difficulty as an ineffective group, rather than as having ineffective procedures for working together. When groups settle for a reduced goal, members generally will tell you privately that the group is no good, it will never get anywhere, and that they would like to get out of the group and join a better one somewhere else.

Setting individualistic goals ("Let's all do what we want to") may come from two or more dominant members' refusing to abandon their own position, or it may result from a general unwillingness to work for consensus. The setting of individualistic goals may be manifest in vote-taking (to avoid working for consensus), appointing one or two members to make a decision involving all, postponing working on decisions, or reluctance to make any decision at all.

When individualistic goals are set, they may or may not have much relevance to the group or to the task, but they will be highly relevant to the individuals concerned. An integrative-synergistic goal will generally have high relevance to the group, the task, and the individual; while the idealistic goal will tend to have high relevance to task but little relevance to the group and the individual. The difference can be noted by observing what happens after decisions are made. Integrative decisions will command acceptance and action by all or most of the members; the members will act individually on what they have worked out collectively. If individualistic goals are set, those who set them will feel most responsible, while others will be halfhearted and apathetic. If idealistic, members will tend to be either quite happy with each other or quite unhappy but will not have much enthusiasm for the product.

5. Change Signals

A. Type
   1. Supportive
   2. Nonsupportive

B. Relevance
   1. To group
   2. To individual

If members of a group are to improve their ability to work together effectively, behavior will change to fit conditions encountered. Changes can come through signalling between members as to desired behavior changes. These signals may be supportive or nonsupportive. A supportive signal might be: "It would help me if you would not speak at such great lengths, as I lose your train of thought after a minute or two." A nonsupportive type might be: "Shape up or ship out."

The supportive signal communicates to the other person, "You can help me if you will do such-and-such." It indicates the desired direction of change and has relevance to the group members working together as a group.

The nonsupportive signal communicates, "I'm disgusted or angered by what you are doing." The signal may not, however, provide any suggestions as to what change is useful or acceptable, as there is no indication of what "shape up" means.

In general, supportive signals result from efforts of members to describe their own feelings and thoughts about themselves and others, such as: "I'm having a hard time paying attention to you"; "I'm having a hard time following you"; "I find myself getting angry with you"; and so forth. The nonsupportive signals result from members' passing judgment on other members, such as: "You're doing a poor job"; or "Do you always take this same stupid approach to what you do?"

When supportive signals are given, it may be observed that groups tend to become more cohesive and that members tend to listen to other members more closely. The reason seems to be that each person begins to find out that others are trying to help him become more effective as an individual. This tends to increase their value in his eyes; hence he listens more attentively.

When nonsupportive signals are given, it may be observed that groups tend to become less cohesive and that members tend to become competitive with one another and to tune each other out. The reason seems to be that individuals feel that their character and personality are under attack, so they tend to devalue what others say and hence to listen less.

The signals emitted by an individual may be relevant to the group or to the person giving them. If relevant to the group, they may be intended to increase the effectiveness of the group in some way. If relevant solely to the individual, the intention may be to satisfy purely personal needs. The difference sometimes can be determined by listening to find out if efforts are made to explain behavior that may appear nonfunctional to others. If someone notices that others are puzzled by what he does or has done, or that his behavior does not seem to make sense to others, he might try to explain how it makes sense to him. If behavior is designed to meet purely personal needs, no explanation might be offered.

6. Analytical Preferences

A. Models of
1. Reality
2. Organization
3. Effectiveness

B. Assumptions about
1. Associational relationships
2. Procedures
3. Control
4. Problem-solving and decision-making
5. Values and the source of values

In general, people hold two contrasting concepts of reality. The first concept, which is by far the most predominant, is that the real world is *external* to the mind; the second concept, which is less prevalent but which is gaining ground, is that the real world is primarily *internal*.[2]

Persons who hold the view that reality is external tend to believe that trustworthy knowledge comes from recording and classifying data. An extreme version of this point of view holds that "If you can't count it or measure it, it isn't worth knowing." Psychologically, those who hold the external view will require experts or

[2] For a discussion of the effect of external and internal views of reality on international relations, see Kissinger, 1966.

authorities to organize the group. They also will want an expert or authority to tell them how effective the group is.

What are often called "unstructured" groups (T-groups, encounter groups, sensitivity training groups, etc.) are often viewed with some alarm by persons who are deeply committed to the view that the real world is external, as the lack of structure is taken to mean that the value of knowledge already gained is being denied. Often they may say: "It's a waste of time to meet just for the sake of meeting," or "What's the point of meeting if no one is able to specify what the problem is?" Such statements appear to stem from the feeling that the real world does have a structure, and that to deny this is mere foolishness.

Persons who adhere to the external view may pay little or no attention to their own feelings and attitudes, or to the feelings and attitudes of those around them. If they do take these into consideration, they may want a formal procedure or request the services of someone who is an expert or authority in determining how others feel.

Persons who hold the view that what is most real is internal to the observer tend to value their own feelings and attitudes as sources for action and judgment. They also tend to believe that valuable knowledge can be produced by processes which do not involve classification and measurement. Thus, they may judge the effectiveness of a group by their own feelings and standards, rather than by standards external to them. Similarly, they may also want to organize group efforts on the basis of the problems they see and feel, rather than on the basis of something external. In short, they see value in structuring their own efforts and hence tend to like unstructured groups.

If there is a designated authority in the group, the observer might look for the following reactions from persons who are externally oriented:

1. Glances toward the authority to get clues as to what to do, or to find approval or disapproval.

2. Questions concerning "What should we do now?" "Is what we are doing right?" "Is what we are doing safe?" "How do we compare with other groups?"

3. More attention to the authority than to anyone else in the group.

From persons who are internally oriented:

1. Questions about what the authority is feeling.

2. Questions about what is happening.

3. Requests to act as a third party or mediator.

When no one is designated as an authority, those who are externally oriented may:

1. Move to elect someone chairman or leader.

2. Ask "What should we do?"

3. Keep quiet until they feel they can speak authoritatively on the subject being discussed.

Those who are internally oriented may:

1. Ask for statements of expectations.

2. Ask for a discussion of problem-solving and decision-making approaches.

3. Volunteer information about their motivation to work issues presented.

Below I have given some elements from the external and internal models. These models indicate values, procedures, and behaviors which are often found in the two. When the observer hears, or sees, preferences such as those listed, he might test to determine to what extent other elements are also present.

Two Models of Reality

INTERNAL ORIENTATION	EXTERNAL ORIENTATION
1. Singing songs written by oneself, composing poetry, producing movies.	1. Singing songs written by professional song writers, reading what poets write.
2. Designing an education to fit personal needs.	2. Taking the education designed by someone else on the basis of what they think is needed.
3. Declaration for life and love.	3. Declaration for life and the pursuit of property.
4. Sacred importance of truth, love, beauty, and interpersonal relationships.	4. Sacred importance of logic and rationality.
5. Respect for person; unwillingness to exploit others.	5. Respect for authority; authority knows what is best for others.

6. Acceptance of individual differences.
7. Positive tolerance, openness, honesty.

8. Unit of change is small group—self propelled, autonomous, exploratory.
9. Influence by local example.

10. Direct personal involvement in change.
11. Personalization of relationships: I–thou
12. Problem orientation; pragmatic; here-and-now focus.
13. Dependence on association and interpersonal relationships.
14. Creating and maintaining the ability to make real choices and real decisions.
15. Noncoercive concern.

16. Effective freedom; fulfillment in experience.
17. Man's value not defined by contribution to production.
18. Being moral means being responsible to one's inner self.
19. Expressiveness encouraged.
20. Ad hoc groupings—disposable organizations centered around tasks.
21. Meanings of propositions tested by their consequences.

6. Acceptance of conformity.
7. Positive acceptance of idea of tolerance, openness, honesty.

8. Unit of change is individual with rights and legal freedom.
9. Influence by ideology and national policy.
10. Representation and proxy.

11. Professionalization of relationships.
12. Theory-ideology orientation; past or future focus.
13. Dependence on fixed and hierarchical roles.

14. Choice between different intellectual constructions.

15. Concern for what is good for others and for what is right.
16. Efficiency; fulfillment in living up to an ideal.
17. Man's value determined by how mercantile he is.
18. Being moral means following a code.
19. Expressiveness repressed.
20. Stable groupings around property, territory, organizations.
21. Meanings of propositions tested against ideology.

Other Possibilities

Additional methods for observing can be developed by looking for the ways in which members of different professions guide their observations. Poets and playwrights, for example, have developed distinctive ways of looking at human behavior. Directing attention to these may be helpful in providing a different perspective. Similarly, architects, urban planners, dancers, and others, have developed methods to fit their needs. Trying to discover what these are and to understand them can be an aid in gaining a deeper insight into human interaction.

REFERENCES

Bugental, J. F. T. (Ed.) *Challenges of humanistic psychology.* New York: McGraw-Hill, 1967.

Kissinger, H. Domestic structure and foreign policy. *Daedalus,* Spring 1966, 528–529.

MacLeish, A. To face the real crisis: Man himself. *The New York Times Magazine,* December 25, 1960.

Rossi, E. L. Game and growth: Two dimensions of our psychotherapeutic *Zeitgeist. Journal of Humanistic Knowledge: Toward a post-critical philosophy* (Harper Torchbooks TB1185). New York: Harper, 1964.

13 / PRESSURES TOWARD CONFORMITY IN GROUP COUNSELING

Warren C. Bonney

The value of the application of group dynamic principles to an understanding of counseling groups has been given recognition in some recent publications. Rosenbaum and Berger (1963) state: "Overemphasis on the individual denies an important facet of human behavior, that the group is both an important conforming force and an impelling force." These writers further state: "Psychotherapists as a group have been remarkably ignorant of the various relevant studies by academic psychologists and sociologists." Many others would agree that an interchange between the disciplines of group psychotherapy or counseling and group dynamics would be mutually profitable. Some, but too few, efforts have been made to make direct application of specific group dynamic principles to the counseling group. One set of principles that has applicability may be found in the literature on conformity to group pressures. Some of the phenomena occurring in group counseling will be explained in this paper according to principles of conforming behavior. This explanation is presented as an example of the application of group dynamics and is not intended to be a comprehensive examination of counseling group processes.

Nature of the Counseling Group

The primary goal of the counseling group is the creation of an interpersonal helping climate (counseling atmosphere) which will

From PERSONNEL AND GUIDANCE JOURNAL, *1965, Vol. 43, pp. 970–973. Copyright 1965, American Personnel and Guidance Association. Reprinted with permission of author and publisher.*

allow each individual to develop insight into himself and to achieve healthier personal adjustment. The vehicle for accomplishing this goal is the discussion of personal concerns at an affective level. Personal openness and honesty in group relationships are stated, or at least suggested, by most counselors as essential ingredients of this process. The members of the group must accept the counselor's suggestions as appropriate norms for the group in order to achieve the goal of a counseling atmosphere. The demand or preference of the counselor is not enough; the group itself must become eventually the source of the influence through the establishment of a group norm. Other norms also will be established by the group, such as confidentiality and trust, as well as others that may be unique to a particular group.

"Group norm" is a well-established concept in the literature of social psychology, and is central to an understanding of group functioning (Sherif, 1936). Since the term norm is so variously defined in psychological usage an explanation of its meaning in the context used in this paper will be stated briefly. Group norms are sets of rules or standards defining the limits of acceptable behavior within the group and sometimes extending to behavior beyond the group. The limits are explicitly stated and agreed upon, or, more often, implicitly established by the majority of the members of the group. The norms determine such major aspects of the group process as subject content of discussions, direction and rate of group movement, and mode of expression. While some alteration or departure from the norm may be allowed, an individual will be punished through some form of rejection or reprimand if his violation of a group norm exceeds the group's tolerance. Much of the non-verbal interaction and social exchange among members and with the counselor during the early phases of the group represents both a conscious and an unconscious testing and exploration to determine norms appropriate for the group. The norms are never totally static but are to some extent in constant process of alteration.

The important point here is that under certain conditions members of a group may be more responsive to the norms of a group than they are to their own internal needs or the influence of the counselor. The significance of group norms may be observed most dramatically when the group develops a norm that demands behavior in opposition to the wishes of the counselor. When this situation arises, counseling progress often becomes impossible.

Functions of Pressures Toward Uniformity

A number of dynamic pressures are operant on members of a group toward norm conformity and uniformity of attitudes. Many of these dynamics are essentially the same in origin and effect in counseling groups as in process or task groups. Excellent research efforts have been made by social psychologists in identifying and explaining the phenomena of conformity in small groups. These concepts can be of value to the group counselor not only in understanding and conducting the counseling group but may serve also the counselor and the theorist as a critical check on the validity of counseling theories and presumed counseling outcomes. A brief review of the principles of conforming behavior that appear to apply most directly to the counseling group will help clarify and illustrate the position taken in this paper.

In their review of the research on group pressures, Cartwright and Zander (1962) state: "It seems clear then that similar behavior, attitudes, and opinions occur among the members of any enduring group." Since a counseling group must be enduring in order to be therapeutic, there is reason to believe that similar behavior, attitudes and opinions occur among the members of therapeutic groups as well. Cartwright and Zander identify three functions that they believe pressures toward uniformity can serve. *The first function is to assist the group in achieving its goals.* The goal of the counseling group is to develop a therapeutic atmosphere. The members soon learn (usually from the therapist either directly or subtly) that certain kinds of behaviors are more or less apt to facilitate movement in this direction and consequently establish norms accordingly. *A second function is to help the group maintain itself as a group.* As the counseling group begins to achieve some degree of cohesiveness, much of the behavior in the group can be attributed to conformity or uniformity of behavior for the sake of group maintenance. Whenever the continuation of the group is seriously threatened (i.e., a challenge to the confidentiality of the group, an open clash between two members), most of the group members will work very hard to lessen the threat by resolving the conflict, reaffirming their faith in the group and their need for it, or even by shifting the group norms to encompass the threat. As the group reaches greater stability, this type of behavior becomes unnecessary. *A third function of pressures toward uniformity is to help the members of the group test the social validity of their opinions.* Some degree of uniformity will be demanded by the need of the group to reach consensus about emotional and social reality. It is important that the counselor be aware that an individual's acceptance of a reality definition may be based primarily on his need to conform to majority opinion rather than on achievement of an insight or a change in attitude.

Cognitive Uncertainty

When an individual is uncertain whether he is right or wrong he becomes highly dependent on either group consensus or authority for his response choice (Sherif, 1936). When a member of a counseling group presents a primarily cognitive problem of choice conflict for discussion, he would be likely to experience this kind of dependency. He would be quite vulnerable to group opinion, particularly if he lacked, or was unsure about, pertinent information. Under these conditions individuals differ greatly in the degree to which they are able to withstand group pressure. The counselor needs to be especially sensitive to these differences. A group member who is easily influenced might be swayed toward a decision before he has fully explored the problem. He might even be inhibited in thinking constructively about alternative choices that he had considered previously or that might be suggested by the counselor. If the therapist suspects that this is the case, he could point out to the individual and the rest of the group the nature of the dynamic in operation. The therapeutic work then expands to include not only the original problem as presented by the individual member but also his ready capitulation to the group pressure and the need of the group to apply such pressure.

Emotionality and Novelty

Other research findings set the counseling group as unusually susceptible to the effects of conformity pressures. Cartwright and Zander's (1962) quotation from Schacter's work, although without reference to counseling groups, fits quite well: "In the case of an emotion, when the precipitating situation is ambiguous or uninterpretable in terms of past experience, pressures arise to establish a social reality" and "since emotion producing situations are often novel and outside our past experience it could be expected that the emotions would be particularly vulnerable to social influence."

Schacter (1959) has suggested that the emotional contagion characteristic of panics, riots, and mobs may be explained according to these dynamics. The novelty of the situation and the intense emotionality generated by it make strong suggestions as to appropriate feelings and actions almost irresistible. In counseling groups the direction and intensity of the emotional state is certainly quite different from that of a mob but the same elements of *emotionality and novelty* are present during the early stages although in somewhat different form. *The counseling group sets out to deal with emotion laden topics in a manner that is generally outside the social experiences of participants.* The group becomes highly susceptible to suggestions that promise a reduction of the anxiety associated with this basically incongruous situation. One would expect members of a therapy group to develop an intense need for a behavioral norm to which they can conform. The resolution of the problem can take the form of a definition by the counselor of the counseling group as essentially different from the social group accompanied by suggestions for the norms that will allow it to be experienced as different. The high level of anxiety during the transition period, as pointed out by Bonney and Foley (1963) will be reduced markedly if the counselor presents a reasonable resolution of the group's sense of the incongruity between therapeutic expectation and social expectation.

Re-interpretation of Some Psychotherapeutic Explanations

An analysis or judgment of the process of a counseling group or of individual gains or changes through group counseling that ignored the effects of pressures toward conformity could be very misleading. A brief re-interpretation according to conformity dynamics of some of the more commonly held explanations of certain phenomena of group counseling may help to illustrate this contention. Two of the most basic concepts in counseling and psychotherapy are therapeutic growth or gain and resistance to therapeutic change. Both of these concepts infer intra-psychic phenomena.

Therapeutic growth is sometimes assumed on the basis of increased talk about oneself that might well be in response to a group norm that developed from the counselor's earlier suggestion that one should talk about personal concerns. The individual may not have experienced or admitted to himself any other need for such self-exploration until pressures to conform to the group norm were present. Therapeutic growth is also claimed for noted changes in specific behavioral patterns. Such changes could result simply from group pressures to abandon certain overt acts and replace them with others. This may be the dynamic explanation for the phenomenon which Bach (1954) refers to as "counterphobic reaction," or a complete counter-polar change in a response pattern with no evidence of insight associated with it.

Three dynamics interpreted by counselors as resistance can be explained also in terms of norm conformity. An individual's apparent *resistance to therapeutic-assistance* could be, instead, a rebellion against pressures to conform. *A total group resistance* might represent adherence to a group norm of which the counselor is unaware and in which he does not participate. *Dependent reactions* to the counselor may signify a need for norm clarification rather than transference.

One could argue readily that, if the ultimate result is therapeutic, it does not really matter whether it resulted from the natural dynamics of intra-group process or the counselor's skill. However, if behavioral or attitudinal changes are primarily in response to conformity pressures one would wonder to what extent and for how long the changes would generalize to situations where similar norms did not exist. The conformity responses to group norms, as described above, might, in part, account for the difficulty of establishing external evidence of behavioral change as a consequence of group counseling.

It is not the intention of this writer to deny the significance or reality of therapeutic change through group counseling, but rather to point up the importance of the dynamics generated by the group because it is a group, and, more specifically in this paper, the need for the counselor to recognize the difference between a reaction or change based on norm conformity and one that grows out of therapeutic insight or intra-psychic perceptual alteration. It should be further stressed that these two kinds of reactions are not at all mutually exclusive. Even though a group member may be pressured into self-revelations, the intrinsic rewards or disturbances for doing so might be sufficient for him to continue self-exploration out of his own needs and eventuate in stable gains. In fact this kind of outcome is frequently reported by members of counseling groups. It is not uncommon for a member of a counseling group to confess that he thought he was just making up a problem because it was expected, but before he was through he found himself revealing genuine feelings in an almost uncomfortable manner. Others report that they partially faked a response in order to gain group approval, then found themselves seriously pursuing the problem area outside the group. These comments in themselves raise a host of ethical and procedural issues. We need to re-examine the process of group counseling through the discipline of group dynamics.

REFERENCES

Bach, G. *Intensive group psychotherapy*. New York: Ronald Press, 1954.

Bonney, W. C., & Foley, W. The transition stage in group counseling in terms of congruence theory. *Journal of Counseling Psychology*, 1963, *10*, 136–188.

Cartwright, D., & Zander, A. *Group dynamics, research and theory*. 2nd ed. Evanston, Ill.: Row Peterson, 1962.

Rosenbaum, M., & Berger, M. *Group psychotherapy and group function*. New York: Basic Books, 1963.

Schacter, S. *The psychology of affiliation*. Palo Alto, Calif.: Stanford University Press, 1959.

Sherif, M. *The psychology of social norms*. New York: Harper, 1936.

14 / THERAPEUTIC INTERACTION IN ADULT THERAPY GROUPS

Ernest E. Andrews

Group therapy with adult outpatients in the psychiatric setting usually takes place within the ninety-minute, once-a-week session. The group consists of seven to eight carefully selected members who are seen by the group therapist several times to prepare them for the group experience. This preparatory period of individual sessions with the therapist lasts as long as is necessary to prepare the patient for his particular group.[1] The sex and age of group members varies somewhat with the particular setting. The most common varieties are:[2]

(a) A heterogeneous grouping of males and females in approximately equal numbers, with a wide age span from early adulthood to retirement age (Mullan & Rosenbaum, 1963). This is most common in exclusively adult services. The age groups for college students are, likewise, heterogeneous but generally have a limited age span of 18 to 25 (Andrews, 1969). Heterogeneous

---

[1] The nature and process of "careful selection" of patients for groups, and their preparation to enter the group experience, is beyond the scope of this paper. (See Mullan & Rosenbaum, 1963; Neighbor, Beach, Brown, Kevin, & Visher, 1958.)

[2] Family therapy groups have been purposefully omitted. The dynamics of a two (or more) generational, natural group—the family—are different from the dynamics of a contrived and artificial adult therapy group. This distinction is dealt with by Handlon and Perloff (1962).

Unpublished paper, February 1969. Copyright 1971 by Ernest E. Andrews. Revised and adapted from "Some Group Dynamics in Therapy Groups of Mothers," INTERNATIONAL JOURNAL OF GROUP PSYCHOTHERAPY, *1962, Vol. 12, pp. 476–491. Printed with permission of author.*

groups of parents whose children are in treatment are utilized in children's treatment services.

(b) Special groups of mothers only (Durkin, 1954), fathers only (Marcus, 1956), and married couples (Leichter, 1962). These groups are common in child treatment services where there is a necessity to treat disturbances in the parents as a prerequisite to improvement in the child. Married couples groups are also utilized in adult treatment service. The age range of parents is most often between 25 and 45.

All of the persons chosen for these groups have neurotic or characterological patterns which have become a significant part of their relationship with others. Therapy is directed toward a reconstruction or dissolution of the pathological patterns of the personality which are dominant in their relationship with others. The therapist utilizes the basic elements of psychotherapy elaborated by Slavson (1960)—transference, catharsis, insight, reality testing, and sublimation in working toward this goal.

In this type of group there appear to emerge certain therapeutic dynamics which work hand in hand with the basic elements of psychotherapy to produce the therapy for each of the group members. These dynamics may be defined as the forces which produce effective action in a field. In this instance, the field is the group of patients and the effective action is the elements of psychotherapy previously enumerated. The group is at all times seen as the vehicle of treatment for its individual members. The dynamics, therefore, do not constitute the therapy but, instead, act as a facilitating agent for effective therapy.

Therapeutic Dynamics

The therapeutic dynamics which will be discussed are (1) group balance, (2) group task orientation, (3) universalization, (4) extensive emotional support, (5) extensive defense confrontation, and (6) experiential validation. Operational definitions and clinical examples will be given for each, as well as a discussion of (a) how each is seen as facilitating the therapy, and (b) the therapist's role in utilizing the dynamics.

The first of these dynamics, *group balance,* may be defined as the proportionate alignment of instigators, neutralizers, neuters, and isolates among the group population in approximately equal numbers. These terms have been fully discussed by Slavson (1952), but will be described here as they apply to adult groups. Instigators are individuals who aggressively involve themselves, make bold statements, show their feelings openly, and are somewhat impulsive individuals. Neutralizers are better integrated members who help to regulate feeling, suggest alternatives, and are frequently conciliators. Social neuters are the rather ineffectual members who accept the group trend as it is and do not affect the group atmosphere. Isolates are persons who seldom express themselves, largely remain silent, but usually listen and follow well. A more subtle factor in group balance is the heterogeneous mixture of characterological defense patterns, passivity, aggressiveness, withdrawal, etc., which underlie these group role descriptions.

The therapist has the responsibility for achieving the most effective group balance through careful selection of group members. Once the group is meeting he can affect the maintenance of the balance somewhat through his verbalizations, but this can never substitute for an initially adequate group balance. His comments can be instigating or neutralizing through focusing on specific material, or neuter in effect by assenting to the group trend, but they must never be isolationist; that is, he must never withdraw his verbal or nonverbal communications, as this might be interpreted as rejection or lack of interest by the members of the group.

The interaction produced by a planned, heterogeneous group balance acts dynamically in the following ways to facilitate the elements of psychotherapy. Initially the instigators produce affective verbalizations which tend to stimulate responses or comments from the neutralizers and neuter members of the group. This establishes the flow of affective verbalizations among the group members. In later meetings, the instigators also frequently draw out the isolates. The neutralizers frequently can tone down the disproportionate affective verbalizations of the instigators. The group balance, therefore, operates in the promotion of affective verbalizations to encourage catharsis, to serve as a comparative sounding board for reality testing, and to stimulate transference reactions.

Perhaps a few clinical examples[3] will illustrate the dynamic effect of group balance.

At an early group session, Mrs. V., an instigator, began the session by stating that she was very mad at her family because they never

---

[3] All examples used in this paper were drawn from mothers' groups in a child guidance clinic.

gave her any sense of appreciation, so she did not go home and fix supper for them after last week's session but, instead, stayed with her sister until 2 a.m. She then associated this feeling of lack of appreciation to her relationship with her mother, recalling how her mother always ranted on about how much she did for all of her kids. Mrs. V. felt guilty and always tried to be "johnny-on-the-spot" with her help, but her mother and siblings took advantage of this and never gave her any credit for what she did for them, which only increased her feeling of nonacceptance. She ended by stating, "Now I realize how angry I must have been at my mother and brothers."

Mrs. S. passively attacked Mrs. V. because her own anxiety was aroused, saying she can recall no resentment toward her parents. She acted the part of the "good child" in this session.

Mrs. L., a withdrawn woman, remarked that she resented her parents when they were divorced after thirty years of marriage because she felt they could have been divorced earlier and prevented the constant state of turmoil and unhappiness which existed at home. She then described the family turmoil with a great deal of feeling.

Then Mrs. T., a neuter thus far, stated how her parents were divorced too, and she lived with her mother, but she always loved her father dearly. He was described as never providing for the family, frequently drunk, but always charming with Mrs. T., who felt accepted by him, while her mother's domineering behavior squelched her.

Mrs. V., the instigator, stimulated the flow of affective verbalizations and catharsis in Mrs. T. and Mrs. L. Although Mrs. S. successfully defended against this focus by denial, the group continued along this avenue for several more sessions until Mrs. S. finally admitted she has angry feelings too. For her this was a reality-testing experience.

In a later session, Mrs. D., a very hostile mother, burst forth with anger about the therapist not seeing her husband: "Don't husbands come in? He ought to be in a father's group. He told me I couldn't come in anymore. He is always against anything I try to do." (She was practically shouting.) Finally, she said dejectedly, "I don't know what to do!" Mrs. M. then said that most husbands have positive feelings but sometimes wives must work to bring them out. She talked about how her husband used to become depressed and anxious at times and she got the children to wake him up in the morning. They would all gather around him, jump on him playfully, and give him lots of attention. Now he was the first one up and not at all as grouchy as he used to be. He seemed a real part of the family now.

Mrs. M., a neutralizer in the group, suggested an avenue of sublimation for Mrs. F.'s anger at her husband. Mrs. M. was angry at her husband's lack of cooperation, too, but basically she handled it with him constructively. The angry tone of Mrs. F.'s voice was largely gone in future sessions. Mrs. F.'s statements also revealed a negative transference toward the therapist which could be dealt with.

These two clinical summaries illustrate how the heterogeneous balance of the group facilitated the flow of affective verbalizations, encouraged catharsis, stimulated transference, and suggested problem-solving sublimation.

The second of the dynamics, *group task orientation,* may be defined as the assumption by the group members of their involvement in their interpersonal disturbances and their acceptance of the value of affective expression of their anxieties, conflicts, and characterological patterns as a method of working toward a solution to these disturbances. This task orientation is at first the responsibility of the therapist, but when accepted by the group members, it becomes a characteristic aspect of the group's functioning. The group task orientation is especially important with mothers, as they are so often reluctant patients because of their unawareness of their involvement in the child's disturbance. However, what at first appears a problem in the clinical management of the resistive patient becomes a valuable dynamic in the form of the group task orientation.

The process by which the therapist instigates this in the members of the group is essentially what Durkin (1954) has so aptly described as "putting the group on a therapeutic basis." The therapist does this in three main ways: first, by structuring the initial session by stating that the reason for their participation is their affective involvement in their own problems and that, therefore, the free expression of their feelings about whatever concerns them is the beginning of working toward a solution; secondly, by dealing with requests for advice and direct questions by focusing on their feeling or thoughts about what they ask; and, thirdly, by always focusing on the affective meaning or content of the patients' statements.

After a period of initial resistance, the members of the group usually accept this *modus operandi* as the group task orientation. The practical effect of this orientation is threefold: (1) it tends to reduce group resistance after the initial phase of therapy; (2) it encourages catharsis through the creation of a permissive atmosphere for expression of feelings; and (3) it facilitates the acquisition of insight through the constant focus on the interrelation of experiences, feelings, and actions.

The following clinical material will illustrate the dynamics of group task orientation.

Mrs. S. began the session by stating she was concerned over a neighbor whom she called a "floozy-type" woman. Mrs. V. questioned why Mrs. S. should feel so concerned. Mrs. S. answered that she felt it was not fair. "What would make you feel that way?" questioned Mrs. L. Then Mrs. S. recalled that her sister, who was more attractive than she, always tried to better herself in every way, including taking away her boyfriends. She felt that this neighbor woman had obtained her husband's loyalty—not that he would be untrue to her, but that he had taken the neighbor's part and suggested Mrs. S. try to understand this woman more. She was hurt because her husband did not automatically support her, and she felt this woman took her husband's loyalty from her. "Just like my sister did with my boyfriends, I guess." Mrs. S. then began to cry softly.

Mrs. V. and Mrs. L. manifested the group task orientation by focusing on the affective meaning of Mrs. S.'s opening statement immediately. This encouraged catharsis of the relationship with her sister, then stimulated insight into why she felt the "unfairness" of this neighbor's presence. At this point, focusing on the affective meaning of her statements was done by group members without the therapist's participation.

The presence of group balance and the group task orientation become fundamental properties of the group's interaction. The therapist's role is paramount in their establishment, but, once established, their effect is group-originated. Without these two basic dynamics, the group would not function as a therapeutic experience and would only be a social experience. It cannot be stressed too much, therefore, that the therapeutic success of a group experience for an individual patient places substantial responsibility upon the therapist for careful selection, balance, and early group direction and structure.

The third dynamic, *universalization,* well known as a dynamic of groups, is here defined as patients' becoming aware of the fact that almost everyone entertains similar negative and ambivalent feelings. In a mothers' group, it is seldom necessary for the therapist to structure the "universalizing experience" in any way, as it comes out of the group interaction spontaneously once the free flow of affective verbalization has begun. The prior establishment of group balance and group task orientation lays the base for significant universalizing experiences within the group. This is a particularly important dynamic with mothers, as many of them feel considerable guilt— partially because of their part in the child's problem but even more so because of their relationship with their own parents. This guilt frequently acts to prevent further therapeutic focusing, but the universalizing experience can serve to initiate the break-up of this pattern. The experience of the universalization of certain feelings, moods, and experiences serves to counteract the feeling of isolation many mothers have and the consequent conviction that many of their feelings and experiences are completely unique.

The therapist's role in the group dynamic of universalization is threefold: (1) he allows the universalizing experiences to occur spontaneously out of the group's interaction, reinforcing its effect by lending his authority as a parent figure to its validity—in other words, by nodding or commenting to imply that he realizes and accepts the presence of negative and/or ambivalent feelings on a universal basis; (2) when necessary, he draws together similar feelings, moods, and experiences of the group members to create the basis for a universalizing experience; (3) when universalization occurs, he focuses upon the emotional relationship of feeling and consequent action.

When the dynamic of universalization is present in the group, several elements of psychotherapy are given impetus. Initially, universalization relieves guilt, which permits certain beginning insights and gives a base for reality testing, while usually opening the gates for extensive emotional support from other group members. As guilt is relieved, members are able to admit to and talk about the underlying feelings, and further catharsis ensues. Then they begin to realize and to see how these feelings are related to their actions, usually toward a series of recipient figures: parents, siblings, husband, and child.

Mrs. S. seemed upset about something. At first, she spoke of her unsureness in dealing with David, her son, and her unsureness in speaking to her husband about his handling of the boy. When asked how she felt about his handling of David, she revealed for the first time angry feelings toward her husband's mother, who was domineering. She then talked quite directly and with a lot of feeling about her husband being like her mother-in-law, in that he was rigid and not accepting of her feelings. Finally, she broke into lengthy sobs. The group was momentarily silent, then strong support came from Mrs. V. and Mrs. D. Mrs. S. said she felt a compulsion to confess what she had said in the group to her husband because she felt so disloyal. Mrs. V. said that she felt guilty, too, when she first talked about her anger, but that it was a great relief to her. Mrs. B. stated, "This is the place we can talk about these things; it's hard to talk about anger, but I guess we all feel it." Mrs. S. admitted she felt very guilty about her anger because it meant stepping out of the role of the "good person" for her. She ended by saying she apparently expected a lot of herself. During the next session a week later, when Mrs. E. was speaking about how positive she felt about her family, Mrs. S. remarked to her, "I have trouble expressing anger, too." Then later in the session Mrs. S. recalled how, as a child, she felt nobody paid attention to her. She was able to recognize her anger toward her parents and its correlate in anger toward her mother-in-law and husband. In later sessions, she began to see how her repression of this anger colored her handling of her son's angry feelings, which she felt was related to his stuttering.

The universalizing experience initially drew support from other group members for Mrs. S.'s feelings, which aided in relieving her guilt. This in turn promoted firmer reality testing and encouraged catharsis in the following session. This was later followed by insight into the genesis of her anger and its relationship to her handling of David.

With the formation of the group task orientation and the presence of universalization, a fourth dynamic, *extensive emotional support,* assumes significance in the group's interaction. This dynamic may be defined as the positive reinforcement of a member's self-esteem by the verbal and/or nonverbal acceptance of that patient's feelings by other group members. This is essentially the same as support given in individual therapy by the therapist. In a group the support is extensive in nature, as it comes from several concurrent sources, and in many ways it seems to be more meaningful coming from peers. In mothers' groups this dynamic is particularly vital, as many of the mothers feel strongly that they receive little real support in their role from their families. The experiencing of extensive emotional support from other members of the group has a "shoring-up" effect on the self-image. Changes, for example, in personal outlook and appearance are sometimes dramatic.

Several elements of therapy are facilitated by extensive emotional support. Though frequently stimulated by catharsis, this dynamic often triggers off further and deeper catharsis. Feeling that others are on their side and will not criticize, reprimand, or slough off her feelings, the patient is able to talk about many guilt- and anger-laden experiences with spouse, siblings, and parents. Positive transference may form between the recipient of the support and the group member who gives the support. The supportive members symbolize the good sibling or parent and throw into juxtaposition negative experiences with the significant "others" of earlier experience who undermined the individual's self-esteem. The positive transference stimulates, through identification, positive avenues of sublimation. The energies released through catharsis and stimulated by the positive transferences permit growth of a more positive self-image.

The therapist may utilize this group dynamic in several ways. Initially, he gives early support to group members to establish this as an appropriate response within the group. It is necessary for extensive emotional support to develop early in the group's interaction in order to facilitate essential focusing and catharsis and to build up ego strength to tolerate interpretation. When support becomes a part of the group's interaction, the therapist joins the other members in their support and then relates the patient's responses to their support to the apparent level of self-esteem, e.g., "You are surprised others sympathize with your feelings"; or "You seem to feel good that others can accept your feelings."

The following clinical summary shows the therapeutic effect on a mother of extensive emotional support over a number of group sessions.

Mrs. S. was quite depressed in appearance, meek, shy, and unable to verbalize to any significant extent. When she did talk, however, there seemed to be a great deal of anger toward her family for their lack of appreciation of her. When someone commented that she seemed to feel very angry about this, it brought forth a lot of material about her relationship at home when she was a child. She felt that her mother had never given her any acceptance or recognition. There was strong sibling rivalry with a younger brother who was the mother's favorite. Mrs. S. said that she would have done anything to win his acceptance, and, crying, she related an experience with the brother involving humiliating sexual play which she acquiesced to in hopes of winning his acceptance. Mrs. S.'s mother caught them in the midst of this and severely blamed Mrs. S., saying nothing to the brother, which again served as further rejection. The sexual experience seemed to serve as a screen memory to cover Mrs. S.'s deep loathing and anger toward her mother; she had degraded herself to win someone's favor only to be further rejected by her mother when discovered. When she expressed guilt over the experience, all the other group members, who had followed her story with deep compassion, expressed with feeling how difficult it must have been for her when her mother blamed her when she was so desperate for acceptance. Mrs. S., who was sitting with her head bowed, looked up with a real sparkle in her eye and a look of relief. After the session several members gathered around her, reiterating their remarks, and Mrs. S. seemed very pleased.

At the next session, Mrs. S. brought cookies for the group. Her manner of dress was decidedly improved; she seemed enthusiastic and was very verbal throughout the session. She said she always felt she could never do much but that she liked to write and she had brought in some examples of a few things published in a religious periodical. After she passed these out, she went on to say that her mother had never taught her to cook, so she had taught herself and entered numerous county fair contests; she then displayed about twenty ribbons she had won. This brought gasps of approval and a bevy of compliments from the other mothers. After the session, the others all gathered around her, complimenting her and talking in a very animated fashion to her. She beamed broadly throughout all this. Further sessions revealed a dramatic transformation of this woman from a meek, passive person who was almost too timid to make comments in the group, to a person who was more outgoing, much more relaxed, and who participated actively and aggressively in the group. She also relaxed some of her demands on her son.

The presence of the first four dynamics which have been described —group balance, group task orientation, universalization, and extensive emotional support—serve as an essential base for the difficult therapeutic work in mothers' groups of assimilating insight and translating it into action. Extensive defense confrontation and experiential validation are the therapeutic dynamics which figure prominently in this process. Their effective functioning depends upon the working effectiveness of the earlier dynamics, especially the group task orientation and extensive emotional support. A person must feel accepted by the others and supported by them if he is to let down his defenses and accept interpretations, and later if he is to experiment within the group to test the "action effectiveness" of his insights.

The fifth dynamic, *extensive defense confrontation*, is the experience of having defenses directly challenged by other group members. Before the group members "confront" another member, extensive support must be prevalent in the group interactions so that the "confrontation" will not be perceived as criticism or ridicule. The extensiveness of the confrontation coming from several members, plus the perceived supportiveness of the group, breaks down the necessity for the defenses without arousing overwhelming anxiety. This seems to be a particular instance in which group therapy works more effectively than individual therapy. The extensive confrontation of defenses usually occurs increasingly directly over a period of time, building up to a firm refutation of the defensive elaboration by several group members.

The therapist, in order to insure the complete usefulness of the group's dynamic interaction, must constantly focus, clarify, summarize, and, finally, interpret. When the group confronts extensively, he must clarify the two-way relationship of anxiety-defense behavior. As the confrontation of a long-established defense is anxiety arousing even in the most favorable circumstances, the therapist must usually be supportive in inverse proportion to the group's support. The defenses which are usually successfully worked through by concurrent extensive confrontation and therapist interpretation are reaction formation, repression, isolation, and undoing.

The therapy is considerably facilitated by the group in several ways: (1) It is easier to deal with the rigid defenses just mentioned, which are usually very difficult to penetrate in individual treatment with patients; (2) insight is hastened by group pressure to relinquish unrealistic defensive modes of handling anxiety; (3) after confrontation, the group serves as a social context for reality testing.

The following is a clinical summary of the building up and emergence of extensive defensive confrontation over a month's time.

Mrs. D. always dressed very stylishly and used large amounts of perfume. She seemed aloof; her participation in the group was considerable but largely on a highly intellectualized level. She appeared calm and controlled. In an early session, another member, Mrs. G., said she felt Mrs. D. "would wear a chic dress to paint the barn in." The others all agreed with Mrs. G. Mrs. D. said she was not like that at all. Some time after this, Mrs. D. said she felt anxious over her facade of calmness, for she did not really feel that way. Sometimes she felt a storm within her. She got angry but could not say no because she feared rejection. Mrs. W. talked about how angry and hostile she feels toward her mother. Mrs. D. quickly said she feels very protective and solicitous toward her mother, that her mother could always depend on her. (Mrs. D.'s parents were divorced when she was about three years old, and her mother gave her into the care of the maternal grandparents. She never saw her father again. Mrs. D. had referred to her mother in an earlier session as a "retarded adolescent." She saw her frequently during her childhood and adolescence, but never lived with her. Her mother remarried and had another daughter whom she pampered and overprotected.) As the session ended the others raised questions as to why Mrs. D. would feel protective toward her mother. Mrs. W. said, "I felt hurt when my mother let me down." Mrs. G. practically shouted at Mrs. D., "How can you feel that way! I'd feel hurt and angry. How can you not feel hurt?"

During the next session, Mrs. D. said that when it was hard for her to talk about her feelings, she would circumvent it by talking around the point. Mrs. G. said, "Yes, you're very clever at that, but I bet you feel angry and want to hurt sometimes, just like us." Others in the group seconded this. Mrs. W. broke in to describe an incident which revealed how undependable her mother was, then added, "I never have been able to depend upon her. She never paid any attention to me. Now it makes me furious. Your mother and mine were a lot alike," she finished, looking at Mrs. D. Mrs. D. then said she really felt the same as Mrs. W. She admitted that her mother had let her down, too, and that she could not depend on her for anything. She said, "I've never been able to trust anyone or depend on them." The therapist summarized. "If you couldn't depend on her, you let her depend on you, by mothering her as you wished she had mothered you. Your relationship could be maintained without your feeling angry or being hurt again by her." Mrs. D. answered, "Yes, I never felt the anger before." Mrs. W. said to Mrs. D., "You put a barrier up to protect yourself from feeling the hurt. That's what I did, too."

At the next session, Mrs. D. told how she had called on her mother for help during the week and was turned down. "I felt so angry at her. I've always known I couldn't depend on her, but this time I really felt mad at her, real mad. I guess I've always felt that if I were of use to her, and others too, then they would like me." "But if you felt angry at her, and others, you thought they wouldn't like you," the therapist said. Mrs. D. answered, "Yes, they wouldn't like me if they knew I was angry. I didn't like myself very much, did I?"

Mrs. D. was first confronted with the group's perception of her inappropriate manner of dress. This aroused anxiety about the efficiency of her defensive facade, which was really designed to keep others from understanding her. Another group member, Mrs. W., displayed anger openly toward her own mother, which led to a momentary tightening of Mrs. D.'s defensive elaboration but clearly revealed her unrealistic behavior in view of what the group already knew of her background. The defense confrontation occurred rapidly within the group on an extensive basis. In the following session, Mrs. D.'s defense dissolved easily, and with support from the group she assimilated interpretations from the therapist and group members. Later, she was able to feel the anger toward her mother without undue anxiety or guilt. The experience of finding out that she could be accepted even when she felt realistic anger was later validated as she worked through her transferences to others in the group. This involved the therapeutic dynamic of *experiential validation.*

The dynamic of experiential validation has both unlearning and relearning aspects. It may be defined either as the abandonment of inappropriate behavioral responses through experiencing their inappropriateness in interpersonal relations within the group, or as the establishment of appropriate behavioral responses through experiencing their appropriateness in interpersonal relations within the group. Essentially, this dynamic is the learning process embodied in working through the multiple transferences which emerge between one member and the other members. The appropriateness or inappropriateness of a patient's behavior responses is validated by the group's response to the behavior both in their actions and in their verbalizations regarding the patient's behavior. The unlearning of negative responses facilitated by experiential validation precedes the learning of more positive, appropriate responses. This is the last hump the person has to get over in order to develop a realistic and appropriate relationship with others. The group serves as an experiential arena for the reality testing of behavioral patterns. Intellectual insight is exposed as being realistically ineffectual without subsequent emotional translation into appropriate action. Gradually, emotionally meaningful insights develop. The presence of negative transferences indicates that the old responses have not been extinguished sufficiently.

The therapist's function in this process is to focus on the multiple transferences which emerge within the group and to relate current transferences to prior insight about the person's life experiences. His role is usually quite active at this point. Emerging behavior responses are clarified and summarized as to their effect on the others in the group. The other members usually express their reactions spontaneously, but cause-and-effect clarification is often necessary. Emphasis on the effectiveness of newly developed appropriate responses is necessary in order to reinforce their integration into ego functioning.

Experiential validation in groups is closely linked to several vital elements of psychotherapy. Its value in the reality testing of behavioral patterns has already been mentioned. The living interpersonal situation which the group provides establishes a firm and realistic "experimental station," as it were, for the translation of insight into action. The multiple transferences within the group are highlighted by the quest for successful validations. Unless negative transference entanglements can be resolved, inappropriate responses continue to exist. The experiential validation of inappropriate responses is aided frequently by the dynamics of extensive defense confrontation and extensive emotional support—the former exerting forces which highlight inappropriate responses, and the latter providing the positive stimulus for renunciation of old patterns as well as encouraging the desire to develop more positive relationship patterns.

Experiential validation as a therapeutic dynamic is illustrated in the following clinical summary.

Mrs. G. was a very outspoken group member. She frequently had a chip-on-the-shoulder attitude, always acted the part of the rebel, and quite openly attempted numerous times to bait the others into arguments. She was a hostile, angry woman. Her mother had been bedridden with many illnesses and controlled the family through her illnesses, frequently experiencing attacks of one thing or another to get whatever she wanted. She was very unaccepting of Mrs. G., who was born illegitimately to the parents before they were married. Her father was a weak, passive, ineffectual man who drank much and was completely dominated by his wife. Mrs. F. felt all males were passive, and she either attacked them or seduced them by trying to be pleasing. She married a passive man whom she alternately attacked and seduced, and did likewise with her son who was becoming a passive, unsure, ineffectual boy. In the early group sessions, Mrs. G. established a pattern in which she attacked others verbally under the pretext of being honest and truthful. At the end of one session, she brought out that she felt she was a "bad" person, at which point Mrs. D. said, "Sometimes you act as if you don't want people to like you." Mrs. G. answered, "I do want them to like me." Then she was quiet. In a subsequent session she brought out that her parents always emphasized "not being bad," which had made her feel she was bad. This was followed by several sessions in which she was the loud center of attention by describing the "bad" thoughts she had. These were in the form of forbidden sexual desires, like being seductive with other men at business parties with her husband or saying how thrilling it would be to have an affair. She then reported that her husband had accused her of an affair, and said, "I really exploded at him. I was deeply insulted." Mrs. D. said to her, "Actually you wouldn't dare do anything of the sort, would you? You just talk like you would." Mrs. S. said, "You're not bad because you think about those things." The interpretation was given that she was trying to make herself seem like a "bad woman" again, the way her parents made her feel.

After this session, she gave up trying to impress the others with her "evilness." But she turned to describing incidents on her job of how she attacked and hurt others with her statements. These were all people she considered weaker than herself, really "no match." She made reference to Mrs. A.—a group member who was passive, timid, and fearful of saying the wrong thing—as "one of that passive kind." The therapist mentioned that Mrs. G.'s father was passive, too, and did not fight back. Mrs. A., while obviously angry, said nothing; but after that she gradually began to make subtle—but pointed—jabs at Mrs. G., who got livid several times but did not say much except that she had "to bite her tongue." However, she frequently disagreed with the others' statements.

Finally, Mrs. E., who had an angry, hostile boy in treatment, said to Mrs. G., "I wish I knew how you felt, because you're so much like David. Maybe I could understand him better then." Mrs. G. looked stunned for a moment, then said angrily, "I resent being a problem child." Mrs. D. chimed in: "Well, you act that way sometimes." Then Mrs. G. launched into a tirade about how she felt—that her parents never really cared about her, that everything she did was never any good, and that she was so angry about this. Mrs. D. responded by saying that even though Mrs. G. acted so hostile all the time, she liked her, and if she knew Mrs. G. better, she thought she would like her very much.

After these episodes, Mrs. G. seemed much less hostile; there was a tone of kindness when she commented on others' remarks. At one point, she related her poor self-image to her aggressiveness and hostility; Mrs. D. and Mrs. W. both said that she seemed to attack because she really feared others would attack her, then interpreted their anger over being attacked as rejection of her. Mrs. G. agreed with them.

Mrs. G.'s early indiscriminate hostility toward all group members was accepted by them with indifference. At this point, they were transference objects for her hostile feelings toward her mother. However, she felt guilty about this and so tried to paint herself as a bad person, which was the expression of her self-image, the result of her early experiences with an openly rejecting mother and passively rejecting father. While her husband's accusation was angrily reacted to as the sought-after rejection, the group saw through the maneuver and, instead of rejecting her, offered support since she had triggered off a common concern over self-images. Her hostility then focused on Mrs. A., who stimulated the negative transference feelings engendered in her relationship to her father. The interpretation of the transference seemed to permit her to attempt some control of it. Mrs. A.'s reaction was to return Mrs. G.'s hostility with more of the same, stimulating Mrs. G. to a beginning repudiation of her character defense of hostility as she began to feel uncomfortable over the perceived consequences of her actions. This was an early experiential validation, which was further re-experienced and reinforced by the transference feelings which Mrs. E. aroused with her comparison of her angry son and Mrs. G. Mrs. D.'s comment that she acted like a problem child was the clinching experiential validation, which opened the way for insight linking her early experiences with her anger. The subsequent positive transference brought out by Mrs. D. for Mrs. G. established the motivation for later attempts at positive experiential validations within the group.

Conclusion

Usually these dynamics develop in the sequence in which they have been discussed here, although at times one can see universalization and extensive emotional support occurring during the development and acceptance of the group task orientation. However, these two are much more effective in their impact on individual members after the group task orientation has been firmly established. Four dynamics—group balance, group task orientation, universalization, and extensive emotional support—are characteristic of the formative stages of the interpersonal interaction within the group. Three dynamics—extensive emotional support, extensive defense confrontation, and experiential validation—are more prominent in the later stages of the interaction within the group.

Heterogeneous group balance is an essential prerequisite for the later effective development of extensive defensive confrontation. The confrontations are partially the result of the heterogeneous characterological defense patterns present in the group. Intragroup "blind spots" are largely eliminated, reducing group-wide resistances. The confrontations can be more easily accepted and assimilated by the individual because of the emotional support received from the group. Assimilation of the defense confrontations then leads naturally to experiential validation. Universalization frequently is the forerunner of the development of extensive emotional support. The group task orientation seems to be a continuous thread throughout. (The relationship between these therapeutic dynamics and the elements of psychotherapy can be seen in Table 1. The "X" indicates the focal areas of collaborative congruence.)

TABLE 1

Relationship Between Therapeutic Dynamics and Elements of Psychotherapy

Interactional Dynamics	Elements of Psychotherapy				
	Relationship (transference)	*Insight*	*Catharsis*	*Reality Testing*	*Reorganization of Defenses*
Group balance	x		x	x	
Group Task orientation	x	x	x		
Universalization	x		x	x	
Extensive emotional support	x		x		x
Extensive defense confrontation		x		x	x
Experiential validation		x		x	x

These dynamics present a conceptual framework for the descriptive analyses of the interactions within a therapy group. They cover the same areas which are of concern to the group dynamicist—co-

hesiveness, group pressures and standards, group goals and locomo-
tion, and structural properties of the group (as stated by Cartwright
and Zander, 1953)—but they uniquely reflect the therapeutic focus
of a particular group setting. For example, it is doubtful whether
cohesiveness exists in a heterogeneous group where the focus is
basically individuation of response; although the group task orientation, extensive emotional support, and universalization might be
construed as elements of a kind of cohesiveness. But this would not
appear to be the same as the group dynamicist's cohesiveness, which
implies common individual needs for protection, security, and affection, predominance of positive affectional ties, shared ideals and interests, etc. (Scheidlinger, 1952). Abstracted out of the context of the
therapy group, the similarity to cohesiveness is apparent; but since
the context is decisive, the doubtfulness of cohesiveness also seems
apparent.

Extensive defense confrontation appears to fit into the area of
group pressures, the group task orientation into the area of group
goals, and group balance into the area of structural properties of the
group. The qualitative difference, however, lies in the intended purpose of a psychotherapeutic group—the acceptance of individual
pathological responses and their eventual reconstruction into positive individual responses, as revealed in interpersonal interaction
within a group setting.

A therapeutic group, in my opinion, has specific "therapeutic
dynamics" of its own, and normal group dynamics need not be imposed on its structure and functioning. The dynamics of the therapeutic groups which have been described are an attempt to conceptualize the working of the elements and techniques of psychotherapy
in an interactional group setting. We do not "therapeutize" groups
or group dynamics, to use Schwartz and Wolf's term (1960); we treat
individuals and their individual psychodynamics in an interactional
group setting.

Summary

In summary, there appear to be certain dynamics present in therapy
groups for adults which arise out of the structuring of the group by
the therapist and the interaction among the group members. These
are not the "group dynamics" of the group dynamicists, but therapeutic dynamics peculiar at least to the type of group approach
which is described. These dynamics facilitate the effectiveness of the

basic elements of psychotherapy: transference, catharsis, insight, reality testing, and sublimation. They generally develop in sequence and are characteristic of the group as an interactional and therapeutically focused assemblage. The therapeutic dynamics discussed were: (1) group balance, (2) group task orientation, (3) universalization, (4) extensive emotional support, (5) extensive defense confrontation, and (6) experiential validation.

The thesis was presented that these dynamics function hand in hand with the basic elements of psychotherapy listed above to produce the therapy. The group structure and functioning as seen in the therapeutic dynamics is the "lubricant" of the therapy. The group is viewed at all times as the vehicle of treatment for its individual members. Frequently, the therapist may utilize the therapeutic dynamics through manipulation to facilitate the therapy for each of the group members.

Operational definitions and clinical examples were given for each of the six therapeutic dynamics, as well as a discussion of how each is seen as facilitating the therapy, and the therapist's role in structuring the group and utilizing the therapeutic dynamics.

REFERENCES

Andrews, E. Some dynamics of college student therapy groups: Identity in transition. Paper presented at the meeting of the American Group Psychotherapy Association, New York, January 1969.

Cartwright, D., & Zander, A. *Group dynamics*. White Plains, N.Y.: Row, Peterson, 1953.

Durkin, H. *Group therapy for mothers of disturbed children*. Springfield, Ill.: Charles C Thomas, 1954.

Handlon, J., & Parloff, M. The treatment of patient and family as a group: Is it group psychotherapy? *International Journal of Group Psychotherapy*, 1962, *12*, 132–141.

Leichter, E. Group psychotherapy of married couples' groups: Some characteristic treatment dynamics. *International Journal of Group Psychotherapy*, 1962, *12*, 154–163.

Marcus, I. Psychoanalytic group therapy with fathers of emotionally disturbed preschool children. *International Journal of Group Psychotherapy*, 1956, *6*, 61–76.

Mullan, H., & Rosenbaum, M. The process of selection and preparation. In *Group psychotherapy*. New York: The Free Press, 1963. Pp. 91–136.

Neighbor, J., Beach, M., Brown, D., Kevin, D., & Visher, J. An approach to the selection of patients for group psychotherapy. *Mental Hygiene,* 1958, *42,* 234–254.

Scheidlinger, S. *Psychoanalysis and group behavior.* New York: Norton, 1952.

Schwartz, E., & Wolf, A. Psychoanalysis in groups: The mystique of group dynamics. *Topical Problems of Psychotherapy,* 1960, *2,* 117–153.

Slavson, S. *Child psychotherapy.* New York: Columbia University Press, 1952.

Slavson, S. When is a therapy group not a therapy group? *International Journal of Group Psychotherapy,* 1960, *10,* 3–21.

15 / THE SELF-DIRECTED THERAPEUTIC GROUP: THREE STUDIES

Betty Berzon and Lawrence N. Solomon

The self-directed therapeutic group is one that meets without a professionally-trained leader present to guide its interaction. The potential of this approach for extending a personal growth experience to many who would never encounter a professional mental health worker is obviously enormous.

Four years of experimentation with self-directed groups at the Western Behavioral Sciences Institute has led to two convictions, (*a*) that such groups are feasible, and (*b*) that stimulus materials could be developed that would significantly enhance their effectiveness.

Study I: Exploration

Initially, the task of researching self-directed groups was approached with great caution (Berzon & Solomon, 1964). Two groups of adult men and women, who had come voluntarily for group therapeutic experience in a research-institute setting, met weekly for 18 weeks. They were observed through a one-way vision window by an "on call" therapist who could be summoned into the group upon unanimous agreement of its members that it was necessary to do so.

During the 18 weeks, the therapist was summoned only 3 times in each group. The subjects saw the experience through, none appeared to have been injured by it and some reported that they had found it helpful. There was none of the physical acting-out that,

From JOURNAL OF COUNSELING PSYCHOLOGY, *1966, Vol. 13, pp. 491–497. Copyright 1966 by the American Psychological Association, and reproduced by permission.*

strangely enough, seemed to be the focus of concern for many professionals who criticized the endeavor. The worst that was envisaged, when the study began, was not that too much would happen, but that too little would happen. And this proved right. Too little did happen. Nevertheless, it was concluded that self-directed therapeutic groups are generally feasible, as judged against the specific criteria of absenteeism and attrition, groups' ability to function without a leader, and subjective evaluation of the experience by the group members.

In the attempt to discover why so little that was therapeutic happened in the pilot study, it became apparent that an important precondition to therapeutic effectiveness was previous experience in some type of therapeutic activity (individual therapy, sensitivity training, etc.). Those group members who were experienced in this activity were more prone to take responsibility for what happened in the group, either to themselves or to their fellow members. Inexperienced members were reluctant to assume this responsibility. From Study I emerged a major variable for further study: previous experience. Additionally, Study I suffered methodologically from the lack of a "control" group with which to compare the findings from the self-directed group. It was decided to design a more elaborate study in which self-directed groups would be compared with professionally-directed groups, and in which the influence of group members' previous therapeutic experience could be evaluated. The two major variables, direction and experience, defined the parameters of Study II.

Study II: Evaluation

Twelve 8-person groups met weekly for 18 weeks. Six of the groups were professionally-directed, with a designated leader who was a qualified professional with significant experience working with groups and whose regular staff assignment included such work. The other 6 groups were self-directed, without a professionally-trained, designated leader present, and with no one "on call" as was the case in Study I. Three of the 6 professionally-directed groups were composed of individuals who had had some kind of previous individual or group therapeutic experience; 3 were composed of subjects who had not had prior individual or group therapeutic experience. The self-directed groups were similarly composed.

The subjects were adult men and women who came voluntarily,

on a non-paying basis, to serve as participants in a research project. The groups were compared on 5 dimensions: (1) personality changes were evaluated with pre- and post-*MMPI* scores; (2) *S*'s perceptions of therapeutic conditions present in the group were measured by a modified form of the *Relationship Inventory* (Barrett-Lennard, 1959) questionnaire; (3) therapeutic process was rated by trained judges on two scales developed to measure the degree of "facilitative behavior" and the level of "intra personal exploration" discernible in 4-minute recorded excerpts from the groups' 2nd, 10th, and 16th sessions; (4) *S*'s subjective reports of "therapeutic events" were quantitatively and qualitatively analyzed; and (5) attendance and attrition rates were computed.

Contrary to what might have been expected, there were no clear-cut differences among the four treatment conditions on any of the five dimensions, with one exception: experienced *S*'s were more facilitating and achieved deeper levels of intrapersonal exploration than did the inexperienced.

The presence or absence of professional leadership did not significantly affect the group's ability to establish facilitative conditions, nor the ability of most of its members to engage in the therapeutic work in a meaningful way. The results of Study II appeared to demonstrate the potential usefulness of the self-directed therapeutic group as an important mental health resource (Berzon, 1964). Still, however, there were some indications that those groups which accomplished the least therapeutically were the self-directed, inexperienced groups. While prior experience seemed to compensate for the absence of a professionally-trained leader, naïve subjects, left entirely on their own, generally did more poorly than their professionally-directed counterparts.

The results of Studies I and II were consistent in affirming the feasibility of self-directed therapeutic groups. They were also consistent in underscoring the need for the development of stimulus materials that could be presented to non-experienced self-directed groups to enhance their effectiveness. Accordingly, in Study III, attention was turned specifically to the task of developing "program" materials which could guide and enhance the therapeutic interaction of non-experienced subjects.

Study III: Programming[1]

First Year

In the first year of this study, an 18-session program of stimulus materials was developed and tested with a vocational rehabilitation client population.[2]

Eight small groups met twice weekly for 9 weeks. Four of the groups were professionally-directed (PD) and did not use the stimulus materials. The other four groups did not have professional leadership and used instead, the materials. These were the self-directed groups (SD).

A basic assumption was made about the vocational rehabilitation client population: that they were, typically, persons with low self-esteem and an unfavorable self-concept. The program was designed, therefore, to increase the probability that the participant would come away from the group with a sense of personal contribution to cohesive group interaction. He would have the opportunity, through identification with peer group interaction, to test his own leadership capability and to perceive himself as a responsible participant. These experiences, it was assumed, would specifically influence his sense of self-esteem and his self-concept in a positive direction.

Structurally, the program consisted of 18 booklets, one for each of 18 sessions. Each group member had a booklet and the contents were read aloud, a paragraph at a time, with the group members taking turns reading around the circle. The program was written in this way to, (a) encourage total participation, and (b) promote a continuing focus on the here-and-now aspect of the group's interaction.

Each session had a cognitive component, or "message" and an interactive component, or "exercise." The exercise followed the reading of the message and required the group to engage in a task specifically designed to provide direct experiencing of the phenomena discussed in the message section. There were also review sections in several of the sessions.

Quantitative assessment was made using a battery of 7 research

[1] This investigation was supported, in part, by a research grant No. RD-1748 from the Vocational Rehabilitation Administration, Department of Health, Education, and Welfare, Washington, D.C.

[2] This program was written by Betty Berzon, Lawrence N. Solomon, and Melinda Sprague.

instruments. They included, (1) pre- and post-tests to measure personality and self-concept change, and counselor-rated progress toward vocational rehabilitation; (2) early and late subject-ratings of the therapeutic conditions perceived to be present in the groups; (3) session-by-session subject-ratings of their degree of self-disclosure; and (4) ratings of group "therapeutic climate," made by observers monitoring the live interaction through one-way vision windows.

Significant findings were two. There was a change in the self-concept in the direction of a more positive evaluation by both the PD and the SD subjects, as compared to control subjects who did not have a group experience. Also, the data revealed a significant increase in self-disclosure from early to late sessions for both the PD and the SD conditions. In both instances, improved self-concept and increased self-disclosure were achieved in the SD condition to the same extent as was possible under the guidance of a professionally-trained leader (Solomon & Berzon, 1965).

From an impressionistic point of view, the following weaknesses and strengths were notable in the program.

Weaknesses. There was, obviously, an attempt to cover too much. The participants' time was overstructured. There was too little time allowed to let the idiosyncratic material come out—the raw material—without which we have, often, only the illusion that something meaningful is happening.

There was too little time allotted to develop themes and to work through conflicts that emerged among group members.

The program was, in general, too cognitive and not experiential enough.

Strengths. On the positive side, there was definitely more dealing with personally relevant material in these groups than in such self-directed groups of naïve persons studied by the writers in the past.

There was also more confrontation in these self-directed groups than in those studied in the past. And, they not only confronted each other, but the experiment as well. They often discussed the value of what they were doing, talked about alternative choices open to them, and expressed the resentment and frustration they felt toward the experimenters when particular sessions did not work at all. In other words, they dealt directly with their own fate. This was not as true of self-directed groups studied in the past, and it is taken as a gain in what the program was able to bring about.

Second Year[3]

In the second year of Study III, major changes were made in regard to research design, and in program format and content.

Since it was felt that the professionally-directed and structured self-directed groups in the first year were sufficiently comparable, the professionally-directed condition was eliminated.

A shift was made from semi-weekly meetings to daily intensive sessions. Groups met for two sessions a day, five consecutive days in one week, and four consecutive days in the following week. The intensity of such scheduling appears to contribute greatly to the increased effectiveness of the program as compared to those previously conducted on a semi-weekly basis.

Another major change from the first year involved the presentation of the program on audio-tape, rather than in booklet form. Group members were told, during a brief orientation period at the beginning of each group, that they would find a new tape on the machine each session and they need only turn on the recorder to begin the session. Instructions for each session's exercise usually took about ten minutes, though the tape continued to run silently for the entire two hours. Also, a Participant's Notebook was provided which included forms needed for certain exercises and some of the material presented on the tapes, made available for the participants' later reference.

In addition to changes in format, the content of the program was completely revised, based on learnings from the first year. The new program is described below in some detail.

General Goal of the Program.   The general goal of the program is to enhance the individual's ability to make fuller use of his social and vocational potential through better understanding and broadened experiencing of himself in relation to other people.

Specific Goals of the Program.   To accomplish the general goal, a set of specific goals was designed, focusing on the impact of feelings and behavior on interpersonal relationships.

The specific goals are for the participant to *experience more fully in awareness:*

[3] This program was written by Betty Berzon, Lawrence N. Solomon, Melinda Sprague, and Clifford Weedman, for use in vocational rehabilitation settings.

1. His own feelings (OF)
2. How his own feelings affect his own behavior (OF → OB)
3. How his own behavior affects another's feelings (OB → AF)
4. How another's feelings affect his behavior (AF → AB)
5. How another's behavior affects his own feelings (AB → OF)

A simple graphic model is used to conceptualize this set of relationships.

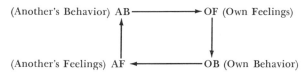

Criterion Behaviors. In order for the specific goals to be met, two things must happen to the individual in the group. He must (1) symbolize what he is experiencing and talk about it, and (2) listen with relatively accurate understanding when others talk.

From the specific goals, a set of criterion behaviors were developed along two dimensions: talking and listening. These are the behaviors to be evoked in the group and they are presented below as they relate to the specific goals.

Goal: To experience more fully in awareness one's own feelings.

Intermediate behavior:
    Talking about public aspects of self.
    Talking about private aspects of self.
    Talking about private aspects of self with description of feelings.

Criterion behavior:
    Talking with direct expression of here-and-now feelings.

Goal: To experience more fully in awareness how one's own feelings affect one's own behavior.

Criterion behavior:
    Talking with recognition of feelings and of their meaning for own behavior in relation to others.

Goal: To experience more fully in awareness how one's own behavior affects another's feelings.

Intermediate behavior:
    Listening with accurate understanding of the content of what others are saying.

Listening with accurate understanding of the feelings others are describing.

Criterion behavior:
Listening with accurate understanding of others' here-and-now feelings and how they have been affected by one's own behavior.

Goal: To experience more fully in awareness how another's feelings affect his behavior.

Criterion behavior:
Listening with an accurate understanding of others' feelings and how they affect their behavior.

Goal: To experience more fully in awareness how another's behavior affects one's own feelings.

Criterion behavior:
Talking with direct expression of own here-and-now feelings and recognizing the effect of others' behavior on these feelings.

It will be noted that on both behavioral dimensions, talking and listening, there is a general sequential movement from (1) public to private, (2) there-and-then to here-and-now, and (3) simple to complex.

Exercises. To evoke the intermediate and criterion behaviors, a series of exercises are presented via the tape recording. (Because the tape continues to run for the entire two hours, it is possible in some exercises to intervene with additional instructions during the session.)

A brief session-by-session outline of exercises appears below. It is obviously not a complete description of program content, but is presented merely to give an idea of the nature of the structuring used.

Session 1A—Orientation. The main purpose of this session is to establish group norms along the lines of trust building and facilitative behavior. This is done by presentation of (1) a set of "Group Ground Rules" and (2) a list of ten characteristics employers look for in a "good employee," the latter heavily weighted with interpersonal factors. The exercise is to rank order the "ten characteristics" in terms of their relative importance. This is a group task and the rank ordering must be a consensual one.

Session 1B—Listening Lab: Triads. In this session, "rules for good listening" are presented and a checklist using these rules is provided in the Participant's Notebook. The exercise is to divide into triads, or three-person groups, in which one person takes the role of the "talker," one the "listener," and one the "observer," who uses the checklist to rate the "listener" on his listening behavior. The "talker's" task is to talk for ten minutes about why he came to the Department of Rehabilitation. The roles are then rotated so that each person has a chance to take each role. During the last 15 minutes of this session, the group consensually rank orders its membership on "good listening" and the results are recorded on a "Feedback Chart" on the wall of the group room.

Session 2A—Paraphrasing. This exercise is built on the previous session's material. Each person tells the group what his "talker" told him about why he came to the agency. This task serves the dual purpose of underlining the importance of listening to understand others, and of making information about each participant available to the entire group.

In this "go around" exercise, as in others to follow, the instruction is for each group member to take a given number of minutes. As he talks, he holds a simple kitchen timer which he has set for the designated time, usually 10 minutes. When the timer goes off, he finishes, and hands it to the next person; in a sense giving up the floor to him and passing on the responsibility of participation. This provides an effective way to encourage active participation and to distribute it equally.

Session 2B—Self-Appraisal. In a "go around" each group member selects one of the "ten characteristics of a good employee" that he thinks he needs to work on to make himself more sought after as an employee.

The last fifteen minutes is spent on the Feedback Chart. This time the group consensually rates each other in terms of "Participation."

Session 3A—Unfortunate Circumstance. In a "go around" group members are asked to tell the most unfortunate circumstance in their life and to discuss their feelings about it.

Session 3B—Listening Lab: Cue Cards. One group member is designated a "talker" and one a "listener." They sit in the center of the room facing a row of "talker's helpers" on one side, and "listener's helpers" on the other. The "talker" continues discussion about the feelings he had during the unfortunate circumstance described in the previous session. The "listener" practices the "rules of good listening" to facilitate the "talker's" job. The "helpers," with the aid of large cue cards, encourage the "talker" and the "listener" to fulfill their roles using the various principles regarding self-disclosure and understanding that have been presented earlier in the program.

Feedback Chart for this day is again for "good listening."

Session 4A—Descriptions: Other. In a "go around" each group member describes every other group member metaphorically, thus initiating here-and-now interpersonal feedback in an indirect way.

Session 4B—Descriptions: Self. In another "go around" each individual describes himself metaphorically, providing an opportunity for group members to make themselves better known to the group. Feedback Chart is for "participation."

Session 5A—Feeling Pooling. In this session, individuals anonymously write out a strong feeling they have about another group member. These are placed in a pile, drawn out one at a time, and read aloud by others who comment on why they think someone would feel that way about the person named. Group members are encouraged to elaborate, using their own feelings toward the person.

Session 5B—Motion Giving. In an effort to build a bridge from the individual's group experience to his life outside, the group gives each member a specific task to do over the intervening weekend. The task is related to a problem that the member has discussed or manifested in the group, and is having difficulty working through. He is asked to at least "go through the motions" of doing something about the problem. Additionally, each group member selects a partner, and then, over the weekend, writes a story about what he hopes his partner will do in carrying out his "motion."

Feedback Chart this session is for "willingness to try to improve self."

Session 6A—Motion Reporting. Participants describe what happened when they tried to go through their "motion," telling particularly what their feelings were. Each "partner" then reads his prediction and discusses his feelings about what the person did in relation to what he thought he would do.

Session 6B—Free Session. In this session, it is suggested that the participants use their time to deal with, or go more deeply into anything that has occurred in the group so far.

Feedback Chart is again for "willingness to improve self."

Session 7A—Secret Pooling.[4] Group members are asked to write anonymously a personal secret. The papers are scrambled, and each

[4] The authors are grateful to Gerald Goodman for this exercise.

person then reads the secret he selected and tells how he thinks it would feel to have a secret like that.

Session 7B—Free Session. Feedback Chart is for "willingness to be known by others."

Session 8A—Confrontation.[5] Group members stand in a circle and one at a time they go around the circle stopping before each person. The instruction is, "look directly at the person, touch him, and tell how you feel about him."

Session 8B—Free Session. Feedback Chart is for "emotional honesty."

Session 9A—Self-Reappraisal. Participants are asked to look again at the list of "ten characteristics of a good employee" and to now select the one they think they need to work on the most, or to talk about any other way in which they think they need to make an effort to change.

Session 9B—Going Home. The instruction is to pretend you are on the way home after the group has ended (this is the last session). Think about the things you did not do or say in the group when you had the chance. Then, tell the group what those things are.

To assist in understanding the relationship of the exercises to the criterion behaviors and the specific goals, an outline is presented on page 182.

In the second year the battery of instruments used to assess the program's effectiveness was modified relative to changes in research design and program format.

Again, the clients who had the group experience showed a positive change in self-concept as compared to a control group, and became more self-disclosing, or congruent, as they went through the sessions. A pre/post measure indicated an increased willingness to be known and increased "transparency," as compared to the control group.

The ratings of therapeutic climate were generally higher than those of the first year, suggesting that the revisions in format and content of the program increased its effectiveness (Berzon & Solomon, 1966).

Plans for the future include further refinement of the present program and another year of testing. Particular attention will be given, in the third year, to assessing the effectiveness of this approach with an economically and educationally disadvantaged population.

It is anticipated that following the third year of the study, the

---

[5] The authors are grateful to William Schutz for this exercise.

Program Design Outline

Session No.	Exercises	Intermediate and Criterion Behaviors	Specific Goals
1A	Orientation		
1B	Listening Lab: Triads	Talking about public aspects of self; listening to understand content.	
2A	Paraphrasing	Talking about public aspects of self; listening for accurate understanding of content.	
2B	Self-Appraisal	Talking about private aspects of self.	
3A	Unfortunate Circumstance	Talking about private aspects of self-description of feelings; listening for feelings.	
3B	Listening Lab: Cue Cards	Listening for accurate understanding of feelings described.	
4A	Descriptions: Other	Talking with indirect expression of own feelings about another.	
4B	Descriptions: Self	Talking about self with indirect expression of own feelings.	
5A	Feeling Pooling	Talking with direct expression of own here-and-now feelings.	Experience more fully in awareness own feelings.
5B	Motion Giving	Understanding how another's feelings affect his behavior.	
6A	Motion Reporting	Talking with recognition of how own feelings affect own behavior; listening with accurate understanding of other's feelings and how they affect his behavior; listening with accurate understanding of other's here-and-now feelings and how they have been affected by one's own behavior.	Experience more fully in awareness how own feelings affect own behavior; experience more fully in awareness how other's feelings affect their behavior.
6B	Free		
7A	Secret Pooling	Understanding how others' feelings affect their behavior relative to more deeply personal material.	Experience more fully in in awareness how others' feelings affect their behavior.
7B	Free		
8A	Confrontation	Talking with direct expression of own here-and-now feelings, recognizing effect of other's behavior on these feelings.	Experience more fully in awareness how other's behavior affects one's own feelings.
8B	Free		
9A	Self-Reappraisal		
9B	Going Home		

program can be made available for general use in mental health and rehabilitation settings.

REFERENCES

Barrett-Lennard, G. T. The relationship inventory: A technique for measuring therapeutic dimensions of an interpersonal relationship. *Psychological Monographs,* 1962, *76* (43, Whole No. 562).

Berzon, Betty. The self-directed therapeutic group: An evaluative study. (Western Behavioral Sciences Institute, La Jolla, California, 1964.) Paper read at American Psychological Association, Los Angeles, Calif., 1964.

Berzon, Betty, & Solomon, L. N. The self-directed therapeutic group: An exploratory study. *International Journal of Group Psychotherapy,* 1964, *14,* 366–369.

Berzon, Betty, & Solomon, L. N. A small group program for continuing personal growth. Paper read at American Psychological Association, New York, 1966.

Solomon, L. N., & Berzon, Betty. The self-directed therapeutic group: A new rehabilitation resource. Paper read at American Psychological Association, Chicago, Ill., 1965.

Group Process
and Development

16 / THE PROCESS OF THE BASIC ENCOUNTER GROUP

Carl R. Rogers

I would like to share with you some of my thinking and puzzlement regarding a potent new cultural development—the intensive group experience.[1] It has, in my judgment, significant implications for our society. It has come very suddenly over our cultural horizon, since in anything like its present form it is less than two decades old.

I should like briefly to describe the many different forms and different labels under which the intensive group experience has become a part of our modern life. It has involved different kinds of individuals, and it has spawned various theories to account for its effects.

As to labels, the intensive group experience has at times been called the *T-group* or *lab group,* "T" standing for training laboratory in group dynamics. It has been termed *sensitivity training* in human relationships. The experience has sometimes been called a *basic encounter group* or a *workshop*—a workshop in human relationships, in leadership, in counseling, in education, in research, in psychotherapy. In dealing with one particular type of person—the drug addict—it has been called a *synanon.*

[1] In the preparation of this paper I am deeply indebted to two people, experienced in work with groups, for their help: Jacques Hochmann, M.D., psychiatrist of Lyon, France, who has been working at WBSI on a U.S.P.H.S. International Post-doctoral Fellowship, and Ann Dreyfuss, M.A., my research assistant. I am grateful for their ideas, for their patient analysis of recorded group sessions, and for the opportunity to interact with two original and inquiring minds.

The intensive group experience has functioned in various settings. It has operated in industries, in universities, in church groups, and in resort settings which provide a retreat from everyday life. It has functioned in various educational institutions and in penitentiaries.

An astonishing range of individuals have been involved in these intensive group experiences. There have been groups for presidents of large corporations. There have been groups for delinquent and predelinquent adolescents. There have been groups composed of college students and faculty members, of counselors and psychotherapists, of school dropouts, of married couples, of confirmed drug addicts, of criminals serving sentences, of nurses preparing for hospital service, and of educators, principals, and teachers.

The geographical spread attained by this rapidly expanding movement has reached in this country from Bethel, Maine (starting point of the National Training Laboratory movement), to Idyllwild, California. To my personal knowledge, such groups also exist in France, England, Holland, Japan, and Australia.

In their outward pattern these group experiences also show a great deal of diversity. There are T-groups and workshops which have extended over three to four weeks, meeting six to eight hours each day. There are some that have lasted only 2½ days, crowding twenty or more hours of group sessions into this time. A recent innovation is the "marathon" weekend, which begins on Friday afternoon and ends on Sunday evening, with only a few hours out for sleep and snacks.

As to the conceptual underpinnings of this whole movement, one may almost select the theoretical flavor he prefers. Lewinian and client-centered theories have been most prominent, but gestalt therapy and various brands of psychoanalysis have all played contributing parts. The experience within the group may focus on specific training in human relations skills. It may be closely similar to group therapy, with much exploration of past experience and the dynamics of personal development. It may focus on creative expression through painting or expressive movement. It may be focused primarily upon a basic encounter and relationship between individuals.

Simply to describe the diversity which exists in this field raises very properly the question of why these various developments should be considered to belong together. Are there any threads of commonality which pervade all these widely divergent activities? To me it seems that they do belong together and can all be classed as focusing on the intensive group experience. They all have certain similar external characteristics. The group in almost every case is small (from eight to eighteen members), is relatively unstructured, and chooses its own goals and personal directions. The group experience usually, though not always, includes some cognitive input, some content material which is presented to the group. In almost all instances the leader's responsibility is primarily the facilitation of the expression of both feelings and thoughts on the part of the group members. Both in the leader and in the group members there is some focus on the process and the dynamics of the immediate personal interaction. These are, I think, some of the identifying characteristics which are rather easily recognized.

There are also certain practical hypotheses which tend to be held in common by all these groups. My own summary of these would be as follows: In an intensive group, with much freedom and little structure, the individual will gradually feel safe enough to drop some of his defenses and facades; he will relate more directly on a feeling basis (come into a basic encounter) with other members of the group; he will come to understand himself and his relationship to others more accurately; he will change in his personal attitudes and behavior; and he will subsequently relate more effectively to others in his everyday life situation. There are other hypotheses related more to the group than to the individual. One is that in this situation of minimal structure, the group will move from confusions, fractionation, and discontinuity to a climate of greater trust and coherence. These are some of the characteristics and hypotheses which, in my judgment, bind together this enormous cluster of activities which I wish to talk about as constituting the intensive group experience.

As for myself, I have been gradually moving into this field for the last twenty years. In experimenting with what I call *student-centered teaching,* involving the free expression of personal feelings, I came to recognize not only the cognitive learnings but also some of the personal changes which occurred. In brief intensive training courses for counselors for the Veterans Administration in 1946, during the postwar period, I and my staff focused more directly on providing an intensive group experience because of its impact in producing significant learning. In 1950, I served as leader of an intensive, full-time, one-week workshop, a postdoctoral training seminar in psychotherapy for the American Psychological Association. The impact of those six days was so great that for more than a dozen years afterward, I kept hearing from members of the group about the meaning it had had for them. Since that time I have been involved in more than forty ventures of what I would like to term—using the label most congenial to me—*basic encounter groups*. Most of these have involved for many of the members experiences of great intensity and considerable personal change. With two individuals, however, in these many groups, the experience contributed, I believe, to a psychotic break. A few other individuals have found the experience more unhelpful than helpful. So I have come to have a profound respect for the constructive potency of such group experiences and also a real concern over the fact that sometimes and in some ways this experience may do damage to individuals.

The Group Process

It is a matter of great interest to me to try to understand what appear to be common elements in the group process as I have come dimly to sense these. I am using this opportunity to think about this problem, not because I feel I have any final theory to give, but because I would like to formulate, as clearly as I am able, the elements which I can perceive at the present time. In doing so I am drawing upon my own experience, upon the experiences of others with whom I have worked, upon the written material in this field, upon the written reactions of many individuals who have participated in such groups, and to some extent upon the recordings of such group sessions, which we are only beginning to tap and analyze. I am sure that (though I have tried to draw on the existence of others) any formulation I make at the present time is unduly influenced by my own experience in groups and thus is lacking in the generality I wish it might have.

As I consider the terribly complex interactions which arise during twenty, forty, sixty, or more hours of intensive sessions, I believe that I see some threads which weave in and out of the pattern. Some of these trends or tendencies are likely to appear early and some later in the group sessions, but there is no clear-cut sequence in which one ends and another begins. The interaction is best thought of, I believe, as a varied tapestry, differing from group to group, yet with certain kinds of trends evident in most of these intensive encounters and with certain patterns tending to precede and others to follow. Here are some of the process patterns which I see developing, briefly described in simple terms, illustrated from tape recordings and personal reports, and presented in roughly sequential order. I am not aiming at a high-level theory of group process but rather at a naturalistic observation out of which, I hope, true theory can be built.[2]

MILLING AROUND

As the leader or facilitator makes clear at the outset that this is a group with unusual freedom, that it is not one for which he will take directional responsibility, there tends to develop a period of initial confusion, awkward silence, polite surface interaction, "cocktail-party talk," frustration, and great lack of continuity. The individuals come face-to-face with the fact that "there is no structure here except what we provide. We do not know our purposes; we do not even know one another, and we are committed to remain together over a considerable period of time." In this situation, confusion and frustration are natural. Particularly striking to the observer is the lack of continuity between personal expressions. Individual A will present some proposal or concern, clearly looking for a response from the group. Individual B has obviously been waiting for his turn and starts off on some completely different tangent as though he had never heard A. One member makes a simple suggestion such as, "I think we should introduce ourselves," and this may lead to several hours of highly involved discussion in which the underlying issues appear to be, "Who is the leader?" "Who is responsible for us?" "Who is a member of the group?" "What is the purpose of the group?"

RESISTANCE TO PERSONAL EXPRESSION OR EXPLORATION

During the milling period, some individuals are likely to reveal some rather personal attitudes. This tends to foster a very ambivalent reaction among other members of the group. One member, writing of his experience, says:

[2] Jack and Lorraine Gibb have long been working on an analysis of trust development as the essential theory of group process. Others who have contributed significantly to the theory of group process are Chris Argyris, Kenneth Benne, Warren Bennis, Dorwin Cartwright, Matthew Miles, and Robert Blake. Samples of the thinking of all these and others may be found in three recent books: Bradford, Gibb, & Benne (1964); Bennis, Benne, & Chin (1961); and Bennis, Schein, Berlew, & Steele (1964). Thus, there are many promising leads for theory construction involving a considerable degree of abstraction. This chapter has a more elementary aim—a naturalistic descriptive account of the process.

There is a self which I present to the world and another one which I know more intimately. With others I try to appear able, knowing, unruffled, problem-free. To substantiate this image I will act in a way which at the time or later seems false or artificial or "not the real me." Or I will keep to myself thoughts which if expressed would reveal an imperfect me.

My inner self, by contrast with the image I present to the world, is characterized by many doubts. The worth I attach to this inner self is subject to much fluctuation and is very dependent on how others are reacting to me. At times this private self can feel worthless.

It is the public self which members tend to reveal to one another, and only gradually, fearfully, and ambivalently do they take steps to reveal something of their inner world.

Early in one intensive workshop, the members were asked to write anonymously a statement of some feeling or feelings which they had which they were not willing to tell in the group. One man wrote:

I don't relate easily to people. I have an almost impenetrable facade. Nothing gets in to hurt me, but nothing gets out. I have repressed so many emotions that I am close to emotional sterility. This situation doesn't make me happy, but I don't know what to do about it.

This individual is clearly living inside a private dungeon, but he does not even dare, except in this disguised fashion, to send out a call for help.

In a recent workshop when one man started to express the concern he felt about an impasse he was experiencing with his wife, another member stopped him, saying essentially:

Are you sure you want to go on with this, or are you being seduced by the group into going further than you want to go? How do you know the group can be trusted? How will you feel about it when you go home and tell your wife what you have revealed, or when you decide to keep it from her? It just isn't safe to go further.

It seemed quite clear that in his warning, this second member was also expressing his own fear of revealing *him*self and *his* lack of trust in the group.

DESCRIPTION OF PAST FEELINGS

In spite of ambivalence about the trustworthiness of the group and the risk of exposing oneself, expression of feelings does begin to assume a larger proportion of the discussion. The executive tells how frustrated he feels by certain situations in his industry, or the housewife relates problems she has experienced with her children. A tape-recorded exchange involving a Roman Catholic nun occurs early in a one-week workshop, when the discussion has turned to a rather intellectualized consideration of anger:

BILL: What happens when you get mad, Sister, or don't you?

SISTER: Yes, I do—yes I do. And I find when I get mad, I, I almost get, well, the kind of person that antagonizes me is the person who seems so unfeeling toward people—now I take our dean as a person in point because she is a very aggressive woman and has certain ideas about what the various rules in a college should be; and this woman can just send me into high "G"; in an angry mood. *I mean this.* But then I find, I. . . .

FACIL.:[3] But what, what do you do?

SISTER: I find that when I'm in a situation like this, that I strike out in a very sharp, uh, *tone,* or else I just refuse to respond—"All right, this happens to be her way"—I don't think I've ever gone into a tantrum.

JOE: You just withdraw—no use to fight it.

FACIL.: You say you use a sharp tone. To *her,* or to other people you're dealing with?

SISTER: Oh, no. To *her.*

This is a typical example of a *description* of feelings which are obviously current in her in a sense but which she is placing in the past and which she describes as being outside the group in time and place. It is an example of feelings existing "there and then."

EXPRESSION OF NEGATIVE FEELINGS

Curiously enough, the first expression of genuinely significant "here-and-now" feeling is apt to come out in negative attitudes toward other group members or toward the group leader. In one group in which members introduced themselves at some length, one woman refused, saying that she preferred to be known for what she was in the group and not in terms of her status outside. Very shortly after

---

[3] The term "facilitator" will be used throughout this paper, although sometimes he is referred to as "leader" or "trainer."

FREDA: Oooh, that's *weird!*

MARY: People have problems, Freda, I mean ya know. . . .

FREDA: Yeah, I know, but *yeOUW!!!*

FACIL. (*to Freda*): You know about these problems, but they still are weird to you.

GEORGE: You see what I mean; it's embarrassing to talk about it.

MARY: Yeah, but it's O.K.

GEORGE: It *hurts* to talk about it, but I know I've got to so I won't be guilt-ridden for the rest of my life.

Clearly Freda is completely shutting him out psychologically, while Mary in particular is showing a deep acceptance.

THE EXPRESSION OF IMMEDIATE INTERPERSONAL FEELINGS IN THE GROUP

Entering into the process sometimes earlier, sometimes later, is the explicit bringing into the open of the feelings experienced in the immediate moment by one member about another. These are sometimes positive and sometimes negative. Examples would be: "I feel threatened by your silence." "You remind me of my mother, with whom I had a tough time." "I took an instant dislike to you the first moment I saw you." "To me you're like a breath of fresh air in the group." "I like your warmth and your smile." "I dislike you more every time you speak up." Each of these attitudes can be, and usually is, explored in the increasing climate of trust.

THE DEVELOPMENT OF A HEALING CAPACITY IN THE GROUP

One of the most fascinating aspects of any intensive group experience is the manner in which a number of the group members show a natural and spontaneous capacity for dealing in a helpful, facilitative, and therapeutic fashion with the pain and suffering of others. As one rather extreme example of this, I think of a man in charge of maintenance in a large plant who was one of the low-status members of an industrial executive group. As he informed us, he had not been "contaminated by education." In the initial phases the group tended to look down on him. As members delved more deeply into themselves and began to express their own attitudes more fully, this man came forth as, without doubt, the most sensitive member of the group. He knew intuitively how to be understanding and acceptant. He was alert to things which had not yet been expressed but which were just below the surface. When the rest of us were paying attention to a member who was speaking, he would frequently spot another individual who was suffering silently and in need of help. He had a deeply perceptive and facilitating attitude. This kind of ability shows up so commonly in groups that it has led me to feel that the ability to be healing or therapeutic is far more common in human life than we might suppose. Often it needs only the permission granted by a freely flowing group experience to become evident.

In a characteristic instance, the leader and several group members were trying to be of help to Joe, who was telling of the almost complete lack of communication between himself and his wife. In varied ways members endeavored to give help. John kept putting before Joe the feelings Joe's wife was almost certainly experiencing. The facilitator kept challenging Joe's facade of "carefulness." Marie tried to help him discover what he was feeling at the moment. Fred showed him the choice he had of alternative behaviors. All this was clearly done in a spirit of caring, as is even more evident in the recording itself. No miracles were achieved, but toward the end Joe did come to the realization that the only thing that might help would be to express his real feelings to his wife.

SELF-ACCEPTANCE AND THE BEGINNING OF CHANGE

Many people feel that self-acceptance must stand in the way of change. Actually, in these group experiences, as in psychotherapy, it is the *beginning* of change. Some examples of the kind of attitudes expressed would be these: "I *am* a dominating person who likes to control others. I do want to mold these individuals into the proper shape." Another person says, "I really have a hurt and overburdened little boy inside of me who feels very sorry for himself. I *am* that little boy, in addition to being a competent and responsible manager."

I think of one governmental executive in a group in which I participated, a man with high responsibility and excellent technical training as an engineer. At the first meeting of the group he impressed me, and I think others, as being cold, aloof, somewhat bitter, resentful, and cynical. When he spoke of how he ran his office it appeared that he administered it "by the book," without any warmth or human feeling entering in. In one of the early sessions, when he spoke of his wife, a group member asked him, "Do you love your wife?" He paused for a long time, and the questioner said, "O.K., that's answer enough." The executive said, "No. Wait a minute. The reason I didn't respond was that I was wondering if I ever loved anyone. I don't think I *ever* really *loved* anyone." It seemed quite dramatically clear to those of us in the group that he had come to accept himself as an unloving person.

A few days later he listened with great intensity as one member of the group expressed profound personal feelings of isolation, loneliness, and pain, revealing the extent to which he had been living behind a mask, a facade. The next morning the engineer said, "Last night I thought and thought about what Bill told us. I even wept quite a bit by myself. I can't remember how long it has been since I have cried, and I really *felt* something. I think perhaps what I felt was love."

It is not surprising that before the week was over, he had thought through new ways of handling his growing son, on whom he had been placing extremely rigorous demands. He had also begun genuinely to appreciate the love which his wife had extended to him and which he now felt he could in some measure reciprocate.

In another group one man kept a diary of his reactions. Here is his account of an experience in which he came really to accept his almost abject desire for love, a self-acceptance which marked the beginning of a very significant experience of change. He says (Hall, 1965):

During the break between the third and fourth sessions, I felt very droopy and tired. I had it in mind to take a nap, but instead I was almost compulsively going around to people starting a conversation. I had a begging kind of a feeling, like a very cowed little puppy hoping that he'll be patted but half afraid he'll be kicked. Finally, back in my room I lay down and began to know that I was sad. Several times I found myself wishing my roommate would come in and talk to me. Or, whenever someone walked by the door, I would come to attention inside, the way a dog pricks up his ears; and I would feel an immediate wish for that person to come in and talk to me. I realized my raw wish to receive kindness.

Another recorded excerpt, from an adolescent group, shows a combination of self-acceptance and self-exploration. Art had been talking about his "shell," and here he is beginning to work with the problem of accepting himself, and also the facade he ordinarily exhibits:

ART: I'm so darn used to living with the shell; it doesn't even bother me. I don't even know the real me. I think I've uh, well, I've

pushed the shell more away here. When I'm out of my shell—
only twice—once just a few minutes ago—I'm really me, I guess.
But then I just sort of pull in the [latch] cord after me when I'm
in my shell, and that's almost all the time. And I leave the [false]
front standing outside when I'm back in the shell.

FACIL.: And nobody's back in there with you?

ART (crying): Nobody else is in there with me, just me. I just pull
everything into the shell and roll the shell up and shove it in my
pocket. I take the shell, and the real me, and put it in my pocket
where it's safe. I guess that's really the way I do it—I go into my
shell and turn off the real world. And here: that's what I want
to do here in this group, ya know, come out of my shell and
actually throw it away.

LOIS: You're making progress already. At least you can talk about it.

FACIL.: Yeah. The thing that's going to be hardest is to stay out of
the shell.

ART (still crying): Well, yeah, if I can keep talking about it, I can
come out and stay out, but I'm gonna have to, ya know, protect
me. It hurts; it's actually hurting to talk about it.

Still another person reporting shortly after his workshop experience said, "I came away from the workshop feeling much more
deeply that 'It is all right to be me with all my strengths and weaknesses.' My wife has told me that I appear to be more authentic,
more real, more genuine."

This feeling of greater realness and authenticity is a very common
experience. It would appear that the individual is learning to accept
and to be himself, and this is laying the foundation for change. He
is closer to his own feelings, and hence they are no longer so rigidly
organized and are more open to change.

The Cracking of Facades

As the sessions continue, so many things tend to occur together
that it is difficult to know which to describe first. It should again be
stressed that these different threads and stages interweave and overlap. One of these threads is the increasing impatience wtih defenses.
As time goes on, the group finds it unbearable that any member
should live behind a mask or a front. The polite words, the intellectual understanding of one another and of relationships, the smooth
coin of tact and cover-up amply satisfactory for interactions outside

are just not good enough. The expression of self by some members of the group has made it very clear that a deeper and more basic encounter is *possible,* and the group appears to strive, intuitively and unconsciously, toward this goal. Gently at times, almost savagely at others, the group *demands* that the individual be himself, that his current feelings not be hidden, that he remove the mask of ordinary social intercourse. In one group there was a highly intelligent and quite academic man who had been rather perceptive in his understanding of others but who had not revealed himself at all. The attitude of the group was finally expressed sharply by one member when he said, "Come out from behind that lectern, Doc. Stop giving us speeches. Take off your dark glasses. We want to know *you.*"

In Synanon, the fascinating group so successfully involved in making persons out of drug addicts, this ripping away of facades is often very drastic. An excerpt from one of the "synanons," or group sessions, makes this clear (Casriel, 1963, p. 81):

JOE (*speaking to Gina*): I wonder when you're going to stop sounding so good in synanons. Every synanon that I'm in with you, someone asks you a question, and you've got a beautiful book written. All made out about what went down and how you were wrong and how you realized you were wrong and all that kind of bullshit. When are you going to stop doing that? How do you feel about Art?

GINA: I have nothing against Art.

WILL: You're a nut. Art hasn't got any damn sense. He's been in there, yelling at you and Moe, and you've got everything so cool.

GINA: No, I feel he's very insecure in a lot of ways but that has nothing to do with me. . . .

JOE: You act like you're so goddamn understanding.

GINA: I was *told* to act as if I understand.

JOE: Well, you're in a synanon now. You're not supposed to be acting like you're such a goddamn healthy person. Are you so well?

GINA: No.

JOE: Well why the hell don't you quit acting as if you were.

If I am indicating that the group at times is quite violent in tearing down a facade or a defense, this would be accurate. On the other hand, it can also be sensitive and gentle. The man who was accused of hiding behind a lectern was deeply hurt by this attack, and over the lunch hour looked very troubled, as though he might break into tears at any moment. When the group reconvened, the members sensed this and treated him very gently, enabling him to tell us his own tragic personal story, which accounted for his aloofness and his intellectual and academic approach to life.

THE INDIVIDUAL RECEIVES FEEDBACK

In the process of this freely expressive interaction, the individual rapidly acquires a great deal of data as to how he appears to others. The "hail-fellow-well-met" discovers that others resent his exaggerated friendliness. The executive who weighs his words carefully and speaks with heavy precision may find that others regard him as stuffy. A woman who shows a somewhat excessive desire to be of help to others is told in no uncertain terms that some group members do not want her for a mother. All this can be decidedly upsetting, but as long as these various bits of information are fed back in the context of caring which is developing in the group, they seem highly constructive.

Feedback can at times be very warm and positive, as the following recorded excerpt indicates:

LEO (*very softly and gently*): I've been struck with this ever since she talked about her waking in the night, that she has a very delicate sensitivity. (*Turning to Mary and speaking almost caressingly*.) And somehow I perceive—even looking at you or in your eyes—a very—almost like a gentle touch and from this gentle touch you can tell many—things—you sense in—this manner.

FRED: Leo, when you said that, that she has this kind of delicate sensitivity, I just felt, *Lord yes!* Look at her eyes.

LEO: M-hm.

A much more extended instance of negative and positive feedback, triggering a significant new experience of self-understanding and encounter with the group, is taken from the diary of the young man mentioned before. He had been telling the group that he had no feeling for them, and felt they had no feeling for him (Hall, 1965):

Then, a girl lost patience with me and said she didn't feel she could give any more. She said I looked like a bottomless well, and she wondered how many times I had to be told that I *was* cared for. By this time I was feeling panicky, and I was saying to myself, "My God, can it be true that I can't be satisfied and that I'm somehow compelled to pester people for attention until I drive them away!"

At this point while I was really worried, a nun in the group spoke up. She said that I had not alienated her with some negative things I had said to her. She said she liked me, and she couldn't understand why I couldn't see that. She said she felt concerned for me and wanted to help me. With that, something began to really dawn on me, and I voiced it somewhat like the following. "You mean you are all sitting there, feeling for me what I say I want you to feel, and that somewhere down inside me I'm stopping it from touching me?" I relaxed appreciably and began really to wonder why I had shut their caring out so much. I couldn't find the answer, and one woman said: "It looks like you are trying to stay continuously as deep in your feelings as you were this afternoon. It would make sense to me for you to draw back and assimilate it. Maybe if you don't push so hard, you can rest awhile and then move back into your feelings more naturally."

Her making the last suggestion really took effect. I saw the sense in it, and almost immediately I settled back very relaxed with something of a feeling of a bright, warm day dawning inside me. In addition to taking the pressure off of myself, however, I was for the first time really warmed by the friendly feelings which I felt they had for me. It is difficult to say why I felt liked only just then, but, as opposed to the earlier sessions, I really *believed* they cared for me. I never have fully understood why I stood their affection off for so long, but at that point I almost abruptly began to trust that they did care. The measure of the effectiveness of this change lies in what I said next. I said, "Well, that really takes care of me. I'm really ready to listen to someone else now." I *meant* that, too.

CONFRONTATION

There are times when the term "feedback" is far too mild to describe the interactions which take place, when it is better said that one individual *confronts* another, directly "leveling" with him. Such confrontations can be positive, but frequently they are decidedly negative, as the following example will make abundantly clear. In one of the last sessions of a group, Alice had made some quite vulgar and contemptuous remarks to John, who was entering religious work. The next morning, Norma, who had been a very quiet person in the group, took the floor:

NORMA (*loud sigh*): Well, I don't have *any* respect for you, Alice. *None!* (*Pause.*) There's about a hundred things going through my mind I want to say to you, and by God I hope I get through 'em all! First of all, if you wanted us to respect you, then why couldn't you respect *John's* feelings last night? Why have you been on him today? Hmm? Last night—couldn't you—couldn't you accept— *couldn't you* comprehend in any way at all that—that *he felt* his unworthiness in the service of God? Couldn't you accept this, or did you have to dig into it today to find something *else there?* And his respect for womanhood—he *loves* women—yes, he does, because he's a real person, but you—you're not a real woman— to me—and thank God, you're not my mother! ! ! ! I want to come over and beat the hell out of you ! ! ! I want to slap you across the mouth so hard and—oh, and you're so, you're many years above me—and I respect age, and I respect people who are older than me, *but I don't respect you, Alice. At all!* And I was so *hurt* and *confused* because you were making someone else feel *hurt* and *confused.* . . .

It may relieve the reader to know that these two women came to accept each other, not completely, but much more understandingly, before the end of the session. But this *was* a confrontation!

THE HELPING RELATIONSHIP OUTSIDE THE GROUP SESSIONS

No account of the group process would, in my experience, be adequate if it did not make mention of the many ways in which group members are of assistance to one another. Not infrequently, one member of a group will spend hours listening and talking to another member who is undergoing a painful new perception of himself. Sometimes it is merely the offering of help which is therapeutic. I think of one man who was going through a very depressed period after having told us of the many tragedies in his life. He seemed quite clearly, from his remarks, to be contemplating suicide. I jotted down my room number (we were staying at a hotel) and told him to put it in his pocket and to call me anytime of day or night if he felt that it would help. He never called, but six months after the workshop was over he wrote to me telling me how much that act had meant to him and that he still had the slip of paper to remind him of it.

Let me give an example of the healing effect of the attitudes of group members both outside and inside the group meetings. This is taken from a letter written by a workshop member to the group one month after the group sessions. He speaks of the difficulties and depressing circumstances he has encountered during that month and adds:

I have come to the conclusion that my experiences with you have profoundly affected me. I am truly grateful. This is different than personal therapy. None of you *had* to care about me. None of you had to seek me out and let me know of things you thought would help me. None of you had to let me know I was of help to you. Yet you did, and as a result it has far more meaning than anything I have so far experienced. When I feel the need to hold back and not live spontaneously, for whatever reasons, I remember that twelve persons, just like those before me now, said to let go and be congruent, to be myself, and, of all unbelievable things, they even loved me more for it. This has given me the *courage* to come out of myself many times since then. Often it seems my very doing of this helps the others to experience similar freedom.

The Basic Encounter

Running through some of the trends I have just been describing is the fact that individuals come into much closer and more direct contact with one another than is customary in ordinary life. This appears to be one of the most central, intense, and change-producing aspects of such a group experience. To illustrate what I mean, I would like to draw an example from a recent workshop group. A man tells, through his tears, of the very tragic loss of his child, a grief which he is experiencing *fully,* for the first time, not holding back his feelings in any way. Another says to him, also with tears in his eyes, "I've never felt so close to another human being. I've never before felt a real physical hurt in me from the pain of another. I feel *completely* with you." This is a basic encounter.

Such I–Thou relationships (to use Buber's term) occur with some frequency in these group sessions and nearly always bring a moistness to the eyes of the participants.

One member, trying to sort out his experiences immediately after a workshop, speaks of the "commitment to relationship" which often developed on the part of two individuals, not necessarily individuals who had liked each other initially. He goes on to say:

The incredible fact experienced over and over by members of the group was that when a negative feeling was fully expressed to another, the relationship grew and the negative feeling was replaced by a deep acceptance for the other. . . . Thus real change seemed to occur when feelings were experienced and expressed in the context of the relationship. "I can't *stand* the way you talk!" turned into a real understanding and affection for you the *way* you talk.

This statement seems to capture some of the more complex meanings of the term "basic encounter."

THE EXPRESSION OF POSITIVE FEELINGS AND CLOSENESS

As indicated in the last section, an inevitable part of the group process seems to be that when feelings are expressed and can be accepted in a relationship, a great deal of closeness and positive feelings result. Thus as the sessions proceed, there is an increasing feeling of warmth and group spirit and trust built, not out of positive attitudes only, but out of a realness which includes both positive and negative feeling. One member tried to capture this in writing very shortly after the workshop by saying that if he were trying to sum it up, ". . . it would have to do with what I call confirmation —a kind of confirmation of myself, of the uniqueness and universal qualities of men, a confirmation that when we can be human together something positive can emerge."

A particularly poignant expression of these positive attitudes was shown in the group where Norma confronted Alice with her bitterly angry feelings. Joan, the facilitator, was deeply upset and began to weep. The positive and healing attitudes of the group, for their own *leader,* are an unusual example of the closeness and personal quality of the relationships.

JOAN (*crying*): I somehow feel that it's so *damned* easy for me to— to put myself *inside* of another person and I just guess I can feel that—for John and Alice and for you, Norma.

ALICE: And it's *you* that's hurt.

JOAN: Maybe I am taking some of that hurt. I guess I am. (*Crying.*)

ALICE: That's a wonderful gift. I wish I had it.

JOAN: You have a lot of it.

PETER: In a way you bear the—I guess in a special way, because you're the—facilitator, ah, you've probably borne, ah, an extra heavy burden for all of us—and the burden that you, perhaps, you bear the heaviest is—we ask you—we ask one another; we grope to try to accept one another as we are, and—for each of us in various ways I guess we reach things and we say, *please* accept me. . . .

Some may be very critical of a "leader" so involved and so sensitive that she weeps at the tensions in the group which she has taken into herself. For me, it is simply another evidence that when people are real with each other, they have an astonishing ability to heal a person with a real and understanding love, whether that person is "participant" or "leader."

Behavior Changes in the Group

It would seem from observation that many changes in behavior occur in the group itself. Gestures change. The tone of voice changes, becoming sometimes stronger, sometimes softer, usually more spontaneous, less artificial, more feelingful. Individuals show an astonishing amount of thoughtfulness and helpfulness toward one another.

Our major concern, however, is with the behavior changes which occur following the group experience. It is this which constitutes the most significant question and on which we need much more study and research. One person gives a catalog of the changes which he sees in himself which may seem too "pat" but which is echoed in many other statements:

I am more open, spontaneous. I express myself more freely. I am more sympathetic, empathic, and tolerant. I am more confident. I am more religious in my own way. My relations with my family, friends, and co-workers are more honest, and I express my likes and dislikes and true feelings more openly. I admit ignorance more readily. I am more cheerful. I want to help others more.

Another says:

Since the workshop there has been a new relationship with my parents. It has been trying and hard. However, I have found a greater freedom in talking with them, especially my father. Steps have been made toward being closer to my mother than I have ever been in the last five years.

Another says:

It helped clarify my feelings about my work, gave me more enthusiasm for it, and made me more honest and cheerful with my coworkers and also more open when I was hostile. It made my relationship with my wife more open, deeper. We felt freer to talk about anything, and we felt confident that anything we talked about we could work through.

Sometimes the changes which are described are very subtle. "The primary change is the more positive view of my ability to allow myself to *hear,* and to become involved with someone else's 'silent scream.' "

At the risk of making the outcomes sound too good, I will add one more statement written shortly after a workshop by a mother. She says:

The immediate impact on my children was of interest to both me and my husband. I feel that having been so accepted and loved by a group of strangers was so supportive that when I returned home my love for the people closest to me was much more spontaneous. Also, the practice I had in accepting and loving others during the workshop was evident in my relationships with my close friends.

Disadvantages and Risks

Thus far one might think that every aspect of the group process was positive. As far as the evidence at hand indicates, it appears that it nearly always is a positive process for a majority of the participants. There are, nevertheless, failures which result. Let me try to describe briefly some of the negative aspects of the group process as they sometimes occur.

The most obvious deficiency of the intensive group experience is that frequently the behavior changes, if any, which occur, are not lasting. This is often recognized by the participants. One says, "I wish I had the ability to hold permanently the 'openness' I left the conference with." Another says, "I experienced a lot of acceptance, warmth, and love at the workshop. I find it hard to carry the ability to share this in the same way with people outside the workshop. I find it easier to slip back into my old unemotional role than to do the work necessary to open relationships."

Sometimes group members experience this phenomenon of "relapse" quite philosophically:

The group experience is not a way of life but a reference point. My images of our group, even though I am unsure of some of their meanings, give me a comforting and useful perspective on my normal routine. They are like a mountain which I have climbed and enjoyed and to which I hope occasionally to return.

SOME DATA ON OUTCOMES

What is the extent of this "slippage"? In the past year, I have administered follow-up questionnaires to 481 individuals who have been in groups I have organized or conducted. The information has been obtained from two to twelve months following the group experience, but the greatest number were followed up after a three- to six-month period.[4] Of these individuals, two (i.e., less than one-half of 1 percent) felt it had changed their behavior in ways they did not like. Fourteen percent felt the experience had made no perceptible change in their behavior. Another fourteen percent felt that it had changed their behavior but that this change had disappeared or left only a small residual positive effect. Fifty-seven percent felt it had made a continuing positive difference in their behavior, a few feeling that it had made some negative changes along with the positive.

A second potential risk involved in the intensive group experience and one which is often mentioned in public discussion is the risk that the individual may become deeply involved in revealing himself and then be left with problems which are not worked through. There have been a number of reports of people who have felt, following an intensive group experience, that they must go to a therapist to work through the feelings which were opened up in the intensive experience of the workshop and which were left unresolved. It is obvious that, without knowing more about each individual situation, it is difficult to say whether this was a negative outcome or a partially or entirely positive one. There are also very occasional accounts, and I can testify to two in my own experience, where an individual has had a psychotic episode during or immediately following an intensive group experience. On the other side of the picture is the fact that individuals have also lived through what were clearly psychotic episodes, and lived through them very constructively, in the context of a basic encounter group. My own tentative clinical judgment would be that the more positively the group process has been proceeding, the less likely it is that any individual would be psychologically damaged through membership in the group. It is obvious, however, that this is a serious issue and that much more needs to be known.

Some of the tension which exists in workshop members as a result of this potential for damage was very well described by one member when he said, "I feel the workshop had some very precious moments for me when I felt very close indeed to particular persons. It had some frightening moments when its potency was very evident and I

4 The 481 respondents constituted 82 percent of those to whom the questionnaire had been sent.

realized a particular person might be deeply hurt or greatly helped but I could not predict which."

Out of the 481 participants followed up by questionnaires, two felt that the overall impact of their intensive group experience was "mostly damaging." Six more said that it had been "more unhelpful than helpful." Twenty-one, or 4 percent, stated that it had been "mostly frustrating, annoying, or confusing." Three and one-half percent said that it had been neutral in its impact. Nineteen percent checked that it had been "more helpful than unhelpful," indicating some degree of ambivalence. But 30 percent saw it as "constructive in its results," and 45 percent checked it as a "deeply meaningful, positive experience." [5] Thus for three-fourths of the group, it was *very* helpful. These figures should help to set the problem in perspective. It is obviously a very serious matter if an intensive group experience is psychologically damaging to *anyone*. It seems clear, however, that such damage occurs only rarely, if we are to judge by the reaction of the participants.

OTHER HAZARDS OF THE GROUP EXPERIENCE

There is another risk or deficiency in the basic encounter group. Until very recent years it has been unusual for a workshop to include both husband and wife. This can be a real problem if significant change has taken place in one spouse during or as a result of the workshop experience. One individual felt this risk clearly after attending a workshop. He said, "I think there is a great danger to a marriage when one spouse attends a group. It is too hard for the other spouse to compete with the group individually and collectively." One of the frequent aftereffects of the intensive group experience is that it brings out into the open for discussion marital tensions which have been kept under cover.

Another risk which has sometimes been a cause of real concern in mixed intensive workshops is that very positive, warm, and loving feelings can develop between members of the encounter group, as has been evident from some of the preceding examples. Inevitably some of these feelings have a sexual component, and this can be a matter of great concern to the participants and a profound threat to their spouses if these feelings are not worked through satisfactorily in the workshop. Also the close and loving feelings which

[5] These figures add up to more than 100 percent since quite a number of the respondents checked more than one answer.

develop may become a source of threat and marital difficulty when a wife, for example, has not been present, but projects many fears about the loss of her spouse—whether well founded or not—onto the workshop experience.

A man who had been in a mixed group of men and women executives wrote to me a year later and mentioned the strain in his marriage which resulted from his association with Marge, a member of his basic encounter group:

There was a problem about Marge. There had occurred a very warm feeling on my part for Marge, and great compassion, for I felt she was *very* lonely. I believe the warmth was sincerely reciprocal. At any rate she wrote me a long affectionate letter, which I let my wife read. I was *proud* that Marge could feel that way about *me*. [Because he had felt very worthless.] But my wife was alarmed, because she read a love affair into the words—at least a *potential* threat. I stopped writing to Marge, because I felt rather clandestine after that.

My wife has since participated in an "encounter group" herself, and she now understands. I have resumed writing to Marge.

Obviously, not all such episodes would have such a harmonious ending.

It is of interest in this connection that there has been increasing experimentation in recent years with "couples workshops" and with workshops for industrial executives and their spouses.

Still another negative potential growing out of these groups has become evident in recent years. Some individuals who have participated in previous encounter groups may exert a stultifying influence on new workshops which they attend. They sometimes exhibit what I think of as the "old pro" phenomenon. They feel they have learned the "rules of the game," and they subtly or openly try to impose these rules on newcomers. Thus, instead of promoting true expressiveness and spontaneity, they endeavor to substitute new rules for old to make members feel guilty if they are not expressing feelings, are reluctant to voice criticism or hostility, are talking about situations outside the group relationship, or are fearful of revealing themselves. These old pros seem to be attempting to substitute a new tyranny in interpersonal relationships in the place of older, conventional restrictions. To me this is a perversion of the true group process. We need to ask ourselves how this travesty on spontaneity comes about.

Implications

I have tried to describe both the positive and the negative aspects of this burgeoning new cultural development. I would like now to touch on its implications for our society.

In the first place, it is a highly potent experience and hence clearly deserving of scientific study. As a phenomenon it has been both praised and criticized, but few people who have participated would doubt that *something* significant happens in these groups. People do not react in a neutral fashion toward the intensive group experience. They regard it as either strikingly worthwhile or deeply questionable. All would agree, however, that it is *potent*. This fact makes it of particular interest to the behavioral sciences since science is usually advanced by studying potent and dynamic phenomena. This is one of the reasons why I personally am devoting more and more of my time to this whole enterprise. I feel that we can learn much about the ways in which constructive personality change comes about as we study this group process more deeply.

In a different dimension, the intensive group experience appears to be one cultural attempt to meet the isolation of contemporary life. The person who has experienced an I–Thou relationship, who has entered into the basic encounter, is no longer an isolated individual. One workshop member stated this in a deeply expressive way:

Workshops seem to be at least a partial answer to the loneliness of modern man and his search for new meanings for his life. In short, workshops seem very quickly to allow the individual to become that person he wants to be. The first few steps are taken there, in uncertainty, in fear, and in anxiety. We may or may not continue the journey. It is a gutsy way to live. You trade many, many loose ends for one big knot in the middle of your stomach. It sure as hell isn't easy, but it is a *life* at least—not a hollow imitation of life. It has fear as well as hope, sorrow as well as joy, but I daily offer it to more people in the hope that they will join me. . . . Out from a no-man's land of *fog* into the more violent atmosphere of extremes of thunder, hail, rain, and sunshine. It is worth the trip.

Another implication which is partially expressed in the foregoing statement is that it is an avenue to fulfillment. In a day when more income, a larger car, and a better washing machine seem scarcely to be satisfying the deepest needs of man, individuals are turning to the psychological world, groping for a greater degree of authenticity and fulfillment. One workshop member expressed this extremely vividly:

[It] has revealed a completely new dimension of life and has opened an infinite number of possibilities for me in my relationship to myself and to everyone dear to me. I feel truly alive and so grateful and joyful and hopeful and healthy and giddy and sparkly. I feel as though my eyes and ears and heart and guts have been opened to see and hear and love and feel more deeply, more widely, more intensely—this glorious, mixed-up, fabulous existence of ours. My whole body and each of its systems seems freer and healthier. I want to feel hot and cold, tired and rested, soft and hard, energetic and lazy. With persons everywhere, but especially my family, I have found a new freedom to explore and communicate. I know the change in me automatically brings a change in them. A whole new exciting relationship has started for me with my husband and with each of my children—a freedom to speak and to hear them speak.

Though one may wish to discount the enthusiasm of this statement, it describes an enrichment of life for which many are seeking.

Rehumanizing Human Relationships

This whole development seems to have special significance in a culture which appears to be bent upon dehumanizing the individual and dehumanizing our human relationships. Here is an important force in the opposite direction, working toward making relationships more meaningful and more personal, in the family, in education, in government, in administrative agencies, in industry.

An intensive group experience has an even more general philosophical implication. It is one expression of the existential point of view which is making itself so pervasively evident in art and literature and modern life. The implicit goal of the group process seems to be to live life fully in the here and now of the relationship. The parallel with an existential point of view is clear cut. I believe this has been amply evident in the illustrative material.

There is one final issue which is raised by this whole phenomenon: What is our view of the optimal person? What is the goal of personality development? Different ages and different cultures have given different answers to this question. It seems evident from our review of the group process that in a climate of freedom, group members move toward becoming more spontaneous, flexible, closely related to their feelings, open to their experience, and closer and more expressively intimate in their interpersonal relationships. If we value this type of person and this type of behavior, then clearly the group process is a valuable process. If, on the other hand, we place a value on the individual who is effective in suppressing his feelings, who operates from a firm set of principles, who does not trust his own reactions and experience but relies on authority, and who remains aloof in his interpersonal relationships, then we would regard the group process, as I have tried to describe it, as a dangerous force. Clearly there is room for a difference of opinion on this value question, and not everyone in our culture would give the same answer.

Conclusion

I have tried to give a naturalistic, observational picture of one of the most significant modern social inventions, the so-called intensive group experience, or basic encounter group. I have tried to indicate some of the common elements of the process which occur in the climate of freedom that is present in such a group. I have pointed out some of the risks and shortcomings of the group experience. I have tried to indicate some of the reasons why it deserves serious consideration, not only from a personal point of view, but also from a scientific and philosophical point of view. I also hope I have made it clear that this is an area in which an enormous amount of deeply perceptive study and research is needed.

REFERENCES

Bennis, W. G., Benne, K. D., & Chin, R. (Eds.) *The planning of change.* New York. Holt, Rinehart & Winston, 1961.

Bennis, W. G., Schein, E. H., Berlew, D. E., & Steele, F. I. (Eds.) *Interpersonal dynamics.* Homewood, Ill.: Dorsey, 1964.

Bradford, L., Gibb, J. R., & Benne, K. D. (Eds.) *T-group theory and laboratory method.* New York: Wiley, 1964.

Casriel, D. *So fair a house.* Englewood Cliffs, N.J.: Prentice-Hall, 1963.

Gibb, J. R. Climate for trust formation. In L. Bradford, J. R. Gibb, & K. D. Benne (Eds.), *T-group theory and laboratory method.* New York: Wiley, 1964.

Gordon, T. *Group-centered leadership.* Boston: Houghton Mifflin, 1955.

Hall, G. F. A participant's experience in a basic encounter group. (Mimeographed) Western Behavioral Sciences Institute, 1965.

17 / AN EXPERIENTIAL APPROACH TO GROUP THERAPY

Eugene T. Gendlin and John Beebe III

The emphasis in this paper is set forth in a series of eleven propositions or *Ground Rules for Group Sessions,* written so that each participant in a group can take a copy home, study it, bring it back, discuss it, and tentatively operate by it. (There is insufficient experience with these rules and group members should be so informed.)

The ground rules cut across the usual orientations in psychotherapy and group methods: they fit both therapeutic and task groups, and they fit various settings: for example, clinic, church, industry, and school. How can one set of rules cut across all these differences and still characterize anything? The answer lies in the theory of experiencing (Gendlin, 1962; 1964): that is to say, in being concerned with the concrete experiential process rather than the different words people use, or the different social roles which different settings involve. The crux of the current group movement is not words and roles, but the experiential process.

The scope of spontaneity has greatly widened in modern society. Almost every situation today requires large portions of spontaneous, direct, unplanned, individually devised behaviors. Some generations ago, prescribed routines were required. Some now view the lack of prescribed routines as a breakdown in social forms and, indeed, the strain on the individual is very great. If there is going to be continuing multiplication of forms and conflicting values (i.e., a breakdown in prescriptions and ever widening scope for spontaneity), then either humans will become very much more proficient at the

From JOURNAL OF RESEARCH AND DEVELOPMENT IN EDUCATION (*Athens, Georgia*), *1968, Vol. 1, pp. 19–29. Copyright 1968, University of Georgia. Reprinted with permission of authors and publisher.*

process of spontaneously revising and devising forms or the percentage of people and portions of each life "not making it" will greatly increase. At present, both trends are discernible. The group trend is the former.

A powerful group process is being discovered and used under different names in different settings. Some of its names are sensitivity group, T-group, brain-storming, creativity group, encounter group, development group, group psychotherapy, marathon group. Some of its settings are schools, churches, industry, campus politics, hospitals, consulting offices, private homes.

The different approaches and settings involve the same experiential process. Of course, people speak differently in a religious group dedicated to more open communication about personal and religious conflicts than they do in a middle management development group devoted to more perceptiveness of others and one's own feelings toward them. But both groups involve expressing and pursuing creative ideas even when at first these may not seem correct, and in both cases individuals are breaking out from routine role behavior. In both instances, direct and spontaneous expression is valued, taught, and made safe. In both cases, individuals discover their own good sense, capacities for originality, sensitivity, interesting reactions, deserving of the respect of others, and so on. In both cases, individuals break through to (and then gain steady control of) a more spontaneous, live, real, experiential manner of process. They still speak the same English words and live in the same American patterns; the content of what is said and done is not always startlingly different, but the manner of process is an interplay between concrete experiencing on the one hand, and roles or words on the other—rather than mere empty roles with minimal deadened, or silent, private, removed experiencing.

Neither group is the same as a psychotherapy group. But these differences in words and roles must not obscure the fact that in each instance, the individuals are seeking one and the same process, variously called "seeking to overcome alienation," "seeking to be more alive in roles and words," and (to make the roles and words stretch to permit this) "seeking to be more open, more in touch with what they live and feel," "more expressive," "more spontaneous," "more real and genuine," "more honest with themselves and others," and "more in the world rather than silent, dumb, isolated, and frozen in mere empty role-playing." Note that each of these phrases refers to the same concrete process occurring in an individual, even though these phrases stem from different fields and verbal contexts and are at home in quite different social settings. The manner of verbal and institutional behavior is changing from alienation to experientially interactive.

Thus, the following analysis of experiential groups, cuts across social settings (i.e., industry, churches, schools, hospitals) and theoretical vocabularies (i.e., group dynamics, psychoanalysis, client-centered therapy, existentialism, sociology).

Experiential Groups

PHASES

One way to characterize the concrete process common to all these settings is by the following phasic descriptions:

Breakthrough phase. This phase lasts from six weeks to six months and consists of an explosive freeing and growth process in the individual. (The individual describes it as one of the most important occurrences in his life, or in many, many years.)

Sustaining phase. If new members come to the group, the old members in the "sustaining phase" consider it valuable to help the new members. For themselves, the older members no longer need the breakthrough experience, but they can help others have it. Although they are convinced of the great value of the group process, these old members get increasingly tired with the repeated arrival and breaking through of new members, since their group is now doing little that is directly meaningful for them. On the one hand, the sustaining phase is both rewarding and needed for new members. On the other hand, a *continuing* life-sustaining group fails to occur in many cases. We think that this failure happens when *different* times and places are not provided for the excitement of inducting new members, and for sustaining feelings of depth when old members meet alone. When this separation is not successful, the sustaining phase (which should continue indefinitely) gives way to the tired phase.

Tired phase. If new members constantly come into a group, and there is not also a quiet continuing group of old members, the old members cannot indefinitely sustain the group. Eventually, the old members get tired of trying to make the breaking through have meaning long after they are done with that phase.

EXPERIENTIAL EXPRESSIVENESS

These three phases (breakthrough, sustaining, tired) can be observed in all types of groups, for example, in the student political groups. The first phase for a new student in the political group is explosive. He discovers he can speak well, have new ideas, influence others, relate meaningfully, reason for himself, help and appreciate others. This is not his usual role-playing way in most of his classes, but a new spontaneous way that is natural, experientially expressive and, it turns out, quite safe—really safer than the routine social controls embodied in his more habitual behavior. Naturally, all this is very exciting. And if the political group is seeking to bring to the society as a whole the same sort of change (participative democracy), then concrete experiences and political programs support each other. And, indeed, politics has developed considerably from the days when the political program was everything and the mode of organizing individuals did not matter at all so that idealistic freedom-oriented programs were agitated for by rigid people in authoritarian groups. In today's left politics, proponents of the Ghandi insight look upon their movement as a miniature of the sort of society they seek to create.

Why the political example in the middle of a psychological article? The shift from words and roles to an experiential manner is itself a shift in current political thinking. But a shift in religious thinking is also brought about by the same experiential trend and the same group process now considered in that setting: it asserts "renewal," the breaking out of the words and routines that have become empty. So also in education where, for example, "the new math" teaches by making sense and not by rote, or in the psychotherapy area where discussion no longer rages so much as to the supposedly basic contents (the patient must talk about sex, self concepts, power drive, life style, separation anxiety), nor so much anymore about the supposedly right therapist role (transference engendering, neutral reflecting). Client's words and therapist's roles have given way to the more basic question of the experiential expressiveness, working through, and real, open interaction of two persons.

These are not separate and unrelated developments in separate and unrelated fields. The same manner of experiential process is being developed in all of them, and it is making one basic change in the manner of living—a change which, if it becomes dominant, can be expected to change thought and action in all these areas from mere roles into an interplay, a zig-zag from role to spontaneous person and back to revised role.

But how can there be a back-and-forth, an interplay between words and roles, and some concretely felt process called experiencing? One seems external and precise, the other neither. To understand this group process one must know that the individual is not an entity, not only a thing inside a box or inside his skin, but the individual is an experiential interplay with the environment. "An experience" is not some thing located in the eye, the mind, or the gut, but an experiencing of something outside, the situation in. It is not really true that we feel our feelings—that repeats the word "feel" as both a verb and then a noun that is the object of the verb. Really we feel our situations. When I am scared I do not fear my fear, but rather I have a fear *of* the thing coming at me. The very nature of a human personality *is* to be this interplay process and not a thing inside. Once we know that, we can grasp how what a person is will be different in different situations, in different relations to others, and hence in a group. To be alive differently is already to have been changed. One does not first have insights and then apply them to oneself. Rather, one could not have that insight the way one was alive before (*that* way of being made *that* insight impossible to have, to feel, to see, to be) for we cannot "grasp" and say "Oh!" or "A-ha!," except physically, bodily, with a breath and a directly felt sense of "making sense." The way one is alive must, therefore, change first before one can have the insight one lacked before (Gendlin, 1964).

Some Safeguards Concerning the Ground Rules

CLOSENESS

Note in the ground rules that contact or closeness is not at all the same thing as revealing intimate facts. The latter is content; we are concerned with process: i.e., a certain manner of process.

Closeness comes before unmasking. Contact or closeness is the sort of experiential sense you have when another person is looking right into your eyes and you into his; it is an unavoidable concrete sense of knowing yourself as seen by another person and has nothing to do with whether or not you know anything *about* him.

The example of looking into another person's eyes and being seen by him is *only* an example. The point is that closeness is independent of what one knows about someone.

Sometimes we take off our masks and thereby become close. But, more often, we feel like taking off our masks with those with whom we already feel close.

It is never necessary or possible to take off another person's mask against his will, and it can never make for closeness to try to do so.

The rule, *closeness comes before unmasking,* phrases for us the learning that it is useless and harmful to claw at another person, insultingly insisting that he is "not being real," "not opening up" as groups unfortunately sometimes try to do. Many of these desires to hear from the other person are highly artificial, throwing the difficulty of the process onto the other person. Sharing oneself becomes a forced parlor game in which facts are shared and inward loneliness is not at all relieved. But, while "opening up" is made into something artificial, the attacks on some members are perfectly real attacks. People claw at some person's supposed "mask," but that is really his face, at least for the moment.

LEADER SUPPORT

The leader supports against too much attack. Whatever the members and leader may think of one member being attacked, someone in the group must support the member who is being attacked. This is best done by quickly inserting time in which the attacked member is asked and helped to state his view, feelings, good sense, intention, honesty, and so forth. Every person makes some sense and, whether one agrees with him or not, one can see his point if one wishes. A member can tolerate being attacked by nearly everyone in the group, if his own good sense also emerges and is recognized by at least someone in the group. It is the leader's obligation to do this.

Anyone can be the leader; he might be elected, his role might be rotated, he might be picked out on some other basis. What counts is that there be someone recognized as the responsible person to make room for a member not then being heard rightfully, that is to say, in the name of the group as a whole.

The ground rules are written to apply to any situation and therefore we also included (under number 8) the situation where the leader really does command more attention (because he is really the teacher, or the doctor). But the leader could be simply any member who, for the time being, has been given the role; and who thus, for that period of time, makes it his first order of business to watch carefully each person in the room and to notice when someone is not being heard, or might want to speak, or is being misunderstood or out-argued. As leader, he is also a member; nevertheless, he may be very busy just paying that sort of responsible attention.

People Before Purpose

People first—and that expedites purposes. A group may have this or that purpose, but when other things are in the way, then those other things must be dealt with or the purpose cannot be served. Thus, putting the individual first permits the same rules for all sorts of groups.

If the group is a therapy group, but a participant is all involved in some event that happened to him, he must first be allowed to talk —thus is he welcomed by the group. Then he can turn with the others to the therapeutic task.

Conversely, if it is a task group, but two participants fight and undercut each other, the task will not be done effectively until their problem is resolved. Or, if a member cannot do well because of some private painful problem, the task will be done better if the group sustains that member when he needs it.

If the purpose is ideological, much more communication and effective arguing will occur if contact and caring for each other come first. The usual discussions never convince, whereas personal closeness makes for being able to see and sometimes adopt the other's outlook.

Quite often it may seem that all this personal self-expression is inappropriate or distracting in a group devoted to completing some task. If the group wants to complete a task and nothing stands in the way, then they will constitute a simple task group. Yet, when or if something is obstructing, the assumption that it will be considered, that anyone's expression of it will be welcomed, is a powerful aid in getting the task itself completed.

Why force a group, by rules, to be only one thing or the other when so evidently any group has times for both? As an example, when a psychotherapy group is devoted only to a therapeutic purpose, the very insistence that everything must be deep and meaningful makes it all somewhat artificial, ruling out the quiet times and the times of sharing seemingly irrelevant things, the things that matter "only" because they matter to someone there.

Consider, as another example, a group of therapist trainees that tries to decide once and for all whether or not their group will be a "process group" or a "case conference group." These seem like two different things. In one they talk about themselves; in the other they talk about their therapy cases. But why would they want to talk about therapy cases? They do so only to learn, to work through difficulties they feel as therapists.

It is necessary, therefore, to have a climate of free expression, openness, and willingness both to express and to listen. If we have trouble with each other, we do not have such a climate; therefore what is the use of playing tapes and using discussions of cases as mere gambits in bad moves between us? On the other hand, once these things are worked through, and as long as no new ones exist, *must* we manufacture issues between us just so we can say we have a "process" group?

Of course, there are often official purposes—for example, the above group may actually be a case conference group, or a therapy group. Other things being equal, we return to our official business, but with the understanding that we must do all these different things as needed.

Ground Rules for Group Sessions

The following series of ground rules for group sessions are promulgated as an informal kind of "constitution" which members of the group can amend, add to or delete from. Each participant in a group is given a copy to take home, study, and bring back. The experiential process starts then.

(One might phrase some of these things differently, and one might find different helpful rules.)

1. *Everyone who is here belongs here just because he is here, and for no other reason.* (This is our top rule. It depends on nothing else. Nothing changes it.)

If everyone in the group is angry at one person, that does not change his belonging in it. If he gives up on himself, the group does not give up on him. If he is unfair to everyone, the group says so and tries to help him with whatever troubles him. If he has something hopeless, the group keeps company with him and it.

(Since this is so basic, it is fitting for anyone to remind us of it, if we seem to act or feel as though it were not so.) The group leader should do the reminding, but sometimes the group may have to re-

mind him. Any person whose belonging is somehow being questioned can and should remind us, but this may be hard for him
just when he is made to feel shaky. (It is easiest for someone who
at the moment is not part of the argument, but it is equally fitting
for anyone to do this reminding.)

2. *For each person what is true is determined by what is in him,
what he directly feels and finds making sense in himself, and the
way he lives inside himself.*

Everyone does a lot of living inside himself. No one knows more
about how a person really is than the person himself. For instance,
when someone says, "I feel pain," no one can say, "You're wrong!"
When someone says, "I like this," no one can say, "No you don't!"
On the other hand, anyone can say (and we will say), "Can you tell
us more? Is that *all* you feel? Don't you feel some other things, too?"

We try to help each person get to know even more clearly what
he feels and thinks. We do this by listening more closely to how he
feels and lives inside himself—and only he can tell us more of this.
We tell each other whatever we think might be useful. Whether or
not it actually turns out to be useful, only the person himself can
determine; he does this through determining if it makes any direct
sense to him in the feelings and meanings of his living inside. When
what we say seems useless to him, we ask him to say more of what
he does feel. Of course, not always will everyone state the truth of
what he feels. Sometimes he will not be able to (though we try to
help him say it). Sometimes he will not want to, and we respect that.
Our living inside cannot all be put into words, anyway. We can
only say a little about it, or from it.

3. *Our first purpose is to make contact with each other. Everything
else we might want or need comes second.*

We will often have other needs or purposes or jobs to get done.
They will get done better, faster, and more fully if we make contact
first. There may be someone in the group who values some aim or
purpose he has above everything else and above all of us. We will
try to make contact with him first. We will respect his purpose just
because it is *his*. Later, when we have contact, it will become possible for him to tell (and for us to feel) what this purpose means to
him. Then we can see (and say) what we feel about it. That will
mean a lot to us, *then*. It would only be empty arguing, *now*.
Contact comes first. Contact is something felt. It is like looking

someone in his eyes and knowing that he sees you. It is a direct feeling for the other person's living inside himself.

Contact occurs despite differences in upbringing, viewpoint, and even when two people cannot speak each other's language. Contact is a feeling for the other human being. Contact, feeling close, and caring occur not because of what someone is like, but for him, for who he is.

If one of us seems to be only pretending, lying, or very cautiously hiding behind a false front, we assume that this person still feels distant. We would like to know him. But we may first have to get across more of ourselves. We hope to make more contact with him and get to the point where we feel some caring for him, and he for us. By that time, he will be more direct with us. When we feel contact, it is because we sense the other person's living inside himself. This may occur without words, with few words, or with many words.

4. *We try to be as honest as possible and to express ourselves as we really are and really feel—just as much as we can.*

My own honest, real self-expression is the fastest way to make contact with others. Any self-expression is always welcome in this group. (In other places, what we feel does not "fit" being said. Here it always fits because making contact as the people we really are is our first aim.) Any expression of anyone's feelings or thoughts is equally welcome whether good or bad, smart or foolish, ugly or pretty, friendly or angry, strong or weak. It is welcome and fitting because he feels it and for no other reason. We try to express what is difficult, hard to say, what hurts or is puzzling, troubling, what we usually cannot say because it is not fitting to say.

If we feel something toward what is happening in the group, or if we see that another person has feelings about it (perhaps from looking at his face), we try to say it. The more difficult it is to say, the more we will all appreciate someone's saying it aloud. We try—and we try to help others—to speak and live here as the people we really are and feel inside.

5. *We listen for the person inside living and feeling.*

We always assume that any person speaking to us is really speaking from a living and feeling place inside. What he says is probably just the first thing, the opener for a lot more which he could say if we invite him to. We tell him what we sense about the way he is living inside at a given moment. When he tells us more, we will have a clearer idea. What he says may not make sense to us at first, but we ask to hear more about it. We know it makes sense to him, and we hope to see the sense it makes. If he says it not at all clearly, we guess at it; perhaps that helps him find better words for it.

We force no one to be more honest than he wants to be at a given moment. If he tells us that he wants to say no more for the time being, we respect it. If we see someone being pressured to talk more, we may say to the group, "Maybe Joe doesn't *want* to say more about it." We let Joe then say if that is so. We try to sense this living and feeling part of each person, and to see what is there at a given instant in time. We know that what is there is always felt, and it is always much more than anything he says.

6. *We listen to everyone.*

Sometimes just from seeing someone's face change, we know he could say something—and might want to. If it seems he might want to, we invite him to do so.

The person who interrupts someone needs to be heard. What does he feel so strongly that made him interrupt? Did what was being said make him angry? Did it scare him? Did he think what Mr. A. was saying was all wet? Did he feel Mr. A. was hurting Mr. B.? But, if we stop to listen to the person now interrupting, and we find out what made him feel so strongly, who will remind us to go back to Mr. A., who was talking and did not get a chance to finish what he wanted to say? Anyone in the group can remind us, and invite Mr. A. to finish if he so desires.

And meanwhile, perhaps I notice Miss C. frowning. I wonder what she is frowning about. *I can say,* "I notice Miss C. frowning. I wonder what she is frowning about. Will you tell us, Miss C.?"

Perhaps one of us makes a comment. Right afterwards someone else makes another comment. We all discuss the second comment. No one paid any attention to the first one. Anyone in the group who remembers can bring us back to the first comment. "Miss D. said earlier that so and so . . . and nobody said anything about it. I didn't really understand why she said that." (Or we may state what we think about what she said.)

We do not bring the group back to every unfinished start, or every uninterpreted facial expression, but we do when we feel it might be important, or when we wonder about it. When we notice people who are usually quiet starting to say something, we make very sure they get heard. We want to be sure that we listen to everyone.

7. *The group leader is responsible for two things only: he protects the belonging of every member, and he protects their being heard if this is getting lost.*

The group leader makes it his special task to pay attention and notice when someone is not being heard, ignored, or attacked to the point where his belonging to the group needs reaffirming. It is the group leader's responsibility not to get his own feelings *so* involved that he can no longer notice these things. (Even so, sometimes he will get so involved that he will miss what is happening to certain members.) All of us do these two things, but we do not have to do them.

The group leader does not speak between *every* two members. He is not a switchboard or funnel through whom everything must go. The group leader does not tell us what to do. He may suggest it, but everyone else has the same right. We do not do anything just because the group leader suggests it. His only special rights are to affirm belonging and to let everyone be heard.

8. *Realism: If we know things are a certain way, we do not pretend they are not that way.*

By being in this group, we do not stop being whatever we are on the outside. Therefore, we do not pretend we are not what we are. If, in our group, there is a husband and wife, a father and daughter, two good friends, or an employee and his boss, we do not expect them to act as if they did not have the relationship they do have.

We do not pretend that the leader is not the leader, and *if* we try to do whatever he wishes, then we do not pretend that we are not trying to do what he wishes. (Of course, we do not have to do it, but if we feel we should, then we say so.) We probably pay more attention to what he seems to want than to what others want.

We do not pretend that we want to do something if we would rather not. For example, we do not pretend that we want to share feelings with each other if we would rather talk ideas or plans.

If there is research going on, or if there are observers present, we do not pretend there is no research or that the observers are not present. It is fair for anyone to know all he wants about any observers or research.

If some people in the group know each other very well, they do not act as if they did not. In fact, we hope they will talk with each other much as they would if we were not present. We hope they will talk intimately and with a feeling of closeness. Of course, this means they may not fill us in on some of the things they introduce. In this group, we do not think this is impolite. We are glad they are permitting us to be present while they are close with each other. (It lets us all feel closer to them than if they saved it until they were alone, and talked here as if they were strangers.)

With these ground rules, one's capacity for deep feelings toward others grows markedly. Since we expect and want this, we will not be surprised when it happens toward others in the group. Realism means that we will not violate the long-term relationships in which we live the major part of our lives, even though growth is slower there. A group member's marriage may currently be hostile, distant, or empty, but he must not damage it further by anything that he does in the group or in relationships engendered by the group. As his new capacities develop further, his marriage will also change and may become closer, although currently it may seem impossible, and another relationship may seem safe and intense. One must know in advance not to act in ways that will introduce long-term damages or obstacles into his marriage, unless he has really decided to leave it.

Similarly, we make realism include any other type of case in which outside consequences might temporarily be lost sight of without really being dealt with. For example, if two competitors for a promotion are in the group, they will be moving to a real closeness only by talking honestly about whatever realistic cautions they must exercise.

These examples illustrate that we try not to pretend anything we know is not so.

9. *What we say here is "confidential": no one will repeat anything said here outside the group, unless it concerns only himself. This applies not just to obviously private things, but to everything. After all, if the individual concerned wants others to know something, he can always tell them himself.*

But will all of us really keep everything confidential? We will have to get to know each other before we can be sure. Meanwhile we will not say anything which would greatly hurt us or hurt others if it were repeated by those here. (We need not tell private facts when we do not want to. We can just say, "There is *something* in my life which makes me feel so and so . . . ," or "Once *something* happened to me which scared me so much that I felt I didn't have any guts, and . . . ," or, "Once *something* happened which hurt me so badly that even now I still. . . ."

Honest expression is not so much a telling of private facts as it is a telling of what we feel and what we are as persons.

But, anything whatever—feelings, events, ideas, plans, troubles, hurts, joys, views—anything that means something to one of us here is welcome and worth telling just because it means something to one of us here. Whatever means the most to you is the most worth telling and welcome, whatever it is.

10. *Decisions made by the group need everyone taking part in some way.*

If a person is quiet throughout the time we make a decision, it means that what is happening is all right with him and he has nothing important to add. If what is decided is unpleasant for anyone, it is his right *and duty* to say so, even if it means backtracking for the rest of the group to hear arguments or opinions we thought we had already finished.

We try to find a way that everyone likes. At least in the beginning it is important to us all to hear what anyone does not like. He might bring in something we forgot that is important to us, also. And, he is part of the group; we cannot make a true group decision without him. We might then have to settle for something not all of us like, but at least something all of us can accept.

If we absolutely have to do so, we might have to agree to a way which some said they could not accept. But we will not be content until we know what they do not like, then we may be able to find a better way. To find such a way, they will have to tell us more and exactly what thing or part of it they cannot accept. Then we will avoid that specific thing and probably find a new way.

Sometimes the group is making a decision which concerns one person more than any other, because it is for him, or because it is his idea, or because he will have more to do with it than anyone else. In such a case, what he wants counts more than what any other group member wants (including the leader), and we remind ourselves of this if we forget.

We are here to be really ourselves, and so in all cases we let the group know when some decision or turn of events makes it hard or impossible for us to be really ourselves in the group. We never let ourselves be twisted into what we are not. We do not let the group become something which will not permit us to be ourselves. We do not put up with it and stew about it later, or never come back. We tell the group (and quickly).

But how do we decide the purpose of the group? The answer is that it is *for us*. This means that when we make decisions about what to discuss or to do, we are guided by what those of us here really feel, need, and care about. We try to help each member with what *he* cares about at the moment. He may want to discuss with us some situation, decision, task, personal feeling, or view of his. He may want to show or tell us something of his life just because it is his.

As a group, we may find that we all come to feel a given purpose. Then we arrange to act together to fulfill it. Therefore, we may sometimes look like a discussion group, an action group, a social group, a therapy group, a political group, a religious group, a task force, a class, or a group of friends—yet throughout we remain really the same kind of group because our purposes come from us and what we come to care about.

11. *New members become members because they walk in and remain. Whoever is here belongs.*

We look at a new person with a feeling of "I want to sense who you are"—perhaps we say something of the sort. We cannot tell new people what we do here, but we can give them the ground rules and we can show them what we do and engage them in it.

But if we constantly have new people, then some of us need to set a time when we can be together without new members, so that we can move in depth . . . not only experiencing the excitement of novelty and new humans. We let that be *another* time of the week, so that we can have *both* new people *and* depth with each other.

If a very large number of new people come, and keep returning so that they are then no longer "new," we may suggest that they too set a different time so that they also can move in depth as another group.

Summary

The essence of the paper is the inclusion of a set of ground rules for group sessions. Preceding the ground rules, certain safeguards in using them are set forth.

The paper includes a brief presentation of the theory of experiencing with special application to the small group. The phases (breakthrough, sustaining, and tired) which characterize the concrete process common to all experiential groups are described briefly, followed by a further explanation of the phases through the use of the paradigm of student political groups.

REFERENCES

Gendlin, E. T. *Experiencing and the creation of meaning.* New York: Free Press of Glencoe, 1962.

Gendlin, E. T. A theory of personality change. In P. Worchel and D. Byrne (Eds.), *Personality change.* New York, Wiley, 1964, 100–118.

18 / A DEVELOPMENTAL MODEL FOR COUNSELING GROUPS

Walter J. Foley and Warren C. Bonney

This paper has two objectives: (*a*) to examine behavior in a group setting in terms of a theoretical model of group development and change; (*b*) to present a method of analysis that delineates the developmental stages of small groups.

Subjects and Procedure

During the second semester of the 1962–63 academic year, students in the group guidance course at the University of Illinois were given an opportunity to participate in group counseling. Participation in the counseling groups was presented to the students as of value in itself as well as a pragmatic corollary to the didactic presentation of group theory and technique. The class was divided into three groups of six persons each. Since the three groups followed very similar developmental patterns, the discussion and analysis presented in this paper will be restricted to one of the groups.

The six members of the counseling group were students in the counselor training program. There were three males and three females. One of the students (male) was a doctoral candidate, while the other five members were master's degree candidates. The counselor was a second-year doctoral candidate and was supervised by a faculty member experienced in group work. In the context of the group, the counselor was attempting to accomplish two goals:

From PERSONNEL AND GUIDANCE JOURNAL, *1966, Vol. 44, pp. 576–580. Copyright 1966, American Personnel and Guidance Association. Reprinted with permission of authors and publisher.*

First, to create an atmosphere that would allow freedom of interaction among the group members and provide an opportunity for therapeutic gain; second, to present a teaching experience, defined as playback, to the group members. To accomplish this, each counseling session was tape-recorded. The playback was intended to be and was structured as that hour of the two-hour time period when significant portions of the tape of the preceding group session would be discussed in terms of group dynamics and counseling technique. This was to be done during each of the group meetings. In practice, two of the 11 playback periods were spent administering and analyzing the group-rating scale and a sociometric device discussed in this paper.

The Development of the Group

The development of the group will be discussed in terms of concepts derived from equilibrium theory (Zojouc, 1960) and the dynamic theory of George Bach (1954). The early meetings of the group follow a pattern best described as stages. The group members during the first stage, the *establishment stage,* reveal individual characteristics through verbal and nonverbal expression and receive feedback from other group members. By the end of this stage, usually one to four meetings, the role and status relationships at the top and bottom have polarized (Sherif & Sherif, 1956).

A counseling group, once through the establishment stage, enters into a *transition stage* that is climaxed by the members' acceptance that the goal of this group is unique. Early in this stage, they realize that the purpose for their existence as a group is to develop a situation that will allow for therapeutic experiences. This realization carries with it a negative connotation about discussing personal problems in groups based on past social experience. There ensues a period characterized by a lack of involvement on the part of the group members for fear of violating the perceived social norm inhibiting the discussion of personal problems in groups. The incongruency is eventually resolved through the acceptance of a new norm that demands the discussion of personal concerns. In an earlier paper by the junior author (Bonney, 1965), the transition period, Stage 2, in group counseling was described as an example of the operation of equilibrium theory.

The early socialization in therapy groups as described by Bach (1954) and here called the establishment stage was, for the most part, nonexistent in the counseling group under discussion. Students in the group began to talk of problem areas and attitudes without the expected socialization period. They also discussed freely the personal meaning of the group and of significant people in their lives. While this was deemed highly desirable, it was also surprising in view of the theoretical development of groups. Since the group described in this paper did not experience the establishment period as the first stage, the transition period did not occur in the usual manner. In this sense the group process and development did not follow the expected stages of development.

Theoretical Explanation

The first objective, that of providing an explanation for the non-occurrence of the expected sequential periods in the early phase of group formation, is presented in terms of group pressures and group standards toward conformity (Bonney & Foley, 1963). The concept of conformity in group counseling is dealt with at greater length in another paper (Bonney, 1965). It was concluded that group members understood and accepted the standard presented by the course instructor. Support for this conclusion was found in the pre-group self-rating scale in which "willingness to discuss personal concerns" was central to the group. There was also evidence based upon the members having experienced: (a) similarity of background in course work (the group guidance course occurs late in the counselor-training sequence), (b) the nature of the group (counselors in training), (c) the initial contact with the group counselor (administration of the pre-counseling rating scale). These data led to the conclusion that the group analysis that did not show an establishment stage was correct and also consistent with group development theory.

Counseling groups formed under more usual conditions (i.e., not as an adjunct to a course in a counselor-training program) are presented with essentially the same standard by the counselor, "discussion of personal concerns," as were the trainee groups discussed here. Nevertheless, these groups characteristically develop through the establishment and transition stages. The difference found appears to be that the perceived authority of a course instructor coupled with conditions (a) and (b) are not operant in the more usual counseling situation. Festinger and Aronson (1962) present a position on group norms and standards that supports the conclusions stated and was reflected by the data. The members were influenced by prior information relating the aspiration and goal of becoming a counselor with the performance and relationships in the group situation.

The effect of group pressure to conform to the norm of discussing personal matters in the group context (shown in the analysis that follows) is also consistent with the findings of Asch (1962), as the situation had little extrinsic structure in terms of the group members' past experiences and the counselor offered little in the way of structure for the group situation. The "majority effect" (following the behavior of other group members) described by Asch was seen to occur under these circumstances. The verbal reports of the participants in the group presented during the playback portion of the experience supported this inference. The students reported that they found themselves talking about personal concerns, even when their desire was not to exhibit this verbal behavior.

Analysis of the Recorded Interview

In keeping with the second objective of the paper, a method of analyzing group tape material on the basis of content is presented as the vehicle for delineating stages in the group. The method noted by Antenen (1963) may be most briefly described as a sequential content-affect classification and yields acceptable interjudge reliability. Agreement among pairs of four judges for topic ranged from 76 percent to 88 percent; for affect from 74 percent to 90 percent. The sequential aspect of the analysis will identify the developmental stages of the group and will help to illustrate more clearly the dynamics discussed earlier in this paper.

Source of the Data

The topics classified were "self," "group," "significant others," and "things and ideas." "Things and ideas" are relatively superficial discussions at an intellectual rather than an affect level. The discussions may represent sincere problem-oriented concerns or, more likely, a defensive avoidance of personal involvement. The topic "group" mostly involved the discussion of group goals, processes by which the goals may be accomplished, and the norms or rules necessary for the group to develop in the desired direction. Talk about "self" is the expression of personal feelings, attitudes, and concerns. Talk about "significant others" usually involves the client's relationship with the significant others and is often as personal as talk about self. "Self" and "significant others" are the topics that most counselors believe contain the potential for therapeutic gain (Rogers & Dymond, 1954).

A frequency count of the verbal output of each group member was obtained from the tape recording of each session, and an affect-topic rating of each of the verbalizations of the group members was made and defined as: positive affect (the subject expresses positive feeling when discussing a topic), negative affect (the subject expresses negative affect when discussing a topic), no affect (the subject does not show a classifiable affect when discussing a topic). This material was treated in two ways for the group as a unit: the total classification of topic discussed across sessions and the affect classification by topic across sessions. The matrices were then pooled to obtain the total classification parameters.

Treatment of the Data and Discussion of Results

The data on the group, in terms of total group parameters, consisted of the classification of verbalization for the four topics classified. A tabulation of these data is shown in Table 1.

TABLE 1
Verbal Output Tabulated by Significant Topic

Topic	Percent
Self	47.5
Group	29.3
Significant others	18.9
Things and ideas	4.2

The group members spent approximately 50 percent of their verbalization on "self." This was taken as a gross indication of the relevance of the topic for the group. The second largest percentage of the group's verbal output was concerned with the "group" itself. This was followed by "significant others" and the least frequent, in terms of percentage of total talk, was "things and ideas."

The other classification of the group data of interest was the analysis of topic, stated as a percentage of the total use of the topic, over the course of the sessions. Figure 1 shows the topic "self" as it was classified with reference to affect classification.

FIGURE 1

Classification of the Use of the Topic "Self" During 10 Group Sessions*

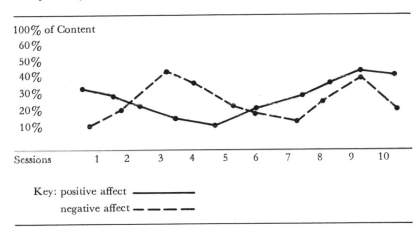

Key: positive affect ——————
     negative affect — — — —

* Bernoulli's theorem based on total probability distributions shows differences greater than ±8% significant at .05 level (Festinger & Aronson, 1962). The *n*'s in Figures 1 and 2 are the number of topics discussed.

FIGURE 2

Classification of the Use of the Topic "Self" Plus "Significant Others" Compared with the Use of the Topic "Group"

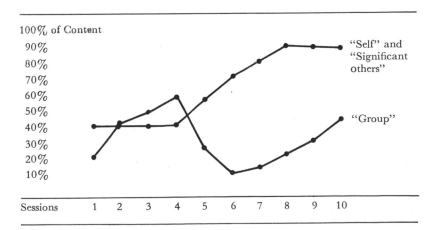

The figure describes graphically the tendency of the group members to describe themselves positively at the beginning of the sessions, negatively during the middle sessions, and positively toward the termination of the group meetings. The pattern of talk about "self" throughout the sessions was consistent with the findings of the analysis of individual client-centered therapy reported by Rogers and Dymond (1954).

An analysis of the affect classification showed that the topic "self" was discussed with positive affect 61 percent of the time, and negatively 30 percent of the time. The remaining 9 percent was classified as either no affect or as no describable affect.

An analysis across sessions of the relationship between topics clearly demonstrates the stage effect of a group's development. In Figure 2 the topics "self" and "significant others" are combined and compared with the topic "group." The percentages are total percentages without regard to sign, since the nature of the affect is not important for this purpose.

An inspection of Figure 2 reveals a median-level discussion of the topics "self" and "others" from Session 1 through 6, and a relatively high level of discussion of topic "group" from Session 2 through 5. This suggests that the topics "self" and "others" remained restricted and perhaps somewhat forced until the concerns about the group were resolved. The peak of "group" discussion at Session 3 represents a kind of transition period involving discussion of goals and procedures. But the high anxiety level that characterizes the transition stage following the usual establishment stage was not present. In a theoretical sense, the transition stage under the unique circumstances of the training situation involved group goals and norms, but was not typical of what has been presented as the transition stage in other writings.

Summary

This analysis method and theoretical discussion are presented to aid in the structuring of group guidance courses in terms of the evidence on group development and to assist the counselor in understanding the behavior that occurs in groups under these unique circumstances through a topic affect classification system. Also, it was felt that students who participated in groups would be better able to cope with the dynamics of the group situation. The outcomes of a process analysis of group development in a training setting were most parsimoniously explained in terms of the operation of group standards and group pressures toward conformity.

REFERENCES

Antenen, W. Changes in topic and affect during group counseling: Its relationship to outcomes of group counseling. Unpublished dissertation, University of Illinois, 1963.

Asch, S. E. Effects of group pressure upon the modification and distortion of judgments. In D. Cartwright and A. Zander (Eds.), *Group dynamics, research and theory*. Evanston, Ill.: Row, Peterson, 1962.

Bach, G. R. *Intensive group psychotherapy*. New York: Ronald Press, 1954.

Bonney, W. C. Pressures toward conformity in group counseling, *Personnel and Guidance Journal*, 1965, *43*, 970–973.

Bonney, W. C., & Foley, W. J. The transition stage in group counseling in terms of congruity theory. *Journal of Counseling Psychology*, 1963, *10*, 136–138.

Festinger, L., & Aronson, E. The arousal and reduction of dissonance in social contexts. In D. Cartwright and A. Zander (Eds.), *Group dynamics, research and theory*. Evanston, Ill.: Row, Peterson, 1962.

Hays, W. L. *Statistics for psychologists*. New York: Holt, Rinehart & Winston, 1963.

Rogers, C. R., & Dymond, R. F. (Eds.) *Psychotherapy and personality change*. Chicago: University of Chicago Press, 1954.

Sherif, M., & Sherif, C. W. *An outline of social psychology*. New York: Harper, 1956.

Zojouc, R. The concepts of balance, congruity, and dissonance. *Public Opinion Quarterly*, 1960, *24*, 280–296.

19 / DEVELOPMENTAL SEQUENCE IN SMALL GROUPS

Bruce W. Tuckman

The purpose of this article is to review the literature dealing with the developmental sequence in small groups, to evaluate this literature as a body, to extrapolate general concepts about group development, and to suggest fruitful areas for further research.

While small-group processes have been given great attention in recent years by behavioral scientists, the question of change in process over time has been relatively neglected. Perhaps the major reason for this is the overwhelming tendency of the small-group researcher to run groups for short periods of time and thus avoid the "problems" created by temporal change. Laboratory studies of developmental phenomena are quite rare. The majority of articles dealing with sequential group development come from the group-therapy setting and human relations training-group setting, neither of which features strict experimental control nor manipulation of independent variables. Moreover, the only major theoretical statements of group development which have appeared are those of Bales (1953), Schutz (1958), and Bach (1954).

In an attempt to bring the facts and the issues into sharper focus, existing research in the area of small-group development will be cited, and a framework within which this phenomenon can be better understood and further investigated will be presented. This framework will also serve to integrate the variety of studies cited in a meaningful way.

From PSYCHOLOGICAL BULLETIN, *1965, Vol. 63, pp. 384–399. Copyright 1965 by the American Psychological Association, and reproduced by permission.*

Classification Model

The classification approach adopted for distinguishing between and within developmental studies is a threefold one. The delineations are based on (a) the setting in which the group is found, (b) the realm into which the group behavior falls at any point in time, that is, task or interpersonal, and (c) the position of the group in a hypothetical developmental sequence (referred to as the stage of development). It is this last delineation that allows not only for the separation and ordering of observations within each setting, but for the development of additional hypotheses as well.

SETTING

Classification according to setting allows for the clustering of studies based on their similarity of features, for example, group size, group problem area, group composition, duration of "group life," etc. More similarity between observations made in the same setting than in different settings is expected.

In the *group-therapy setting* the task is to help individuals better deal with their personal problems. The goal is individual adjustment. Such groups contain from 5 to 15 members, each of whom has some debilitating personal problem, and a therapist, and the group exists for 3 months or more. The developmental data for such groups consist of the observations of the therapist and those professional observers that are present, usually as trainees. Such data are highly anecdotal in nature and reflect the clinical biases of the observers. Furthermore, such accounts are usually formulated after the fact and based on the observation of a single group. Since the bulk of the literature reviewed comes from this setting, its generality must be limited by the limitations of the setting and the mode of data collection.

In the *human relations training-group (T-group) setting*, the task is to help individuals interact with one another in a more productive, less defensive manner, and to be aware of the dynamics underlying such interaction. The goal is interpersonal sensitivity. Such groups contain ordinarily from 15 to 30 members, usually students or corporation executives, and one trainer or leader, and endure from about 3 weeks to 6 months.

The most striking differences between therapy- and training-group settings are in the areas of group composition, task, goal, and duration of group life. Such differences can account for different findings in the two settings. The most striking similarity is in the manner of data collection. Data in the training-group setting are highly anecdotal, subjective, collected by the trainer and his co-workers, and often based on the observations of a single group. Again, this serves to limit the generality of these findings.

The *natural-group setting* is distinguished on the basis that the group exists to perform some social or professional function over which the researcher has no control. Members are not brought together for self-improvement; rather, they come together to do a job. Such groups may be characterized either by appointed or emergent leadership. Presidential advisory councils and industrial groups represent examples of natural groups. Similar limitations to generalization based on the manner of data collection and number of groups observed applies in this setting as in the previous settings.

The *laboratory-task setting* features groups brought together for the purpose of studying group phenomena. Such groups are small (generally under 10 members), have a short life, and may or may not have leaders. In this setting, groups are given a task or tasks which they are to complete. Quantitative data are collected and analyzed based on multiple-group performances.

The last two settings have been combined due to the small number of studies in each (the dearth of group development studies in the industrial area is notable), and also because theoretical statements are reviewed which are generalized to cover both areas. All studies will be classified into one of the three setting categories according to best fit.

Realm: Interpersonal versus Task

Within the studies reviewed, an attempt will be made to distinguish between *interpersonal* stages of group development and *task* behaviors exhibited in the group. The contention is that any group, regardless of setting, must address itself to the successful completion of a task. At the same time, and often through the same behaviors, group members will be relating to one another interpersonally. The pattern of *interpersonal relationships* is referred to as *group structure* and is interpreted as the interpersonal configuration and interpersonal behaviors of the group at a point in time, that is, the way the members act and relate to one another as persons. The content of interaction as related to the task at hand is referred to as *task activity*. The proposed distinction between the group as a social entity and the group as a task entity is similar to the distinction between the task-oriented functions of groups and the social-emotional-integrative functions of groups, both of which occur as simultaneous aspects of group functioning (Bales, 1953; Coffey, 1952; Deutsch, 1949; Jennings, 1947).

In therapy groups and T groups, the task is a personal and interpersonal one in that the group exists to help the individuals deal with themselves and others. This makes the interpersonal-task distinction a fuzzy one. A further problem with this distinction occurs because the studies cited do not distinguish between the two realms and often talk about interpersonal development at one point in the sequence and task development at another point. The distinction will be maintained, however, because of the generic difference between the reaction to others as elements of the group task versus the reaction to others as social entities. Failing to separate stages by realm obscures the continuity of the developmental process. While the two realms differ in content, as will be seen, their underlying dynamics are similar.

Proposed Developmental Sequence

The following model is offered as a conceptualization of changes in group behavior, in both social and task realms, across all group settings, over time. It represents a set of hypotheses reflecting the author's biases (rather than those of the researchers) and the perception of trends in the studies reviewed which become considerably more apparent when these studies are viewed in the light of the model. The model of development stages presented below is not suggested for primary use as an organizational vehicle, although it serves that function here. Rather, it is a conceptual statement suggested by the data presented and subject to further test.

In the realm of group structure the first hypothesized stage of the model is labeled as *testing and dependence*. The term "testing" refers to an attempt by group members to discover what interpersonal behaviors are acceptable in the group, based on the reactions of the therapist or trainer (where one is present) and on the reactions of the other group members. Coincident to discovering the boundaries of the situation by testing, one relates to the therapist, trainer, some powerful group member, or existing norms and structures in a dependent way. One looks to this person, persons, or standards for guidance and support in this new and unstructured situation.

The first stage of task-activity development is labeled as *orientation to the task,* in which group members attempt to identify the task in terms of its relevant parameters and the manner in which the group experience will be used to accomplish the task. The group must decide upon the type of information they will need in dealing with the task and how this information is to be obtained. In orienting to the task, one is essentially defining it by discovering its "ground rules." Thus, orientation, in general, characterizes behavior in both interpersonal and task realms during this stage. It is to be emphasized that orientation is a general class of behavior which cuts across settings; the specifics of orientation, that is, what one must orient to and how, will be setting-specific.

The second phase in the development of group structure is labeled as *intragroup conflict.* Group members become hostile toward one another and toward a therapist or trainer as a means of expressing their individuality and resisting the formation of group structure. Interaction is uneven and "infighting" is common. The lack of unity is an outstanding feature of this phase. There are characteristic key issues that polarize the group and boil down to the conflict over progression into the "unknown" of interpersonal relations or regression to the security of earlier dependence.

Emotional response to task demands is identified as the second stage of task-activity development. Group members react emotionally to the task as a form of resistance to the demands of the task on the individual, that is, the discrepancy between the individual's personal orientation and that demanded by the task. This task stage will be most evident when the task has as its goal self-understanding and self-change, namely, the therapy- and training-group tasks, and will be considerably less visible in groups working on impersonal, intellectual tasks. In both task and interpersonal realms, emotionality in response to a discrepancy characterizes this stage. However, the source of the discrepancy is different in the different realms.

The third group structure phase is labeled as the *development of group cohesion.* Group members accept the group and accept the idiosyncracies of fellow members. The group becomes an entity by virtue of its acceptance by the members, their desire to maintain and perpetuate it, and the establishment of new group-generated norms to insure the group's existence. Harmony is of maximum importance, and task conflicts are avoided to insure harmony.

The third stage of task activity development is labeled as the *open exchange of relevant interpretation.* In the therapy- and training-group context, this takes the form of *discussing oneself and other group members,* since self and other personal characteristics are the basic task inputs. In the laboratory-task context, exchanged interpretations take the form of opinions. In all cases one sees information being acted on so that alternative interpretations of the information can be arrived at. The openness to other group members is characteristic in both realms during this stage.

The fourth and final developmental phase of group structure is labeled as *functional role-relatedness.* The group, which was established as an entity during the preceding phase, can now become a problem-solving instrument. It does this by directing itself to members as objects, since the subjective relationship between members has already been established. Members can now adopt and play roles that will enhance the task activities of the group, since they have learned to relate to one another as social entities in the preceding stage. Role structure is not an issue but an instrument which can now be directed at the task. The group becomes a "sounding board" off which the task is "played."

In task-activity development, the fourth and final stage is identified as the *emergence of solutions.* It is here that we observe constructive attempts at successful task completion. In the therapy- and training-group context, these solutions are more specifically *insight* into personal and interpersonal processes and constructive self-change, while in the laboratory-group context the solutions are more intellectual and impersonal. Here, as in the three preceding stages, there is an essential correspondence between group structural and task realms over time. In both realms the emphasis is on constructive action, and the realms come together so that energy previously invested in the structural realm can be devoted to the task.

The next section presents a review of relevant studies separated according to setting. The observations within each study are separated according to stage of development and realm.

Stages of Development in Therapy Groups

STAGE 1

Group Structure: Testing and Dependence. Of the 26 studies of development in therapy groups which were reviewed, 18 identified a beginning stage as either testing or dependence or both. Bach (1954) speaks of *initial situation testing* to determine the nature of the therapy environment and discover the kinds of relationships the therapist will promote, followed closely by *leader dependence* where group members relate to the therapist dependently. Barton (1953), Beukenkamp (1952), and Mann and Semrad (1948) identify an initial stage in which the group tests to determine the limits of tolerance of the therapist and the group.

Researchers emphasizing the more dependent aspects of this initial stage are Bion (1961), who describes groups operating with the basic assumption of *dependency*, Cholden (1953), who has observed dependency in therapy groups of blind individuals, and Stoute (1950), who observed dependency in larger classroom therapy groups.

Others have observed this stage and have used a variety of names to label it. Corsini (1957), in an integration of other studies, identifies *hesitant participation* as an initial stage, in which members test the group and therapist to discover how they will respond to various statements. Grotjahn (1950) refers to an initial period of orientation and information, while King (1959) labels initial testing and orienting behavior in activity-group therapy as *acclimatization*. Powdermaker and Frank (1948) and Abrahams (1949) describe the initial period as one of orientation and testing where group members attempt to relate to the therapist and to discover the structure and limits of the therapy group. Schindler (1958), using bifocal-group therapy, labels the initial stage as *attachment to the group,* in which individuals discharge old ties and establish new ones. Taylor (1950) talks about qualifying for acceptance by the group at the start of therapy which implies both testing and conforming.

Four of the studies reviewed describe a stage preceding the testing-dependence stage which will be referred to as Prestage 1. Thorpe and Smith (1953) and Osberg and Berliner (1956), in therapy with hospitalized narcotic addicts, describe an initial stage of resistance, silence, and hostility followed by a testing period where patients attempt to discover what behaviors the therapist deems acceptable. Shellow, Ward, and Rubenfeld (1958), who worked with institutionalized delinquents, described two such stages of resistance and hostility preceding the testing stage, while Martin and Hill (1957) theorized about a stage of isolation and "unshared behavior" preceding one of stereotypic responding to fellow group members and a dependent orientation toward the therapist.

Three of the four studies identifying a Prestage 1 were specifically based on observations of groups of antisocial individuals (drug addicts and delinquents) who probably must be won over to the situation and their initial extreme resistance overcome before the normal sequence of therapy-group development can begin. This would account for Prestage 1.

The remaining studies did not identify an initial stage of testing-dependence but dealt either with task development (to be discussed below), or offered as an initial Stage 1 which is postulated here as a second stage. Finally, a study by Parker (1958) described an initial stage of *cohesive organization* in which subgroups are formed, rules followed, and harmony maintained—a description which is difficult to fit into the testing-dependence category.

Task Activity: Orientation and Testing. During the initial stage, task development is characterized by indirect attempts to discover the nature and boundaries of the task, i.e., what is to be accomplished and how much cooperation is demanded, expressed specifically through (a) the discussion of irrelevant and partially relevant issues (Bion, 1961; Coffey, Freedman, Leary, & Ossorio, 1950; Martin & Hill, 1957; Osberg & Berliner, 1956), (b) the discussion of peripheral problems (Stoute, 1950), (c) the discussion of immediate behavior prbolems (Abrahams, 1949), (d) the discussion of symptoms (Bach, 1954; Taylor, 1950), (e) griping about the institutional environment (Mann & Semrad, 1948; Shellow et al., 1958; Thorpe & Smith, 1953), and (f) intellectualization (Clapham & Sclare, 1958; Wender, 1946).

This stage is also characterized by more direct attempts at orientation toward the task as illustrated (a) a search for the meaning of therapy (Cholden, 1953), (b) attempts to define the situation (Powdermaker & Frank, 1948), (c) attempts to establish a proper therapeutic relationship with the therapist through the development of rapport and confidence (Dreikurs, 1957; King, 1959; Wolf, 1949), (d) mutual exchange of information (Grotjahn, 1950), and (e) suspiciousness of and fearfulness toward the new situation which must be overcome (Corsini, 1957).

STAGE 2

Group Structure: Intragroup Conflict. Thirteen of the 26 studies of group therapy reviewed identified a stage of intragroup conflict (in 11 cases as a second stage and in 2 as a first stage). Abrahams (1949) identifies an interaction stage typified by defensiveness, competition, and jealousy. Bion (1961) discusses a *fight-flight* period in which members conflict with the therapist or attempt to psychologically withdraw from the situation. Grotjahn (1950) identifies a stage of increasing tension, while Parker (1958) talks about a *crisis period* where friction is increased, anxiety mounts, rules are broken, arguments ensue, and a general structural collapse occurs. Powdermaker and Frank (1948) discuss a second stage featuring sharp fluctuation of relationships, sharp reversals of feelings, and "intense but brief and brittle linkages." Schindler (1958) talks about a stage of psychodramatic acting-out and localization of conflicts in the group, while Shellow et al. (1958) describe a stage characterized by ambivalence toward the therapist which is expressed through the formation of conflicting factions in the group. Stoute (1950) describes a second stage beginning with derogation and negativity, while Thorpe and Smith (1953) describe a stage beginning with disintegration, distance, defenses out of awareness, and disrupted communication. King (1959), in activity-group therapy, describes a second stage of *benign regression* characterized by extreme acting-out and unacceptable behavior. Martin and Hill (1957) theorize about a stage of polarization featuring the emergence of subgroups following a stage of interpersonal exploration.

Coffey et al. (1950) identify an initial stage of defensiveness and resistance where members clash with one another. However, these authors also see "pecking orders" being established during this period; perhaps their initial stage includes Stages 1 and 2 as postulated in this review. Mann (1953) describes an initial phase of "working through of hostility" followed by a stage of "working through of anxieties." The hostility phase is characterized by disruption and fragmentation which are reduced gradually in the anxiety phase.

The remaining studies fail to identify this stage. Some of them jump from Stage 1 directly to Stage 3, while others deal with task development as concerns the first two stages of therapy-group development.

Task Activity: Emotional Response to Task Demands. The outstanding feature of this second task stage appears to be the expression of emotionality by the group members as a form of resisting the techniques of therapy which require that they "expose" themselves and of challenging the validity and usefulness of therapy (Bach, 1954; Barton, 1953; Cholden, 1953; Clapham & Sclare, 1958; Mann, 1953; Mann & Semrad, 1948; Martin & Hill, 1957; Stoute, 1950; Wender, 1946). Furthermore, mention is made of the fact that this is a period of extreme resistance to examination and disclosure (Abrahams, 1949; Barton, 1953), and an attempt at analysis of this resistance is made (Wolf, 1949). Others emphasize ambivalence toward the therapist (Shellow et al., 1958), the discussion of sensitive areas (Powdermaker & Frank, 1948), psychodrama (Schindler, 1958), and resistance via "putting one on" (Thorpe & Smith, 1953).

STAGE 3

Group Structure: Development of Group Cohesion. Twenty-two of the 26 studies reviewed identified a stage in which the group became a cohesive unit and developed a sense of being as a group. Bach (1954), Barton (1953), and Clapham and Sclare (1958) identify a stage during which ingroup consciousness is developed and establishment and maintenance of group boundaries is emphasized. Bion (1961) discusses the basic assumption of *pairing* in which the emphasis is on cohesion, but the unit is the pair as opposed to the whole group. Coffey et al. (1950), Corsini (1959), and Taylor (1950) describe a stage following the stage of intragroup hostility in which the group becomes unified and is characterized by the existence of a common goal and group spirit. Parker (1958) and Shellow et al. (1958) see the stage of crisis and factions being followed by one featuring consensual group action, cooperation, and mutual support. Mann and Semrad (1948), Grotjahn (1950), and Powdermaker and Frank (1948) describe a third stage characterized by group integration and mutuality. Noyes (1953) describes a middle stage of group integration, while Stoute (1950) and Thorpe and Smith (1953) see the stage of intragroup hostility grading into a period of unity, support, and freedom of communication. Martin and Hill (1957) theorize about a stage featuring awareness that the group is an organism preceding the final stage of development. Abrahams (1949) describes the development of "we-consciousness" in the third stage, while Mann (1953) sees the third stage as one of personal mutual exploration and analysis during which the group attains unity.

The notion that the group becomes a simulation of the family constellation (that is, through transference members react to one another as members of their family), with the unity and cohesion generally accepted in that structure, fits as a close parallel to the stage of development of group cohesion being postulated. Beukenkamp (1952) describes the middle stage of *reliving the process of the family constellation* where the group becomes a familylike structure, while King (1959) utilizes a similar description (that is, family unity in the group) for the final stage in activity-group therapy. Wender (1946) and Wolf (1949) both describe a stage preceding the final stage in which the group becomes the new family through the displacement of parent love.

Studies that fail to identify this stage are those that deal primarily with task development or those that integrate it as part of the final stage.

Task Activity: Discussing Oneself and Other Group Members. Many researchers observed probing and revealing by group members at a highly intimate level during this period and labeled it as (*a*) confiding (Clapham & Sclare, 1958; Coffey et al., 1950; Thorpe & Smith, 1953), (*b*) discussing personal problems in depth (Corsini, 1957; Mann & Semrad, 1948; Osberg & Berliner, 1956; Taylor, 1950), (*c*) exploring the dynamics at work within the individual (Dreikurs, 1957; Noyes, 1953), and (*d*) exploring the dynamics at work within the group (Bach, 1954; Martin & Hill, 1957; Powdermaker & Frank, 1948).

Beukenkamp (1952) observed that recalled material was related to the family; Abrahams (1949) observed the process of common ideation; and Shellow et al. (1958) and Wolf (1949) emphasized patients' discussion of topics related to transference to the therapist and to other group members which took place during this period.

STAGE 4

Group Structure: Functional Role-Relatedness. Only 12 of the therapy studies are at all explicit in their identification of this stage. Almost all of the therapists discuss the final stage of development of the therapy group in task terms as the therapeutic stage of understanding, analysis, and insight. The group is seen as serving a therapeutic function, but the nature of this therapeutic function is not spelled out. This is a stage of mutual task interaction with a minimum of emotional interference made possible by the fact that the group as a social entity has developed to the point where it can support rather than hinder task processes through the use of function-oriented roles.

Bach (1954) and Bion (1961) both refer to the group in its final stage as the *work group*. As such it serves a function supportive of therapy. Wender (1946) and Abrahams (1949) see the group as creating a therapeutic atmosphere in the final stage, while Wolf (1949), Stoute (1950), and Corsini (1951) describe this stage as one of *freedom and friendliness* supportive of insightful behavior and change. Both Coffey et al. (1950) and Dreikurs (1957) see the group as a therapeutic force producing encouragement and integrating problems with roles. Martin and Hill (1957) identify the group as an *integrative-creative-social instrument* in its final stage which facilitates problem solving, diagnosis, and decision making. Osberg and Berliner (1956) describe the self-starting stage where the group environment supports analysis, while Mann (1953) discusses a final stage of *personal mutual synthesis.*

Other therapy researchers failing to specifically delineate this final stage in social development have tended to lump the third and fourth stages together and not make the distinction between the development of cohesion and the "use" of cohesion (via functional roles) as a therapeutic force. Such descriptions were included in the section on the third stage. The small number of investigators identifying this final stage is most likely due to the high visibility of task functions occurring during this time period which obscure and minimize social processes occurring simultaneously.

Task Activity: Emergence of Insight. There seems to be overwhelming agreement among the observers of therapy-group development that the final stage of task development is characterized by attainment of the desired goal, insight into one's own problems, an understanding of the cause of one's abnormal behavior and, in many cases, modification of oneself in the desired direction (Beukenkamp, 1952; Bion, 1961; Clapham & Sclare, 1958; Coffey et al., 1950; Corsini, 1957; Dreikurs, 1957; King, 1959; Noyes, 1953; Schindler, 1958; Stoute, 1950; Thorpe & Smith, 1953; Wender, 1946; Wolf, 1949). Others (Abrahams, 1949; Bach, 1954; Barton, 1953; Cholden, 1953; Grotjahn, 1950; Shellow et al., 1958; Taylor, 1950) place more emphasis on the processes of attempting to develop insight and change during this last period as opposed to the development of such insight and change itself.

Two additional therapy-group studies are worthy of inclusion, both of which utilized a technique for collecting and analyzing data which was highly dissimilar to the approach used in the other therapy-group studies, namely, interaction-process analysis (Bales, 1950). Psathas (1960) found that groups phase from *orientation* to *evaluation* to *control,* based on an analysis of early, middle, and late sessions. Talland (1955) failed to observe this phase movement based on an analysis of the first eight sessions.

Stages of Development in Training Groups

Stage 1

Group Structure: Testing and Dependence. Nine of the 11 training-group studies reviewed that deal with the development of group structure identify an initial stage characterized at least in part by testing and dependence, with the emphasis on the dependent aspect of this stage.

Herbert and Trist (1953), Bennis and Shepard (1956), Bradford and Mallinson (1958), and Bradford (1964a) describe the initial group phase as one characterized by the strong expression of dependency needs by the members toward the trainer, and attempts at group structuring to work out authority problems by the quick acceptance of and dependence on such structure and arbitrary norms. Thelen and Dickerman (1949) discuss initial stage establishment of a leadership hierarchy catering to the dependency needs of the members. Hearn (1957) sees group members making an attempt to structure the unknown and to find their position in the group in the earliest group stage. Here again, structure reflects the expression of dependency needs.

Miles (1953) describes a first stage characterized by *establishment of the situation* through interpersonal exploration and testing, while Semrad and Arsenian (1961) identify an initial phase during which group members "test" the central figure and "test" the situation.

Whitman (1964) describes a beginning stage in which the chief "vectors" are dependency and hostility. It would appear that Whitman has identified a first stage which combines the first two stages proposed in this article.

The two studies that do not yield an exact fit to the proposed scheme are those of Barron and Krulee (1948) and the Tulane Studies in Social Welfare (1957) which identify an initial period characterized by the emergence of leadership and orientation, respectively. Insofar as these authors see the authority area as being of central concern and emphasize the orientation aspects of the first stage, there is overlap with the scheme proposed herein. Moreover, orientation as a first stage fits the hypothesized initial stage for task activities; perhaps the observation in the Tulane studies (1957) of a member orientation as an initial stage is better classified in the task-activity area.

Task Activity: Orientation. Bradford (1964b) identifies an initial stage of *learning how to learn* which is characterized by acceptance of the group's goal and orientation to the techniques to be used. Herbert and Trist (1953) label their initial stage as *discovery,* in which the members orient themselves to the consultant or trainer who serves an interpretive and educational role. Stock and Thelen (1958) discuss an initial stage characterized by little "work" and a variable amount of "emotionality," during which time the members are concerned with defining the directions the group will pursue.

As can be seen, initially interpersonal problems are dealt with via dependence, while task problems are met with task-orienting behavior (i.e., what is to be accomplished and how).

STAGE 2

Group Structure: Intragroup Conflict. Ten of the 11 studies identify intragroup conflict as a second stage, while the remaining study (Whitman, 1964) describes an initial stage encompassing both dependence and hostility, in that order.

Barron and Krulee (1948) and Bradford (1964a) discuss a second stage characterized by group cleavage and conflict. Both studies identify the emergence of polarities during this stage—members favoring a more active, less defensive approach versus those who are more passive and defensive and seek "safety" via structure. Thelen and Dickerman (1949), Hearn (1957), the Tulane studies (1957), and Bradford and Mallinson (1958), as well, identify a similar polarization and resultant conflict, frustration, and disruption during the second stage.

Herbert and Trist (1953) describe a second stage characterized in part by resistance, while Miles (1953) identifies anarchic rebellion during this stage of *anxiety, threat, and resistance.* Semrad and Arsenian (1961) identify rivalry for the position of central figure and emotional struggles in this period, while Bennis and Shepard (1956) see a similar power struggle in which counterdependents seek to usurp the leader, resulting in a conflict between counterdependents and dependents.

There appears to be general agreement that the dependency stage is followed by a stage of conflict between warring factions representing each side of the polarized issue: dependence versus independence, safe retreat into the familiar versus risky advance into the unfamiliar, defensiveness versus experimenting.

Task Activity: Emotional Response to Task Demands. Bradford (1964b) identifies a second stage in which individuals *learn how to give help* which requires that they remove blocks to learning about themselves, reduce anxiety, and express real reactions. Stock and Thelen (1958) see emotionality occurring in considerable excess of work during this period. The Tulane studies (1957) describe the second stage as one of experimental aggressiveness and hostility where individuals express themselves freely.

Thus, self-change and self-denial necessitated by the learning task is reacted to emotionally, as is the imposition of the group on the individual. Often the two (representative of the two realms) are difficult to separate.

STAGE 3

Group Structure: Development of Group Cohesion. All of the relevant T-group development studies see the stage of conflict and polarization as being followed by a stage characterized by the reduction of the conflict, resolution of the polarized issues, and establishment of group harmony in the place of disruption. It is a "patching-up" phase in which group norms and values emerge.

Hearn (1957), Miles (1953), and Thelen and Dickerman (1949) identify a third stage characterized by attempts to resolve conflict and the consequent development of group cohesion and mutual support. Semrad and Arsenian (1961) and the Tulane studies (1957) each describe two phases in their temporal sequences which would be included in Stage 3. In the case of the former, their first cohesion phase is characterized by group cohesion processes and their second by the development of affection bonds; in the latter, the first cohesion stage features the emergence of structure, roles, and "we-feeling," while the second features increased group identification on a conscious level and vacillation in role acceptance. Whitman (1964) talks about a middle phase, following conflict, described as the development of a new group culture via the generation of norms and values peculiar to the group as an entity. Bradford and Mallinson (1958) describe Stage 3 as one of reorganization, in which reforming and repair take place and a flexible organization emerges.

Bradford (1964a) describes a third stage in which the group norm of "openness" emerges, and a fourth stage in which the group generates additional norms to deal with self-revelation and feedback. Furthermore, Bradford (1964b) identifies a third stage as one of developing a group climate of permissiveness, emotional support, and cohesiveness in which learning can take place. This description would appear to subserve both interpersonal and task realms.

Bennis and Shepard (1956) describe a third stage in which resolution of authority problems occurs, and a fourth stage characterized by smooth relations and enchantment as regards the interpersonal sphere of group functioning. Finally, Barron and Krulee (1948) identify the third stage as increasing member responsibility and changing faculty role in which a definite sense of structure and goal orientation emerge in the group.

Task Activity: Discussing Oneself and Others. Herbert and Trist (1953) identify a second stage labeled as *execution,* in which the group settles down to the description of a single basic problem and learns to accept "the examination of what was going on inside of itself as a regular part of the task . . . ." Stock and Thelen (1958) describe a third task phase in which the group shows a new ability to express feelings constructively and creatively. While emotionality is still high, it now contributes to work.

While the social function of the third stage is to cause a unique and cohesive group structure to emerge, the task function is to attempt to use this new structure as a vehicle for discovering personal relations and emotions by communicating heretofore private feelings.

STAGE 4

Group Structure: Functional Role-Relatedness. There is some tendency for T-groupers, as there was for the therapy groupers, to emphasize the task aspects of the final stage, namely, the emergence of insight into the interpersonal process. In doing this, it is made implicit that the group as a social entity characterized by task-oriented role-relatedness makes the emergence of such insight possible by providing support and an opportunity for experimentation and discovery.

Bradford (1964a) sees the group becoming a work organization which provides member support, mutual acceptance, and has strong but flexible norms. Hearn (1957) discusses mutual acceptance and use of differences in the collaborative process during the fourth and fifth group stages, while Miles (1953) sees group structure as tending "to be functional and not loved for itself alone" as it was in the preceding stage. The support function is further emphasized by Miles when he says,

In groups where the interpersonal bonds are genuine and strong . . . members give one another a great deal of mutual evaluative support, which seems to be a prime requisite for successful behavior change. (p. 94)

Semrad and Arsenian (1961) describe a final phase of productive collaboration, while Thelen and Dickerman (1949) identify the group as an effective social instrument during this period. Barron and Krulee (1948) see, as one group function occurring during the final two meetings, the sharing and refining of feelings through the group process.

Bennis and Shepard (1956) see the stage of group cohesion being followed by another period of conflict, in which the issue is intimate social relations versus aloofness. The final stage is then one of consensual validation in which group interpersonal problems are solved and the group is freed to function as a problem-solving instrument.

The Tulane studies (1957) describe the stage following the emergence of cohesion as one in which behavior roles become dynamic, that is, behavior is changed as a function of the acceptance of group structure. An additional stage is also identified in this study in which structure is institutionalized by the group and thus becomes rigid. Perhaps this stage, not identified by other researchers, would most apply to groups with a long or indefinite group life.

The remaining T-group studies describe task development exclusively during the final group phase.

Task Activity: Insight. Bradford's (1964b) fourth stage is one in which members discover and utilize various methods of inquiry as ways of group development and individual growth, while, in his fifth and final stage, members learn how to internalize, generalize, and apply learnings to other situations. Herbert and Trist (1953) label their final stage as *evaluation*. Stock and Thelen (1958) describe the fourth and final stage as one characterized by a high degree of work in the absence of affect. The issues are dealt with in a less excited way.

The overall fit between stages of development postulated in this paper for application in all settings and those delineated by T groupers is highlighted in the fourfold scheme presented by Golembiewski (1962), based on his examination of some T-group development studies already reviewed in this paper. Golembiewski describes his stages as: (a) establishing the hierarchy; (b) conflict and frustration; (c) growth of group security and autonomy; (d) structuring in terms of problems facing the group rather than in terms of stereotypic role prescriptions.

Stages of Development in Natural and Laboratory Groups

Few studies or theoretical statements have concerned themselves with the developmental sequence in natural groups or laboratory groups.

STAGE 1

Group Structure: Testing and Dependence. Modlin and Faris (1956), studying an interdisciplinary professional group, identify an initial stage of *structuralization,* in which members are dependent upon roles developed outside of the group, well-established traditions, and a fixed hierarchy of responsibility.

Schroder and Harvey (1963) describe an initial stage of *absolutistic dependency,* featuring the emergence of a status hierarchy and rigid norms which reduce ambiguity and foster dependence and submission.

Theodorson (1953) observed a tendency initially for only one leader to emerge and for group members to categorize one another so that they could define the situation and reduce ambiguity.

Schutz (1958)[1] sees the group dealing initially with problems of *inclusion*—to join or not to join; to commit oneself or not. The group concern, thus, is boundary problems, and the behavior of members is individually centered. This description is somewhat suggestive of testing.

Task Activity Orientation. Bales and Strodtbeck (1951) and Bales (1953), using Bales' (1950) interaction-process categories, discovered that leaderless laboratory groups begin by placing major emphasis

---

[1] The classification of Schutz's theory as one primarily descriptive of natural and laboratory groups is arbitrary. Some would argue that Schutz is working in the T-group tradition.

on problems of *orientation* (as reflected in Bales' categories: "asks for orientation" and "gives orientation"). This orientation serves to define the boundaries of the task (i.e., what is to be done) and the approach that is to be used in dealing with the task (i.e., how it is to be accomplished).

Stage 2

Group Structure: Intragroup Hostility. Modlin and Faris (1956) describe *unrest* characterized by friction and disharmony as the second stage, while Schroder and Harvey (1963) identify a second stage of *negative independence* featuring rebellion, opposition, and conflict. In this stage the greater emphasis is on autonomy and individual rights. Theodorson (1953) observed more friction, disharmony, and animosity early in the group life than during later periods.

Schutz (1958) postulates a second stage in which the group deals with problems of *control*. This entails a leadership struggle in which individual members compete to establish their place in the hierarchy culminating in resolution.

In the task area, the stage of *emotional response to task demands* is not delineated, presumably due to the impersonal and non-threatening nature of the task in these settings. When the task does not deal with the self at a penetrating level, extreme emotionality in the task area is not expected.

Stage 3

Group Structure: Development of Group Cohesion. Modlin and Faris (1956) identify *change* as the third stage, characterized by the formation of the concept of the group as a functioning unit and the emergence of a team "dialect." Schroder and Harvey (1963) refer to Stage 3 as *conditional dependence,* featuring a group concern with integration and an emphasis on mutuality and the maintenance of interpersonal relationships.

Theodorson (1953) observed the following group tendencies over time (i.e., tending to occur later as opposed to earlier in group development): (*a*) discovering what is common to the members and developing a within-group "parochialism"; (*b*) the growth of an interlocking network of friendship; (*c*) role interdependence; (*d*) mutual involvement and identification between members with a concomitant increase in harmony and solidarity; and (*e*) the establishment of group norms for dealing with such areas as discipline.

Schutz (1958) postulated a third stage wherein problems of *affection* are dealt with. Characteristic of this stage are emotional integration, pairing, and the resolution of intimacy problems.

Task Activity: Expression of Opinions. Bales and Strodtbeck (1951) and Bales (1953) observed that the orientation phase was followed by a period in which major emphasis was placed on problems of *evaluation* (as reflected by categories: "asks for opinion" and "gives opinion"). "Evaluation" as a descriptor of the exchange of opinions appears to be comparable to the third task stage in therapy- and training-group development which was heretofore labeled as "discussing oneself and others." Because the therapy and training tasks are personal ones, task opinions must involve self and others. When the task is an impersonal one, the content of task opinions varies accordingly.

STAGE 4

Group Structure: Functional Role-Relatedness. Modlin and Faris (1956) identify integration as the fourth and final stage in which structure is internalized and the group philosophy becomes pragmatic, that is, the unified-group approach is applied to the task.

Schroder and Harvey (1963) postulate a final stage of *positive interdependence,* characterized by simultaneous autonomy and mutuality (i.e., the members can operate in any combination, or as a unit), and an emphasis on task achievement which is superordinate to social structure.

Theodorson (1953) sees the group as developing into a subculture over time, along with the development of member responsibility to the group.

Schutz (1958) does not identify a fourth stage; rather, he sees his three postulated stages in continually cycling over time.

Task Activity: Emergence of Solution. The third and final phase observed by Bales and Strodtbeck (1951) and Bales (1953) is one in which major emphasis is placed on problems of *control* (as reflected by categories: "asks for suggestion" and "gives suggestion"). The purpose of suggestions is to offer solutions to the task based on information gathered and evaluated in previous developmental periods. This then represents an analogue to final stages in therapy-

and training-group task development where the emergence of insight yields solutions to personal problems.

These authors do not identify a period of task development in laboratory groups comparable to the second task stage in therapy- and training-group development which features the expression of emotional material. Again, because therapy and training tasks are personal ones, this will be reflected in the content of discussion, specifically by the manifestation of resistance prior to dealing with the personal task at a level of confidence and honesty. This task stage does not appear to be quite relevant in laboratory discussion groups, and its existence has not been reported by Bales and Strodtbeck (1951) or Bales (1953).

Philp and Dunphy (1959) have further substantiated the findings of Bales and Strodtbeck (1951) and Bales (1953) by observing the same phase-movement pattern in groups working on a different type of discussion problem.[2] Furthermore, Philp and Dunphy (1959) present evidence which indicates that sex of the participants does not affect the pattern of phase movements.

Finally, Smith (1960) has observed that experimental groups show early concentration on matters not related to the task, and, only later in the development sequence, concentrate on task-relevant activities. Again, this finding suggests a strong similarity between task development in laboratory groups and in therapy and training groups, since, in the latter settings, constructive task-relevant activity appears only late in the developmental sequence.

Discussion

The literature that has been reviewed can be criticized on a number of grounds. First, it may be pointed out that this literature cannot be considered truly representative of small-group developmental processes, since certain settings have been overrepresented, primarily the therapy-group setting, and others underrepresented, primarily the natural-group and laboratory-group settings. This shortcoming cannot be rectified within the existing literature; rather, it must serve as a stimulus for further research in the latter group settings. Furthermore, the inequality of setting representation necessitates caution in generalizing from this literature. Generalization

[2] As mentioned earlier, Psathas (1960), working with therapy groups, observed the same phase movement, namely, orientation to evaluation to control. However, Talland (1955) failed to get this phase movement in therapy groups.

must, perforce, be limited to the fact that what has been presented is mainly research dealing with sequential development in therapy groups.

A second source of criticism concerns the extent of experimental rigor characteristic of the majority of studies cited in this review. Most of the studies carried out in the therapy-group, training-group, and natural-group settings are based on the observation of single groups. Furthermore, these observations are qualitative rather than quantitative, and as such are subject to the biases of the observer, ordinarily the therapist or trainer. This is not to suggest that the therapy-group setting is not appropriate for studying group processes, but that the study of such processes should be more subject to methodological considerations. A good instance of the application of such considerations is the study of Psathas (1960) conducted in the therapy-group setting. Psathas coded group protocols using Bales' (1950) scheme of interaction-process analysis. After satisfactory reliabilities were obtained, the data could be considered as highly quantitative and objective, and could then be subjected to statistical analysis. Approaches of equal rigor are recommended for other studies conducted in the therapy-group setting and other settings as well.

A final criticism concerns the description and control of independent variables. Since most of the studies in the therapy-, training-, and natural-group settings used a single group, the control and systematic manipulation of independent variables was impossible. In the absence of the manipulation of independent variables and the consequent discovery of their differential effects within studies, these effects can only be approximately discerned by comparing studies. However, many independent variables are likely to vary from study to study, for example, group composition, duration, etc., and little light will be shed on the effects of these variables on the developmental process. Therefore, no conclusions about the specific effects of independent variables on developmental phenomena will be drawn, and further work along these lines is encouraged.

In order to isolate those concepts common to the various studies reviewed (across settings), a developmental model was proposed. This model was aimed at serving a conceptual function as well as an integrative and organizational one. The model will be summarized here.

Groups initially concern themselves with orientation accomplished primarily through testing. Such testing serves to identify the boundaries of both interpersonal and task behaviors. Coincident with testing in the interpersonal realm is the establishment of dependency relationships with leaders, other group members, or preexisting standards. It may be said that orientation, testing, and dependence constitute the group process of *forming*.

The second point in the sequence is characterized by conflict and polarization around interpersonal issues, with concomitant emotional responding in the task sphere. These behaviors serve as resistance to group influence and task requirements and may be labeled as *storming*.

Resistance is overcome in the third stage in which ingroup feeling and cohesiveness develop, new standards evolve, and new roles are adopted. In the task realm, intimate, personal opinions are expressed. Thus, we have the stage of *norming*.

Finally, the group attains the fourth and final stage in which interpersonal structure becomes the tool of task activities. Roles become flexible and functional, and group energy is channeled into the task. Structural issues have been resolved, and structure can now become supportive of task performance. This stage can be labeled as *performing*.

Although the model was largely induced from the literature, it would seem to withstand the test of common sense as well as being consistent with developmental theory and findings in other areas. It is not unreasonable to expect "newness" of the group to be greeted by orienting behavior and resultant unsureness and insecurity overcome through dependence on an authority figure, as proposed in the model. Such orienting responses and dependence on authority are characteristic of the infant during the first year (Ilg & Ames, 1955), the young child when first apprehending rules (Piaget, 1932), and the patient when first entering psychotherapy (Rotter, 1954).

After the "newness" of the group has "worn off," the members react to both the imposition of the group and the task emotionally and negatively, and pose a threat to further development. This proposal is mirrored by the rebelliousness of the young child following his "obedient" stages (Ilg & Ames, 1955; Levy, 1955).

Such emotionality, if overcome, is followed by a sense of "pulling together" in the group and being more sensitive to one another. This sensitivity to others is mirrored in the development of the child (Ilg & Ames, 1955; Piaget, 1932) and represents an essential aspect of the socialization process (Mead, 1934).

Finally, the group becomes a functional instrument for dealing with the task. Interpersonal problems lie in the group's "past," and its present can be devoted to realistic appraisal of and attempt at solutions to the task at hand. This interdependence and "marriage to reality" is characteristic of the "mature" human being (Erikson, 1950; Fromm, 1941) and the "mature" 9-year-old child (Ilg & Ames, 1955).[3]

The suggested stages of group development are highly visible in the literature reviewed. The fit is not perfect, however. Some of the studies identify some but not all of the suggested stages. In some of these cases, two of the suggested stages have been welded into one by the observer. For instance, Barton (1953) describes three stages; the first and second fit the first two conceptual stages closely, while Barton's third stage is descriptive of the third and fourth conceptual stages insofar as it is characterized by both the emergence of cohesiveness and the working through of problems. In other cases, one or more of the hypothesized stages have been clearly missing, and thus not recognized in the group or groups being observed. For instance, Powdermaker and Frank (1948) identify three stages that fit the first three conceptual stages fairly closely, but they do not identify any fourth stage. Perhaps cases like this can be accounted for on the basis of independent variables such as duration of group life.

A few studies identify more than four stages. Some of these additional stages represent a greater degree of differentiation than that of the model and are of less generality (i.e., highly specific to the independent conditions of the study). For instance, therapy-group studies with delinquents and dope addicts identify a stage prior to conceptual Stage 1 in which the antisocial group members must be won over to the point where they will take the therapy seriously.

Some of the studies identify a stage that is clearly not in the model. Parker (1958) describes a first stage of cohesive organization. This divergence from the model may reflect a different way of describing much the same thing or may reflect an unusual set of independent conditions. Parker was observing a ward population of about 25, rather than a small weekly therapy group. It may be that the hypothesized first stage is somewhat inappropriate for larger, living-together groups.

While the suggested sequence appeared to hold up under widely varied conditions of group composition, duration of group life, and specific group task (i.e., the sequence held up across settings), it must be assumed that there is a finite range of conditions beyond which

[3] A more detailed model of individual development (similar to the group model proposed here), along with many citations of supporting literature, may be found in Harvey, Hunt, and Schroder (1961).

the sequence of development is altered, and that the studies reviewed did not exceed this assumed range to any great extent. Setting-specific differences and within-setting differences may affect temporal change as regards the specific content of the stages in the developmental sequence, the rate of progression through the sequence, or the order of the sequence itself. In the therapy-group setting, for instance, task information in the third stage is considerably more intimate than it is in the laboratory-group setting, and this stage may be attained at a later chronological time in therapy groups than in laboratory groups.

Certainly duration of group life would be expected to influence amount and rate of development. The laboratory groups, such as those run for a few hours by Bales and Strodtbeck (1951), followed essentially the same course of development as did therapy groups run for a period of a year. The relatively short life of the laboratory group imposes the requirement that the problem-solving stage be reached quickly, while no such imposition exists for the long-lived therapy group. Consequently, the former groups are forced to develop at a rapid rate. The possibility of such rapid development is aided by the impersonal and concrete nature of the laboratory task. Orientation is still required due to the newness of the task but is minimized by task rules, players' manuals, and the like, that help to orient the group members. Emotionality and resistance are major features of therapy-group development and represent personal and interpersonal impediments to group development and solution attainment as a function of the highly emotionally charged nature of the therapy-group task. The impersonal laboratory task features no such impediments and consequently the stage of emotionality is absent. The exchange of relevant information is as necessary to the laboratory task as it is to the therapy task, but the information to be exchanged is limited in the laboratory task by the nature of the task and time considerations. The behavior of "norming" is common to both settings but not so salient in the laboratory where the situation is so task-oriented. Finally, the problem-solving or "performing" stage is an essential stage in both settings.

One would expect the laboratory group to spend relatively more time in the fourth stage relative to the first three stages because of the task orientation in the laboratory setting. In the therapy task, with its unavoidable deep interpersonal penetration, we would expect relatively equal time to be spent in each stage. This, however, can undoubtedly be further modified by group composition as well as by the duration of group life and specific nature of the laboratory task. Undoubtedly there is an interaction between setting and development such that the sequence proposed here will be altered.

Unfortunately, the above hypotheses cannot be substantiated with available data, though certain of the studies are suggestive of the explanations offered. The articles reviewed do not deal with rate of temporal change nor do they give sufficiently complete and detailed time data associated with each stage to make calculations of rate possible. Furthermore, they do not systematically describe their independent variables nor relate them to the developmental phenomena through systematic variation and the observation of cause and effect. The major task of systematically studying the effects of a variety of appropriate independent variables on development still remains. The value of the proposed model is that it represents a framework of generic temporal change within which the above explorations can be nested and which should lead to the derivation of many specific hypotheses relating independent variables to the sequence of temporal change. Such quantitative explorations will undoubtedly lead to refinements and perhaps major modifications of such a model.

REFERENCES

Abrahams, J. Group psychotherapy: Implications for direction and supervision of mentally ill patients. In Theresa Muller (Ed.), *Mental health in nursing*. Washington, D.C.: Catholic University Press, 1949. Pp. 77–83.

Bach, G. R. *Intensive group psychotherapy*. New York: Ronald Press, 1954. Pp. 268–293.

Bales, R. F. *Interaction process analysis: A method for the study of small groups*. Cambridge, Mass.: Addison-Wesley, 1950.

Bales, R. F. The equilibrium problem in small groups. In T. Parson, R. F. Bales, & E. A. Shils (Eds.), *Working papers in the theory of action*. Glencoe, Ill.: Free Press, 1953. Pp. 111–161.

Bales, R. F., & Strodtbeck, F. L. Phases in group problem-solving. *Journal of Abnormal and Social Psychology*, 1951, *46*, 485–495.

Barron, M. E., & Krulee, G. K. Case study of a basic skill training group. *Journal of Social Issues*, 1948, *4*, 10–30.

Barton, W. E. Group psychotherapy of the psychoses. *Digest of Neurology and Psychiatry*, 1953, *21*, 148–149.

Bennis, W. G., & Shepard, H. A. A theory of group development. *Human Relations*, 1956, *9*, 415–437.

Beukenkamp, C. Some observations made during group therapy. *Psychiatric Quarterly Supplement,* 1952, *26,* 22–26.

Bion, W. R. *Experience in groups.* New York: Basic Books, 1961.

Bradford, L. P. Trainer-intervention: Case episodes. In L. P. Bradford, J. R. Gibb, & K. D. Benne (Eds.), *T-group theory and laboratory method.* New York: Wiley, 1964. Pp. 136–167. (a)

Bradford, L. P. Membership and the learning process. In L. P. Bradford, J. R. Gibb, & K. D. Benne (Eds.), *T-group theory and laboratory method.* New York: Wiley, 1964. Pp. 190–215. (b)

Bradford, L. P., & Mallinson, T. Group formation and development. In *Dynamics of group life.* Washington, D. C.: National Education Association, National Training Laboratories, 1958.

Cholden, L. Group therapy with the blind. *Group Psychotherapy,* 1953, *6,* 21–29.

Clapham, H. I., & Sclare, A. B. Group psychotherapy with asthmatic patients. *International Journal of Group Psychotherapy,* 1958, *8,* 44–54.

Coffey, H. S. Socio and psyche group process: Integrative concepts. *Journal of Social Issues,* 1952, *8,* 65–74.

Coffey, H., Freedman, M., Leary, T., & Ossorio, A. Community service and social research—group psychotherapy in a church program. *Journal of Social Issues,* 1950, *6*(1), 14–61.

Corsini, R. J. *Methods of group psychotherapy.* New York: McGraw-Hill, 1957. Pp. 119–120.

Deutsch, M. A. A theory of cooperation and competition. *Human Relations,* 1949, *2,* 129–152.

Dreikurs, R. Group psychotherapy from the point of view of Adlerian psychology. *International Journal of Group Psychotherapy,* 1957, *7,* 363–375.

Erikson, E. H. *Childhood and society.* New York: Norton, 1950. Pp. 213–220.

Fromm, E. *Escape from freedom.* New York: Rinehart, 1941.

Golembiewski, R. T. *The small group.* Chicago, Ill.: University of Chicago Press, 1962. Pp. 193–200.

Grotjahn, M. The process of maturation in group psychotherapy and in the group therapist. *Psychiatry,* 1950, *13,* 63–67.

Harvey, O. J., Hunt, D. E., & Schroder, H. M. *Conceptual systems and personality organization.* New York: Wiley, 1961.

Hearn, G. The process of group development. *Autonomous Groups Bulletin,* 1957, *13,* 1–7.

Herbert, E. L., & Trist, E. L. The institution of an absent leader by a student's discussion group. *Human Relations,* 1953, *6,* 215–248.

Ilg, F. L., & Ames, L. B. *Child Behavior.* New York: Harper, 1955.

Jennings, H. H. Sociometric differentiation of the psychegroup and socio-group. *Sociometry*, 1947, *10*, 71–79.

King, C. H. Activity group therapy with a schizophrenic boy—follow-up two years later. *International Journal of Group Psychotherapy*, 1959, *9*, 184–194.

Levy, D. M. Oppositional syndromes and oppositional behavior. In P. H. Hoch and J. Zubin (Eds.), *Psychopathology of childhood*. New York: Grune & Stratton, 1955. Pp. 204–226.

Mann, J. Group therapy with adults. *American Journal of Orthopsychiatry*, 1953, *23*, 332–337.

Mann, J., & Semrad, E. V. The use of group therapy in psychoses. *Journal of Social Casework*, 1948, *29*, 176–181.

Martin, E. A., & Hill, W. F. Toward a theory of group development: Six phases of therapy group development. *International Journal of Group Psychotherapy*, 1957, *7*, 20–30.

Mead, G. H. *Self, mind and society*. Chicago: University of Chicago Press, 1934.

Miles, M. B. Human relations training: How a group grows. *Teachers College Record*, 1953, *55*, 90–96.

Modlin, H. C., and Faris, M. Group adaptation and integration in psychiatric team practice. *Psychiatry*, 1956, *19*, 97–103.

Noyes, A. P. *Modern clinical psychiatry*. (4th ed.) Philadelphia: Saunders, 1953. Pp. 589–591.

Osberg, J. W., & Berliner, A. K. The developmental stages in group psychotherapy with hospitalized narcotic addicts. *International Journal of Group Psychotherapy*, 1956, *6*, 436–447.

Parker, S. Leadership patterns in a psychiatric ward. *Human Relations*, 1958, *11*, 287–301.

Philp, H., & Dunphy, D. Developmental trends in small groups. *Sociometry*, 1959, *22*, 162–174.

Piaget, J. *The moral judgment of the child*. New York: Harcourt Brace, 1932.

Powdermaker, F. & Frank, J. D. Group psychotherapy with neurotics. *American Journal of Psychiatry*, 1948, *105*, 449–455.

Psathas, G. Phase movement and equilibrium tendencies in interaction process in psychotherapy groups. *Sociometry*, 1960, *23*, 177–194.

Rotter, J. B. *Social learning and clinical psychology*. New York: Prentice-Hall, 1954.

Schindler, R. Bifocal group therapy. In J. Masserman & J. E. Moreno (Eds.), *Progress in psychotherapy*. Vol. 3. New York: Grune & Stratton, 1958. Pp. 176–186.

Schroder, H. M., & Harvey, O. J. Conceptual organization and group structure. In O. J. Harvey (Ed.), *Motivation and social interaction.* New York: Ronald Press, 1963. Pp. 134–166.

Schutz, W. C. *FIRO: A three dimensional theory of interpersonal behavior.* New York: Rinehart, 1958. Pp. 168–188.

Semrad, E. V., & Arsenian, J. The use of group processes in teaching group dynamics. In W. G. Bennis, K. D. Benne, & R. Chin (Eds.), *The planning of change.* New York: Holt, Rinehart & Winston, 1961. Pp. 737–743.

Shellow, R. S., Ward, J. L., & Rubenfeld, S. Group therapy and the institutionalized delinquent. *International Journal of Group Psychotherapy,* 1958, *8,* 265–275.

Smith, A. J. A developmental study of group processes. *Journal of Genetic Psychology,* 1960, *97,* 29–39.

Stock, D., & Thelen, H. A. *Emotional dynamics and group culture.* Washington, D.C.: National Education Association, National Training Laboratories, 1958.

Stoute, A. Implementation of group interpersonal relationships through psychotherapy. *Journal of Psychology,* 1950, *30,* 145–156.

Talland, G. A. Task and interaction process: Some characteristics of therapeutic group discussion. *Journal of Abnormal and Social Psychology,* 1955, *50,* 105–109.

Taylor, F. K. The therapeutic factors of group-analytic treatment. *Journal of Mental Science,* 1950, *96,* 976–997.

Thelen, H., & Dickerman, W. Stereotypes and the growth of groups. *Educational Leadership,* 1949, *6,* 309–316.

Theodorson, G. A. Elements in the progressive development of small groups. *Social Forces,* 1953, *31,* 311–320.

Thorpe, J. J., & Smith, B. Phases in group development in treatment of drug addicts. *International Journal of Group Psychotherapy,* 1953, *3,* 66–78.

Tulane Studies in Social Welfare. *The use of group methods in social welfare settings.* New Orleans, La.: Tulane University School of Social Work, 1957.

Wender, L. The dynamics of group psychotherapy and its application. *Journal of Nervous and Mental Disease,* 1946, *84,* 54–60.

Whitman, R. M. Psychodynamic principles underlying T-group processes. In L. P. Bradford, J. R. Gibb, & K. Benne (Eds.), *T-group theory and laboratory methods.* New York: Wiley, 1964. Pp. 310–335.

Wolf, A. The psychoanalysis of groups. *American Journal of Psychotherapy,* 1949, *3,* 16–50.

Part Three

APPLICATIONS: ILLUSTRATIVE STUDIES AND DESCRIPTIONS

Part Three provides answers to several questions: For what purposes have group experiences been used? What methods have been employed? To what extent have goals been attained in various types of groups? These questions have been posed vigorously for many years by the general public, prospective group members, and even group practitioners.

Until recently, definitive answers were scarce. During the late 1960's, however, reports on applications of group methods began to appear in the professional literature of education, psychology, sociology, and human relations training. Few empirical documentations were offered—the majority of reports were theoretical or allegorical in nature. Part Three contains the best of these articles selected for their descriptions of purpose, composition, procedure, and outcomes. Many are eloquent in their presentations of people and events. More important, perhaps, these selections offer well-articulated explanations of the rationale and goals of the group experience as well as the relationship between group purposes and outcomes.

Part Three deals with the problems and concerns of students from first grade through college. It should be noted that research in the application of group procedures to these non-laboratory settings is still in the infancy stage. It is not surprising, therefore, that the hypotheses and research questions posed by several of the studies were not confirmed by the results. In more than one instance the authors were content to speak of the general trends in the data.

The studies included in this part represent something different from systematic inquiry in the usual sense. The reader will find that in each study the authors were committed not only to research but also to providing an appropriate, worthwhile experience for the participants. Some of the rigor of sophisticated empirical research has been tempered with consideration for the people involved and the practical realities of the settings. The studies and projects in Part Three may be regarded as field trials of some of the thoughts and theories presented in Part Two. The various authors describe attempts to establish the validity of the group experience in both theoretical and practical terms.

The focus of Part Three is on group work conducted in educational settings. Schools and colleges—the counselor's "natural habitats"—have been selected as the most appropriate sites for examining the application of concepts to lives. Three of the selections report the use of group methods in elementary schools, three describe the efforts of high school counselors, and three illustrate the use of groups to respond to the typical concerns of the college student. Diversity has been maintained by including reports which involve people of various ages and which emphasize personal growth, situational problems, developmental concerns, or therapy.

Group work has found a ready market in the elementary school. In fact, it appears that counselors in elementary schools often prefer to counsel students, parents, or teachers in groups rather than individually. Other innovative efforts besides group-centered techniques have also been successful in elementary school guidance. In an article entitled "Group Counseling with Children: A Cognitive-Behavioral Approach" (1969), Mayer, Rohen, and Whitley describe a cognitive-behavioral approach, and Stormer, in "Milieu Group Counseling in Elementary School Guidance" (1967), provides a comprehensive evaluation of a project based upon milieu group counseling.

The selections in Part Three focus on problems typically encountered by students. In so doing, the readings represent a commentary on the current status of counseling and mental health services in schools. Since academic achievement is so greatly prized in society, it is important for students who fail to perform academically as well as they could to be given special attention. Counselors are expected to help students improve their academic performance and find greater personal satisfaction in the complex social system of the school.

In some instances in the group experience the emphasis has been on personal growth and development rather than remediation. Examples of the growth-centered focus are seen in "A Time for Feelings" (1967), by Anderson and Schmidt; "Milieu Group Counseling in Elementary School Guidance" (1967), by Stormer; "Small Group Counseling with Negro Adolescents" (1968), by Gilliland; "Evaluation of Developmental Counseling with Groups of Low Achievers in a High School Setting" (1967), by Benson and Blocher; and "Transitional Adolescents, Anxiety, and Group Counseling" (1966), by Clements. The use of the group experience for growth, awareness, and organizational change has become common practice in such nonschool settings as industry, community service, and graduate schools. The therapeutic potential of the group has also been recognized and employed in virtually every type of mental health service. Counselors in schools and colleges are in a good position to use group experiences for the benefit of a large number of people; yet their efforts most often are directed toward improving the achievement or behavior of a small number of students. As knowledge of group techniques increases from experience and research, perhaps both growth and therapy applications will achieve greater prominence.

The rich variety in purpose, composition, and methodology evident in the following selections shows innumerable possibilities for the use of group experiences. Anderson and Schmidt, for example, describe a program for pupils in grades one through three which centers on personal awareness, problem-solving capabilities, and pupil-teacher relationships. Their program is a rare example in which a school acknowledges its responsibility for personal as well as intellectual growth.

During recent years, learning theory approaches to behavior have been revitalized. Mayer, Rohen, and Whitley demonstrate the applicability of a cognitive model for working with children in a group setting. The Adlerian orientation has found contemporary relevance in the milieu as practiced and described by Stormer. His report is unique in that the project is evaluated both qualitatively and quantitatively. Research in the area of group work poses several real challenges for counselors who wish to validate their work. However, the methodology employed by Stormer is highly appropriate and has been encouraged as a means of compensating for the lack of suitable instrumentation. (See Part Four for more on this topic.)

Gilliland explains his attempt to inject relevance in the lives of students attending a typical high school. He clearly defines the project and its research outcomes. The reader should pay particular attention to the final section in which the author discusses the extended impact of the study.

The next two selections, "Group Counseling for Gifted Under-Achieving High School Students" (1969), by Finney and Van Dalsem, and the article by Benson and Blocher, are characteristic of the remedial use of group methods. One questions, however, whether achievement is ever the real issue for counselors and students in experiences such as these. In any case, it appears certain that the benefits might encompass several additional variables, each broader than the criterion offered in the titles.

The last three articles in Part Three illustrate the use of groups in college and university settings. In addition, each article has particular merits of its own. Clements, for example, demonstrates the viability of the group experience in responding to anxiety concerning college entry—feelings experienced by approximately one-half of the students who graduate from our high schools. Gilbreath, in "Group Counseling with Male Underachieving College Volunteers" (1967), compares the effectiveness of leader- versus group-structured groups in dealing with academic underachievement, which he believes to be causally related to an underlying emotional syndrome. The study by Ofman, "Evaluation of a Group Counseling Procedure" (1964), is a classic example of a program conceived and conducted so that it could be comprehensively evaluated. In this respect it serves as a model for other counselors who want to insure their program of credibility.

The selections in Part Three—in contrast to the other four parts —are full, rational accounts of *what actually happens* in groups, rather than theories of what ought to be. The articles are pragmatic, with an emphasis on results. The field of group work is richer because of these authors, who were willing to relate not only their goals and methods but also the extent to which their objectives were achieved.

20 / A TIME FOR FEELINGS

Joann Anderson and Wesley I. Schmidt

The School: Counseling's Reason to Be

Group guidance activities are an integral part of an effective elementary guidance program. Within an organized, systematic guidance program, group guidance activities contribute directly to the goals of students and faculty by implementing and supplementing the counseling and consulting roles of the elementary guidance worker.

Elementary school guidance, as described in this context, is a continuous educational program that contributes to each child's positive use of the school and its facilities. The program is directed toward helping teachers and students create a nurturing environment in which children may feel and enjoy their development of those skills, knowledge, and attitudes that are the *raison d'être* of our schools.

Group guidance classes are not only inherently efficient in terms of the number of persons served per unit of time spent, but they also provide excellent opportunities for the guidance consultant to accomplish the consultative tasks considered to be part of his role. This emphasis on group guidance classes was described as early as 1947 by Bullis and O'Malley. They described tools and techniques designed to help teachers utilize the principles of guidance in their total instruction role.

Today, the guidance worker is placed at the disposal of the teacher to support and facilitate good teaching. He brings his spe-

From ELEMENTARY SCHOOL GUIDANCE AND COUNSELING, *1967, Vol. 1, pp. 47–56. Copyright 1967, American Personnel and Guidance Association. Reprinted with permission of authors and publisher.*

cialized knowledge to the faculty from a multi-disciplined background in the behavioral sciences. As teachers and counselors mesh their specific skills and talents, complementing one another, each child is helped to know himself and to understand his purpose within the school setting.

An Approach: Storybook Counseling

The approach described here is one that has been found useful in the Elementary Guidance Demonstration Project in Rockford, Illinois. Within this project each child in grades one, two, and three spends one-half hour every third week in a group guidance activity. He comes to the guidance room with half of his classmates, a specific group of companions selected by his teacher from her observation of friendship patterns.

Stories describing children in a wide variety of typical, difficult or pleasurable situations, are presented by the counselor. The children are then given the opportunity to anticipate their own behavior as well as its consequences in similar situations. They are encouraged to express their reactions to the story situation fully. Then they are challenged to consider the impact of their behavior on others as well as themselves. Each meeting is recorded in its entirety, with the children's knowledge, so that the teacher may review the ideas and feelings expressed by her children. The teacher thereby perceives her children in a new and more objective light. By hearing the counselor's responses, the teacher learns to become a consistent reinforcer of positive self-referent remarks, as she works with her children between guidance sessions.

In the main, the material used for these activities is based on the work of Ralph Ojemann et al., in "A Teaching Program in Human Behavior and Mental Health" (Ojemann, Hawkins, & Chowning, 1961a), a graded series developed by the Preventive Psychiatry Research Program at the State University of Iowa. This material includes stories and pictures prepared for use at specified grade levels and around defined causal relationships. Dr. Ojemann contends that:

We tend to take it for granted (and there is evidence to support our assumption) that using a causal approach toward our *physical* environment helps the child in living and adjusting to that environment. The teaching of a causal approach to the *social* environment is not so well developed. . . . Only in recent years has there been a growing interest in helping the child understand more about *why* people do what they do and what some of the effects tend to be of alternative ways of working out social situations.

In the second-grade series, for example, is a story called "Jack's Workbook." This narrative opens with a forthright discussion of cheating, manipulation of parents, sibling problems, the reasons for poor grades, feelings about school, tests and their purposes, and how it feels to have adults tell children, "You are too little to do that" (Ojemann, Hawkins, & Chowning, 1961b).

PETER RABBIT AND FAMILY RELATIONS

Many children's stories that are among the so-called *classics* are equally appropriate for use as stimulus materials, once the counselor and teacher grasp the causal approach to understanding human behavior. As the children discussed the exciting adventures of Peter Rabbit, each responded in his own way to the tale of this mischievous, bold, little rabbit who hopped so complacently into Farmer McGregor's garden, both disobeying his mother and experiencing a pleasurable sense of apprehension or fear. The children delighted in his clever escape and then agreed that Peter had to be punished before his mother tucked him snugly into his bed. The guidance group wondered where Peter's father was and discussed their own fathers; they talked of their problems with their brothers and sisters; they talked of the reasons for not listening and for disobeying; they discussed the kinds of limits and punishments set for them at home and at school and their feelings about these limits and their consequences. *Children and Books,* by Arbuthnot (1957), offers many suggestions for other classics that may be used by counselors and teachers in this manner.

A Group in Action

A transcript containing excerpts from one of the thirty-minute sessions illustrates the dynamics of these guidance groups and their potential as a learning opportunity for children, teachers, parents, and the guidance worker. This recording was made by a third-grade group from a school in a middle-class neighborhood. The class had a Negro teacher and two Negro girls, one of whom was present during the recording. This is the second session, which was based upon the *Story of Ming Fu,* a fat Chinese boy. (C—Counselor; Cн—Children)

Ming Fu, the Fat Chinese Boy

C. What do you remember about Ming Fu?

Cн. He was fat! (*The entire group laughs loudly.*)

C. And he felt badly about that, didn't he?

Cн. He is a boy.

Cн. He is shy.

C. Why was he shy? Sherry, how did he feel about himself? Did he like himself very well?

Cн. No, because the other boys call him names and say he is fat.

Cн. He is very unhappy.

Cн. He didn't think that anybody loved him.

C. He thought he couldn't be as good as he thought he should be. What did he say about himself?

Cн. That he was different from everybody else. He thought, "I can't do anything right; I can't do anything at all."

Cн. I read a book about Ben Franklin and he invented things, and they made a chapter called "Ben is different" because he was always inventing things while the other boys were fishing.

C. We talked yesterday about our differences, and do you remember how all of us were so happy that we were not all alike?

Cн. I don't like school.

Cн. I don't either.

C. What bothers you? There are some things that you would change.

Cн. Only one thing that bothers me! I would like to be the teacher and boss everybody around. They are always bossing us around.

C. You would like to be boss.

Cн. Yeah!! No!! I don't want to be boss, but I want to be a teacher.

C. Why?

Cн. Then I could teach them and they couldn't teach me. They couldn't tell me then. I could tell them.

C. You could feel more important then and bigger.

Сн. No—not that.

C. I was wrong thinking that.

Сн. I don't know what I am going to say; I am going coo-coo. I would like to say this about Ming Fu (I think that is his name). Other kids make fun of him because they say he is fat, and that he is dumb, but Mr. M. (*our principal*) isn't dumb, but he is fat. And other kids don't laugh at him.

C. That's right. That has started you thinking *why*, hasn't it? He is heavy, but we don't laugh at him.

Сн. It will make him feel quite sad.

C. But I never look at him and think of laughing. What has he shown me?

Сн. He helps other people and he is the principal.

C. You think that his helpfulness is more important than what he looks like?

Сн. I like school because I like my teacher.

C. When you like your teacher, school is a very pleasant place.

Сн. Yes! I love her.

Сн. She is a nice teacher.

Later, during a discussion of worthless feelings . . .

Сн. Yes, maybe if you don't look so good on the outside, you may know things that they don't know.

C. That is so true. How many of you choose your friends by the way you think they are on the inside?

Сн. Hmmmmmm. (*As a group*)

C. We make guesses about the kinds of people they are from the way they behave, don't we?

Сн. It's more important to be nice on the inside than to just look pretty.

Сн. Debbie and Mary . . . well . . . they are Negroes in our class and my mommy she said for me to be nice to them—real nice because they are different—and just because they are a different color doesn't mean that they are not the same on the inside and that's just what I thought. Just because they are brown on the outside doesn't mean they haven't got red blood on the inside.

Сн. They have the same feelings we have.

C.   I guess I agree with you in certain ways. You're saying that you don't need to be any nicer to Debbie and Mary—you don't treat them any differently, do you? You are nice to them if they are nice to you. If they are mean and ugly to you, you are probably going to find it hard to think of them as special friends. Do you think as I do, but as other adults might not, that people earn our respect regardless of their color, like Mr. M., myself, your teacher, Debbie, Mary—or you, too!!

Ch.   Yes! (*A general agreement*)

Discussion continuing about a boy in another class who constantly teases the girl sitting in front of him . . .

C.   Why did Albert make fun of her? We might think of some reasons.

Ch.   Because he just didn't stop and think about it.

C.   That might be a reason. How does Albert feel about Albert?

Ch.   Albert feel about Albert?!???!! (*Shocked*)

C.   Yes, each of us has feeling toward himself. How does he feel?

Ch.   He feels that he is the grandest in the room.

C.   He might. I don't agree with you, however.

Ch.   Yes! Yes! Yes! (*All of the children, loudly*)

C.   You really don't agree with me, but I still don't think that.

Ch.   I think he feels like he is the best in the room.

C.   Do any of you know what kind of grades Albert gets?

Ch.   Oh, Oh, Oh, Oh, Man!!! (*Entire group responding negatively*)

C.   Do you think maybe he wants to be a good reader like you are, Aileen, or so good in arithmetic like you are, Jared?

Ch.   Hmmmmmmm. (*Tentative agreement among children*)

C.   Do you suppose that he might poke fun at others because he is mad at himself?

Feelings and Behavior—A Message System

Within this group the children are learning the dynamics of human behavior. They are learning that all behavior is caused by some personal desire, that what now seems to be the best solution can be changed as circumstances change, and that each act operates as a message system that is learned or may be relearned.

The children become positively conditioned to the experience of helping each other to explore problems that may interfere with their growth and learning. It is often helpful to children just to know that they are not the only ones who have difficulty solving specific problems or resolving feelings, that there is a sameness among all children "in this village we call the world" (Adlai Stevenson).

From the typescript it is evident that each child is encouraged to explore his thoughts and feelings about himself—his strengths and weaknesses, his likes and dislikes, his beliefs and attitudes, and his own mental picture of himself vis-à-vis others. The children are learning to discuss and to accept many kinds of behavior and to explore alternatives. In the environment of acceptance, openness, and nonjudgmental interplay, which are characteristic of the guidance room, most children begin to feel a freedom which permits them to examine themselves and their world. They begin to understand their problem-solving capabilities as they learn new, coping responses by role-playing the situations that demand "mastery behaviors, value-relevant behaviors, and work-relevant behaviors" (Blocher, 1966).

As the children begin to respect, accept, like, and value themselves, they are able, as a consequence of these positive feelings to respect, accept, like, and value others and to achieve more successfully the developmental tasks appropriate to their particular stage of development (Havighurst, 1953).

Also, as the children learn more effective behavior and are able to drop some of their self-defeating patterns, they are able to understand the consequences of their behavior—the extent to which each of them is held accountable for his actions even by those persons who love and respect him most. The narratives give them many opportunities to explore the meaning of the signals they themselves send, as well as the reactions of teachers, parents, and peers to these signals.

During these group sessions the children learn that they can communicate on the feeling level with a trusted adult who will not allow them to be hurt needlessly or unbearably by their openness. They learn that when feelings are brought into the open and are discussed in a safe climate, it is easier to concentrate on school tasks.

Assistance to the Teachers

Although assistance to the children is the primary objective of these group activities, teachers also broaden their understandings of behavior, its causes, and the conditions of effective behaving and growing. Many of them increase their skill in creating an educational environment in which children feel free to learn and "try out" different behaviors. Teachers gradually learn to understand and *trust* a democratic classroom organization. Many teachers also increase their ability to allow a real group spirit to form with its attendant *esprit de corps,* cohesiveness, and power.

The feelings and comments of the children often help the teacher to recognize and deal with individual differences, to personalize or individualize instruction within the classroom, and to understand the needs of the individual child. Certain kinds of behavior are often modified as teachers increase their understanding of the etiology of maladjustive behavior forms.

Greater knowledge of the child's perceptions of himself and his world allows the teacher to communicate in more depth with the child's parents and to understand them as individuals with needs. Thus a focus for parental redirection in helping the child to grow is often found. Seminars or adult classes in child development practices for parents of first and second graders, led by the elementary counselor or other specialists, are more successful because the guidance workers "know" the children and parents.

Feelings and the Need for Help

Often, the kinds of feelings communicated by the children during these sessions provide clues that enable the counselor to have greater understanding of the learning or emotional difficulties that the child may be experiencing in school. Together, the teacher and counselor watch for signs of emotional difficulties: an inability to learn that seems to defy explanation, an inability to maintain satisfying relationships with peers and teachers, inappropriate or immature types of behavior, a general mood of unhappiness or depression, or a tendency to develop physical symptoms. The information they gather often suggests, or confirms, to the teacher and guidance worker that the child could benefit from individual counseling, group counseling, or referral to other specialists within the school or community.

Conclusion: A Time for Feelings

Group guidance classes in elementary schools help teachers and guidance people to build meaningful relationships with each other and with children. These close relationships of mutual understanding and purpose provide our children genuine opportunities for growth. A *time for feelings* is an integral, effective part of the elementary guidance program.

REFERENCES

Arbuthnot, M. H. *Children and books.* Chicago: Scott, Foresman, 1957.

Blocher, D. H. *Developmental counseling.* New York: Ronald Press, 1966. P. 54.

Bullis, H. E., & O'Malley, E. E. *Human relations in the classroom.* Delaware: The Delaware State Society for Mental Hygiene, 1947.

Havighurst, R. J. *Human development and education.* New York: Longmans, Green, 1953. P. 2.

Ojemann, R. H., Hawkins, A., & Chowning, K. *A teaching program in human behavior and mental health.* Iowa City: University of Iowa Press, 1961. (a)

Ojemann, R. H., Hawkins, A., & Chowning, K. *Handbook for kindergarten and first grade teachers.* Iowa City: State University of Iowa, 1961. P. 7. (b)

Stone, L. J. & Church, J. *Childhood and adolescence.* New York: Random House, 1957. Pp. 260–261.

21 / GROUP COUNSELING WITH CHILDREN: A COGNITIVE-BEHAVIORAL APPROACH

G. Roy Mayer, Terrence M. Rohen, and A. Dan Whitley

Attempts at group counseling with elementary school children are presently being undertaken by pupil-personnel workers in elementary schools throughout the nation. However, evidence regarding the school counselor's relative effectiveness when employing various group-counseling procedures with elementary school children is almost nonexistent. The intent of the present paper is to initiate further thought, discussion, and research concerning the applicability of a cognitive-behavioral approach to group counseling with elementary school children.

Mayer and Cody (1968) and Rohen and Mayer (1968) have illustrated the apparent applicability of aspects of Festinger's theory of cognitive dissonance (Festinger, 1957) to individual counseling. Several individuals (Krumboltz, 1966; Krumboltz & Hosford, 1967) have also illustrated the applicability of aspects of social learning theory to counseling. Both approaches have implications for group counseling with children.

Festinger's (1957) theory is primarily concerned with the necessary conditions for attitudinal and, to a lesser degree, behavioral changes persisting as a consequence of a given behavior or commitment. Social learning theory (Bandura & Walters, 1963) is less concerned with attitudinal consequences. Its major concern appears to be with bringing about behavior change while usually ignoring attitudes. The present paper presents salient segments from the two empirically oriented approaches, social learning theory and dissonance theory, and applies them to elementary school group counseling.

From JOURNAL OF COUNSELING PSYCHOLOGY, 1969, Vol. 16, pp. 142–149. Copyright 1969 by the American Psychological Association, and reproduced by permission.

The segments are integrated and are presented as complementary to one another along with several findings from research in group dynamics.

Research findings from both approaches suggest that the probability of an attitudinal and/or behavioral change occurring is enhanced when a counselee "sees" a model or models do something that is contrary to or different than his (the counselee's) opinion or previous behavior (Bandura, 1965a, 1965b, 1965c; Bandura & Walters, 1963; Brehm & Cohen, 1962; Brock & Blackwood, 1962; Cohen, Terry, & Jones, 1959; Elms & Janis, 1965; Festinger & Carlsmith, 1959; Hovland & Pritzker, 1957; Janis & King, 1954). A "model," for the present purposes, is a fellow group member or counselor.

A state of dissonance (Festinger, 1957) will result if an individual sees another do something that is contrary to his private opinion. Dissonance is purported to be a prerequisite if attitudinal and behavioral change is to occur. It refers to a motivated state characterized by feelings of conflict and tension during which an individual experiences contradictory perceptions either about himself or his environment. Any two items of information which psychologically do not fit together are said to be in a dissonant relation to each other.

Counselors, then, can foster dissonant-enhancing situations from which attitudinal and/or behavioral changes are likely to occur by providing opportunities for their clients to observe contradictory items of information. The items can relate to behaviors, feelings, opinions, or events in the environment. Several examples should serve to illustrate how dissonance could be created through observation.

1. Jim had the opinion that "adults tell me what to do." In counseling, he observed that the counselor, an adult, did not tell him what to do.

2. Mike had the opinion that "adults don't listen to kids." During group counseling he observed that the counselor did listen to children.

3. Tom constantly interrupted when others talked. (He may have had the opinion that others did not mind when he interrupted.) He later observed that the group turned their back on him when he interrupted.

Each of the above individuals experienced dissonance as a consequence of "seeing" or experiencing contradictory items of information, that is, "adults tell me what to do. This adult does not tell me what to do." Such a state would motivate each of them to change or reduce the incompatibility of their perceptions in that dissonance represents an uncomfortable state of affairs, or feelings of tension and conflict, which individuals attempt to reduce or alleviate (Brehm & Cohen, 1962; Festinger, 1957).

Research findings suggest that the probability of an attitudinal and/or behavioral change occurring is enhanced when a counselee "hears" something from a model or models that is contrary to his opinions (Brehm, 1959; Brodbeck, 1956; Hovland, 1959; Salzinger, Feldman, Cowan, & Salzinger, 1967).

A verbal expression of a group member's perception or experiencing could introduce an attitude, behavior, or some other item of information inconsistent with the opinion or attitude held by an individual or the group, thus creating dissonance. Several examples should serve to illustrate how dissonance could be created through the sense of hearing.

1. A counselee may express doubt concerning a group member's respect for him. The group member then may verbally state his personal experiencing of high respect for the counselee.

2. A third-grade client may feel no remorse relative to his stealing activities at school. However, during a group guidance or counseling session conducted by the counselor the client and the other group members are exposed to the Ojemann (1967) story "Andy Can't Play." The significant others in the story disapprove of the stealing activities which the central character performs and this position is endorsed in the ensuing discussion by the group members.

3. A client might believe that he should not discuss his difficulties at school. During group counseling he hears another group member talking about his difficulties, and also hears the counselor and other group members accepting this behavior.

In each of the above examples a dissonance-creating situation, which is conducive to attitudinal or behavioral change, would have been created due to the introduction of contradictory items of information.

Research findings suggest that the probability of an attitudinal or behavioral change occurring is enhanced when the counselee "says" something that is contrary to his opinion or previous behavior (Festinger & Carlsmith, 1959; Keirsey, 1965; Krumboltz & Schroeder, 1965). Counselors can foster dissonance-enhancing situations, which could result in attitudinal and/or behavioral changes, by providing opportunities for their clients to say contradictory items of information. For example, one of the authors did some counseling with a group of six children in a camp setting. One of the children was reported to be urinating on the sleeping bags of his fellow campers. The counselor asked each of the six campers their opinion about the behavior. He also asked each one if he felt that whoever was doing it should stop it or not. The suspected camper's opinion was not asked for first, a procedure likely to create dissonance and one which has been indicated to be effective in modifying behavior through experimental group work by Asch (1951, 1956). Each group member verbalized a negative attitude toward the urination behavior and felt that whoever was doing it should stop it. In this example, the counselor would have increased the likelihood that the violator would have experienced dissonance concerning his behavior by eliciting from him a verbal statement which was contradictory to his previous behavior—that is, previous behavior: urinating on sleeping bags; verbal statement: "urinating on sleeping bags is wrong."

The counselor in the above example also provided the violator with a dissonance reducing alternative—stop urinating. The cessation of the behavior would be in agreement with the new attitude of "it is wrong to do." Thus, dissonance reduction would be achieved upon the cessation of the urinating behavior. The urination behavior ceased.

Role playing (Corsini, 1966; Moreno, 1946), a procedure often employed in group work with children, also provides opportunities for clients to "say" something contradictory to previous behavior or attitude. It follows, then, that role playing is another mode of creating dissonance (Janis & Mann, 1965), a state conducive to change.

Research findings also suggest that the probability of an attitudinal or behavioral change occurring is enhanced when the counselee "does" something that is contrary to his opinion or previous behavior (Allen, Henke, Harris, Baer, & Reynolds, 1967; Aronson, 1959; Bandura & Walters, 1963; Margolius & Sheffield, 1961; Mills, 1958).

Counselors can foster dissonance-enhancing situations by providing opportunities for their clients to do something contrary to their previous behavior or opinion. Dissonance could be enhanced if a client joined in and participated with a small group concerning something he previously felt he could not or would not do. That is, if a client perceived that he was not able to perform a task and then discovered himself as a participating group member doing the task, he would experience dissonance (Festinger & Aronson, 1953). For example, suppose Tom is not completing his modern math homework. During an intake interview with the counselor Tom described his opinion as, "Modern math is for the birds." If Tom was provided the opportunity to join in and participate with a group who was using and enjoying some sort of "play object," which employed new math concepts, he would experience dissonance provided he recognized that his opinion and new behavior were not congruent with one another (Brehm & Cohen, 1962; Festinger, 1957). As indicated earlier, this dissonance would motivate Tom to promote consonance by changing his items of information to a congruent state. Because Tom is doing and enjoying the new math in a group it is suggested that his dissonance would be reduced by a modification of his opinion toward the new math. Similar analogies could be drawn with groups employing role playing (Corsini, 1966; Janis & Mann, 1965) or other kinds of play media (Ginott, 1961).

Conditions Conducive to Dissonance and Resultant Behavior Changes

The effectiveness of such dissonance-creating events in producing counselee change, a change which is congruent with the event or newly obtained item of information, appears to be enhanced if the following conditions are met:

Condition 1

An environment is provided which is characterized by minimal (not a complete absence, but minimal) pressure and/or rewards while maintaining an accepting nonthreatening environment (Brehm & Cohen, 1962; Brock, 1962; Cohen, et al., 1959; Festinger, 1957; Festinger & Carlsmith, 1959; Janis & King, 1954; Mayer & Cody, 1968). Minimal reward or pressure seems necessary to evoke the desired behavior, or to motivate the student. Large reward or pressure can also evoke the desired behavior but tends to serve as a justification for the behavior (Festinger & Aronson, 1953). Thus, when experiencing large reward and/or pressure the client is likely to reduce his dissonance, not by changing previously held attitudes or beliefs, but perhaps by denying, distorting, or rationalizing away the dissonance-creating item(s) of information. An environment, then, characterized by minimal pressure and/or rewards while maintaining an accepting atmosphere, appears more effective in promoting attitudinal or behavioral change than one characterized by an absence or excess of pressure or rewards.

CONDITION 2

The counselor or group member who is emitting the dissonance-creating act is perceived by the counselee as similar to himself (Bandura, 1965a; Bandura & Walters, 1963; Burnstein, Stolland, & Zander, 1961; Festinger, 1957; Landfield & Nawas, 1964; Mendelsohn, 1966; Mendelsohn & Geller, 1963; Stotland & Dunn, 1963; Stotland & Patchen, 1961). Individuals tend to be influenced by and interact more with those who are like themselves (Zander & Havelin, 1960). Moreover observers who believe themselves to be similar to models in some attributes are more likely to match other classes of responses of the models than are observers who believe themselves to be dissimilar (Bandura & Walters, 1963). Similarity, then, among clients and between counselor and client, appears positively related to interaction and behavioral change.

Too much similarity, however, appears to handicap the group's ability to function as a change agent. Dissonance apparently cannot be introduced in relation to an item of information if the group members are in complete agreement with one another concerning the item (Festinger, Riecken, & Schachter, 1956; Mitnick & McGinnies, 1958). For example, if the group members have the same prejudice or belief they will tend to reinforce one another's viewpoints (Festinger et al., 1956; Mitnick & McGinnies, 1958). Such behavior effectively maintains their consonance and prevents the introduction of desired dissonance. Thus, little, if any dissonance can be created about a topic or item unless there are differing viewpoints and/or behaviors represented within the group concerning the item. Group members, then, should probably be similar in some aspects, but should not have a similar or identical attitude if the goal is to change that attitude or resultant behavior.

Counselors can often increase group interaction, and thereby dissonance-enhancing situations by pointing out existing similarities among group members. Group size also appears to influence interaction. Mayer and Baker (1967) have advocated that for maximal interaction group size should probably not exceed six for children from the upper elementary grades, and group sizes of less than six would be more appropriate for relatively immature or younger elementary school students.

Condition 3

Verbalizations or behaviors should not be too complex for the counselee to comprehend and imitate (Bandura, 1965c, 1969). This condition is similar to Condition 2 in that verbalizations and behaviors emitted by a counselee are not likely to be too complex for fellow counselees to imitate if they are similar to one another. An attitude or behavior is more likely to be rapidly acquired by a counselee if the complexity of the stimulus is not too difficult, if the stimulus is not presented too rapidly for him to comprehend, and if it possesses some components which he has already learned previously (Bandura, 1956a, 1965b, 1965c). For example, a counselee may observe or hear a dissonance-creating behavior and not be able to imitate it due to its complexities. In such a situation, the complex behavior must be broken down into its components before accurate imitation can occur. In addition, if a behavior or attitude exceeds the comprehension level of a counselee, it may not even arouse dissonance because its existence will not be meaningfully acknowledged. Consequently, the counselor needs to help his counselees become aware of and understand the attitudes and behaviors of the other group members so that they will be able to incorporate such items into their attitudinal and behavioral repertoires. At times, this will mean that the counselor will need to simplify or verbalize in a clearer fashion various counselee behaviors or attempts at communicating with one another.

Condition 4

A model's behavior or statement (in this case the behavior or statement of the counselor or group member) receives positive consequences (Bandura & Kupers, 1964; Bandura, Ross, & Ross, 1963a, 1963b; Walters, Leat, Marion & Mezei, 1963). A model's statement or behavior which receives positive consequences is more likely to be imitated than a statement or behavior which does not (Bandura, 1969). Perhaps a statement or behavior which receives positive consequences appears to the observer to be more effective or better than his own attitude or behavior thus contributing to his dissonance or motivation to change.

Studies also suggest that an individual, or in this case, a counselee, is more likely to imitate another item of information if it is emitted by an individual who is perceived by the counselee as being attractive, important, or having high prestige. (Asch, 1948; Bandura, Ross, & Ross, 1963a; Lefkowitz, Blake, & Mouton, 1955; Toch & Schulte, 1961.) It would seem that in order for an individual to appear attractive, important, or prestigious he would have had to receive positive consequences for his previous and/or current behaviors. Perhaps, then, an individual would be more likely to imitate the behavior of a model referred to as attractive, important, or prestigious simply because he emits more effective behaviors (behaviors which receive positive consequences).

An example should help to illustrate: A client believed that he should not discuss his difficulties when at school. During the group session he heard another member discussing his school difficulties and he observed that this behavior was accepted and perhaps reinforced (positive consequences) by the counselor and the group. In the context of this condition, the client's dissonance would be enhanced because he heard a group member emit an effective act which was dissonant to his attitude. That is, the model's act of discussing his school difficulties, which the client felt should not be done, was probably perceived as effective by the client because it was accepted and reinforced by the counselor and the other group members. Furthermore, the positive consequences the group member received could have enhanced the prestige or importance of his behavior to the client. Such an event would enhance the likelihood that the group member's behavior would be imitated.

CONDITION 5

The counselee has a history of experiencing positive consequences for imitating or adopting the attitudes and/or behaviors of others (Lanzetta & Kanareff, 1959; Miller & Dollard, 1941; Toch & Schulte, 1961). That is, if a client has learned from his past experiences that he will receive positive consequences for imitating or adopting the behaviors and attitudes of others it is likely that he will continue to do so. However, if this has not occurred in the past he would be less likely to imitate a statement or behavior emitted from another regardless of the consequences it received. He is not likely even to attend to it (Bandura, 1965c, 1969). In such a situation dissonance would not have been created.

Condition 6

The counselee receives positive reinforcement for an emittance of his newly obtained item of information, statement, or behavior from the counselor and/or group members (Bandura, 1965c, 1969; Bandura & Walters, 1963; Toch & Schulte, 1961). Once responses occur, the consequences to the behavior will largely determine whether these responses are strengthened, weakened, or inhibited (Millenson, 1967). Reinforcement appears to be particularly effective when applied to the responses of individuals experiencing dissonance (Corrozi & Rosnow, 1968; Kanareff & Lanzetta, 1960; Lesser & Abelson, 1959; Walters & Ray, 1960). In the group setting this condition could be employed by having the counselor or another group member give positive reinforcement to a client for expressing an attitude or for exhibiting a behavior that was known to cause him dissonance. In an earlier example, a client did not think he should discuss his difficulties at school. Assuming that this attitude was known by the counselor, the client's eventual behavior change could be enhanced if the counselor reinforced the client when he did discuss his difficulties at school. As the client was reinforced this behavior would be strengthened, that is, the probability of it occurring again would be greater. As the reinforcement continued for each occurrence, the behavior would tend toward stability and gradually become a part of the client's repertoire.

Discussion

The preceding suggests that dissonance theory can be combined with social learning theory in a manner which may prove to be highly effective in bringing about client behavioral and attitudinal changes through group counseling. Assuming that some or all the above conditions are met, a client seems likely to reduce his dissonance by changing his behavior and/or attitude so that it would become congruent with his newly obtained item of information. If the conditions are not met he is likely to reduce his dissonance, not by changing previously held attitudes, but perhaps through denial, distortion, or rationalization, thereby reducing or avoiding the dissonance-creating item(s) of information. However, such behavioral changes are usually not considered to be positive nor relatively permanent. Thus, if a behavior change is obtained without a corresponding change in attitude, the behavior may not persist. The conditions, then, might be important if persistent attitudinal and behavioral changes are desired.

Group counseling appears to offer an excellent environment for the creation of dissonance through the aid of segments of social learning theory. In such a setting more than one model is provided for each student to listen to, observe, and interact with. As a result of this interaction among members contradictory items of information are likely to be introduced in the group. Furthermore, group counseling provides several potential sources of reinforcement that could be used to aid clients in behavioral change. It would appear, then, that group counseling, as viewed by the authors, could be a powerful instrument for assisting students in their developmental process. The reader should be cautioned, however, to view the conclusions reached as tentative and suggestive. The intent of this paper has not been to present absolutes but to present a point of departure for discussion and applied research. It is hoped that further research may delete, further substantiate, or add to some of the conditions and ideas which were briefly outlined.

REFERENCES

Allen, K. E., Henke, L. B., Harris, F. R., Baer, D. M., & Reynolds, N. J. Control of hyperactivity by social reinforcement of attending behavior. *Journal of Educational Psychology,* 1967, *58,* 231–237.

Aronson, E. The effect of effort on the intrinsic attractiveness of a stimulus. Unpublished doctoral dissertation, Stanford University, 1959.

Asch, S. E. The doctrine of suggestion, prestige, and imitation in social psychology. *Psychological Review,* 1948, *55,* 250–276.

Asch, S. E. Effects of group pressure upon the modification and distortion of judgment. In H. Guetzkow (Ed.), *Groups, leadership and men.* Pittsburgh: Carnegie Press, 1951.

Asch, S. E. Studies of independence and conformity. A minority of one against a unanimous majority. *Psychological Monographs,* 1956, *70,* (9, Whole No. 416).

Bandura, A. Behavioral modifications through modeling procedures. In L. S. Krasner & L. P. Ullman (Eds.), *Research in behavior modification.* New York: Holt, Rinehart & Winston, 1965. (a)

Bandura, A. Influence of model's reinforcement contingencies on the acquisition of imitative responses. *Journal of Personality and Social Psychology,* 1965, *1,* 589–595. (b)

Bandura, A. Vicarious processes: A case of no-trial learning. In L. Berkowitz (Ed.), *Advance in experimental social psychology.* Vol. 2. New York: Academic Press, 1965. Pp. 1–55. (c)

Bandura, A. Social learning theory of identificatory processes. In D. A. Goslin & D. C. Glass (Eds.), *Handbook of socialization theory and research,* Chicago: Rand McNally, 1969.

Bandura, A., & Kupers, C. J. The transmission of patterns of self-reinforcement through modeling. *Journal of Abnormal and Social Psychology,* 1964, *69,* 1–9.

Bandura, A., Ross, D., & Ross, S. A. A comparative test of the status envy, social power, and the secondary-reinforcement theories of identificatory learning. *Journal of Abnormal and Social Psychology,* 1963, *67,* 527–534. (a)

Bandura, A., Ross, D., & Ross, S. A. Vicarious reinforcement and imitation. *Journal of Abnormal and Social Psychology,* 1963, *67,* 601–607. (b)

Bandura, A., & Walters, R. H. *Social learning and personality development.* New York: Holt, Rinehart & Winston, 1963.

Brehm, J. W. Increasing cognitive dissonance by a *fait accompli. Journal of Abnormal and Social Psychology,* 1959, *58,* 379–382.

Brehm, J. W., & Cohen, A. R. *Explorations in cognitive dissonance.* New York: Wiley, 1962.

Brock, T. C., & Blackwood, J. E. Dissonance reduction, social comparison and modification of others' opinions. *Journal of Abnormal and Social Psychology,* 1962, *65,* 319–324.

Brodbeck, M. The role of small groups in mediating the effects of propaganda. *Journal of Abnormal and Social Psychology,* 1956, *52,* 166–170.

Burnstein, E., Stotland, E., & Zander, A. Similarity to a model and self-evaluation. *Journal of Abnormal and Social Psychology,* 1961, *62,* 257–264.

Cohen, A. R., Terry, H. I., & Jones, C. B. Attitudinal effects of choice in exposure to counterpropaganda. *Journal of Abnormal and Social Psychology,* 1959, *58,* 388–391.

Corrozi, J. F., & Rosnow, R. L. Consonant and dissonant communications as positive and negative reinforcements in opinion change. *Journal of Personality and Social Psychology,* 1968, *8,* 27–30.

Corsini, R. J. *Roleplaying in psychotherapy: A manual.* Chicago: Aldine, 1966.

Elms, A. C., & Janis, I. L. Counternorm attitudes induced by consonant versus dissonant role playing. *Journal of Experimental Research in Personality,* 1965, *1,* 50–60.

Festinger, L. A., *A theory of cognitive dissonance.* Evanston, Ill.: Row, Peterson, 1957.

Festinger, L. A., & Aronson, E. The arousal and reduction of dissonance in social contexts. In D. Cartwright & A. Zander (Eds.), *Group dynamics research and theory.* New York: Harper & Row, 1953.

Festinger, L. A., & Carlsmith, J. M. Cognitive consequences of forced compliance. *Journal of Abnormal and Social Psychology,* 1959, *58,* 203–210.

Festinger, L., Riecken, H., & Schachter, S. *When prophecy fails.* Minneapolis: University of Minnesota Press, 1956.

Ginott, H. G. *Group psychotherapy with children.* New York: McGraw-Hill, 1961.

Hovland, C. Reconciling conflicting results derived from experimental and survey studies of attitude change. *American Psychologist,* 1959, *14,* 8–17.

Hovland, C., & Pritzker, H. Extent of opinion change as a function of the amount of change advocated. *Journal of Abnormal and Social Psychology,* 1957, *54,* 257–261.

Janis, I. L., & King, B. T. The influence of role-playing on opinion changes. *Journal of Abnormal and Social Psychology,* 1954, *49,* 211–218.

Janis, I. L., & Mann, L. Effectiveness of emotional role-playing in modifying smoking habits and attitudes. *Journal of Experimental Research in Personality,* 1965, *1,* 84–90.

Kanareff, V. T., & Lanzetta, J. T. Effects of success-failure experiences and probability of reinforcement upon the acquisition and extinction of an imitative response. *Psychological Reports,* 1960, *7,* 151–166.

Keirsey, D. W. Transactional casework: A technology for inducing behavior change. Paper presented at the Annual Convention of the California Association of School Psychologists and Psychometrists, San Francisco, 1965.

Krumboltz, J. D. *Revolution in counseling: Implications of behavioral science.* Boston: Houghton Mifflin, 1966.

Krumboltz, J. D., & Hosford, R. E. Behavioral counseling in the elementary school. *Elementary School Guidance and Counseling,* 1967, *1,* 27–40.

Krumboltz, J. D., & Schroeder, W. W. Promoting career planning through reinforcement and models. *Personnel and Guidance Journal,* 1965, *44,* 19–26.

Landfield, A., & Nawas, M. Psychotherapeutic improvement as a function of communication and adoption of therapist's values. *Journal of Counseling Psychology,* 1964, *11,* 336–341.

Lanzetta, J. T., & Kanareff, V. T. The effects of a monetary reward on the acquisition of an imitative response. *Journal of Abnormal and Social Psychology,* 1959, *59,* 120–127.

Lefkowitz, M. M., Blake, R. R., & Mouton, J. S. Status factors in pedestrian violation of traffic signals. *Journal of Abnormal and Social Psychology,* 1955, *51,* 704–706.

Lesser, G. C., & Abelson, R. P. Personality correlates of persuasibility in children. In I. L. Janis & C. I. Hovland (Eds.), *Personality and persuasibility*. New Haven, Conn.: Yale University Press, 1959.

Margolius, G. J., & Sheffield, F. D. Optimum methods of combining practice and filmed demonstration in teaching complex response sequences: Serial learning of a mechanical-assembly task. In A. A. Lumsdaine (Ed.), *Student response in programmed instruction: A symposium*. Washington, D.C.: National Academy of Science–National Research Council, 1961.

Mayer, G. R., & Baker, P. Group counseling with elementary school children: A look at group size. *Elementary School Guidance and Counseling*, 1967, *1*, 140–145.

Mayer, G. R., & Cody, J. J. Aspects of Festinger's theory of cognitive dissonance applied to school counseling. *Personnel and Guidance Journal*, 1968, *47*, 233–239.

Mendelsohn, G. Effects of client personality and client-counselor similarity on the duration of counseling: A replication and extension. *Journal of Counseling Psychology*, 1966, *13*, 228–234.

Mendelsohn, G., & Geller, M. Effect of counselor–client similarity on the outcome of counseling. *Journal of Counseling Psychology*, 1963, *10*, 71–77.

Millenson, J. R. *Principles of behavioral analysis*. New York: Macmillan, 1967.

Miller, N. E., & Dollard, J. *Social learning and imitation*. New Haven, Conn.: Yale University Press, 1941.

Mills, J. Changes in moral attitudes following temptation. *Journal of Personality*, 1958, *26*, 517–531.

Mitnick, L. L., & McGinnies, E. Influencing ethnocentrism in small discussion groups through a film communication. *Journal of Abnormal and Social Psychology*, 1958, *56*, 82–90.

Moreno, J. L. *Psychodrama*. New York: Beacon House, 1946.

Ojemann, R. O. *A teaching program in human behavior and mental health:* Book III. *Handbook for third grade teachers*. (Rev. ed.) Cleveland, Ohio: Educational Research Council of Greater Cleveland, 1967.

Rohen, T. M., & Mayer, G. R. Public commitment and dissonance: Cognitive counseling. Southern Illinois University, 1968. (Mimeo)

Salzinger, K., Feldman, R. S. Cowan, J. E., & Salzinger, S. Operant conditioning of verbal behavior of two young speech-deficient boys. In L. Krasner & L. P. Ullman (Eds.), *Research in behavior modification*. New York: Holt, Rinehart & Winston, 1967.

Schein, E. H. The effect of reward on adult imitative behavior. *Journal of Abnormal and Social Psychology*, 1954, *49*, 389–395.

Stotland, E., & Dunn, R. Empathy, self-esteem, and birth order. *Journal of Abnormal and Social Psychology,* 1963, *66,* 532–540.

Stotland, E., & Patchen, M. Identification and changes in prejudice and in authoritarianism. *Journal of Abnormal and Social Psychology,* 1961, *62,* 265–274.

Toch, H. H., & Schulte, R. Readiness to perceive violence as a result of police training. *British Journal of Psychology,* 1961, *52,* 389–394.

Walters, R. H., Leat, M., & Mezei, L. Response inhibition and disinhibition through empathetic learning. *Canadian Journal of Psychology,* 1963, *17,* 235–243.

Walters, R. H., & Ray, E. Anxiety: Social isolation and reinforcer effectiveness. *Journal of Personality,* 1960, *28,* 358–367.

Zander, A., & Havelin, A. Social comparison and intergroup attraction. *Human Relations,* 1960, *13,* 21–32.

22 / MILIEU GROUP COUNSELING IN ELEMENTARY SCHOOL GUIDANCE

G. Edward Stormer

A Guidance Program Tailor-made for the Elementary School

Should the elementary school counseling and guidance program be patterned after the model developed in the secondary school program? The answer to this question given by counselors and counselor educators consistently turns out to be *no*. However, as we examine existing programs of elementary school guidance, the parallel to the secondary program is all too overpowering to accept the position that the two levels involve distinct programs. A unique program tailored to fit the needs of the elementary school curricula must be developed if elementary school counseling is to be a distinct program. The study reported here is of such a program.

It is unique in that it deals with the milieu forces acting on the individual in his environment—those influences of peers, school, and home, but in a counseling setting under the auspices of the public school. That is, it deals with the interpersonal relationships between the student, his peers, his teachers, his principal, and his parents. Weekly sessions were conducted with each of these groups in an attempt to synthesize the problems and difficulties experienced by individuals and their respective groups. Central to the goals of the program is the desire to help children be independent and self-productive, that is, to help them assume the responsibilities that they are capable of, thus helping them to be self-activating and responsible for the improvement of their own achievement.

From ELEMENTARY SCHOOL GUIDANCE AND COUNSELING, *1967, Vol. 1, pp. 240–254.* *Copyright 1967, American Personnel and Guidance Association. Reprinted with permission of author and publisher.*

This program was conducted as a demonstration center for the Department of Program Development for Gifted Children in Illinois. At the outset of the study, approximately 110 pupils in grades 3–5 in six elementary schools were referred by teachers as possible talented underachievers or dysfunctioning children.

Final screening methods for these 110 students included the use of IQ scores, cumulative records, teachers' recommendations, and other previously administered test materials. These materials were reviewed in light of a Wechsler Intelligence Scale for Children (WISC) test given at this time to the students referred by the teachers. Each of the six schools was found to have from nine to 13 students in grades 3–5 who met the criterion of talented underachievers. For the purpose of this study, the gifted underachiever was a student who scored in the upper 20 per cent on intellectual ability as measured by the WISC, and was only average in achievement. A *significant* consideration for inclusion was the manifestation of social and emotional adjustment disturbing to the principal, teacher, parents, classroom, or peers. Many of the students appeared post facto to be those that the teachers felt inadequate to cope with either because they were withdrawn, verbally hostile, or aggressive. A series of pre-tests were administered to each student including the following:

Perceived Parent Attitude Scale

California Test of Personality (CTP)

General Anxiety Scale

Sequential Test of Educational Progress (STEP)—arithmetic and social studies

Iowa Every Pupil Silent Reading Comprehension Test (ISRT)

Current academic grades: arithmetic, social studies, language, and spelling

Behavioral Description Chart: a teacher rating of withdrawal, aggression, leadership, and friendship

Of the students referred by the teachers, 70 were selected for the project. They were randomly divided, by drawing numbers out of a hat, into an experimental group and a control group, the exception being that two siblings were not included in the same group. Each school contained both experimental and control students.

Weekly group counseling sessions of 45 minutes' duration were conducted in each school in groups ranging from 5–7 students each. Teachers of the experimental pupils met weekly for one hour in

a seminar session discussing problems of the students they had referred to the experimental group or discussing general classroom
problems relating to learning or behavior.

Parents met weekly for a two-hour period in a large group of
30–60. In this meeting individual parents were interviewed about
specific problems with their own children; at times a general session
was held in which the counselor dealt with the questions or subjects
the parents brought up in regard to understanding children and
dealing effectively with their behavior.

The crucial factor in the total process of the elementary school
counseling program was the determination of purposes of behavior
and recommendations toward more desirable behavior. This was
brought about through the counseling of these three interrelated
groups: students, teachers, and parents. The degree of success was
dependent upon the cooperation and participation of all three
groups. The counseling procedure included looking at one's self
and one's attitude toward others in a non-threatening, reality-testing
setting. It allowed opportunity to express ideas or feelings without
shame or fear of ridicule. It facilitated growth of an individual
through better understanding of the motives and purposes of that
individual by peers, teachers, and parents.

The recommendations made by the counselor were based on the
evaluation of the individual case. The psychological dynamics of
each child, his attitudes and his personality, were considered along
with his predominant mistaken concepts. There were specific recommendations made that were geared to the problems of one particular
child, teacher, parent, or to their total inter-relationship pattern.
There were also non-specific recommendations given to parents and
teachers which were applicable to *any* child, recommendations which
embodied the promises of a democratic relationship.

These recommendations were based on an overall principle,
namely, the assumption of democratic equality, with its call for
mutual respect. Many of the principles suggested to parents and
teachers apply to all human relationships. A mother, father, or
teacher who is acquainted with these principles and knows what to
do and why is in a better position to deal with a given situation
effectively for the best interest of the child.

The role of the elementary school counselor in this model program is uniquely different from the typical secondary school counselor. He spends roughly one-third of the time with students (largely
in groups), one-third of the time with teachers, and one-third of
the time with parents or community groups.

Evaluation

Most research studies turn to statistics when the outcomes of a study are somewhat in question and objective evidence is needed to show that those persons subjected to the experimental variable did change more often than by chance. The examples that follow show several changes in behavior so obvious that fine testing and analysis were not needed to discern them. Furthermore, testing for the changes observed was not adequately incorporated into the original design. This obviously does not imply that statistical evaluation was replaced by observation, nor that similar changes could not have been achieved through different means.

It does indicate that observable change in behavior in elementary age school children is achieved through a process of group counseling. Following are illustrations of the types of behavioral change observed in the 11-month duration of the project.

Joe was an extremely intelligent student but was also severely withdrawn, lacking any strong peer relationships. Bob had many friends but wasn't doing so well in school. They combined as one interdependent team; Joe depended on Bob to provide social relationships and the techniques needed to gain friends, and Bob in turn depended on Joe for help in academic areas. They sat together, ate together, and were generally inseparable.

At the time the study terminated, both Bob and Joe had achieved a substantial degree of independence.

Tommy was large for his age and was constantly reminded that he was dumb and clumsy. He never accepted his own ideas as worthwhile and turned to belligerence and fighting to protect his self-image.

As the sessions concluded Tommy was handing in written assignments, his fighting had dropped off to a minimum, and he began accepting his own ideas without depreciating himself constantly.

Kathy was excessively withdrawn and apparently unable to cope with a group, never offering her ideas or contributing in the classroom or in the counseling group.

Kathy changed from a withdrawn child to a very aggressive and rebellious child and then shifted again to a median position of openness and free interaction with the group. She became quite sensitive to problem-solving situations and very adept at offering insights into problem areas.

Alfred was so aggressive at home and at school that he was thoroughly obnoxious. He would not allow a group discussion unless he controlled it. Student interaction in initial sessions was dominated 70 to 80 per cent by Alfred. He became angry and resentful when anyone questioned him or didn't accept what he said.

Alfred went through a remarkable change at home and in school. He was able to let others control the group discussion and classroom activities, his fighting and bullying ceased, and he acquired a number of friends. The belligerent attitude changed in all but extremely trying situations.

Donna was so timid and shy that tears came to her eyes if she was asked simple questions such as "What do you think about it?" She never handed in school work, and was constantly making excuses for her lack of preparation.

As the program continued she came to take an active part in the group sessions, inviting other girls in and taking a real responsibility for her homework. Most remarkable was her change from fear and withdrawal around boys to taking an active verbal and physical stand against their attempts to intimidate her.

Billy appeared effeminate in mannerisms, played with girls, and was entirely dependent on the teacher to help him individually.

Billy was in the group only four months, but showed considerable improvement in turning to boy activities and stopped being a discipline problem in the classroom. His school work began showing significant signs of improvement, and fighting with siblings lessened dramatically.

These are real examples of behavior changes that were easily observable. Similar changes were observed in other schools where similar group programs have been conducted.

Statistical Evaluation

The pre- and post-tests indicated on page 293 were administered to the entire group. Pre- and post-scores were tested by a design out-

TABLE 1

Significance of Difference in Gain Scores From Pre- to Post-Testing Between Control and Experimental Groups

Test No.	Z Score	Significance Level*	
1	4.289	.001	General Anxiety Scale
3	1.150	.15	STEP Social Studies Achievement Test
9	1.765	.05	Behavior Description Chart, Aggression Scale
10	2.695	.01	Perceived Parent Attitude Scale
16	1.850	.05	CTP 1-A Self Reliance (California Test of Personality)
19	1.615	.06	CTP 1-B Feeling of Belonging
21	2.068	.05	CTP 1-F Nervous Symptoms
27	1.460	.08	CTP 2-E School Relations
28	1.178	.12	CTP 2-F Community Relations

* Significance levels are based on a one-sided test which is preferred in this case due to the one-tailed hypothesis of improved behavior on the post-test.

lined by Guilford (1965) for testing difference in mean gain scores. This procedure yields a Z score reflecting the significance of mean gains from pre- to post-testing, between experimental and control groups. The data are reported in Table 1.

It became very difficult to achieve significance on most of the test items due to a contamination of the design. This evolved in selection of the control group. It happened in the random selection of experimental and control groups that some of the students in the control group were in the classrooms of teachers involved in the program. Many suggestions and techniques discussed in the teacher's seminar were tried on the whole class. Thus control students also gained indirectly from the teachers' participation. The result was that differences between the two groups were lessened and the experimental group was required to make very strong gains to overcome this influence. Therefore, the small number of items reaching a desirable level of significance is not surprising.

The data in Table 1 indicate very strongly that a reduction in general anxiety took place. Secondly, a definite change was noted in the student's perception of the parents' attitudes toward the student. The change was in the direction of less strained and more desirable perception of the student by the parents.

A change was also verified of an increase in self-reliance scores on the CPI and freedom from nervous symptoms on the CPI.

Change was also indicated in a decrease in the aggression score of the Behavior Description Chart and an increase in Feelings of Belonging, CPI, and School Relations CPI. The trend toward higher performance on the STEP Social Studies Test and the improved relations indicated by scores on Community Relations are also worth considering as an outcome of this type of program.

Grades did not show a significant improvement during the experimental period. Reports of progress the following year indicated stronger academic achievement. The criterion of improvement in grades, however, is not the most immediately achievable criterion. Improvement in grades happens *after* changes in behavior and attitudes occur. Improvement in adjustment and interrelationship patterns were the most immediate concern of the program with improvement in grades and achievement as a secondary goal.

Table 2 reports data from a second phase of evaluation in which the Behavior Attitude Inventory Check List was distributed to teachers and parents at the close of the experimental study. Thirty teachers rated all 70 students, controls and experimentals; twenty-six parents rated their own children who were the experimental students. The Parent Check List contained 68 items, and the Teacher Check List, 80 items. The majority of the statements used in each were the same items; however, the check list was differentiated. Approximately one-fourth of the items in each test referred to the home *or* to the classroom, respectively.

The BAI was developed during the course of the study from two sources: from the 40 concepts of good mental health as extracted by Jahoda in an extensive review of the literature, and from basic premises of Adlerian psychology. The ratings were made on a six-point scale including change for the worse, no change, and change for the better.

Preliminary analysis using the binomial test referred to by Siegel in *Non Parametric Statistics* indicated a strong bias in the responses. It was then decided to continue the analysis by using a chi square test, but with a correction for the Hawthorne effect. To adjust for this bias, the theoretically expected normal distribution was arbitrarily altered by shifting the expected mean one-half standard deviation to the right. This has the effect of making a statistically significant positive change in behavior more difficult to achieve but it seemed a logical procedure after examining the data. The chart on page 300 indicates the difference in percentages expected in each cell by shifting the expected mean. Expected percentages were derived from symmetrical distribution using 4.0 as the mean instead of 3.5.

TABLE 2

Results of Items Common to Teacher and Parent Check Lists

Item No.	Item with Significance Level of Chi Square	Desirable Changes	
		Teachers' Rating Exp. Grp.	Parents' Rating Exp. Grp.
7	Less withdrawn	—	.05
8	Better in school	.001	.001
9	Respects rights of others	.001	.01
10	Less conflict with self	—	.10
12	Does as much as he feels capable of	—	.02
14	Seeks help for tasks beyond his ability	—	.10
16	Understands why he acts as he does	.05	.001
18	Rebels against group norms	—	—
19	Able to accept failure and/or mistakes	.01	.001
21	Adapts to day-to-day ups and downs	.02	.001
22	Often feels discouraged	—	.001
23	Looks at self objectively	—	.02
25	Relates warmly to others	—	.01
28	Participates in more activities	.001	.02
29	Strong ethical attitudes	.01	.02
30	Flexible, adjusts to situations	—	.001
34	Confidence and reliance on self	—	.001
37	Freer in expression in classroom	—	.02
38	Accepts mistakes without excuses	.001	—
39	Correctly interprets attitudes and intentions of others	—	.05
41	Greater consistency in actions	.02	.001
42	Internalized standards regulating behavior	—	.05
46	Good relationships with authority	—	.001
48	Acknowledges his problems	—	.001
49	More spurts of interest in schoolwork	.001	—
50	Hands in papers	.001	—
54	Seems happier and smiles often	.05	—
55	Volunteers in class	.05	—
58	Willing to negotiate disputes	−.001	—
59	Self-confidence in academic subjects	.001	—
60	Does thoughtful, helpful things	—	.10
62	Responsible for getting in assignments	.001	—
63	Participates more freely in class discussion	.01	—
65	Is more willing to work on school lessons	.001	.001
67	Uses problem-solving techniques	.001	—
68	Shows initiative in beginning work	.01	.001
70	Is friendly in class	—	.05
72	Evidence of self-control	.001	.001
73	Assumes responsibility for written work	.001	—
75	Uses constructive activities during playtime	.05	—
76	Reduction in "clowning"	.05	—

Categories of Behavior Change	1	2	3	4	5	6
Normal Distribution Expected	2%	14%	34%	34%	14%	2%
Adjusted Distribution Expected		7%	24%	38%	24%	7%

Table 3 summarizes results of the items found only on the parent check list.

TABLE 3
Results of Chi Square Test on Items Found Only on the Parent Check List

Item No.	Significance Level	
6	.05	Seeks revenge, tries to hurt people
15	.05	Responsibility in handling money
34	.02	Good relationship with father
36	.001	An ability to love
38	.02	Good relationship with neighborhood children
46	.001	Less talk and more action regarding behavior problems in home
47	.001	Good relations with mother
48	.001	Father is more accepting of child
49	.001	More tolerance to let children face natural consequences
50	.001	Family functions as a unit
51	.001	Relationship between parents is not strained
52	.001	Children manage own fights without parents' stepping in
54	.001	Parents do not act on first impulse
55	.001	Family members feel free to bring up any subject
56	.001	Less conflict, more pleasant in the home
59	.001	Better attitude toward mistakes
68	.001	Mother is more accepting of the child

Conclusion: A Positive Effect

From the data provided by the teachers and the parents on their respective check lists, it was evident that, from their perceptual frame of reference, (*a*) there were several significant changes in behavior and attitudes of the experimental students, and (*b*) changes were observable and identifiable when compared with the control group.

Although the present study has some obvious weaknesses, there can be little doubt that changes in attitudes and behavior have occurred. A follow-up is planned to determine if such changes will have permanency. Nonetheless, it can be concluded that this group counseling program in the elementary school which utilized the milieu forces of interpersonal relationships has had a very positive effect on students and parents and to a lesser degree on teachers.

The amount of time required to produce change varied with individuals. Concomitantly, significant change was not observable in every student. As compared to other techniques used at the elementary school level, this model seems to be particularly effective in dealing with problems of behavior and attitudes, and in producing change in self-concept.

Observing the program in action had led several schools to implement the program in their own systems. This would seem to indicate that it does meet some of the needs of the elementary school guidance program. The key to such a program is the inter-relatedness of the three milieu groups—students, teachers, and parents. Without doubt this approach develops a Hawthorne effect.[1] But contrary to those who wish to eliminate this effect, the investigator feels that elementary school programs should strive to strengthen and accentuate it.

As the structure of the model program described indicates, the elementary school counselor should rely heavily, though not entirely, on groups. Much of the work-load should include individual and group consultation with teachers and parents. The counselor must help them to better understand the goals and purposes of children's behavior and provide practical assistance that will lead to improved behavior and classroom performance. The counselor's role as reported in this study appears to be a model for the role that seems to be emerging for the counselor in the elementary school.

Summary

A model elementary school counseling program was initiated in which talented underachievers from grades 3–6 were screened from teacher referrals and placed in a control group (N = 35) or into an experimental group (N = 35). The latter met weekly for 45 minutes

[1] The Hawthorne effect increases positive results in a research study through the feeling of importance transmitted to the people involved in the study by the act of experimentation or institution of special programs.

302 / Applications: Illustrative Studies and Descriptions

in five separate counseling sessions. Teachers of these students met weekly in a one-hour seminar related to problems with these children. Their parents also met weekly in a two-hour session in which specific parents were interviewed before the large group, or in which a general question and discussion period was held.

Pre- and post-testing indicated that the experimental group felt less anxiety, were more self-reliant and less nervous, and saw their parents as accepting them more "as they are." They also were less aggressive, had more of a feeling of belonging, and had better school relations. Furthermore, they tended toward improved community relations and higher achievement on the STEP social studies achievement test.

Post-testing with a behavior and attitude inventory revealed a much healthier attitude and behavior around home, less conflict and anxieties, more responsibility taken, and better intra-family relations. In school there were shifts in a desired direction from both withdrawn and aggressive behaviors of students. There was also more participation in class, fewer disturbances, better classroom atmosphere, development of self-respect and confidence, and improved classroom work and study habits. There was also less fear of making mistakes and a tendency to be more flexible and open. Generally parents saw a stronger improvement in their children than did the teachers. Although there was a trend toward improved achievement on the STEP social studies test, no significant change in grades was reported.

It is evident that (a) several desirable changes took place, and (b) this procedure fits extremely well into the typical elementary school program. The program described here is the core of a model elementary school guidance and in-service training program, meeting many of the existing needs that the elementary school staff reflects. But more important it reflects the role of the elementary school counselor that seems to be emerging in practice, such as in the Illinois Demonstration Projects for Elementary School Counseling. Many theoreticians such as Merle Ohlsen and Henry Kaczkowski of the University of Illinois are also describing a very similar role for the elementary school counselor.

23 / SMALL GROUP COUNSELING WITH NEGRO ADOLESCENTS IN A PUBLIC HIGH SCHOOL

Burl E. Gilliland

Recent experiments evaluating the results of small group counseling within educational settings have produced divergent results (Broedel, 1958; Ofman, 1963; Ohlsen, 1960). Differences in results should not be attributed to group techniques (as a method of counseling), but rather should be viewed as productions of variation in such factors as process, content, setting, counselor-counselee personalities, length of time, frequency of sessions, group size, and purpose (Cass & Norton, 1951; Gilliland, 1966). However, the value of group methods as an effective counseling technique has been credibly established over a wide range of experimentation and practice (Gordon, 1951; Rosenbaum & Berger, 1963; Slavson, 1964; Spielberger & Weitz, 1964).

The present study sought to evaluate the outcomes of counseling with small groups of Negro high school students in the technical and scientific community of Oak Ridge, Tennessee. The Negro population constituted a minority of approximately 6% in a large competitive and academically oriented high school. Specific objectives were to determine the effects of small group counseling on: (*a*) achievement in verbal skills of vocabulary, reading, and English usage as measured by the Cooperative English Achievement Tests (CEAT); (*b*) GPAs; (*c*) occupational aspiration as measured by the Occupational Aspiration Scale (OAS; Haller & Miller, 1963); (*d*) attitude toward vocations as measured by the Vocational Development Inventory (VDI; Crites, 1965); (*e*) self-concept as measured by

From JOURNAL OF COUNSELING PSYCHOLOGY, *1968, Vol. 15, pp. 147–152. Copyright 1968 by the American Psychological Association, and reproduced by permission.*

the Index of Adjustment and Values (IAV; Bills, undated); (f) school attendance; (g) affective and feeling behavior; and (h) degree of change or movement of counselees' expression of feeling or involvement between periods in the study as determined by independent raters using the seven-point Experiencing Scale (EXP; Tomlinson & Hart, 1958).

Method

The Ss were drawn and assigned to groups at random from the Negro population of the high school. Ages ranged 15–19 for the boys and 14–17 for the girls. There were two experimental groups— one group of seven boys and another group of seven girls; random control groups—eight boys and eight girls—were selected. No attempt was made to equate for factors such as age, ability, achievement level, GPA, grade level, or attendance percentages. The two experimental groups received small group counseling in addition to their normal school experiences; the two control groups received only their normal school experiences—no group counseling. Experimental groups met 1 hour each week with the same male counselor (the investigator) for one academic year—four 9-week marking periods. All sessions, recorded on sound-taped protocols, were conducted in a group counseling room in the guidance suite of the school. Some factors considered in choosing the CEAT were (a) appropriateness in measuring verbal skills which are so crucial in successful school achievement (an especially critical area for southern Negroes); (b) simplicity of directions, administering, and scoring; (c) brevity (an important factor in testing culturally deprived persons, who often manifest short interest span); (d) favorable validity and reliability; and (e) availability of matched equated forms. The OAS, VDI, and IAV were selected because of (a) suitability in assessing student aspiration, attitudes toward the world of work, and self-concept; (b) successful results reported by both the test developers and others; (c) scarcity of other instruments for testing these particular variables; and (d) ease of administration, scoring, and using results. The EXP was employed because of (a) effectiveness as demonstrated by Tomlinson and Hart (1958), (b) appropriateness in assessing sound-taped protocols, and (c) simplicity of administration and use of results.

Although the research design was formulated on the basis of comparing pre- and posttest data for an academic year, a decision was made after the project began to administer the OAS, VDI, and IAV to experimental Ss at midyear. While such data were not considered vital to stated purposes, these tests were inserted to reflect trends, rather than to draw major conclusions or test specific hypotheses.

The conceptual basis for the group counseling was essentially the group-centered approach. A conscious attempt was made to provide counselor behavior which would be perceived by the students as being "congruent, as empathic, and as having unconditional positive regard" (Rogers, 1961, p. 40). This mode of counselor behavior presupposes that each person in the group seeks, and is capable of attaining, self-fulfillment and self-enhancement, that experience "occurs in a feeling climate, with an emotional tone, in an affective state" (Morgan, 1965, p. 11), and that "the most effective group will be the one in which there is participation of all group members, each member making his most creative contribution" (Gordon, 1951, p. 63). Tomlinson and Hart's (1958) significant findings (that congruent, empathic, acceptant counselor behavior, which transmits a feeling of unconditional positive regard for the client, has a positive effect on the counselee, which reflects in improved client coping behavior in terms of movement away from static, unfeeling, fixed, impersonal types of functioning toward more fluid, changing, acceptant, experiential patterns of functioning) provided a rational basis for following the group-centered concept.

Data from evaluative instruments and school records were taken at the times shown in Table 1, page 306. The statistical system used for testing for significance of the various sets of objective data was the least-squares analysis of data with unequal subclass numbers (United States Department of Agriculture, 1960), employing the matrix-inversion method of solving for the partial regression coefficients (Anderson & Bancroft, 1952). Conventional experimental designs such as analysis of variance formulae were rejected because of the difficulties in maintaining constant subclass numbers for the year. The least-squares method efficiently accomplished the comparison of the means, and the familiar analysis of variance table was still the end result.

Results and Discussion

An essential distillation of the findings was that group counseling enhanced both the achievement level and the personal functioning

TABLE 1
Sequence of Testing

Instrument	Male Experimental			Male Control			Female Experimental			Female Control		
	Pretest	*Midyear*	*Posttest*	*Pretest*	*Midyear*	*Posttest*	*Pretest*	*Midyear*	*Posttest*	*Pretest*	*Midyear*	*Posttest*
Cooperative English Achievement Tests	x		x	x		x	x		x	x		x
Occupational Aspiration Scale	x	x	x	x		x	x	x	x	x		x
Vocational Development Inventory	x	x	x	x		x	x	x	x	x		x
Index of Adjustment and Values	x	x	x	x		x	x	x	x	x		x
Grade-point average	x	x	x	x	x	x	x	x	x	x	x	x
Attendance percentage	x	x	x	x	x	x	x	x	x	x	x	x
Experiencing Scale[a]	x	x	x	x			x	x	x	x		
Protocol evaluations	x	x	x	x			x	x	x	x		

[a] Protocol ratings.

of the Negro adolescent. The experimental groups excelled the control groups on all measures of scholastic endeavor and all personal scales and inventories except the IAV.

FINDINGS BASED ON ANALYSIS OF OBJECTIVE DATA

Table 2 contains an analysis of experimental, control, and sex data for the CEAT (Vocabulary, Reading, and English Usage subtests), OAS, IAV, VDI, and GPA. The experimental groups, compared with control groups, showed gains at the .01 level of significance in Vocabulary, Reading, English Usage, OAS, and VDI. Gain in GPAs approached significance. That the experimental groups reg-

TABLE 2

Analyses of Variance for Group and Sex Effects Based on Raw-Score Total Differences Between Pre- and Posttest

	Source		
Instrument	Groups[a]	Sex	Error
Vocabulary			
MS	1281.51	36.30	40.71
F	31.48*	0.89	
Reading			
MS	2338.42	97.20	132.33
F	17.67*	0.73	
English Usage			
MS	1115.67	19.20	57.04
F	19.56*	0.34	
OAS			
MS	1109.17	32.03	112.46
F	9.86*	0.28	
IAV			
MS	1305.70	156.32	355.11
F	3.68	0.44	
VDI			
MS	998.33	64.53	36.92
F	27.04*	1.75	
GPA			
MS	633160.60	28705.56	154127.30
F	4.12	0.19	

NOTE: Abbreviated: OAS = Occupational Aspiration Scale; IAV = Index of Adjustment and Values; VDI = Vocational Development Inventory; GPA = Grade-point average.
* Experimental group gain significantly greater than that of control group; $p \leq .01$, $df = 1/27$.
[a] Protocol ratings.

istered a decline on the IAV between pre- and posttesting was not surprising in light of a number of recent reports (Blake, 1960; Dentler, 1966; Patterson, 1965; Rainwater, 1966; Wey, 1966) indicating that the Negro's personality and behavior may manifest unusual changes in the desegregated school. Wey (1966) further suggested that "although Negro students have lower aptitude scores on standardized tests, they have higher aspirations than comparable white students in regard to educational training. Blake concluded that the higher levels of aspirations of some Negroes are attempts to maintain self-esteem in the face of discrimination" (p. 510).

The group counseling seems to have brought on a reappraisal of experimental students' self-concepts, suggesting that these students came to perceive the realities of the limited opportunities available to Negroes in their particular environmental setting, and, no longer seeking to deceive themselves, they did not fall back into the trap of overcompensating in attempts to maintain self-esteem. The midyear tests (data not included in this report) yielded only one significant difference—the experimental boys showed a decline in self-rating between pretest and midyear test ($p < .01$). In effect, the midyear tests suggest that (a) the effectiveness of short-term group counseling as measured by the OAS, VDI, and GPA was shown to be minimal; and (b) the degree of decline on the experimental boys' IAV was greater between pretest and midyear test than between pre- and posttests, indicating that the boys perceived themselves more negatively at midyear. Whether experimental group members experienced a decline in self-concept, developed a tendency to withstand the impulse to overcompensate, or whether some other factor intervened, is subject to debate. That a marked discrepancy did develop was the important thing—perhaps the most vital finding of the study. Since barriers to Negro opportunity are rapidly being removed, counselors and educators are in a key position to guide and to encourage young Negroes to aspire to further their education, and it is clear that for one to distort his self-esteem—in either direction—is to his disadvantage. One's motivation, aspiration, initiative, goals—indeed, his every behavioral characteristic—are governed by how he views himself. Probably no other factor is so crucial to the education of Negro youth.

No significant gain on any test was attributed to sex.

Table 3 shows the analysis of ratings of spaced segments of early, middle, and late sound-taped protocols by four independent raters whose judgments were done blind; that is, they were not told which were the early and late segments. Although the EXP was designed

TABLE 3

Mean Differences in Counselee Involvement at Three Intervals as Rated on the Experiencing Scale

Experimental Group	M_D Early–Middle	M_D Middle–Late	M_D Early–Late
Boys	5.9*	18.38**	24.88**
Girls	14.88**	−1.25	13.63**

* $p < .05$, $df = 7$.
** $p < .01$, $df = 7$.

for use in rating the movement of counselees' experiential relationships in one-to-one counseling, no difficulty was encountered in applying it to group counseling protocols. The data demonstrate a positive change in the movement of counselees' expression of feeling or involvement between periods in the experiment. The EXP ratings indicate that the Negro girls had achieved a level or degree of involvement by Session 18 which the boys did not attain until 30 or more sessions. This is an interesting result; it correlates with counselor observation as well as with protocol evaluations; it indicates that, from the standpoint of degree of involvement or expression of feeling, 18 sessions represent an optimum length of time for a series of group counseling sessions with Negro girls, while the optimum number for Negro boys is 30 or more. The inferred conclusions about the EXP seem to be: (*a*) Small group counseling enhances the *degree* to which counselees manifest inward reference in their verbalizations; that is, they show positive movement (as measured on a continuum from no personal involvement toward freedom to move among feelings and to internalize their significance from an experiential frame of reference); and (*b*) in small group counseling adolescent Negro girls show maximum positive movement much sooner than do adolescent Negro boys.

FINDINGS BASED ON ANALYSIS OF TAPED PROTOCOLS AND COUNSELOR OBSERVATION OF GROUP SESSIONS

It was found that one of the primary expressed concerns of adolescent Negro males was vocations and vocational planning; adolescent Negro females verbalized greater concern regarding social adjustment and social acceptance. These findings seem to correlate with the unrest of Negroes nationally, and it is interesting that the *girls* later requested multiracial groups. Although the expressive actions of Negro adolescents portrayed predominantly noncognitive, blustery, physical patterns of behavior, there emerged a manifest desire for successful scholastic attainment which had been carefully masked by overt activities. Group counseling appeared to produce in males a revised conceptual model of the ideal self, prompting them to acquire and use, near the end of the year, such academic skills as listening and studying to the degree that functional classroom success was achieved. The implication for counselors and educators is that such educational endeavors as group activities, counseling, remedial study skills, and vocational information projects may be appropriate for Negro adolescents even though they appear unwanted at first.

A longer period was required to achieve productive rapport with Negro boys than with Negro girls. A stark result of the matriarchal influence was that girls shed their inhibitions more quickly and seemed to possess keener, more valid perceptions of interpersonal relations than the boys. Counseling and educational programs should consider that the matriarchal system tends to produce positive affective behavior in girls and overt and/or suspicious behavior in boys.

The ambivalence of low self-esteem versus pride in accomplishment of Negro groups was displayed in the behavior of experimental students. Also, predominantly Negro cultural patterns appeared to provide a vital haven of security. Thus, the divided feeling—desire for integration or acceptance in all phases of society versus "safety" of the all-Negro culture—provides a real problem in achieving equality in the larger society. One unique feature of the group counseling was the provision of role-playing opportunities which worked to dispel fears of failure and to serve as catalysts in propelling Negro adolescents toward greater self-involvement in the total life of the school. Such experience should enhance the progress toward improved interracial understanding by persons of any group, regardless of race, who exhibit fear of cross-cultural interaction.

The involvement of Negro adolescents in group counseling led to the formation of spontaneous counseling groups. It was concluded that satisfying group experiences created a demand for group counseling among peers who apparently had not recognized the desire or need for it.

Spontaneous Groups

Near the end of the year, requests from the non-group-counseled Negro students (boys and girls) led to the formation of spontaneous

Negro student groups, open to any student wishing to participate. These groups met during evenings throughout the following summer, but, because of the initiative of Negro girls who had been experimental subjects during the previous year, selected white students were invited to participate during the latter part of the summer. The interracial communication proved to be of such quality that expansion of the program was necessary.

About 50 students and 8 teachers on the school staff began weekly multiracial group counseling sessions during evenings in September 1966. These multiracial groups (open to all students of all races) received impetus and effective cohesion through the common desire to achieve better interracial understanding. The experiences in these groups afforded Negro youth the unique opportunity to verbalize feelings concerning racially connected problems, grievances, and anxieties in an atmosphere of acceptance by their teachers and their multiracial peers. The groups, which continued to meet throughout the 1966–67 school year, proved to hold a magnetic appeal to both white and Negro youth, leading to the unconditional sharing of feelings and understandings. As students' interests expanded, they began periodically to invite outside resource persons— both white and Negro experts in the human relations field—into the groups. Student representatives of the groups were also invited into history classes which were studying units on racial integration. Fruits of the project have been evidenced by improved intergroup school and community social relations. Positive effects have been recognized by students, school authorities, the local Community Relations Council, the Human Relations Advisory Board of the City Council, and the Community Actions Committee.

REFERENCES

Anderson, R. L., & Bancroft, T. A. *Statistical theory in research.* Chap. 2. New York: McGraw-Hill, 1952.

Bills, R. E. Index of adjustment and values. Unpublished paper, University of Alabama, undated.

Blake, E., Jr. A comparison of intraracial and interracial levels of aspiration. Unpublished doctoral dissertation, University of Illinois, 1960.

Broedel, J. W. A study of the effects of group counseling on the academic performance and mental health of underachieving gifted adolescents. Unpublished doctoral dissertation, University of Illinois, 1958. Pp. 114–121.

Cass, B. M., & Norton, F. T. M. Group size and leaderless discussion. *Journal of Applied Psychology*, 1951, *35*, 397–400.

Crites, J. O. Measurement of vocational maturity in adolescence: 1. Attitude test of the Vocational Development Inventory. *Psychological Monographs*, 1965, *79* (2, Whole No. 595).

Dentler, R. A. Barriers to northern school desegregation. *Daedalus*, 1966, *95*, 45–63.

Gilliland, B. E. An evaluation of the effects of small group counseling with Negro adolescents. Unpublished doctoral dissertation, University of Tennessee, 1966.

Gordon, T. Group-centered leadership and administration. In C. R. Rogers (Ed.), *Client-centered therapy*. Boston: Houghton Mifflin, 1951. Pp. 323–329.

Haller, A. O., & Miller, I. W. The occupational aspiration scale: Theory, structure, and correlates. Technical Bulletin No. 288, 1963, Michigan State University, Agricultural Experiment Station, Department of Sociology and Anthropology.

Morgan, H. G. Introduction. In M. Rassmussen (Ed.), *Feelings and learning*. Washington, D.C.: Association for Childhood Education International, 1965, 10–11.

Ofman, W. Evaluation of a group counseling procedure. Unpublished doctoral dissertation, University of California (Los Angeles), 1963.

Ohlsen, M. M. Counseling within a group setting. *Journal of the National Association of Women Deans and Counselors*, 1960, *23*, 104–109.

Patterson, F. K. *Negro self concept: Implications for school and citizenship*. New York: McGraw-Hill, 1965.

Rainwater, L. Crucible of identity: The Negro lower-class family. *Daedalus*, 1966, *95*, 172–216.

Rogers, C. R. The process equation of psychotherapy. *American Journal of Psychotherapy*, 1961, *15*, 40–41.

Rosenbaum, M., & Berger, M. *Group psychotherapy and group function*. New York: Basic Books, 1963.

Slavson, S. R. *A textbook in analytic group psychotherapy*. New York: International Universities Press, 1964.

Spielberger, C. D., & Weitz, H. Anxiety, group counseling, and college achievement. *Psychological Monographs*, 1964, *78* (13, Whole No. 590).

Tomlinson, T. M., & Hart, J. T., Jr. A validation study of the process scale. Madison: University of Wisconsin, 1958 (Mimeo). Cited by W. F. Gross, Jr., A process approach to the evaluation of short-term counseling. Unpublished doctoral dissertation, University of Tennessee, 1964, Pp. 26–29, 67–71.

United States Department of Agriculture, Agricultural Research Service. *Least-squares analysis of data with unequal subclass numbers.* (ARS-20-8) Washington, D.C.: Government Printing Office, 1960.

Wey, H. W. Desegregation and integration. *Phi Delta Kappan,* 1966, *9,* 508–514.

24 / GROUP COUNSELING FOR GIFTED UNDERACHIEVING HIGH SCHOOL STUDENTS

Ben C. Finney and Elizabeth Van Dalsem

Bright and academically able students who fail to live up to their potential are a concern to their parents and teachers and a challenge to their counselors, who hope to help these students "find themselves" and to be able to use their abilities and educational opportunities. Group counseling, with the potential of enabling counselors to reach more students, and perhaps of using adolescent peer-consciousness in a constructive way, has obvious appeal in dealing with this problem.

Several studies have been conducted evaluating the effectiveness of group counseling with underachieving high school students. Baymur and Patterson (1960) selected a group of underachievers and compared about 12 weeks of individual counseling, group counseling, a one-session "motivational counseling," and no counseling. None of the separate groups showed significant improvement, but with only eight students in each group, the small N limits the conclusions. However, when the individual and group counseling were combined into a "counseled group," which seems a reasonable procedure, there were modest increases in grades and some evidence of personality improvement. Broedel, Ohlsen, Proff, and Southard (1960), working with a gifted underachieving group of high school freshmen, compared a counseled and a control group, with a total N of 34. The counseled group was given group counseling twice a week for 8 weeks, and then the control group was counseled, serving as its own control. Projective measures indicated an improvement of self-acceptance and affective expression, and ratings of parents and

From JOURNAL OF COUNSELING PSYCHOLOGY, *1969, Vol. 16, pp. 87–94. Copyright 1969 by the American Psychological Association, and reproduced by permission.*

counselors showed an improvement toward sounder personality development. But the counseling seemed, if anything, to lower rather than raise grades. Shaw (1962) reported on the results of 14 small groups with able underachieving high school students, meeting once a week for eight sessions, with parents participating. He found no significant differences from the control Ss on grade-point averages, changes in self-concept, or changes in the teachers' attitudes toward the students.

These results suggest that brief group counseling is not likely to show improvement in grades. The results are a little more encouraging in the area of desirable personality changes, but an evaluation of the potential of group counseling from these studies is limited by the small samples and the length of time the students were counseled. The present research was aimed at evaluating group counseling for underachievers, using larger samples, with a number of different groups and counselors, and extending over a long enough period to allow a maximum opportunity for the group process to be effective.

Method

Subjects

All of the sophomore students of the six high schools of the Sequoia High School District were given the Differential Aptitude Test Battery (DAT). Those students with a DAT composite Verbal-Numerical score at or above the seventy-fifth percentile were selected as the academically gifted population. In order to get enough Ss for the matched groups, it was necessary to set the criteria for underachieving so that some students were included who would not ordinarily be thought of as underachievers. Students whose grade-point average (GPA) for their freshman year was below the mean for all students at their DAT level were classified as academic underachievers. Thus students at the ninety-ninth percentile on the DAT were placed in the underachieving group if the GPA was below 3.0 or a "B" average. The cutting point for the ninety-fifth percentile was 2.8, the ninetieth at 2.6, the eighty-fifth at 2.4, the eightieth at 2.2, and the seventy-fifth at 2.0 or below. Approximately half of all these gifted students were classified as academic underachievers.

These students within each school were divided according to sex, and then randomly assigned to either the control or the counseling groups to make up two paired same-sexed groups of similar size. Within the limitations of random selection, the control and counseling groups were comparable. Each of the counseling groups was paired with a same-sexed control group from the same high school, so that their conditions were similar except for the exposure to group counseling.

Four groups of girls were assigned to counseling ($N = 52$) and four to the control conditions ($N = 46$). There were four counseling groups ($N = 40$) and four control groups ($N = 58$) of boys. The groups ranged in size from 5 to 15, with an average of 12. By the end of the study, the size of the counseling sample had shrunk to 69, either through failure to attend the groups or by moving, and the control group was down to 85. In the tables comparing the groups on the various measures there is some variation in the Ns listed due to the fact that on any particular measure one or more of the students might not be included because of extraneous factors such as being ill the day the tests were given, errors in filling out tests, etc.

The effect of the shrinkage of the sample needs to be considered to see if it introduced any bias; although the groups might be comparable on the basis of random selection, the students who persevered and continued with the counseling groups might have different characteristics from those who continued in the control groups. However, inspection of the initial scores of the remaining counseling and control groups shows minimal and nonsignificant differences in the group means. The differences between the groups at the end of the study were not due to differences between the groups in their initial scores due to selection factors.

Group Counselors

The counselors, who are mostly the regular high school counselors, ranged in experience from 2 years to none, but all had had at least 1 year of a weekly seminar in techniques of group counseling. Fourteen leaders served over the 2 years of the study, with some dropping out and being replaced at the end of the first year. In the year prior to the beginning of the study, once a week seminars had been conducted in each of the five participating high schools, led by a psychologist experienced in group counseling. These seminars served to recruit and train leaders, to interest the school administrators, and to prepare a receptive climate for group counseling in the schools. During the first year about half of the counselors met regularly for a 2-hour weekly seminar, discussing their technical problems with their student groups, and also using the seminar group to explore their own personal feelings and reactions. The leaders not attending this seminar met with the consultant in groups of two or three every other week. During the second year the pattern of monthly or semimonthly consultation was the typical one.

The leaders all became involved in the success of the experiment, sometimes to the point of feeling personally responsible for seeing that it was a success. This motivation kept them meeting regularly with their groups, although they were often hard-pressed to find time from their other work commitments, and it helped them to continue in the face of the often discouraging behavior of their student groups. They agreed that leading a student counseling group was a demanding task, often involving their own personal feelings—but also a rewarding one. It became quite clear during the study that regular consultation and the opportunity to discuss their feelings and experiences with other leaders was essential, and that support during discouraging or stormy phases was important. However, they also expressed the feeling that the experience had been of real benefit to them, both as counselors and as persons, and that the experiment was of value no matter how the data came out.

GROUP COUNSELING PROCESS

After the counseling groups had been selected, they were called together by the leader and the plans and the reason for the study were explained frankly; in general the situation was accepted positively and matter-of-factly. The groups met regularly each week during the school year from late in the fall semester of their sophomore year until May of their junior year. The hours were staggered so that absences were spread out among the different classes and they were absent from any one class about once a month. The fact that class time was taken for the counseling process added complications to the normal group process, for the counselors often felt a need to see more progress in the group to justify class absence and sometimes wondered if the attraction of the group was only to get out of class. Similarly, when the students skipped the group with the excuse that they needed the class time, it was hard to decide whether they were being resistive or showing progress.

After the initial uneasiness and questions as to why they had been selected for counseling, they did not seem bothered about being treated specially or about explaining their absences from class to their peers. The parents seemed to react favorably to the attention given their children.

Aside from the hour each week in the counseling group, no special effort was made to treat the counseling students differently from the control group. The control group was told about the aims of the study and that they were serving as controls, which they accepted matter-of-factly. Being in the study did not affect their regular routine, for while the counseling students were meeting they remained in the classroom with the rest of the students, most of whom were not in the study. The teachers knew who were in the two groups, since the counseling students were excused from class about once a month and they rated both the control and counseling students at the end of the semester; about 4–8 students in a class of 30 would be in the study. It is difficult to evaluate how much this knowledge influenced their handling of the students and their ratings; informal observations and conversations indicated that for the most part the teachers were not particularly concerned about the study and the students in it.

In addition to the usual adolescent difficulty in thinking about or discussing their feelings, the counseling groups seemed to treat the group counseling situation much in the same way as they dealt with school; they were inclined to waste the time while trying to shift the responsibility for not using the opportunity to someone else. Typically, at the beginning they spent much group time criticizing—often with devastating accuracy—teachers, parents, adults, the school, the social system, but delicately avoiding any inspection of the part which they played in their academic difficulties—or the feeling behind the actions. With continued experience they became more comfortable, as did the leaders, and began more often to share personal feelings—about themselves, their families, their classmates, and eventually, toward other members of the group. They did not get into "deep" material, but most of them did talk more frankly than they ever had before in a group and began to look at the feelings and motives behind the behavior.

An important variable in the experiment was the relatively long duration of the group counseling. Although the study had been originally planned for only 1 year, at the end of that time the changes were very modest, and it was decided to continue the experiment for another year. Both the observations of the leaders and the magnitude of the changes during the second year support the view point that for group counseling to have significant impact, it needs to continue over a considerable time.

MEASURES

One hypothesis was that group counseling would help these students with their academic problem, their relatively poor grades. Changes in this area were measured by the GPA.

A second hypothesis was that there would be positive changes in some of their attitudes and behaviors toward school and study. Three different measures were used to register changes in this area:

1. The California Study Methods Survey (CSMS), a self-report inventory to reveal the study methods and attitudes of the student toward school and learning, was administered.
2. Absences and deportment referrals, obtained from the school records, were used as another measure of attitude toward school and acceptance of school responsibilities. The numbers of students who had more than nine absences during the semester or one or more referral to the Dean for a deportment difficulty were compared between the two groups.
3. The Student Behavior Questionnaire (SBQ) was devised for this study to get a measure of the teachers' opinions of classroom attitudes and behavior. It consists of 33 true-false questions which were checked by all four classroom teachers at the end of each semester. The sum of all the negative items tallied for the student constituted the score on the questionnaire.

The California Psychological Inventory (CPI) was used as a measure to test the hypothesis that the group counseling experience would produce desirable changes in personal and social functioning. The counseling and control groups were compared on the basis of change scores, the difference between the initial and final scores for each individual. Only 17 males and 35 females of the counseling group and 41 males and 35 females in the control group had taken both the initial and the final testing.

In addition to the 18 scales of the CPI, three factor scores were computed which were based on the work of five recent factor analyses of the test (Crites, Bechtoldt, Goldstein, & Heilbrun, 1961; Hicks, 1960; Mitchell & Pierce-Jones, 1960; Nichols & Beck, 1960; Nichols & Schnell, 1963). These factor scores, obtained by averaging the standard scores of several of the scales, seemed to give a more clear and comprehensive picture when trying to understand the patterns of the individual scales which discriminated between the counseling and the control groups.

The first factor, termed "Factor 1, Social Poise," includes five of the six scales of Gough's Class I, excluding Wb, and is defined by Sociability, and includes Dominance, Capacity for Status, Social Presence, and Self-Acceptance. Gough has described it as indicating "Improvement in poise, social adequacy, and confidence in being able to cope with interpersonal situations." [1]

The second factor, called "Factor 2, Social Conformity," is defined by Self-Control, and includes Good Impression, Achievement through Conformity, and Well-Being. This factor appeared in all five of the factor studies, with some variability in the scales included.

In four of the factor analysis studies there was a factor including, or defined by, Achievement through Independence and a good deal of overlap among the other scales. This factor includes Flexibility, Tolerance, and Intellectual Efficiency and is called "Factor 3, Independent Thought and Action." Mitchell and Pierce-Jones (1960) say, ". . . this factor suggests a complex of qualities which might augur well for success in a wide range of human activities. Common to all of these qualities is an emphasis on intellectuality, broad interests, perspective, and thoroughgoing independence" (p. 454).

A fourth factor, Gough's Class II, was included although it did not emerge in these factorial studies. Gough, however, reports that these scales have clustered together in several cluster analyses he did in developing the tests (see footnote 1). In this study it will be called "Factor 4, Maturity and Responsibility," and includes Responsibility, Socialization, Self-Control, Tolerance, Good Impression, and Communality.

Results

Grade-Point Average

Table 1 shows the GPA for the counseling and control groups at the end of the freshman year, which was the beginning of the study, and at the end of the sophomore and junior years. There were no significant differences in grades, either over time or between the two

[1] H. G. Gough, personal communication, June 1962.

TABLE 1
Grade-Point Average

Year	Counseling Group[a]		Control Group[b]		
	M	SD	M	SD	t
Freshman	2.15	.49	2.16	.51	ns
Sophomore	2.14	.72	2.25	.70	ns
Junior	2.29	.77	2.17	.76	ns

[a] $N = 69$.
[b] $N = 85$.

groups, and the hypothesis that group counseling would produce improvement in grades was not supported.

California Study Methods Survey

Table 2 shows the results from the CSMS. There were no significant changes with time or between the groups. Starting at about the average for high school students in general, they remained unchanged.

Absences and Deportment Referrals

Table 3 shows the number of students who were absent more than nine times during a semester or who were referred to the Dean for deportment difficulty. While there were nonsignificant trends favoring the counseling group in the sophomore year, it was only in the

TABLE 2
California Study Methods Survey

Year	Counseling Group[a]		Control Group[b]		
	M	SD	M	SD	t
Freshman	46.08	9.60	49.00	9.13	ns
Sophomore	48.48	9.75	47.35	9.80	ns
Junior	47.89	8.21	48.01	10.68	ns

[a] $N = 66$.
[b] $N = 73$.

TABLE 3
Number of Absentees and Deportment Referrals

Year	Counseling Group[a]		Control Group[b]		χ^2 for Absences
	Absent	Deportment	Absent	Deportment	
Sophomore	27	12	42	28	ns
Junior	26	21	51	33	6.72*

[a] $N = 69$.
[b] $N = 85$.
* $p < .01$ (one tailed).

junior year that there were significant differences in the number of students who were absent more than nine times during the semester. Of the 85 students in the control group, 51 were absent more than nine times while in the counseling group of 69, only 26 were absent that often ($\chi = 6.72$, $p < .01$, one-tailed). There were no significant differences in referrals for deportment.

STUDENT BEHAVIOR QUESTIONNAIRE

Table 4 shows the results of the two groups on the SBQ at the end of each of the four semesters during the study. Starting with an average of 10 items which had been marked as unsatisfactory by at least two of their four teachers, at the end of the sophomore year there had been improvement in both groups, barely significantly

TABLE 4
Student Behavior Questionnaire

Semester	Counseling Group[a]			Control Group[b]			t
	N	M	SD	N	M	SD	
Low sophomore	72	10.2	4.9	103	10.6	5.8	ns
High sophomore	72	7.0	5.4	101	8.0	6.3	1.90*
Low junior	68	6.0	6.0	84	7.3	5.6	1.34
High junior	68	5.6	5.6	84	8.0	6.5	2.43**

[a] $N = 68$.
[b] $N = 84$.
* $p < .05$ (one tailed).
** $p < .01$ (one tailed).

more in the counseling group. At the end of the last junior semester, the counseling group had continued to improve and was clearly significantly superior to the control group, as observed by their teachers.

Table 5 shows for each individual item of the SBQ the percentage of students in the two groups who were given a negative evaluation by at least two of their teachers at the end of their junior year. The chi-square of the difference, computed on the basis of the number of students being given or not given a score on that item, significantly favored the counseling group on 11 of the 33 items. It should also be noted that on only 2 of the 33 did the control group get fewer negative responses, and those differences were not significant. It should be noted that neither the counseling nor the control groups were characterized by open rebellion; only 3% of these students were considered "rebellious, surly, or disrespectful." The behavior which they showed could be better described as subtle or "quiet" opposition. However, the counseling group showed superiority in their willingness to seek help, to accept suggestions, to pay attention, and became less disruptive, less rebellious against the rules, and less quietly resistive. They were tardy and absent less often, and less likely to put off doing their work, and, significantly, there was a change toward enjoying learning for its own sake. It is interesting that Items 21, 23, 25, 27, and 28, which were most obviously related to psychological disturbance, inner conflict, and group relationships, did not change. It may be that these items reflect deeper, more stabilized phases of the personality, or that they may simply be less directly observable and more inferential than classroom behavior and thus changes were not so readily perceived by the teachers. However, the lack of change on these items does provide some indirect evidence that the behavior improvement was real and not simply the result of positive bias by the teachers. If the improvement reported had merely reflected the hopeful expectations of the teachers that group counseling would help, one would expect these more "psychological" items to be the ones to reflect this bias.

Table 6, page 325, shows the mean scores on the CPI of the control group at the beginning of the sophomore year and at the end of the junior year, and significance of the differences, using the t test for correlated measures. Only one scale, Sense of Well-Being, improved significantly and three scales, Responsibility, Socialization, and Communality, deteriorated. Factor 4, Maturity and Responsibility, was also significantly lower.

TABLE 5

Percentage of Group Checked on Each Student Behavior Questionnaire Item

Item (Abbreviated)	Counseling[a]	Control[b]	χ^{2c}
1. Not paying attention	18	34	4.61*
2. Restless, fidgets	15	20	
3. Doesn't ask for help he needs	29	45	3.35*
4. Does not participate in class	28	42	
5. Puts off doing studies	31	46	3.18*
6. Lacks confidence in class	28	31	
7. Fails to get homework properly done	28	42	
8. Work lacks organization	32	45	
9. Has to be reprimanded	10	17	
10. Acts silly to get attention	7	20	4.05*
11. Reacts poorly to any suggestions	1	11	3.83*
12. Too much in awe of me	6	2	
13. Tardy or absent more than most	4	19	6.08**
14. Does not accept help or suggestions	1	13	5.48**
15. Does not like or trust me	6	11	
16. Has trouble working under pressure	25	19	
17. Rebellious, surly, or disrespectful	3	2	
18. Disrupts the class	6	18	3.89*
19. Resists me in a quiet, covert way	6	12	3.80*
20. Breaks school rules	1	9	
21. Withdrawn and isolated	18	21	
22. Acts or talks without thinking	9	12	
23. Has an unhappy expression	10	12	
24. Antagonizes other students	4	7	
25. Inhibited, timid, and cautious	20	21	
26. Gives excuses why doesn't work	7	9	
27. Uncomfortable with a group	18	14	
28. Has inner problems	19	24	
29. Asks for too much help	1	7	2.75*
30. Makes interested contributions (F)	44	54	
31. Gets homework done on time (F)	35	43	
32. Talks to me about herself (F)	57	64	
33. Enjoys learning for its own sake (F)	34	51	3.93*

[a] $N = 68$.

[b] $N = 84$.

[c] Computed from number of cases.

* $p < .05$ (one tailed).

** $p < .01$ (one tailed).

TABLE 6

California Psychological Inventory Changes from Low Sophomore to High Junior for Control Group

	Mean		
Scale	Low Sophomore	High Junior	t (Correlated)
1. Dominance	49.05	49.71	
2. Capacity for Status	45.50	46.81	
3. Sociability	49.42	49.05	
4. Social Presence	53.40	55.17	
5. Self-Acceptance	54.60	57.27	2.38*
6. Sense of Well-Being	43.71	41.14	
7. Responsibility	46.90	43.83	−2.55*
8. Socialization	51.30	46.98	−3.61**
9. Self-Control	42.13	39.92	
10. Tolerance	47.18	47.18	
11. Good Impression	41.28	39.98	
12. Communality	50.89	48.02	−1.98*
13. Achievement via Conformance	42.34	41.03	
14. Achievement via Independence	51.28	51.63	
15. Intellectual Efficiency	46.86	47.53	
16. Psychological-Mindedness	47.40	47.15	
17. Flexibility	56.88	56.42	
18. Femininity	48.87	46.35	
19. F-1, Social Poise	50.00	51.22	
20. F-2, Social Conformity	41.98	40.18	
21. F-3, Independent Thought and Action	50.15	50.31	
22. Maturity and Responsibility	46.21	43.92	−2.74**

NOTE: $-N = 76$.
* $p < .05$ (two tailed—no predicted direction).
** $p < .01$ (two tailed—no predicted direction).

Table 7, page 326, shows the same CPI measures for the counseling group, and eight scales have improved, Capacity for Status, Sociability, Social Presence, Self-Acceptance, Tolerance, Achievement via Independence, Intellectual Efficiency, and Psychological Mindedness. Also, there was improvement on Factor 1, Social Poise, and on Factor 2, Independent Thought and Action. There was a drop in Femininity, which is not necessarily negative. Thus while the control group seems to have lost some ground, the counseling group appears to have gained.

The crucial test of the effectiveness of counseling is the comparison of the two groups at the end of the study, shown in Table 8 on page 327. The groups were compared on the basis of change scores,

TABLE 7

California Psychological Inventory Changes from Low Sophomore to High Junior for Counseling Group

| | Mean | | |
Scale	Low Sophomore	High Junior	t (Correlated)
1. Dominance	49.86	51.86	
2. Capacity for Status	45.38	50.88	4.86**
3. Sociability	50.67	53.32	2.14*
4. Social Presence	51.94	57.26	4.48**
5. Self-Acceptance	55.78	58.44	2.14*
6. Sense of Well-Being	43.30	44.07	
7. Responsibility	47.05	45.63	
8. Socialization	48.84	47.17	
9. Self-Control	41.48	40.53	
10. Tolerance	46.67	49.71	2.52*
11. Good Impression	41.46	41.21	
12. Communality	52.80	50.94	
13. Achievement via Conformance	43.05	44.96	
14. Achievement via Independence	49.26	54.36	4.23**
15. Intellectual Efficiency	47.50	50.40	2.08*
16. Psychological-Mindedness	47.13	50.11	2.43*
17. Flexibility	55.36	57.59	
18. Femininity	49.78	45.96	−3.25**
19. F-1, Social Poise	50.28	53.92	4.18**
20. F-2, Social Conformity	41.98	42.32	
21. F-3, Independent Thought and Action	49.36	52.65	4.26**
22. F-4, Maturity and Responsibility	46.00	45.42	

NOTE: — $N = 52$.
* $p < .05$ (two tailed—no predicted direction).
** $p < .01$ (two tailed—no predicted direction).

the change for each individual from the sophomore to the junior year. There were significant differences in the predicted direction (one-tailed test) favoring the counseling group, in seven of the scales, Capacity for Status, Sociability, Social Presence, Tolerance, Achievement via Conformance, Achievement via Independence, and Psychological Mindedness. On two of the factors, Social Poise and Independent Thought and Action, there was also significant improvement.

Discussion

The results from the study demonstrate that group counseling can produce some desirable changes in gifted underachieving high

TABLE 8

California Psychological Inventory—Differences Between Control and Counseling Groups Using Change Scores—High Junior

Scale	Diff. in Mean Change Scores	t
1. Dominance		
2. Capacity for Status	4.2	2.64**
3. Sociability	3.0	1.80*
4. Social Presence	3.6	2.10*
5. Self-Acceptance		
6. Sense of Well-Being		
7. Responsibility		
8. Socialization		
9. Self-Control		
10. Tolerance	3.0	1.81*
11. Good Impression		
12. Communality		
13. Achievement via Conformance	3.2	1.76*
14. Achievement via Independence	4.8	2.84**
15. Intellectual Efficiency		
16. Psychological-Mindedness	3.2	1.78*
17. Flexibility		
18. Femininity		
19. F-1, Social Poise	2.4	1.91*
20. F-2, Social Conformity		
21. F-3, Independent Thought and Action	3.1	2.83**
22. F-4, Maturity and Responsibility		

* $p < .05$ (one tailed).
** $p < .01$ (one tailed).

school students. Furthermore, this can be done by school counselors whose training and experience are within the practical possibilities of a progressive high school counseling program. The significant differences in the final group means reflect the effect of group counseling, since the students were randomly assigned to the control and counseling groups from the population of sophomore students in the upper quartile of the DAT and having a GPA below the average for their percentile on the DAT.

The two groups started out the same, as indicated by similar mean scores on the measures at the beginning of the study. The differences in the final scores were not due to a biasing effect of differences of the characteristics of the students who dropped out of the study, since the initial mean scores of the two groups remained very similar. However, the changes were modest, around a fourth to a half a standard deviation on the CPI, and those changes that did occur happened slowly. Originally planned for 1 year, the project was extended to 2 years because at the end of the first year changes were just beginning to occur. It may be that the lack of changes, or very minimal ones, in some of the other studies are due to the short period of counseling. It takes time for high school students to adjust to the new situation of group counseling and to begin to use it constructively, especially with a group characterized by not applying themselves and wasting their opportunities in school.

The changes which were measured by the CPI were interesting in their pattern. The changes in Factor 1, Social Poise, parallel the results of other studies on the effect of therapy, and reflect an improvement in social confidence, with more resourcefulness in dealing with stress (Nichols & Beck, 1960). Factor 3, Social Conformity, the factor on which they were relatively low in the beginning, and which may reflect some of the reasons for their performance difficulty in class, did not change. However, on Factor 3, Independent Thought and Action, both the control and counseling groups were superior to the average high school student at the beginning of the study, as might be expected, since it is probably associated with superior intellectual and socioeconomic status, but it was this factor which showed the most marked improvement of the four factors. In fact, on the scale which defines the factor, Achievement via Independence, which predicts getting superior grades in college, the counseling group was about a full standard deviation superior to the average high school student. The improvement in this area of personality characteristics should be of some significance to these students, for as Mitchell and Pierce-Jones (1960) comment, "This factor suggests a complex of qualities which might augur well for success in a wide range of human activities."

But despite the fact that their teachers observed positive behavior changes in class which would seem to be associated with a more positive attitude toward school and learning, their GPA did not change. Initially both groups were rated by their teachers as showing quite a bit of behavior which could be characterized as quiet opposition; at the end of the study the counseling group had improved more and seemed more identified with adults and adult values. These kinds of changes would seem to be congruent with having had the opportunity to establish a close relationship with their adult counselor and a chance to ventilate and work through their resentments toward school and adults, as well as becoming less anxious with their peers and more able to express their feelings in words rather than actions. And yet their grades did not improve.

Why these observed changes and improvement in attitudes did not get translated into more effective use of their abilities remains unanswered.

The personality changes produced by long-term group counseling were modest, but involved personal characteristics which should stand them in good stead in life, and in college too, if their original and unsolved problem, poor grades, does not keep them from going.

REFERENCES

Baymur, F. B., & Patterson, C. H. A comparison of three methods of assisting underachieving high school students. *Journal of Counseling Psychology*, 1960, 7, 83–89.

Broedel, J., Ohlsen, M., Proff, F., & Southard, C. The effects of group counseling on gifted underachieving adolescents. *Journal of Counseling Psychology*, 1960, 7, 163–170.

Crites, J. O., Bechtoldt, H. P., Goodstein, L. D., and Heilburn, A. B., Jr. A factor analysis of the California Psychological Inventory. *Journal of Applied Psychology*, 1961, 45, 408–414.

Hicks, R. A. Factor analytic studies of the California Psychological Inventory. Unpublished master's thesis, San José State College, 1960.

Mitchell, J. V., Jr., & Pierce-Jones, J. A factor analysis of Gough's California Psychological Inventory. *Journal of Consulting Psychology*, 1960, 24, 453–456.

Nichols, R. C., & Beck, K. W. Factors in psychotherapy change. *Journal of Consulting Psychology*, 1960, 24, 388–399.

Nichols, R. C., & Schnell, R. R. Factor scales for the California Psychological Inventory. *Journal of Consulting Psychology*, 1963, 27, 228–235.

Shaw, M. C. Group counseling fails to aid underachievers. Research Brief No. 4, California State Department of Education, 1962.

25 / EVALUATION OF DEVELOPMENTAL COUNSELING WITH GROUPS OF LOW ACHIEVERS IN A HIGH SCHOOL SETTING

Ronald L. Benson and Don H. Blocher

The general question, "Is counseling effective?", has haunted personnel workers for many years. Relatively little clear-cut research evidence has been accumulated around this question despite the many studies that have attempted to deal with it in one way or another. One very good reason for this dearth of solid evidence lies in the fact that the question itself has relatively little real meaning. "Is counseling effective?" The question itself is more rhetorical than real. The productive issues involved are: What type of counseling is effective? When? With whom? For what? Under which conditions?

This study attempted to answer several of the latter type of question. The type of counseling evaluated is termed *developmental counseling* (Blocher, 1966). Developmental counseling is aimed at helping clients perform more effectively in one or more social roles. It is primarily concerned with helping clients to master developmental tasks and consequently to acquire a more adequate repertoire of coping behaviors.

Developmental counseling is not focused primarily on producing "insight," nor upon effecting global changes in "personality." It treats the client as a learner who needs to develop a more effective set of behaviors, rather than as a patient who needs to be cured, rehabilitated, or adjusted. Consequently, a wide range of techniques is employed, including those which are traditionally considered both "educative" and "therapeutic."

From School Counselor, *1967, Vol. 14, pp. 215–220. Copyright 1967, American Personnel and Guidance Association. Reprinted with permission of authors and publisher.*

Purpose of the Study

The purpose of the study was to evaluate the effectiveness of a program of developmental counseling in helping a selected group of high school students to cope more effectively with their roles as students. The particular population studied was made up of students who are typically termed "underachievers." The students loosely described under this label present one of the most frequently encountered and most challenging problems in counseling. The problems of wasted potential, delinquent behavior, school dropout, etc., which usually surround this type of counseling problem, are well known.

Design of the Study

All teachers of 10th-grade students in a suburban senior high school were asked to identify students who were well described by both the following terms: (1) "low achievers, supposedly equipped to do more satisfactory school work," and (2) "those who have negative feelings and attitudes about school, and who may be a disturbing element in the classroom." The teachers were asked to identify such students for a study being conducted by the guidance department. They were not to refer any such students for counseling. It was felt that this procedure would identify a population that was very marginal in terms of the adequacy of coping behavior for the social role of student.

All 10th-grade teachers responded by identifying one or more students. The 28 most frequently nominated students (all boys) were contacted and invited to participate in a voluntary project designed "to help sophomores with problems of school and grades." It was explained that the project would involve meeting once a week with other sophomores who had concerns similar to their own. All 28 students agreed to participate in the study.

Twelve of the students were randomly drawn to constitute the experimental (counseled) group. Twelve others were drawn for the control (non-counseled) group. The remaining four students were held in reserve in case of attrition in either group.

Two counseling groups of six students each were formed from the experimentals. These groups were formed primarily on the basis of convenience of schedules so that counseling sessions could be conducted as much as possible during study halls.

The control and reserve groups were told that students had been selected randomly for counseling and that because of time limitations, no further groups would be formed. All subjects agreed to take the S.R.A. Youth Inventory before and after the study.

Criteria

Behavior changes in the population were studied under four basic criteria: (1) changes in achievement-oriented coping behaviors as measured by academic grades: (2) changes in social coping behavior as measured by disciplinary referrals (disciplinary referral was viewed as a situation in which the student's coping behaviors are grossly inadequate to meet role expectations); (3) changes in personal feelings of adequacy of coping in social roles as measured by the S.R.A. Youth Inventory; and (4) persistence in the role of student as measured by rate of drop-out between 9th and 10th grades.

Description of the Population

Scholastic ability of each student was determined by combining Numerical Ability–Verbal Reasoning scores of the Differential Aptitude Test. The experimental group ranged from the third percentile to the 63rd percentile (Minnesota norms) with a mean at the 26th percentile (derived from the mean of the raw scores). The control group similarly ranged from the sixth percentile to the 62nd percentile with a mean at the 24th percentile. The first-semester 10th-grade average on a 12-point scale for experimentals was 1.57 (2.0 = D). The average for the controls was 1.33. These differences were not statistically significant.

Further descriptive information on the members of the experimental group provides an understanding of the nature of the population. Eleven of the 12 experimental subjects were reading below grade level as measured by the Gates Reading Test. Four of these subjects were reading below the fifth-grade level. One member was repeating 10th grade. Five had been expressly labelled as potential dropouts by the ninth-grade counselor. Two were from families so disorganized that these students were living with neither parent. All had records of failing grades, and all had exhibited varying degrees of acting-out behavior. For example, two students had past juvenile court records and one was currently on probation. Eight had been referred to the principal at least once during the previous semester, and four had been suspended from school during that period. The control group was, of course, similar in composition.

The Experimental Treatment

The experimental treatment consisted of one 55-minute group counseling session per week for the 18 weeks of the second semester. The groups met in a 12' x 17' conference room, usually during the hour that group members would have been in study hall. All sessions were tape recorded. The counselor neither insisted upon, nor guaranteed, strict confidentiality. Members were asked to use common sense and discretion in talking about anything that happened during the meetings. Members were informed that they had the privilege of withdrawing from the group at any time.

The counselor for both groups was the senior author who is a counselor of several years' experience and who has completed a supervised counseling practicum.

The Counseling Process

The initial counseling sessions were structured primarily around the concerns for which the groups were originally formed, that is, to help students with "problems of school and grades." Both test information and the comments of the students themselves indicated that they felt, and in fact were, woefully inadequate in terms of educational skills generally and study skills in particular. Accordingly, one entire session and the opening 10 to 15 minutes of 11 others were devoted to helping students master key developmental tasks in these areas.

The counselor led discussions on massed versus distributed practice, the SQ3R study method, study scheduling, concentration, homework, word meanings, test preparation, and effects of recitation on reading retention. Four short "how to study" films were shown. The district remedial reading specialist was invited in for one full session with each group.

In addition to these "group guidance" approaches, however, the counselor constantly encouraged members to express freely their feelings and ideas as these were relevant to the goals of the group. He attempted to create a climate of "mutuality" and commitment to group goals.

As the group began to cohere and members began to express feelings in the early sessions, the dominant theme was one of strong resentment toward and frustration with school. These early sessions focused on school, teachers, parents, and adults generally. Hostility and negativism characterized these early meetings. Interactions were spontaneous, and clearly audible in adjacent rooms. Members tended to view parents, teachers, and authority figures as primarily responsible for their problems.

The topics and interactions during the first four sessions were typically repetitive, and members seldom pursued a single line of thought for more than a few minutes. At this point, the members recognized that they were marking time with the same general theme. All indicated that they desired to continue meeting but felt a need to move in more positive directions.

At this stage, the counselor suggested that a crucial developmental task for the groups might be to learn to deal with the obvious feelings of hostility that they held for authority figures in more effective and acceptable ways. The group decided to role-play a series of incidents dramatizing conflicts between adolescents and parents and teachers. In the first of these role-playing sessions, members were quite self-conscious and inhibited. As the sessions progressed, they were able to project more and more of their feelings into the situation.

The counselor replayed the tape recordings of these role-playing sessions for the groups and together they analyzed the dynamics of these situations and particularly the ways in which students and teachers were perceived to cope with authority roles.

As these interactions were discussed, the groups began to verbalize more clearly their complaints about authority figures, particularly teachers. The counselor at this point suggested that they confront a real authority figure, the school principal, with their perceptions. The groups agreed to this and further stipulated that no teacher be individually identified during their discussion. They then compiled a list of observations about school that served as a basis for a full session in which the principal became a participant.

About half way through the 18 weekly sessions, the interaction within the groups began to change markedly. The members began to focus on one another rather than on outside people or situations. There was less effort at overtalking one another and more attempts at listening to other members. The counselees seemed more willing to look at their own behavior and that of other group members as a possible source of difficulty.

The counselor suggested that one important developmental task involved learning to understand how one's behavior is perceived by others. He suggested that the group could become a situation in which members could get "feedback" about their own behavior. The group agreed that this was desirable.

At this point, for several sessions, procedures were developed by which group members confronted each other with their perceptions of the members' behavior. The tenor of these remarks was sincere but sometimes brutal and frequently staggering to the recipient. Despite this, each member appeared to welcome the opportunity to hear others' perceptions of him.

These "feedback" sessions were followed by discussions of values and moral decisions. At this point, several members requested and received individual sessions with the counselor.

In the final sessions, group members evaluated the group experience. They felt overwhelmingly that it was worthwhile and remarked that they felt freer in the group and felt more responsibility for the group than in other school situations.

After each session the counselor replayed the tape recording of the session and tallied the approximate time distribution spent on each of seven general topic areas. Table 1 below gives the approximate percentage of time spent on each area over the entire 36 sessions for both counseled groups.

Evaluation of Results

Results were evaluated under the four types of criteria mentioned earlier.

TABLE 1

Percent of Time Spent in Each of Seven Areas During 18 Group Sessions

Area	Percent
Myself	25
Study Improvement	16
School and Teachers	15
Social Concerns	13
Things in General	13
Family	11
Looking Ahead	7

TABLE 2

Mean Grade-Points of Experimental and Control Groups During 1st and 2nd Semesters

Group	Semester I	Semester II	Difference
Experimental	1.57	2.08	+.51*
Control	1.33	.86	−.47*

* Significant at the .02 level (or $p > .02$).

1. Changes in academic grades. The mean changes in grade-point averages between first semester (pre-counseling) and second semester (post-counseling) were computed for both experimental and control groups. These means were compared using a *t* test. The mean differences for the two groups are shown in Table 2. The differences were in favor of the counseled group and were statistically significant at the .02 level of confidence.

2. Changes in disciplinary referrals. The number of disciplinary referrals to the principal during the second semester was obtained for each group. These differences are shown in Table 3. Eight control group students were referred for a total of 17 times, while five experimentals were referred for a total of 10 times. These differences, while in favor of the experimental group, were not statistically significant. They are obviously of *practical* significance, however.

3. Changes in feelings of adequacy of coping. Changes in the subjects' feelings of adequacy in coping were assessed using the S.R.A. Youth Inventory. This problem checklist that inventories common adolescent problems was considered a rough indicator of the subject's feeling of adequacy of coping within each of the eight areas measured. Table 4 shows the changes for experimental and control groups in terms of change in numbers of individuals who scored above the 75th percentile on each area. Scores above this point are

TABLE 3

Referrals to Principal Due to Acting-Out Behavior

Group	Number of Referrals			Total No. of Pupils Referred	Total No. of Referrals
	Once	*Twice*	*Three Times*		
Experimental	2	1	2	5	10
Control	2	3	3	8	17

TABLE 4

SRA Youth Inventory Pre- and Post-Test Comparison of Number of Control and Experimental Group Members Who Marked More Items as Problems in Each of Eight Areas than 75 Per Cent of High School Pupils in the Nation

Area	Pre-Test		Post-Test		Change	
	Exp. Gp.	*Cont. Gp.*	*Exp. Gp.*	*Cont. Gp.*	*Exp. Gp.*	*Cont. Gp.*
School	11	10	8	11	−3	+1
Looking Ahead	7	4	3	5	−4	+1
About Myself	6	5	5	8	−1	+3
Getting Along with Others	9	3	3	4	−6	+1
Home and Family	7	9	5	10	−2	+1
Boy Meets Girl	4	4	2	3	−2	−1
Health	9	7	4	9	−5	+2
Things in General	8	5	2	5	−6	0
Total	61	47	32	55	−29	+8

usually considered "high." A 2×2 chi square statistic was computed comparing the number of control and experimental scores above the 75th percentile pre-counseling and post-counseling. The chi square indicated a difference in favor of the experimental (counseled) group significant beyond the .01 level.

4. Persistence in school. Perhaps the most crucial indicator of success of the developmental counseling program lay in the degree to which it affected the school-staying behavior of the subjects. The counseling treatment terminated at the end of the subjects' 10th-grade year. All 12 of the experimental (counseled) students returned the following fall to enter 11th grade. Three, or 25 percent, of the control (non-counseled) group dropped out of school during the summer. This difference was not tested statistically but has obvious practical significance in terms of the drastic social consequences associated with dropping out of school.

Discussion

This study has a number of obvious limitations. The *n*'s are very small. Only one counselor was involved. Although steps were taken to minimize contamination of the grade and disciplinary criteria, some was possible if teachers became aware of the nature of the project. Despite these limitations the study does indicate that developmental counseling which is focused on changing rather specific coping behaviors can produce results that are both statistically and practically significant. It also suggests the usefulness of a combination of techniques and approaches not typically used by counselors.

REFERENCE

Blocher, D. H. *Developmental counseling.* New York: Ronald Press, 1966.

26 / TRANSITIONAL ADOLESCENTS, ANXIETY, AND GROUP COUNSELING

Barton E. Clements

Studies attempting to determine the efficacy of group counseling have yielded diverse results depending upon the variables investigated, the subjects counseled, and the procedures utilized. Some (Bilovsky, McMasters, Shorr, & Singer, 1953; Froehlich, 1958; Hoyt, 1955) report group counseling to be of value equal to individual counseling while others (Hewer, 1959; Biersdorf, 1957) report the process to be no better than an absence of treatment. Few have evaluated small group counseling alone and found positive results.

Though the problem of aiding students through transitional periods has been dealt with in group situations, no study was noted prior to this paper which used small group counseling as a vehicle. Aid has been offered through courses (Lowenstein & Hoppock, 1955; Arbuckle, 1949), clinics (Matteson, 1951; Goodrich, 1953), and large formal group discussions (Farmer, 1958).

The intent of this study (Clements, 1964) was to evaluate small group counseling by determining its specific usefulness in aiding the college-bound adolescent in his preparation for the college environment. Students fail to reach college and others leave prematurely for a variety of stated reasons, and a feeling of anxiety concerning self in relation to the new environment probably contributes substantially to a majority of these reasons. Therefore, the evaluation was in terms of anxiety concerning self during the transitional period. It was hypothesized that counseled students would exhibit less anxiety prior and subsequent to college entrance.

From PERSONNEL AND GUIDANCE JOURNAL, *1966, Vol. 45, pp. 67–71. Copyright 1966, American Personnel and Guidance Association. Reprinted with permission of author and publisher.*

Procedure

One hundred-eighty students were randomly selected from a population of 225 college-bound high school seniors in Mesa High School, Mesa, Arizona. Sixty students formed the experimental group and were randomly assigned to six sub-groups of 10 individuals each. Two counselors, full-time doctoral students, met with three groups each. Six 50-minute sessions were scheduled, one each week, in the spring prior to high school graduation. All sessions were held during school time on school property. Following the spring counseling and testing, the experimental groups were contacted by letter during the summer and again after they had enrolled at Arizona State University in the fall. The contacts offered additional group counseling in the fall if desired by the students, and 33 students (of 38 enrolled) availed themselves of one or more group sessions. The remaining 120 students comprised two control groups of 60 each and received no group counseling.

GROUP COUNSELING

The group counseling was structured for the purpose of allowing the direction of the sessions to be determined by the interests of the students. It was felt that college-bound youths, who were in the second semester of their senior year, would need little external motivation to discuss with their peers their immediate concern—college attendance. Structure was therefore applied for the purpose of creating an accepting, permissive atmosphere freeing students to discuss what they wanted to discuss.

In the initial sessions the counselor proposed that the groups center their discussions on their preparation for the college environment. He further suggested to the groups that they list the aspects of college attendance which concerned them most, group them into five units, and decide in what order they wished to deal with them. They identified such topics as college admission, registration, curriculum, selection of a major field of study, social activities, extracurricular activities, financial assistance, and vocational opportunities related to major fields of study.

Beyond this initial structure, the counselors acted as contributing members of the groups rather than group leaders. Direction of individual sessions was made the responsibility of the group members, except when discussion ranged far afield. In such cases, the counselor inquired as to the relationship of the discussion to college attendance. If the group wished to continue, they did so, though this occurred infrequently. It was occasionally difficult for the counselor to avoid prolonged question-and-answer periods with the students asking him for information of the college environment. When it appeared that such a session was developing, the counselor simply "did not know the answers" and suggested that the students contact the University for information. The purpose of this avoidance was to aid the student in establishing a contact with the University on his own.

For the most part, the groups were concerned with attitudes, fears, aspirations, and plans concerning college. Nearly all students regarded their initial contact with college as frightening and fraught with pitfalls. They felt that they must get the courses they wanted, the professors they wanted, the schedule they needed, and the opportunity for freedom to choose a field of study and its resultant vocational goal, or they would be forever lost. They regarded the college as cold, rigid, impersonal, confusing, and awesomely huge. They seemed to want support and assurance that their fears were unfounded. It was not always forthcoming, but the disappointment seemed easier to bear when shared with nine peers. However, when a student reported a personal contact with the University, the effect on the other members of the group was one of exhilaration. A sort of "By George, it can be done!" feeling permeated the group atmosphere.

The members served as excellent "reality testers" for each other in discussing educational and vocational plans. They quickly became adept at finding and pointing out flaws in the plans of group members and, somewhat later, began to evidence some of this facility in making their own plans.

INSTRUMENTS

Following the final session in the spring, two instruments were administered to the experimental and control students. An adaptation of the Bills Index of Adjustment and Values (IAV) and an unpublished Self Concept Inventory (SCI) (Faust & Daane, 1964) were used to measure anxiety concerning self. The Bills instrument yields a self-concept discrepancy score from a comparison of self and ideal-self concepts—the lower the score the less the anxiety. The SCI yields a congruence score which indicates the agreement of "present self" and "wanted self" concepts, minus a third "unwanted self" concept—the higher the score the less the anxiety. Following the

sixth session in the fall, the anxiety measures were again administered to the experimental students and to those of the second control
group who had enrolled in Arizona State University.

Findings

The data from the IAV and the SCI were subjected to an analysis
of variance to test for differences in anxiety through the following
comparisons: (1) experimental and control groups, (2) spring and
fall groups, (3) interaction among groups, and (4) spring experimental groups separated according to counselor (A and B). For all
comparisons the two-way analysis of variance was used, with means
adjusted for disproportionate group sizes. Because the individuals of
the fall experimental group responded to the instruments twice and
each of the separate control groups only once, the analysis of variance did not yield an estimate of the learning effects of the previous
testing. The F values were therefore submitted to the conservative
F test to minimize the effects of repeated measures with the experimental group (Geisser & Greenhouse, 1958).

Table 1 presents the mean scores and standard deviations of the
experimental and control groups on the spring and fall administrations of the SCI. The analysis of variance of SCI scores with means
adjusted for disproportionality is presented in Table 2. An F value
equal to or exceeding 3.90 was needed for significance at the .05
level of confidence.

In Table 2, one notes that the F values reached the .05 level of
significance for three comparisons: (1) experimental and control
groups, (2) spring and fall groups, and (3) interaction among groups.
Inspection of the SCI means in Table 1 reveals that (1) the congruence scores of the experimental groups were significantly higher
than those of the control groups, (2) the congruence scores of the

TABLE 1
Means and Standard Deviations of All Administrations of the Self Concept Inventory

Group	N	Mean	S.D.
Spring experimental	58	31.74	6.4
Spring control	58	29.57	6.8
Fall experimental	33	25.36	5.4
Fall control	30	20.76	5.4

TABLE 2

Analysis of Variance of SCI Scores with Means Adjusted for Disproportionality

Source of Variation	d.f.	Sum of Squares Unadjusted	Adjusted	Mean Square	F
Experimental-Control	1	366.1	381.6	381.6	13.7*
Spring-Fall	1	2284.7	2300.2	2300.2	82.4*
Interaction	1	167.1	151.6	151.6	5.4*
Within	175	4887.1		27.9	
Total	178	7705			

* Indicates significance at the .05 level of confidence or better.

spring groups were significantly higher than those of the fall groups, and (3) the means of the groups were significantly farther apart in the fall than in the spring. Significantly less anxiety was exhibited by the experimental groups as compared with the control groups and by the spring groups as compared with the fall groups as measured by the SCI.

The mean scores and standard deviations of the experimental and control groups on the spring and fall administrations of the IAV are presented in Table 3. Table 4, page 344, shows the analysis of variance of IAV scores with means adjusted for disproportionality. An F value equal to or exceeding 3.90 was needed for significance at the .05 level of confidence.

As shown in Table 4, a significant F value was reported in comparison of experimental and control groups. No significant differences were indicated for the comparison of spring and fall administrations or for the interaction among groups. Inspection of the means in Table 3 shows the discrepancy scores of the experimental

TABLE 3

Means and Standard Deviations of All Administrations of the Index of Adjustment and Values

Group	N	Mean	S.D.
Spring experimental	58	43.25	13.0
Spring control	58	48.27	15.6
Fall experimental	33	40.81	16.2
Fall control	30	50.36	16.1

TABLE 4
Analysis of Variance of IAV Scores with Means Adjusted for Disproportionality

Source of Variation	d.f.	Sums of Squares		Mean Square	F
		Unadjusted	*Adjusted*		
Experimental-control	1	2223.5	2228.4	2228.4	9.7*
Spring-Fall	1	45.4	50.3	50.3	.22
Interaction	1	336.2	331.3	331.3	1.4
Within	175	40169.9		229.5	
Total	178	42770.0			

* Indicates significance at the .05 level of confidence or better.

groups to be significantly lower than those of the control groups. The individuals of the experimental groups exhibited significantly less anxiety concerning self both prior to and subsequent to college entrance as measured by the IAV.

A comparison of the mean scores of the SCI and the IAV was made between the two experimental groups, A and B, to determine the effect of the counselor variable. No significant differences were found between the mean scores of the experimental groups led by different counselors on either the SCI instrument or the IAV instrument. In each case there is less than one full point difference between the mean scores and less than two full points difference between the standard deviations.

Conclusions

Following the six weeks of group counseling in the spring, the individuals of the experimental groups were significantly less anxious about themselves than were the individuals of the control group, as measured by both the SCI and the IAV. The conclusion was drawn that the group counseling with high school seniors resulted in a significant decrease in their self-concern anxiety.

At the conclusion of the program, the individuals of the experimental group were significantly less anxious about themselves in their new environment than were individuals of the control group, as measured by both anxiety estimates. The conclusion was made that the decrease in anxiety reported by the instruments in the spring was sustained by minimal counseling in the fall.

Although two counselors were utilized, each counseling half of the experimental group, no significant differences were observed between the anxiety scores of their respective groups, A and B. It was concluded that the effect of the counselor variable was controlled through carefully planned and executed group procedures.

It appears that a high school counselor, working half days for six weeks, can expect to contribute significantly to the college adjustment of 150 college-bound seniors. In addition, a concurrent study (McKendry, 1964) which used the same sample and group procedures reported significant gains in information about college, increased academic achievement, and increased appropriateness of vocational choice. While research providing further refinements of criteria is needed, it is suggested that group counseling, as described above, is particularly appropriate and highly relevant for high school seniors prior to college entrance.

REFERENCES

Arbuckle, D. S. A college experiment in orientation. *Occupations*, 1949, *28*, 112–117.

Biersdorf, K. R. The effectiveness of two group vocational guidance treatments. Unpublished doctoral thesis, University of Maryland, 1957.

Bilovsky, D., McMasters, W., Shorr, J. E., & Singer, S. L. Individual and group counseling. *Personnel and Guidance Journal*, 1953, *31*, 363–365.

Clements, B. E. The effects of group counseling with college-bound high school seniors on their anxiety and parent-child empathy. Unpublished doctoral dissertation, Arizona State University, 1964.

Farmer, R. A. A group discussion approach in freshman orientation. In H. I. Driver, *Counseling and learning through small group discussion.* Madison, Wisc.: Monona, 1958.

Faust, V., & Daane, C. J. Unpublished self-concept inventory, Arizona State University, 1964.

Froehlich, C. P. Must counseling be individual? *Educational and Psychological Measurement*, 1958, *18*, 681–689.

Geisser, S., & Greenhouse, S. W. An extension of Box's results on the use of the F distribution in multivariate analysis. *Annals of Mathematical Statistics*, 1958, *29*, 885–891.

Goodrich, T. A. Gains in self-understanding through pre-college clinics. *Personnel and Guidance Journal*, 1953, *31*, 433–438.

Hewer, Vivian H. Group counseling, individual counseling, and a college class in vocations. *Personnel and Guidance Journal*, 1959, *37*, 660–665.

Hoyt, D. P. An evaluation of group and individual programs in vocational guidance. *Journal of Applied Psychology*, 1955, *39*, 26–30.

Lowenstein, N., & Hoppock, R. High school occupations course helps students adjust to college. *Personnel and Guidance Journal*, 1955, *34*, 21–23.

Matteson, R. Counseling clinics for high school grads. *Occupations*, 1951, *29*, 502–505.

McKendry, A. W. The effects of group counseling on the educational planning of college-bound high school seniors. Unpublished doctoral thesis, Arizona State University, 1964.

27 / GROUP COUNSELING WITH MALE UNDERACHIEVING COLLEGE VOLUNTEERS

Stuart H. Gilbreath

Recent acts by both public and private agencies in the United States indicate a growing concern about the nation's failure to fully use its existing talent and manpower resources (Wrenn, 1962). The most critical waste of these resources is among underachieving students of high ability who leave school early, who do not go to college, or who drop out of college prematurely. As a result, the nation's educational institutions have responded to this need and increased their efforts to develop effective methods that will enable the underachieving student to develop his resources to the fullest (Educational Policies Commission, 1956).

In recent years, numerous investigators have studied the effect of group dynamics on the problem of academic underachievement. Of 13 investigations (Sheldon & Landsman, 1950; Caplan, 1957; McCarthy, 1959; DeWeese, 1959; Baymur & Patterson, 1960; Broedel, Ohlsen, Proff, & Southard, 1960; Duncan, 1962; Winborn & Schmidt, 1962; Spielberger, Weitz, & Denny, 1962; Maroney, 1962; Speegle, 1962; Clements, 1963; Hart, 1963), only one (Broedel et al., 1960) produced significant changes on any personality dimension and only two (Spielberger et al., 1962; Hart, 1963) produced significant changes in academic achievement.

In almost every study the method of group counseling was of a non-directive, unstructured nature in which the students were generally free to discuss the topic of their choice. No investigation was designed to specifically focus on the underlying, emotional dynamics

From PERSONNEL AND GUIDANCE JOURNAL, 1967, Vol. 45, pp. 469–476. Copyright 1967, American Personnel and Guidance Association. Reprinted with permission of author and publisher.

of the underachiever, or to purposefully discuss at each session the manner in which these dynamics could affect academic performance.

The Problem

The present study was an investigation of the effects of two different methods of group counseling on certain personality characteristics and on grade-point average of the male college underachiever who volunteers for counseling. One method of group counseling (directive, leader-structured) was designed to focus specifically on the underlying personality dimensions that theoretically lead to low academic performance, while the other method (non-directive, group-structured) was designed to allow the group to have as much freedom as possible in determining the topic for discussion.

Design and Methodology

SAMPLE

A male underachiever was defined as a freshman or sophomore student who was attending the university during the academic year 1963–64, who scored at the 50th percentile or higher on the College Qualification Test (CQT), and whose cumulative grade-point average at the end of the fall term, 1963, was below 2.00 (2.00 was a C or passing average on a 4.00 grading scale).

Of 683 male students who were classified as academic underachievers, 96 responded to a mailed invitation to participate in the program and were separated into 12 groups on the basis of common times available for meetings. Four groups were then randomly selected to serve as a no-treatment control group while the remaining eight groups were randomly divided into those who would experience the leader-structured method of group counseling and those who would experience the group-structured method. Two competent counselors were then assigned to two groups within each treatment cell on a random basis (by flip of a coin) in order to obtain replication within the design.

Although the random assignment of subjects to treatment group and counselor would indicate a homogeneous population across all groups as to aptitude and academic achievement, it was decided to test this assumption by use of the analysis of variance (Edwards,

1960). The results of this analysis yielded an F value of 3.05 (2.78 d.f.) for the fall term GPA and an F value of 1.09 (2.78 d.f.) for CQT aptitude. Both F values were nonsignificant and supported the assumption of homogeneity.

Eight one-and-a-half to two hour sessions of group counseling were conducted during the academic term. Of the 96 students who participated in the study, 15 were not included in the final analysis due to illness or failure to attend the minimum number of five sessions of group counseling. Eighty-one students were consequently left for statistical analysis at the conclusion of the experiment.

TREATMENT

Two methods of group counseling were used in the investigation. The directive method, designated leader-structured (LS), placed emphasis on topics that relate to the underlying emotional patterns in the underachiever as discussed in the more recent descriptive and theoretical literature (Kirk, 1952; McClelland, Atkinson, Clark, & Dowel, 1953; Berger & Sulker, 1956; Gebhart & Hoyt, 1958; Farquhar, 1963; Roth & Meyersburg, 1963; Taylor, 1964; McKenzie, 1964), e.g., a strong need for dependent relationships, a concept of self that is inadequate and inferior, a high degree of anxiety and depression, an inability to overtly express feelings of anger, an overall weakness in ego strength, and ambiguous or unrealistic purposes, goals, and values.

At each LS group session the counselor presented one of the topics concerning the dynamics of underachievement to the group and gave a realistic example of how this particular facet of their personality could affect academic behavior. The group was then given the opportunity to freely discuss their feelings and experiences as they related to the particular topic under discussion. Throughout each session the group counselor would actively relate personality patterns to scholastic skills in order to hasten group movement and increase awareness.

The topics, listed below and briefly describing the content of discussion, were organized and presented to the LS groups in the following order:

Academic Underachievement. A discussion of the feelings surrounding academic underachievement in general and, more specifically, the feelings associated with the study habits, attitudes, and discipline necessary for effective study.

Goals and Purposes. Feelings associated with purposes and goals were discussed and questions raised concerning the reasons behind the particular goals and purposes of the group members. Feelings surrounding the expectations of others, particularly parents, were also discussed.

Dependence-Independence. Discussion focused on conflict over dependence and independence and its effect on the achievement of the group members.

Self-Feelings. This involved both self-concept and self-experience. Under self-concept the students explored their self-concepts and beliefs about adequacy and potency. Under self-experience, feelings of anxiety and guilt were discussed as well as depressed feelings. These were then related to achievement and their role in interfering with scholastic endeavors.

Expression of Anger and Hostility. Feelings about the expression of anger and hostility were discussed, and an exploration was made of their particular interfering influence on academic achievement.

Impulses and Controls. Feelings of fear about impulses and their control were discussed, and the role they have in the life of the individual and on his achievement were explored.

The second method of group counseling, a non-directive approach, was labeled group-structured (GS) and placed emphasis on topics that spontaneously originated within the group. The group counselor was an active participant in the group discussion but the examination of what seemed to be a significant area for exploration, the frequency and degree of digression, and the time spent on particular problems were all determined by the group rather than by the group counselor.

The students in the GS groups, in contrast to the subjects in the LS groups, spent the major portion of their time discussing study habits, work schedules, better methods of outlining text books, concentration problems, concerns related to their vocational choice, and feelings about their inability to achieve academically.

INSTRUMENTS

In order to determine whether the two methods of group counseling were perceived differently by the respective groups, a questionnaire was prepared and administered to all groups just prior to the last session. (Interested readers can obtain copies of the questionnaire from the author, if desired.) The questionnaire was composed of 24 items designed to discriminate between the two methods of treatment. For example, the subjects were asked to determine whether the leader or the group initiated and directed the topics for discussion, who determined the amount of time spent on a particular problem, who controlled the overall pace of the group, etc.

A statistical analysis (t test) of the results of the questionnaire supported the contention (at the .01 level of confidence) that the two counselors were consistent in maintaining the difference between the leader-structured and group-structured methods throughout the experimental period.

At the conclusion of the experimental period, all subjects were administered the Stern Activities Index (SAI) and the Minnesota Multiphasic Personality Inventory (MMPI). Selected scales within these two tests were used to measure the degree of change along each personality dimension under study. The Dependency scale (Navran, 1954) of the MMPI was used to measure change in the need to be dependent, and the Abasement scale of the SAI, defined as measuring the degree of self-depreciation and devaluation, was used to detect changes in self-concept. The Anxiety scale (Taylor, 1953) of the MMPI was used to measure the degree of anxiety, and depression was measured by the MMPI Depression scale. The Aggression scale of the SAI, defined as measuring the degree to which a person can overtly and directly express hostile feelings, was used to detect changes in aggression, and the SAI Diffidence-Egoism scale, which indicates the degree to which ego functions are tenuous and underdeveloped, was used to measure ego strength. Improvement in academic achievement was measured by changes in GPA at the conclusion of the experiment and three months after its completion.

Hypotheses

1. The dependency, anxiety, depression and abasement of men in the LS group would be less than that of men in either the GS or control group at the completion of the experiment.

2. The aggression and ego strength of men in the LS group would be greater than that of men in either the GS or control group at the completion of the experiment.

3. The academic achievement of men in the LS group would be greater than that of men in either the GS or control group at the conclusion of the experiment.

4. The academic achievement of men in the LS group would be greater than that of men in either the GS or control group three months following the conclusion of the experiment.

Results

A one-way analysis of variance was computed to determine whether a significant difference in means existed between the LS, GS, and control groups in dependency, anxiety, depression, abasement, and aggression at the conclusion of the study. The results of the analysis did not reveal F values that were significant at the .05 level of confidence. Differences between the respective treatment groups on these dimensions were therefore attributed to chance variation within a common population and not to the effects of experimental treatment, although statistical evidence will be presented in the discussion section that supports the view that group counseling per se does enable male underachievers to more overtly express hostile and aggressive feelings.

A one-way analysis of variance was also computed to determine whether a significant difference in means existed between the LS, GS, and control groups in ego strength. The results of this analysis are summarized in Table 1.

In order to determine how the three group means differ, an extension to group means with unequal numbers of Duncan's New

TABLE 1

Analysis of Variance of SAI Diffidence-Egoism Scores for the Leader-Structured, Group-Structured and Control Groups

Source of Variation	Sum of Squares	d.f.	Mean Square	F
Between treatment	109.00	2	54.50	3.116*
Within treatment	1364.96	78	17.49	
Total	1473.96	80		

* Significant at the .05 level.

TABLE 2

Kramer's Extension of Duncan's New Multiple Range Test of SAI Diffidence-Egoism Scores for the Leader-Structured, Group-Structured and Control Groups

Means	Leader Structured 19.81 A	Group Structured 20.19 B	Control 22.36 C	Shortest Significant Ranges
LS—19.81		1.82	13.00*	$R_2 = 12.17$
GS—20.19			11.69	$R_3 = 11.78$
C—22.36				

* Significant at the .05 level.

Multiple Range Test was used (Kramer, 1956). The results of this analysis are summarized in Table 2.

An examination of the means in Table 2 indicates that the ego strength of the subjects who experienced the LS method of group counseling was significantly greater than the ego strength of the control subjects, whereas no differences were found between the GS subjects and the control subjects.

A two-by-two analysis of variance was computed to determine whether differences in ego strength were due to experimental treatment, different counselors, or an interaction between counselor and type of treatment. No significant effects were found.

The analysis of covariance was used to test for differences in winter-term GPA between subjects who received group counseling and subjects who received no counseling.

It was found in computing the analysis of covariance that the slopes of the regression lines for the three groups (LS, GS, and control) were significantly different (F < .05). Since the analysis of covariance assumes that the regression lines for the experimental groups are parallel within the limits of random sampling, i.e., they all have a common slope, it was not possible to conclude the covariance analysis.

A test of the differences between the three regression coefficients was therefore made and the results are summarized in Table 3.

Inspection of Table 3 validates the results of the *F* test above and indicates that the rate of change in grade-point average between the three experimental groups was significantly different. It was also found that both the regression coefficients for the LS group

TABLE 3

Test of the Significance of the Regression Coefficients for the Leader-Structured, Group-Structured, and Control Groups at the End of the Treatment Period

	sy.x		sy.x	t	p
Leader structured	.419	Group structured	.028	1.845	.05
Leader structured	.419	Control	−.339	5.699	.001
Group structured	.028	Control	−.339	3.35	.01

and controls differed significantly from zero, whereas this was not true for the GS group regression coefficient.

The analysis of covariance was also computed to test for differences between the three groups (LS, GS and control) on spring-term GPA, and the regression lines were again found to be significantly different. A test of the differences between the group regression coefficients was made and the results are reported in Table 4.

Inspection of the table indicates that the rate of change in the LS group was significantly different from and greater than the rate of change in the control group three months following the experiment, whereas no differences occurred between the GS group and the control group in rate of GPA change. It was also found that the LS regression coefficient was significantly different from zero whereas the regression coefficients of the GS and control groups were not significantly different from zero.

It should be emphasized that the mean GPA's for both counseling groups (LS and GS), three months following the experiment, were

TABLE 4

Test of the Significance of the Regression Coefficients for the Leader-Structured, Group-Structured, and Control Groups Three Months after the Completion of the Experiment

	sy.x		sy.x	t	p
Leader structured	.435	Group structured	.102		n.s.
Leader structured	.435	Control	−.087	3.20	.01
Group structured	.102	Control	−.087		n.s.

over the crucial 2.00 mark and the mean of the control group was below this mark.

Discussion

The results of the study indicate that a method of group counseling that focuses upon the underlying, emotional syndrome of the male underachiever will produce a significant and positive change in ego strength when compared to a no-treatment control group when the subjects are volunteers for counseling.

The data in the Stern Activities Index manual include the scores for a sample of 558 normal college males who were randomly selected from 21 colleges and universities across the nation. A t test ($t = 2.63 < p$ .005) between the mean score for the no-treatment control group on the Diffidence-Egoism Scale and the mean score for the SAI college sample indicated that the controls differed significantly and in the direction of an underdeveloped and tenuous ego structure, whereas tests between the LS group and the normal sample, as well as the GS group and the normal sample, did not indicate significant differences. Both treatment groups, therefore, improved in the direction of healthier ego functioning, with differences between the LS and control groups being large enough to be significant, while differences between the GS and control groups were not.

The data do not indicate that either method of group counseling significantly affected any of the other personality dimensions under study, although there is evidence that group counseling itself (in contrast to either method) enables subjects to more overtly express their feelings of anger.

The analysis of variance technique is a conservative test and does not always reveal the fact that some differences between groups may actually exist even though the obtained F value is not large enough to reject the null hypothesis.

Although it was not appropriate to compute three different t tests and separately compare each treatment group, because this procedure increases the probability of obtaining significant t values, it was appropriate for the sake of further research to combine the treatment groups into one group and compare all subjects who experienced group counseling with subjects who received no counseling.

Such a comparison was made and a significant difference on the SAI Aggression scale between subjects who received group treatment and subjects who did not was found ($t = 2.31 < p$ .015). This high t value indicates that the experience of group counseling does allow the male underachiever to express his feelings of anger in a more direct and overt manner.

Kirk (1952), it should be noted, suggests that the academic underachiever is unable to overtly express hostile feelings toward a member of the family who demands academic success, and unconsciously expresses these feelings through academic failure. If this is true, to extend the argument, any increase in ego strength would theoretically lead to an increase in ability to express negative feelings, since a strengthening of the ego implies a reduction in the need to repress hostile impulses. In view of this possibility the mean scores on aggression and ego strength were compared across all three groups in order of rank. The results of this comparison (Table 5) support Kirk's hypothesis and lend further credence to the efficacy of the leader-structured method of group counseling.

Conclusion

The data on the achievement as well as personality dimensions indicate that the less ambiguous, more highly structured LS method of group counseling which specifically focused on the underlying personality patterns of the underachiever and related them to scholastic difficulties produced greater change in ego strength when compared across groups and a higher rate of change in academic achievement.

TABLE 5

Mean SAI Aggression and Diffidence-Egoism Scores for Leader-Structured, Group-Structured and Control Groups

	Control	Group-Structured	Leader-Structured	
Low aggression	4.08	5.08	5.18	High aggression
Low ego-strength	22.36	20.19	19.81	High ego-strength

Any two treatment means not underscored by the same line are significantly different.

Any two treatment means underscored by the same line are not significantly different.

The data also indicated that group counseling, in comparison with a no-treatment control group, enabled these underachievers to more overtly express their hostile feelings.

Both counselors concluded that the one-and-a-half to two hour sessions were more helpful than the usual period of one hour. Often, according to their experience, the most productive period came during the last hour when the intensity of the group interaction seemed to increase considerably.

The lack of any significant change on other dimensions may be due to the following:

1. The topics discussed in the LS sessions, it will be recalled, were based upon a synthesis of the male underachiever's emotional characteristics as described in previous research, descriptive research that does not make a distinction between motivated and non-motivated students. There is a possibility that a basic difference exists between underachievers who are motivated to seek help and underachievers who either will not seek help or who will reject it when it is offered. If these are in fact two separate populations, then the topics used in the study for group discussion may at times have been inappropriate for volunteer subjects, thus lowering the effectiveness of the LS method. A replication of the study but with non-motivated students would help answer the question.

2. It is also possible that different methods of identifying the underachiever actually produce different populations (Farquhar & Payne, 1964). If this is true, then the data derived from a study using one method of selection would not be applicable to a study using another method of selection, and any synthesis of information across such groups would not be as effective as possible in either understanding or altering the underachievement syndrome.

REFERENCES

Baymur, F. B., & Patterson, C. H. A comparison of three methods of assisting underachieving high school students. *Journal of Counseling Psychology*, 1960, 7, 83–88.

Berger, I. L., & Sulker, A. R. The relationship of emotional adjustment and intellectual capacity to the academic achievement of college students. *Mental Hygiene*, 1956, 40, 65–77.

Broedel, J., Ohlsen, M., Proff, F., & Southard, C. The effects of group counseling on gifted underachieving adolescents. *Journal of Counseling Psychology*, 1960, *7*, 163–170.

Caplan, S. W. The effects of group counseling on junior high school boys' concepts of themselves in school. *Journal of Counseling Psychology*, 1957, *4*, 124–128.

Clements, T. H. A study to compare the effectiveness of individual and group counseling approaches with able underachievers when counselor time is held constant. Unpublished doctoral dissertation, University of Southern California, 1963.

DeWeese, H. L. The extent to which group counseling influences the academic achievement, academic potential, and personal adjustment of predicted low-achieving first semester college freshmen. Unpublished doctoral dissertation, University of Illinois, 1959.

Duncan, D. R. Effects of required group counseling with college students in academic difficulty. Unpublished doctoral dissertation, University of Florida, 1962.

Educational Policies Commission. *Manpower and education.* Washington, D.C.: National Education Association, Association of School Administration, 1956.

Edwards, A. L. *Experimental design in psychological research.* New York: Holt, Rinehart & Winston, 1960.

Farquhar, W. W. *Motivation factors related to academic achievement.* Cooperative Research Project 846, January, 1963. East Lansing: Office of Research and Publications, College of Education, Michigan State University, 1963.

Farquhar, W. W., & Payne, D. A classification and comparison of techniques used in selecting under- and overachievers. *Personnel and Guidance Journal*, 1964, *42*, 874–884.

Gebhart, G. G., & Hoyt, D. P. Personality needs of under- and over-achieving freshmen. *Journal of Applied Psychology*, 1958, *42*, 125–128.

Hart, D. A study of the effects of two types of group experiences on the academic achievement of college underachievers. Uupublished doctoral dissertation, Michigan State University, 1963.

Kirk, Barbara. Test versus academic performance in malfunctioning students. *Journal of Consulting Psychology*, 1952, *16*, 213–216.

Kramer, C. Y. Extension of multiple range tests to group means with unequal numbers of replications. *Biometrics*, September, 1956, 307–310.

Maroney, K. A. Effectiveness of short-term group guidance with a group of transfer students admitted on academic probation. Unpublished doctoral dissertation, North Texas State University, 1962.

McCarthy, M. V. *The effectiveness of a modified counseling procedure in promoting learning among bright underachieving adolescents.* Research Project ASE-6401. Washington, D.C.: Department of Health, Education, and Welfare, 1959.

McClelland, D. C., Atkinson, J. W., Clark, R. A., & Dowel, E. L. *The achievement motive.* New York: Appleton-Century-Crofts, 1953.

McKenzie, J. D., Jr. The dynamics of deviant achievement. *Personnel and Guidance Journal,* 1964, *42,* 683–686.

Roth, R. M., & Meyersburg, H. A. The non-achievement syndrome. *Personnel and Guidance Journal,* 1963, *41,* 535–546.

Sheldon, W. D., & Landsman, T. An investigation of non-directive group therapy with students in academic difficulty. *Journal of Consulting Psychology,* 1950, *14,* 210–215.

Speegle, P. T. The effectiveness of two techniques of counseling with students on academic probation. Unpublished doctoral dissertation, North Texas State University, 1962.

Spielberger, C. D., Weitz, H., & Denny, J. P. Group counseling and the academic performance of anxious college freshmen. *Journal of Counseling Psychology,* 1962, *9,* 195–204.

Taylor, R. G. Personality traits and discrepant achievement: A review. *Journal of Counseling Psychology,* 1964, *11,* 76–82.

Winborn, B., & Schmidt, L. G. The effectiveness of short-term group counseling upon the academic achievement of potentially superior but underachieving college freshmen. *Journal of Educational Research,* 1962, *55,* 169–173.

Wrenn, C. G. *The counselor in a changing world.* Washington, D.C.: American Personnel and Guidance Association, 1962.

28 / EVALUATION OF A
GROUP COUNSELING PROCEDURE

William Ofman

There is an increasing recognition among professional workers that the quality of work required for academic attainment is qualitatively different from that required in prior academic settings. As Robinson (1961, p. 11) put it, "college requires higher level work skills." It is also recognized that lack of appropriate performance (performance consistent with the student's academic potential) is often a function of more than a mere lack of strategic study skills. Shaw (1955, p. 465) aptly points out that ". . . students fail in their course work because of social and emotional disturbances. Therefore, an adequate how to study program must offer assistance to the individual student beyond the mere teaching of study techniques." This point is compellingly illustrated by one student's communication to us, "I know I can do it, I know what I have to do . . . I've read the study books, but I just can't seem to get myself to set down and do it now." There are, then, problems in areas of motivation, goal definition, commitment, personal difficulties and conflicts which impinge upon, mitigate, and interfere with the adequate utilization of time and ability (Neugeboren, 1958; Rust, 1958).

The group counseling experience with which this research deals, the Study Habits Seminar (shs), is based on the recognition of the complex variables of which scholastic performance is a function. It is addressed to students who feel they need an approach to their university experience which is more consistent with the higher level demands that exist there. It also concerns itself with the needs of

From JOURNAL OF COUNSELING PSYCHOLOGY, *1964, Vol. 11, pp. 152–159. Copyright 1964, American Psychological Association. Reprinted with permission of author and publisher.*

students who have the capacity to perform in an academic setting where the demands for independent work are great and the competition keen but who, for reasons not directly related to their ability, do not perform at a level consistent with their potential.

The aim of helping persons to fulfill their potential through the exploration and learning of new attitudes, values and skills has traditionally been within the province of individual counseling. That which is relatively new is the group or multiple aspect of counseling: a method wherein a trained psychologist works in a group setting with several counselees who manifest several common concerns. Goldman (1962) cogently points out the confusion that exists in the group counseling field between the process and content dimensions, and the confounding of teaching, guidance, group or multiple counseling, and psychotherapy. Group counseling as we conceive of it "weds" the insights of group dynamics, group psychotherapy, and psychological counseling (Ofman, 1963b).

The Problem

Based on students' reports of their experiences in such a group setting, psychologists working with counseling groups as well as with individuals who had been participants, felt that the study habits seminar helped persons to deal with scholastic demands in a more satisfactory fashion. Students who participated in group counseling reported gains in grades, seemed to find more purpose in their work, felt that, "it was more an important part of me," seemed to find their work more satisfying and less of a burden.

For many reasons it was important to assess the overall effectiveness of this group counseling procedure. An extensive review of the literature on the effectiveness, in scholastic settings, of group counseling revealed a dearth of clear-cut finding in the area, for as Entwisle (1960, p. 246) points out, many of the studies ". . . express expert opinion rather than the results of empirical findings." Importantly, a variable of central importance, motivation, was not controlled in many of the reported studies. Some studies included no control groups at all. Hewer, for example, evaluated group and individual counseling on vocational problems, but decided, "no definite conclusion can be drawn . . . . Should further experimentation . . . be undertaken, a control group should be used, drawn from the same population from which the class comes" (Hewer, 1959, p. 665).

The difficulty in evaluating the literature on outcomes in unequivocal terms stems in the main from its methodological deficits.
One finds lack of good experimental design, failure to use the
proper control groups for motivation or baseline factors (Charles,
1951; Gazda & Ohlsen, 1961; Hoyt, 1955; Ransom, 1955; Shaw, 1955;
Stewart, 1958; Tresselt & Richlin, 1951; Winborn & Schmidt, 1962),
or failure to use control groups altogether (Arbuckle, 1949; Calia,
1957; Froehlich, 1958; Hewer, 1959; McGowan, 1962; Robinson,
1945; Wittenborn, 1944). There is a heavy reliance upon "before-
after" studies and an almost predominant use of immediate rather
than long-term criterion measures.

Clearly the problem of assessing the effectiveness of a group
counseling procedure has much in common with problems inherent
in outcome research in psychotherapy. The important issues relate
to control of variables which might covary with behavior change in
order to "tease out" those changes which are a function of the treatment: in this case, the experience in the group (Frank, 1959; Parloff
& Rubinstein, 1959; Strupp & Luborsky, 1962). Nevertheless, the
majority of authors report that group procedures are effective in
influencing behavior in a positive direction.

We might mention two critical issues. It has been pointed out
and commonly noted that the motivation to improve—the person's
recognition of a concern, a difficulty or a problem—can often stimulate his thinking in a constructive way about it so that this recognition can, on its own, be "therapeutic" in that it can lead to more
effective behavior. Students who perceive their need for developmental work around their reading habits, study procedures, their
resistive or unrealistic attitudes towards scholastic demands, may
become more receptive to the utterances, advice and thoughts of
others and may, via their increased motivation to improve, re-
evaluate their position in such a manner as to constitute a substantial change in behavior. The treatment variable has to be effective,
then, in light of the sources of motivation that are provided by the
recognition of the problem alone and desire to improve.

Another relevant issue is students' tendency to improve without
any expressed motivation or acceptance of the existence of a difficulty. A plot of grades for a random group of students over their
undergraduate semesters indicates that, for a variety of reasons,
their grades rise. A baseline control group is therefore essential to
a well-controlled study. In effect, this research is concerned with
the control of relevant motivational factors, with the aim of arriving
at relatively unequivocal results.

Method and Procedure

We chose as our criterion for effectiveness the grade point average (gpa). It is held that the gpa earned during the semester in which the student is a member of the group, or the semester immediately following it (a criterion used in most of the investigations to date), is insufficient. Rather a better measure of the effectiveness of the Study Habits Seminar (shs) is its effect, if any, over the total undergraduate stay.

Control Variables

Scholastic aptitude: The scores on the American Council on Education Psychological examination (ACE) for Ss in the various groups will act as controls for this variable (Ofman, 1963a).

Motivation: As was mentioned earlier, motivational factors must be controlled if unequivocal statements are to be made regarding treatment effectiveness. The control of motivational factors was accomplished by the selection of appropriate control groups which will now be described:

The Experimental Group consisted of the eight-semester gpa of a sample of Ss who volunteered for the shs and were accepted as participants. A number of Ss who volunteered for the shs had to be excused from participating on administrative grounds.[1] This group of excused volunteers—those who showed the desire to improve—served as the *Control Group* for motivation. Three other control groups were included. One group served as a *Baseline Control* and consisted of Ss, chosen at random, whose gpa was plotted for eight semesters at the university. Another group consisted of the gpa of Ss who volunteered for the shs and were accepted, but who dropped out from the shs before the third session. This Dropout Group permitted an evaluation of the shs in a quantitative fashion. The last group was in reality a subgroup of the motivation control, and constituted a *Wait Group*. It consisted of the gpa of volunteers who were refused admission to the shs but who became participants in

---

[1] Students came voluntarily to "sign up" for the seminar, and all who wished were allowed to sign into the seminar. About twice as many students signed up as accommodations permitted. When all the sections were filled, those who could not be accommodated were told that due to space limitations, the sections were closed. There is no reason to suspect that any systematic factor affected the choice of students who were excused because of space limitations.

the seminar two semesters later. It is held that these five groups helped to control most of the contingencies of which improvement might be a function.

The Sample

Group A: *Baseline Control.* Gpa of 60 Ss,[2] randomly selected, over eight semesters.

Group B: *Experimental Group.* Eight-semester gpa of 60 volunteers who remained in the shs for at least 80% of its duration.

Group C: *Dropout Group.* Eight-semester gpa of 60 volunteers who dropped out before the fourth session and did not re-enter.

Group D: *Control Group.* Eight-semester gpa of 60 volunteers who were refused admission for administrative reasons and who did not enter the shs.

Group E: *Wait Group.* Eight-semester gpa of 60 volunteers who were refused admission for administrative reasons to the shs but who re-entered and participated in the shs two semesters later.

Hypotheses

1. Volunteers should not differ from a random selection of students at the university in their initial grade point averages: gpa of Experimental Group is not different from gpa of the Baseline Group.

2. Scholastic aptitude as measured by the ACE should be comparable for the five groups.

3. The Experimental Group should show a significantly different pattern of grades during its eight semesters than the four other groups.

4. The Experimental Group will have higher gpa than the other groups in semesters following the shs.

5. Gpa of the Experimental Group will be higher than that of the Control Group over eight semesters.

---

[2] Since the numbers in the several groups varied naturally, and it was desirable to have equal numbers in all the groups, the total number in the smallest group (Dropout group N = 60) was taken as the standard and the other groups were reduced (their data cards shuffled and the first 60 chosen) to 60 each.

6. Gpa of the Dropout Group will be higher than that of the Control Group over eight semesters.

7. Gpa of the Wait Group will show significant difference in gpa before and after the experience.

8. Gpa of the Wait Group will, in semesters seven and eight, be comparable to that of the seventh and eighth semester gpa of the Experimental Group.

Results

The design of the experiment was such that it permitted the testing of differences among the curves of the Experimental, Baseline and Control Groups.

Figure 1, page 366, presents a graph of the curves of gpa for the different groups per semester for eight semesters. Volunteers participated in the shs in their first year. It will be noted that the Baseline Group began its career at a higher level than volunteers for the shs. The Control Group and the Dropout Group curves are essentially flat. The Experimental Group, on the other hand, began to improve its gpa in the second semester and by the fourth semester the curve of its gpa departs from that of the Control and Dropout Groups and approaches that of the Baseline Group. The curve of the Wait Group is not different from that of the Control or Dropout Groups during the first four semesters, but it rises to join the curves of the Baseline and Experimental Groups in semesters seven and eight.

In evaluating hypothesis No. 1 (Table 1, page 367) it was found that there were significant differences between initial gpa of the Baseline Groups and that of the Experimental and Control Groups. There were no significant differences in the initial gpa among the volunteering groups. The initial gpa of the Experimental and Control Groups, while not significantly different from each other, are significantly lower than the gpa of the Baseline Group in the first semester of college.

Hypothesis No. 2 was upheld. (Table 2) Since an analysis of variance of ACE scores for the five groups yielded an insignificant F, it was concluded that scholastic aptitude was essentially comparable for the *five* groups. That is, while the volunteers for the shs began their academic career at a lower level of performance than the Baseline Group, they did not do so as a function of lower scholastic potential.

An analysis of variance of the gpas for each group per semester (Table 3) tested hypothesis No. 3. The highly significant Fs for Interaction and for Groups indicated that the curves of grades were neither proportional nor parallel. It was therefore asserted that the differential treatment had different effects upon the several groups.

In terms of hypothesis 4, the results indicated that the Experi-

FIGURE 1

A plot of the mean gpa per semester for Baseline, Experimental, Dropout, Control, and Wait Groups

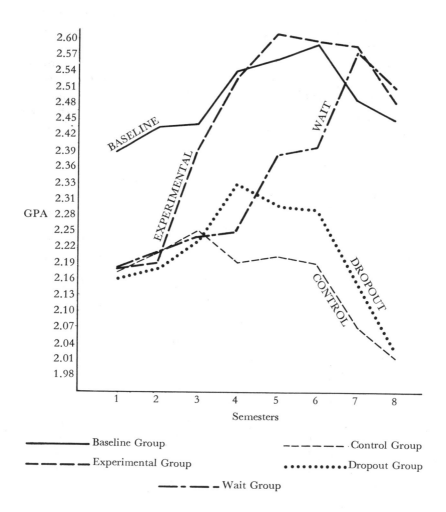

TABLE 1
Critical Ratios of Initial Semester Gpas

Groups	CR	Significance
Base.—Exp.	2.01	.05
Base.—Control	2.08	.05
Exp.—Control	1.01	N.S.

TABLE 2
Summary of Analysis of Variance of ACE Scores for Baseline, Experimental, Dropout, Control and Wait Groups

Source	df	MS	F
Between Groups	4	192	0.362*
Within Groups	225	592.88	
Total	229		

* Not significant.

TABLE 3
An Analysis of Variance of Gpas of Baseline, Experimental, Dropout, Control and Wait Groups for Eight Semesters

Source	df	SS	MS	F
Groups	4	35.68	8.920	5.304**
Semesters	7	10.48	1.497	
Interaction	28	51.28	1.830	4.800**
Within Cells	2360	815.22	0.345	
Total	2399	912.66		

** Significant at .01 level.

mental Group, while beginning significantly lower than the Base-line Group in gpa, did not improve to a degree which significantly superceded the gpa of the Baseline Group (Table 4). In effect, in the last semesters, the gpa of the Experimental Group and the Baseline Group are comparable. However, hypothesis No. 5 was upheld: the Experimental Group's gpa was significantly higher than the Control Group's and Dropout Group's gpa.

TABLE 4

Critical Ratios of Gpas, Semesters 2–8 of Baseline, Experimental, Dropout, Control and Wait Groups

Groups	C.R.	Sig.
Base.—Exp.	1.00	N.S.
Exp.—Drop.	2.508	.05
Exp.—Control	3.438	.01
Exp.—Wait	1.312	N.S.

Hypothesis 6 was not upheld. The Dropout Group evidently did not receive help from the four or fewer sessions of the shs in a manner sufficient to raise its gpa (Table 4). The gpa of the Dropout Group taken over the last seven semesters is comparable to that of the Control Group which did not participate in the shs at all.

Hypothesis 7 was upheld. The results (Table 5) indicated that the gpa of the Wait Group during its wait period—before taking the shs—was significantly lower than its gpa in semesters after participation in the shs.

Further, hypothesis 8 was supported: there was no significant difference in the last two semesters between the gpa of the Wait Group and that of the Experimental Group (Table 4).

Discussion

The findings indicated that those students who volunteered for the shs exhibited inappropriate performance in their first semester: their grades were significantly lower than those of the Baseline Group; but in the light of comparable ACE scores for all the groups, this was not a function of lower scholastic aptitude. It appears that those students who volunteered for the shs (it should be noted that

TABLE 5

Critical Ratios Between Gpa of Wait Group Before and After the SHS

Groups	Gpa	s.d.	C.R.	Sig.
Wait (before)	2.222	.533	2.516	.05
Wait (after)	2.478	.568		

they were not on probation at this point, nor had they been likely to have visited an academic counselor) perceived themselves correctly: they recognized their need for help, and this was a correct perception.

As a result of participation in group counseling, the Experimental Group's gpa became comparable to that of the Baseline Group's gpa and significantly higher than the gpa of the Control and Dropout Groups which, while comparable in other respects, were subjected to lesser amounts of the group counseling experience.

It might be interesting to note that the Experimental Group did not begin its improvement until the third semester. Evidently it takes some time before the results of the newly gained insights, as a result of the group counseling, are translated into action. This is one of the important reasons for the use of long-range rather than immediate criterion measures. Though some students do exhibit a "transference cure" and exhibit immediate marked behavior changes, most of them seem to do better in the "long pull" as a result of the counseling experience.

The improvement of scholastic behavior on the part of the inappropriately performing (underachieving) Experimental Group cannot logically be accounted for by the natural tendency to regress towards the mean. The Control Group, Dropout Group and the Wait Group do not indicate this phenomenon. Therefore, the change in behavior on the part of the Experimental Group (and later the Wait Group) can only be accounted for in terms of our treatment variable.

Further findings lend support to the effectiveness of the shs in influencing gpa. The Dropout Group evidently did not receive help from its limited participation in the shs in a fashion sufficient to significantly raise its gpa. The gpa of the Dropout Group taken over the last seven semesters is essentially similar to that of the Control Group which did not participate in the seminar at all. This is a useful finding. It is often said that students tend to gain as much from the "inspiration" of being stimulated by an ameliorative experience as by the process and content of the procedure itself. This is not the case in this investigation. The first three sessions of the shs are of this introductory, somewhat inspirational nature. Characteristically, there is a discussion of the basic reasons for being at the university, the commonly shared need for higher-level work skills, the basic goals and values consistent with university achievement, and the relationship between the student's goals, the aims of the university, and the aspirations that the student's relatives and parents have *for* the student (Ofman, 1963b). The findings clearly indicate that such a process alone was not sufficient to significantly raise the Dropout Group's gpa. Evidently what is needed is, as McGowan (1962), put it, ". . . therapy plus content."

More light is shed on the motivational variable by an inspection of the gpa curve of the Wait Group. It will be recalled that this group is comparable in gpa, semester of entry, and scholastic aptitude to that of the Experimental and Control Groups. The Wait Group was composed of *S*s who volunteered for the shs, were refused admission and became participants two semester hence. During the wait period, this group exhibits a curve of grades essentially similar to that of the Control Group. No improvement was exhibited during the wait period. After participating in the shs, however, its gpa became significantly different from that of the before period, and from the Control Group's gpa. In the last semester it becomes comparable to that of the Experimental and Baseline Groups. The implications of this finding lend further support to the fact that motivation to improve alone is not sufficient to change the scholastic performance of students who indicate a desire to change. This finding also sheds light on the "when is it too late?" question. Apparently students who are motivated to improve, if given the appropriate treatment, can improve rapidly—it took the Wait Group approximately two semesters to improve to a level comparable to that of the Experimental Group.

As a result, we can state with a high degree of certainty that in the findings of an investigation which concerned itself with long-range results, and which controlled ability and motivational variables, indicated that students of comparable ability who began their scholastic career with inappropriately lower grades, who recognized and expressed their need for help, and participated in group counseling were indeed aided to perform in a manner more consistent with their ability. In contrast, those *S*s who were in the same circumstance, but were refused help, or dropped out of the group, continued to perform in a consistently inappropriate manner: they did not improve their grades even though they were motivated to do so.

The outcome of this investigation supports the results of many studies of the effectiveness of group procedures in academic settings. The critical issue to which this research was addressed was the establishment of controls and the manipulation of variables in a manner which was consistent with conclusions of an unequivocal nature—an aim which former studies accomplished only in small part. It dealt with, at once, a group procedure which focused on personality variables and scholastic skills simultaneously. It provided control for motivational variables, and it used an objective criterion for measurement over a prolonged period of time.

In the light of the design, the findings indicated that such group counseling procedures which take into account the whole person are effective in changing scholastic behavior in a positive direction.

Summary

The effectiveness of a group counseling procedure concerned with students' adjustment to the university which dealt simultaneously with issues related to attitudinal, motivational and specific skills, was assessed in terms of its influence on the gpa of five groups of 60 students. These groups consisted of a Baseline Group of randomly chosen Ss, an Experimental Group of volunteers who participated in the seminar, a Control Group of volunteers who were refused admission to the seminar, a Dropout Group of Ss who participated in the seminar for less than three sessions, and a Wait Group of volunteers who were refused admission but who became participants two semesters later.

The grade point averages for each of these groups was plotted for each of their eight semesters.

The results indicated that students volunteering for the seminar, while comparable to the Baseline Group in scholastic aptitude, were significantly lower than the Baseline in first semester grades. As a function of group counseling, the Experimental Group improved its grades to a level comparable to that of the Baseline Group, and significantly above that of the Control and Dropout Groups. The Wait Group remained static during its wait period, but as a result of the subsequent counseling, improved its gpa to a level not different from the Experimental or Baseline Groups. Gpas did not improve for the Control and Dropout Groups.

It was concluded that the Study Habits Seminar as a group counseling procedure was effective in improving scholastic performance.

REFERENCES

Arbuckle, D. S. A college experiment in orientation. *Occupations*, 1949, *28*, 112–117.

Calia, V. F. A group guidance program in action. *Junior College Journal*, 1957, *27*, 437–442.

Charles, D. C. College reading and study improvement. *Journal of Higher Education*, 1951, *22*, 265–267.

Entwistle, D. R. Evaluation of study skills courses. *Journal of Educational Research*, 1960, *7*, 246–251.

Frank, J. D. Problems of controls in psychotherapy as exemplified in the psychotherapy research project of the Phipps Psychiatric Clinic. In E. Rubinstein, & M. Parloff (Eds.), *Research in psychotherapy*. Washington: American Psychological Association, 1959.

Froehlich, C. P. Must counseling be individual? *Educational and Psychological Measurement*, 1958, *18*, 681–689.

Gazda, G., & Ohlsen, M. The effects of short-term group counseling on prospective counselors. *Personnel and Guidance Journal*, 1961, *39*, 634–638.

Goldman, L. Group guidance: Content and process. *Personnel and Guidance Journal*, 1962, *40*, 518–522.

Hewer, V. H. Group counseling, individual counseling and a college class in vocations. *Personnel and Guidance Journal*, 1959, *37*, 660–665.

Hoyt, D. P. An evaluation of group and individual programs in vocational guidance. *Journal of Applied Psychology*, 1955, *39*, 26–30.

McGowan, B. Group counseling of university students: Group therapy plus content. Unpublished paper, University of California (Los Angeles), 1962.

Neugeboren, B. Clinical study of academic underachievers. In B. M. Wedge (Ed.), *The psycho-social problems of college men*. New Haven, Conn.: Yale University Press, 1958.

Ofman, W. A cross-validation of the Z-scale and a further exploration. *Journal of Educational Research*, In press 1963. (a)

Ofman, W. The study habits seminar—A statement of viewpoint and method. *Personnel and Guidance Journal*, June 1964, *42*, 1027–1029. (b)

Parloff, M. B., & Rubinstein, E. Research problems in psychotherapy. In E. Rubinstein, & M. Parloff (Eds.), *Research in psychotherapy*. Washington, D.C.: American Psychological Association, 1959.

Ransom, M. K. An evaluation of certain aspects of the reading and study program at the University of Missouri. *Journal of Educational Research*, 1955, *48*, 443–454.

Robinson, F. P. Two quarries with a single stone. *Journal of Higher Education*, 1945, *16*, 201, 208.

Robinson, F. P. *Effective study*. New York: Harper, 1961.

Rust, R. Personality and academic achievement: A questionnaire approach. In B. M. Wedge (Ed.), *The psycho-social problems of college men*. New Haven, Conn.: Yale University Press, 1958.

Shaw, J. G. An evaluation of study skills course. *Personnel and Guidance Journal*, 1955, *33*, 465–468.

Strupp, H., & Luborsky, L. *Research in Psychotherapy*. Vol. II. Washington, D.C.: American Psychological Association, 1962.

Stewart, C. C. Attitude change following a counseling seminar. *Personnel and Guidance Journal*, 1958, *37*, 273–275.

Tresselt, M. E., & Richlin, M. Differential prognosis in a college study methods course. *Journal of Psychology*, 1951, *31*, 81–89.

Winborn, B., & Schmidt, L. G. The effectiveness of short-term group counseling upon the academic achievement of potentially superior but underachieving college freshmen. *Journal of Educational Research*, 1962, *55*, 169–173.

Wittenborn, J. P. Classes in remedial reading and study skills. *Journal of Educational Research*, 1944, *37*, 571–586.

Wright, W. E. Multiple counseling; Why, when, how. *Personnel and Guidance Journal*, 1959, *37*, 551–557.

Wright, W. E. Group Procedures. *Review of Educational Research*, 1963, *33*, 205–213.

Part Four

OUTCOMES:
RESEARCH AND
EVALUATION

Part Four is addressed to both the creators and the consumers of research on group procedures. Experience has shown that important research challenges are inherent in group experiences and procedures. This is true whether research is viewed as an empirical process solely dependent on "hard data" or as an organized but more subjective study. We believe that the group experience and the process of research can be compatible. Research designs will most likely be improved by researchers who are familiar with major methodological problems and the extensive literature on groups.

Many research studies related to the use of groups have been undertaken, some of which are currently in process. Gradually, well-designed research and evaluative efforts have evolved, and research findings today seem somewhat less equivocal. The literature on group research suggests three areas of concern for the group leader and the group research worker. First, more attention must be devoted to developing relevant questions for research. Second, our knowledge of research design needs to be applied with greater care. Finally, current and future research must be related to past research in order to develop a more useful and accepted body of knowledge on groups. Replication and extension studies should be encouraged.

Relevant questions need to be formulated in at least four areas. There is a need for sophisticated descriptive studies and naturalistic accounts which would lead to the identification of *independent variables*. The findings from these studies should permit further research in which the planned manipulation of independent variables would shed light on the complexity of group *processes*. Process studies should seek to identify the relative contributions of independent variables. In addition, more questions need to be asked about *outcomes*. To date, little attention has been given to observable changes. Another area in which relevant questions should be developed relates to *theory development*. The current state of research on groups is such that outcome studies are more apt to collapse on theoretical issues than on methodological problems. The relationship between a sound theoretical framework and relevant research efforts may seem obvious, but it is often overlooked by novices and experts alike.

Part Four presents five extended reviews and discussions of generalizations from research on group procedures. Taken as a whole, these selections represent an extensive survey and evaluation of research literature from 1938 to 1968. The readings clearly communicate the kinds of difficulties encountered in the design and interpretation of group research in both the past and present.

One of the group leader's primary considerations in goal-setting should be to provide evaluative procedures related to the stated goals of the group which will reflect whether these goals are attained. Researchers who have made formal attempts to identify and evaluate the effects of a particular group experience have often been disappointed when the analysis of the data proved inconclusive or even negligible. Hindsight in most instances has indicated that the true impact of the group experience can be overlooked either by making an evaluation predicated on unrealistic criteria, or by using inappropriate or inadequate evaluative procedures. Many different sources of information and assessment methods are available for use by the counselor.

The opening article by Zimpfer, "Some Conceptual and Research Problems in Group Counseling" (1968), calls attention to criteria problems. He points out that group practitioners have no organized treatise on which to base procedures, objectives, and evaluative criteria. Zimpfer suggests that research efforts are particularly slow and difficult because of the complexity of variables with which the researcher works. Harrison, in "Problems in the Design and Interpretation of Research on Human Relations Training" (1967), highlights problems involving the provision of adequate control groups, the temporal process of change being studied, and the real difficulty of defining treatments or experiences. In a previously unpublished paper entitled "Laboratory Education: Research Results and Research Needs" (1968), Campbell reviews empirical research results in laboratory education through 1967 and suggests some needed directions in future research undertakings. Although his suggestions are difficult to implement, they are sound and appropriate. Campbell's distinction between internal and external criteria is a highly useful concept.

In general, research on the use of groups supports the claim that group experiences do have growth-producing effects. Group programs have resulted in changes in personal and interpersonal sensitivity, the ability to manage feelings, self-determination, attitudes toward self and others, and interdependence. Research reports also indicate that there is little support for the widespread concern about the traumatic effects of the group experience.

The survey articles by Gazda and Larsen, "A Comprehensive Appraisal of Group and Multiple Counseling Research" (1968), and Anderson, "Group Counseling" (1969), are informative for the novice as well as the experienced researcher. These selections provide the reader with research synopses, conclusions, and implications in an attempt to contribute to the improvement of group research. Gazda and Larsen present an unusually comprehensive analysis of ten process studies and ninety-four outcome studies of group counseling. Of particular interest is the section which deals with research design models. Anderson, in the latest group counseling review to appear in the *Review of Educational Research,* arranges his evaluative study according to a counselor's concerns in setting up and conducting a counseling group. This survey is based on some 240 pertinent articles and identifies trends and needs. The studies by Gazda and Larsen, Anderson, and Campbell represent only a few of the summaries of past research that are available. (See, for example, the reviews cited in the article in Part One by Eddy and Lubin, "Laboratory Training and Encounter Groups" (1971), and the recent survey of existing research by Gibb.[1])

---

[1] Gibb, J. R. The effects of human relations training. In A. E. Bergin and S. L. Garfield (Eds.), *Handbook of Psychotherapy and Behavior Change.* New York: Wiley & Sons, 1970. Pp. 2114–76.

Evaluation carefully conceived and executed plays a vital role in a group's effectiveness and increases the counselor's knowledge and understanding of the process of the group. Evaluation is essential in understanding and utilizing group procedures. A group practitioner needs to be knowledgeable and sophisticated in his efforts to interpret existing knowledge and to plan and conduct innovative research. By carefully studying the selections included in Part Four, the student will discover that a counselor can evaluate the experience of a group more comprehensively than he might have thought possible.

29 / SOME CONCEPTUAL AND RESEARCH PROBLEMS IN GROUP COUNSELING

David G. Zimpfer

In general, group counseling is a process for aiding students in their vocational, educational, social, and personal development and adjustment; it uses the medium of small group interaction under the leadership of a trained counselor. Over the past few years, the process has been called, variously, group counseling, multiple counseling, group therapy, and small group discussion. The objective of this paper is to comment critically on the present scene in group counseling, focus on some of its great problems, and offer, at least through implication, possible suggestions for amelioration of those problems.

Group counseling in educational settings was first initiated largely out of the desperation of counselors who had extremely large caseloads. They were anxious to offer more counseling more often to their counselees, and seeing them in groups seemed a reasonable alternative to individual counseling.

The fact that group counseling was seen as a substitute for individual counseling forced practitioners to make two assumptions: first, that the goals of individual counseling were also appropriate for counseling in groups; and secondly, that the groups counseled were best composed of students who had a common problem, thus rendering them "treatable" in unison by a single counselor. It is the position of this paper that each of these assumptions has held back the development of group counseling as a process which has its own reason for being and its own potential outcomes.

From SCHOOL COUNSELOR, 1968, Vol. 15, pp. 326–333. Copyright 1968, American Personnel and Guidance Association. Reprinted with permission of author and publisher.

The first assumption, that the goals of individual counseling were appropriate for counseling in groups, persists even today. The typical criteria for individual counseling, such as improvement of students' grade point averages, congruence of real and ideal self concept, and realism of vocational choice, have been transported bodily into the group counseling research literature. Little concern has been given to the appropriateness of the group setting for achieving these objectives.

Similarly, the second assumption—that groups needed to be focused on a common problem in order to be treated simultaneously by a single counselor—has also persisted. It has done so under the guise of "assisting the group to relate effectively with each other on an issue of mutual concern," but the common problem requirement has really worked to the disadvantage of groups in counseling. The literature stresses, for groups, the freedom of members to talk about the real issues which concern them, and grants them the right to diverge, to switch, to progressively evolve topics and solutions to problems. The common problem assumption seems to ignore the very permissiveness that theorists endorse and denies the right of the individual to identify his unique concerns and to make his own decisions about whether or not to focus on them.

In brief, then, the history of group counseling has been one of borrowing from the field of individual counseling the objectives, the singularity of treatment, and the criteria of individual counseling. This has even been extended to borrowing the very instruments by which counseling effectiveness is most commonly assessed. Further, a certain rigidity which devotion to research methodology can impose has affected outcome research in group counseling.

Several problems can be identified in the areas of (1) conceptualization and theorizing about group counseling, and (2) the relationship of research to conceptualization.

Conceptualization Issues

Nowhere in the published literature is there yet a true theory of group counseling. There are several published pieces which tell how, for example, group counseling might function in the schools (Wright, 1959), and how a counselor might function (Cohn, Combs, Gibian, & Sniffen, 1963); but there is no organized treatise which systematically examines and presents a concept of the nature of man, premises regarding human growth and development, the change agentry to be applied, the procedures, the objectives, and the criteria for evaluation in group counseling. Some theories in the literature of group psychotherapy have been developed (Slavson, 1964; Satir, 1964; Berne, 1966) and the group dynamics literature presents many possibilities for research on process and outcome variables; but group counseling has not as yet developed a literature of its own in this regard. This has caused particular stress in research in group counseling. A researcher, for example, cannot be sure if the several counselors he may use are well qualified in light of any particular theoretical formulation, or whether they will perform similarly enough to control the counselor input variable while he examines other factors.

There probably cannot be a single theory of group counseling. There are too many philosophical positions about the nature of man, too many psychological bases for human growth and development and the ways by which change is effected, too many variations in counselor personality and style of functioning interpersonally, and too many possible ways for groups to form and develop uniquely for a singular group counseling theory. The fact that there are several possible theoretical positions becomes quite clear when one examines the positions writers take regarding the group counseling process: Should the counselor focus on the individual within the group or on the dynamics of the total group? Those who contend that the focus is on the individual seem to be doing individual counseling in a group setting, using the group largely as an incidental resource for support or questioning. To illustrate with the analogy of a ping-pong game, the pattern of interaction of such a group might show that the counselor would serve on one side, the other members taking their turns one by one opposite the counselor. By contrast, the interaction in a group-dynamics-oriented counseling group would appear more like a multi-sided game of ping-pong, with the ball being transferred quite freely and rather equally among all members as if there were several teams or members participating simultaneously. In this latter position, the leader's keen awareness of and competency in handling group processes is a prime requirement; he is constantly working with these to the advantage of the group and may be interpreting them to the group as an important learning objective of the counseling process.

In their demand that participants be centered on a common problem, group counselors usually impose the same criteria and evaluative instruments on all members of their group. In imposing such a uniform evaluative standard, they judge the quality and effectiveness of their series of encounters on the basis of pre-selected and common objectives, as if only on these could group counseling for the participants be successful. Similarly, the selection of criterion measures before the fact of counseling does injustice to the potential of group counseling for progressively altering its course toward more significant personal experiences. It is convenient for research purposes to invoke the requirement of pre-treatment choice of criteria and of outcome measures to be applied uniformly to all members of a group. But this is an unnecessary and rigid worship of traditional research methodology. It ignores the existence of those evolutionary forces in freely-structured counseling groups which preclude attention to single or pre-determined themes and uniform outcomes. (This is true also, of course, of research on individual counseling.) Objectives and criteria rather should be thought of as constantly in process, steadily evolving rather than fixed from the outset. If need be let the attainment of some goals be determined along the way in order to clear the way for other goals; but let not the introduction and substitution of new criteria be denied.

Often, once a particular counselee problem has been selected for treatment, only reduction of incidence of his specific symptom is taken as an index of success. The counseling of underachievers, for example, is regularly evaluated in terms of change in grade point average. This seems to be an unduly narrow and self-punishing imposition of criteria in the search for success in group counseling. Similarly, in group counseling there is no imperative need on conceptual or research grounds that the criteria and measurement instruments be identical for all individuals. Again, if the objectives of counseling be individualistic regardless of the treatment to which one is exposed, then the outcome criteria and evaluations of success must be individualized. The relatively poor showing that group counseling has made in the research literature may thus be due to the three problems of imposing common criteria on all, lack of mobility of criteria, and selection in advance of single bases for evaluation.

Since there are varieties of theoretical positions and practices in group counseling, it becomes significant to note the lack in typical research literature of virtually any specification of what *has* gone on in the process of counseling. Goldman (1962) has tried to specify the nature of group counseling in terms of its relatively unstructured, free-discussion, affectively-oriented process and in terms of its focus on topics of non-school or school-related nature, such as study habits, vocational plans, dating behavior, etc. Zimpfer (1962) applied

Goldman's matrix to all the possible group counseling studies in educational settings extant in the literature at that time and found that fewer than half of the 30- or 40-odd reports could be classified with confidence as group counseling. Too little descriptive data were provided.

Let journal editors allow space for research contributors to discuss the rationale on which their procedures are based and to elaborate on the very processes themselves. Kagan, in a recent issue of the *Review of Educational Research,* deplored the fact that the nature of the group procedures used in given research articles was not specified—a "confounding source of confusion and the greater obstacle to discovery" (1966, p. 274). After commenting favorably on one article in which the authors did elaborate what went on in their groups, Kagan moaned: "How many studies have led to confusion because such descriptive detail . . . was not offered?" (1966, pp. 276–277).

The lack of theory and adequate conceptualizing and the withholding of relevant descriptive data in research articles have resulted in proliferation of effort and lack of standardization, without concomitant testing of the value of different procedures. Other problems abound. (1) The many labels being used for group counseling —each perhaps with a different intent (most prefer "group counseling," according to Gazda and others (Gazda, Duncan, & Meadows, 1967); but Hansen and others (Hansen, Zimpfer, & Easterling, 1967) found justification for the term "multiple counseling" in the greater perceived relationships with peers than with the counselor); (2) Different writers conceiving of one counselor or more than one; (3) Groups of 3–5 members or as many as 30 or more members; (4) Focus on individuals versus focus on the dynamics of the group; (5) Cognitive versus affective content; (6) Disagreement on the most appropriate type of leadership. It is in this condition that conceptualization on counseling with groups finds itself in the late sixties.

Relationship of Research to Conceptualization

The next area concerns the relationship of research to conceptualization—questions of design, instrumentation, procedures.

Whatever the advantages of the group setting in counseling, the outcomes selected for focus are not typically those which draw on these advantages. As Kagan wrote in reviewing studies of group counseling: "The most frequently employed criterion was improve ment in school functioning" (1966, p. 275). Specifically, the grade point criterion was commonly used.

Either researchers are blissfully unaware of the special advantages enjoyed by groups in counseling—the chance to evolve outcomes quite different from those attainable from individual counseling and really very important all by themselves—or they assume that in the process of enjoying these advantages the counselees should move on to the more ultimate, more generalized goals for which all counseling strives.

What seems quite clear is that there are unique properties of groups which of themselves claim recognition in the process of counseling with groups and that it makes particularly good sense to capitalize on them as a basis for this kind of counseling. Only in a group can a student identify with other students who are working on similar problems; only in a group can an individual test out the reality of and get reactions to his positions, his ideas, and his behaviors from his peers; only in a group can one broaden the scope of the interpersonal roles he plays; only in a group can an individual learn what is involved in assuming leadership functions. No equivalent experience can be presented in an individual counseling session. While there may not be able to be a single theory of group counseling, there is no call for it to be tied to the procedures or objectives of individual counseling.

It seems almost self-defeating to impose ultimate criteria on one's limited efforts. Group counseling outcome research often concludes with null results. Most of the research has been conducted with relatively short-term counseling: 8 to 16 sessions. Perhaps it is unrealistic to expect large positive gains on the criteria often used— gains in self concept or in grade point average—from such relatively short-term experiences. Eight or 16 sessions may not be appropriate to the task of changing attitudes or behaviors that have been built up and reinforced over years of life experience. The commonly advanced argument in null-result research in group counseling is that the counseling seemed to be proceeding in trends toward the desired outcome, and that it only needed to be a longer series of experiences. Such an argument assumes that the nature of the treatment is correct and that adjusting the duration of counseling will suffice to bring about greater change. Such a position has not been tested in the research through replication studies, in which the time variable was the only consciously altered condition.

There are practical problems, too, to increasing the duration of counseling exposure. Given the time limitations of most school counselors, and even of college counselors, it may be inappropriate and unrealistic to expect more than fifteen or so sessions of group counseling with the same participants. If this is so, it demands a re-appraisal of the kinds of goals counselors set for themselves and for counselees in groups. Perhaps more immediate goals, dealing with decisions, plans, and other cognitive outcomes may be more ap-propriate in light of the limited impact of even fifteen sessions. Even such limited outcomes as a simple commitment to examine the possibility of change in one's conception of self, his relation-ships with other persons, his behavior in school, and the like, seem very reasonable. They are preconditions to effective over-all be-havioral change and are worthy in themselves as goals of develop-mental counseling.

If one is tempted to protract the counseling process into longer duration, he may well ask some sobering questions. Is this intense exposure truly appropriate to the developmental stage and tasks of the counselees, or am I submitting to a warped desire to produce the mature product in one extended series of sessions? Do I have the competence to handle the increasingly basic revelations and self discoveries which a long contact can promote? Do I, if I work in an institution such as a school or college, have the mandate to attempt to make rather basic modifications in attitude, value commitment, and behavior?

Another question one must ask is: When should evaluation of counseling take place? Most studies examine results on the criterion measures immediately after counseling. This works to the disadvan-tage of the researcher, especially if he is looking for longer-range behavioral outcomes. Take, for example, the grade-point criterion. What are the chances that an individual who has relatively low grades at the outset of a couple of months of counseling will change those grades by the post-test? He must first undergo a counseling process through which he evaluates his position regarding grades, or in which he attempts to understand his very self; he must somehow internalize these assessments and understandings and translate them into willingness to consider new behaviors; he must search for means of changing and then actually change. His teachers, who may have become accustomed to seeing him as performing in a certain way, must bring themselves to see that he is different and must take this into account in awarding grades for new marking periods. This is not possible by the post-test, even over a span of several months. One recent study (Ofman, 1964) indicated that it took three semes-ters for grade point averages to be affected subsequent to group counseling. Measurement only at the post-test point ignores the possibility of delayed or cumulative effects accruing as a result of counseling.

Very little attention has been given in the research literature to the question of composition and matching of groups. Much of the early research used the group as a setting, comparing the one seemingly discrete dimension—the fact that one had a group—with other settings such as individual counseling or no counseling. Some recent studies have advanced at least to the point of comparing group treatments (Krumboltz & Thoresen, 1964; Chestnut, 1965; Cahoon, 1965). But scarce indeed is the study that reassures the reader that the several experimental groups which may be combined, or the several groups involved in varying experimental conditions, are matched on any dimensions really crucial to group functioning. Traditional matching based on age, IQ, and sex are common. But little concern has been shown for matching on motivation for change, congeniality of members, degree of sociometric status, cooperativeness, attitude toward other members, succorance, nurturance, and other personal and interpersonal variables. These may be vital to an understanding of what is happening in groups and may be the significant variables in distinguishing effectiveness from lack of effectiveness. Such factors related to group composition have not been used in attempting to establish similarly behaving groups. (This would seem essential if one expects to combine data from several groups as he assesses results.) Nor have they been used as independent variables in plumbing the depths of the group process in counseling. It is granted that while these are identifiable variables, they are also uncertainly predictable forces at this point in time; but the fact remains that group counseling research hasn't really begun to test them or to tap their potential.

The group-composition issue is also related to the objectives one has for his group counseling. If the counselor were to seek and reinforce adaptive, adjusting behavior of certain group members, the group membership might ideally include several member-models of the desired behavior, whose influence could then be brought to bear to pressure for change. On the other hand, if the counselor sought to help individuals to test and examine the impact of their behavior on others, he might choose a group whose members were especially willing to be frank with others about how they felt they were treated, and who had diverse backgrounds to serve as resources for offering suggestions for change. The counselor (and similarly the researcher of groups) must carefully think through his rationale in such a way that his objectives and procedures will be consistent with each other.

It is also vital that there be consistency of objectives and the tools with which to assess their attainment. Often, in the flush of eagerness to use new and promising evaluative instruments, researchers adopt devices for which group counseling may be inappropriate or irrelevant. An example of this may be in the use of Q-sort methodology to determine the effectiveness of group counseling on the self concept of counselees.

Q-sorts have been most associated with treatment based on self or phenomenological theory, in which acceptance and understanding and safety of environment are prerequisite to successful outcomes and in which self report is a most important source of evaluation. Group counseling among adolescent peers often becomes the battleground of reality testing, confrontation and challenge rather than the haven of empathy and the opportunity for patient self-examination. While it is true that the counselor seeks to provide the necessary warmth, and while in a sense the total counseling atmosphere of the group is secure ("We can talk about private things and react fankly with each other here"), the environment the counselor has constructed when he adopts group counseling is one which highlights social reaction and feedback, not self exploration, sharpening of perception and insight development. As a result, the use of Q-sort methodology to assess outcomes may be too far removed from the basic activity of the group. This is especially true if the Q-sort focuses on perceptions of the inner self rather than on the interpersonal self.

It could be said that the most constructive changes to come about as a result of group counseling may be those which focus on the individual's competence to deal effectively with social situations; to evaluate the agenda and objectives of a group, the pressures being brought to bear and his own relationship to those objectives and pressures; to develop skills to move the group toward its goals; and to make the group a viable medium for his own personal purposes. Research instrumentation in this case would be quite different from the tools commonly used for evaluation in group counseling.

Group counseling research is slow, partly because of the complexity of the variables being dealt with. The unknown valence of compositional factors; the difficulty of standardizing group climate and interaction; the sheer labor of performing process analyses of a moment-to-moment nature; the dazzling number of combinations of member-member, member-subgroup, subgroup-subgroup, member-group and other interactions, both verbal and nonverbal, make the researcher quail in spite of his interest and concern. It is hoped that some issues and problems of formulation, practice, and research have been dealt with helpfully here.

REFERENCES

Berne, E. *Principles of group treatment.* New York: Oxford, 1966.

Cahoon, D. D. A comparison of the effectiveness of verbal reinforcement applied in group and individual interviews. *Journal of Counseling Psychology,* 1965, *12,* 121–126.

Chestnut, W. J. The effects of structured and unstructured group counseling on male college students' underachievement. *Journal of Counseling Psychology,* 1965, *12,* 388–394.

Cohn, B., Combs, F., Gibian, E. J., & Sniffen, A. M. Group counseling, an orientation. *Personnel and Guidance Journal,* 1963, *42,* 355–358.

Gazda, G. M., Duncan, J. A., & Meadows, M. E. Group counseling and group procedures—Report of a survey. *Counselor Education and Supervision,* 1967, *6,* 305–310.

Goldman, L. Group counseling: Content and process. *Personnel and Guidance Journal,* 1962, *40,* 518–522.

Hansen, J., Zimpfer, D., & Easterling, R. A study of the relationship in multiple counseling. *Journal of Educational Research,* 1967, *60,* 461–463.

Kagan, N. Group procedures. *Review of Educational Research,* 1966, *36,* 274–287.

Krumboltz, J. D., & Thoresen, C. E. The effect of behavioral counseling in group and individual settings on information-seeking behavior. *Journal of Counseling Psychology,* 1964, *11,* 324–333.

Ofman, W. Evaluation of a group counseling procedure. *Journal of Counseling Psychology,* 1964, *11,* 152–159.

Satir, V. *Conjoint family therapy.* Palo Alto, Calif.: Science and Behavior Books, 1964.

Slavson, S. *A textbook in analytic group psychotherapy.* New York: International Universities Press, 1964.

Wright, E. W. Multiple counseling: Why? When? How? *Personnel and Guidance Journal,* 1959, *37,* 551–557.

Zimpfer, D. An analysis of certain factors contributing to outcomes reported in studies of multiple counseling. Unpublished manuscript, 1962.

30 / PROBLEMS IN THE DESIGN
AND INTERPRETATION OF RESEARCH
ON HUMAN RELATIONS TRAINING

Roger Harrison

The measurement of processes of learning and the evaluation of the outcomes of the teaching-learning process have always posed major problems in research design. This is especially true where the desired outcomes are broadly defined as changes in interpersonal behavior: a complex of knowledge, values, perceptions, and behavioral skills. Until recently, behavioral scientists have tended to avoid research on human relations training in favor of more "researchable" topics which lend themselves to rigorous experimental design.[1] In addition to or because of the difficulties in constructing respectable designs, there have been relatively few available publication outlets for such research, and this has further restricted the number of studies which have come to light.

Recently, however, there has been a substantial increase in published research on human relations training, and there appears to be increased interest among behavioral scientists in conducting studies in this area. This paper is written in part to provide these investigators with a review of the problems which should be thought through when planning and conducting such studies.

Unlike much research in the behavioral sciences which is primarily intelligible and of interest only to other researchers, research

[1] A notable exception is the classic study by Fleishman (1951). This study showed that it is possible to construct rigorous training evaluation designs, given sufficient access to the trained subjects.

From EXPLORATIONS IN HUMAN RELATIONS TRAINING AND RESEARCH, 1967, Report No. 1, pp. 1–9. Copyright © 1967, NTL Institute for Applied Behavioral Science. Reprinted with permission of author and publisher.

on human relations training is frequently written for and read by administrators and practitioners who may base important action decisions on the findings of the research. This latter group has an important need for guidelines which will aid them in evaluating the soundness and applicability of research reports to their practical decisions on the planning and conduct of training. This paper is equally addressed, then, to the creators and consumers of research on human relations training.

Much of the research in this area is concerned with the special variation of training known as "sensitivity training," T-group training, or laboratory training in human relations. My own experience and familiarity with the literature are also focused on this approach, and the examples and references in this paper will be drawn from the literature on laboratory training. An attempt will be made to review thoroughly the problems of method in this area.

These problems, however, are general to research on human relations training, not specific to sensitivity training as a special method. The discussion should be of utility to those interested in conducting or interpreting research on any of the various techniques of human relations education.

In this paper I shall try to suggest a number of problems which I feel have some currency in research on human relations training. I do not wish to discourage research on training or to suggest that we postpone investigation until the ambiguities inherent in this area can be resolved by clever research designs or ingenious statistical manipulation. On the contrary, my aim is to point out some ways of avoiding difficulty as well as to indicate some difficulties which we cannot yet do much about other than simply to be aware of them. I hope that this modest catalogue may stimulate others to attack the problems to which solutions appear to be in the offing, but I hope that we shall have the courage to go ahead with the search, even in those areas where we appear doomed to live for the present with lack of rigor in design and with ambiguous, inconsistent, or even misleading findings. When all is said and done, scientific progress has never been stimulated by an unwillingness to launch investigation in the face of uncertainty or the lack of elegant tools.

I shall try, where possible, to indicate ways in which methodological barriers can be circumvented and ambiguities resolved by supplementary investigations. It is to be hoped that where I am unable to do this, others may find a way.

The Problem of Controls

The provision of adequate control groups for research on training is one of the most persistent methodological problems in this area. The fact that a person is in a control group biases his self-image and the perception of him by others; the fact that a person has participated in training inclines him and others to look for change in his behavior.

To compound the problem, there often is administrative or self-control over the division of a group of otherwise equivalent members of an organization into a trained group and a control group. That is, there is other than random selection as to who receives the training and when. Usually, someone makes a decision to send to training a group which is judged more likely to benefit or more willing to participate than those who are not trained. Since there is nearly always some such selection of who is to be trained, this problem is an ubiquitous one.

This problem cannot be resolved by enforced randomness of assignment to training. Sensitivity training programs are usually designed for participants who are at least nominally volunteers. If, for the purposes of research design, assignment to a training or control group is made a matter of administrative fiat, it changes the nature of the training itself. Those who have worked in nonvoluntary laboratory training settings know that the participants show a much higher degree of resistance and mistrust than is the case where attendance is strictly voluntary.

One method of administrative control which preserves a degree of voluntariness has been suggested by Massarik (1965). It involves delaying the participation of some volunteers and using them as a control group in the interim. While this method is theoretically feasible, I have found in practice that it is generally impossible to prevent at least a few persons' joining the control group who have delayed their participation in the laboratory out of ambivalence or reluctance to attend.

There are two ways around the control group problem which appear to me to be both genuinely valid and practical. Both require that we study the *process* of training as well as the outcomes. Instead of simply measuring participants before and after their passage through a "black box" called training, we must make some hypotheses about what it is that happens to the person which causes us to predict one outcome rather than another.

The first solution to be suggested is feasible where it is possible to give comparable groups of participants training which differs systematically along some important training process dimension. For example, the dimension might be depth of personal involvement. The variations (from right to left) might be lectures, case studies, role playing, group-oriented T-groups, person-oriented T-groups, "personal growth" laboratories. One such study by Byrd (1966) compared participants in a T-group laboratory with those in a "nongroup" situation that used personal growth activities as the basic learning setting. Each of the groups was seen by participants and others as having undergone a significant learning experience, yet it was possible to demonstrate differential outcomes consistent with Byrd's predictions.

Another example of the use of this kind of control is a study by Bunker and Knowles (1967) in which the effects of laboratories of different lengths were compared. Bunker and Knowles also compared the kinds and amounts of change occurring for participants of different occupational backgrounds.

The assumption behind these designs is that if the amount and kind of training outcome vary systematically and predictably as functions of some input (whether the design, the type of participant, the behavior of training staff, or whatever), then the obtained changes can be viewed as "real." Because all groups being compared have been through a training experience, the design eliminates the biasing of perception which occurs when an untrained control group is used.

A variation on this theme introduces control by prediction of training outcomes through independent process variables. If we can measure some important difference in the behavior of participants or in the quality of their experience while in training, then this type of control can be achieved.

This design is illustrated by a study by Bunker in which it was found that the number of reported changes for participants in laboratory training was associated with ratings of active involvement in the T-group (Bunker, 1965). Similarly, the author found significant relationships between active involvement in training and change in categories of interpersonal perception following training (Harrison, 1966). In another study, the ratings of involvement predicted posttraining increases in consideration, as rated by organizational associates (Harrison & Oshry, 1967). This predictability of change was found even though there was no significant *overall* change in rated organizational behavior. If third variable prediction had not been used, the study would have resulted in a misleading negative finding rather than a finding of differential change.

Temporal Change in Training Outcome

One process which has been little investigated is the progressive change in outcome with time following training. We ordinarily give some lip service to the importance of longitudinal changes but few researchers have gathered longitudinal data. The importance of doing so is illustrated by one study the author conducted in which data were collected at two points following training. In this study of cognitive change, the changes were progressive over a surprisingly long period of time. It was predicted that changes would be greatest immediately after the laboratory and would decay with time. Change was assessed six weeks after the conclusion of training and again after six months in order to measure temporal deterioration. The results were opposite to the prediction: The changes were positive but insignificant at the six-week mark, increasing to higher and statistically significant levels only after six months (Harrison, 1966).

I believe that there is a tendency for us to study outcomes without thinking deeply about the temporal process of change. What theory there is about this process suggests that this is unwise. For example, Schein and Bennis (1965) have elaborated a three-stage temporal theory of change originally conceptualized by Lewin. According to this model, the T-group laboratory has an initial "unfreezing" effect. The individual is "shaken up" by dissonance and disconfirmation of his self-concept through the feedback which he receives from others. The unfreezing process creates, to a greater or lesser degree, a *need for change*.

This is followed by a period of search and experimentation during which the individual tries out new conceptualizations, experiments with new behavior, and attempts to gather information about the effectiveness of alternate ways of relating to others. This second phase covers the period during which behavioral *change* actually takes place. It is followed by *refreezing* of behavior due both to internal forces stemming from improved adaptation and/or defense and to external forces generated by the social environment. With refreezing, the individual's behavior again comes to a quasi-stable equilibrium as close to a steady state as behavioral patterns usually come. The forces which produced the original imbalance have resulted in change up to the point where counter forces are generated within or external to the person which oppose the change and eventually restabilize behavior.

This is a reasonable though not an empirically demonstrated model of the change process. As yet no one knows how long the phases may be expected to last nor how to identify, in practice, the transition from one to another. What is clear, however, is that if this model is correct the phase a person is in makes a great deal of difference in the kind of changes we should look for as training outcomes. What we usually mean when we talk about outcomes is the "refrozen" state, in which the individual has integrated and stabilized new patterns of cognition, perception, and behavior.

What we may often measure is the process of change itself. During this phase we should expect rather different outcomes if the training has been successful. Rather than stabilized behavior patterns, we should expect to find such changes as higher activity levels and rates of interaction; greater risk taking in attempting new behavior with others; greater variability and inconsistency in behavior, values, and perceptions; and a higher level of aspiration for the quality of inter-personal relationships. These might well be accompanied by higher levels of anxiety and discomfort around the individual's self-concept and his interpersonal relationships.

It is not immediately clear what instruments or methods would best get at these qualitative aspects of behavior, but it is clear that they have not been explicitly investigated in recent studies of training outcome.

Dimensions and Directions of Change

A related problem has to do with the number of dimensions on which our design allows us to measure changes in participants. The number and kinds of degrees of freedom in our design are an implicit statement of the position we take regarding the aims and goals of training. In designing a study of outcome we express our point of view about the kinds and directions of change which we will classify as desirable outcomes. We may study only a narrow range of dimensions, in which case we are by implication narrowing the goals of training, or we may include any conceivable kind of change, in which case we are implying that one kind of change is as good as another.

The classic studies by Bunker (1965), Miles (1965), and Valiquet

(1968) are examples of the latter approach. They all use a design of very wide focus. Each asked participants and their associates to give free responses describing any changes which took place in the participant's behavior during the preceding year. The obtained responses from a trained and a control group were then classified inductively, and the number of changes in each category were compared to determine the kinds of changes on which laboratory participants differed significantly from controls.

This method not only does not specify in advance the dimensions on which change is to be measured but it also tends to count a change as equally significant whether it is up or down on a given dimension. For example, it would be possible, using this method, to find significant differences between trained subjects and controls on both *self-control* and *spontaneity*, qualities of behavior which are generally considered polar opposites on a single dimension.

By contrast, a study by Harrison and Oshry (1967) of changes in organizational behavior following laboratory training used an instrument constructed deductively from Argyris' two-dimensional theory of organizational behavior (Rational-Technical Competence and Interpersonal Competence). Through factor analysis of the items derived from the theory, three dimensions were actually found and studied. Changes not measured by this instrument were, by implication, classified as irrelevant.

Furthermore, only unidirectional changes were assessed. That is, if half the participants showed increases in Rational Technical Competence and half showed decreases of equal magnitude the net effect of the training was considered to be zero.

A Classification Scheme for Training Outcomes

These studies are examples of two of the three major categories into which research designs may be classified according to the kinds and directions of change for which the design permits assessment. Harrison and Oshry's (1967) study would be classified as *normative* with respect to outcome. It is *restrictive* with respect to the dimensions on which change was assessed and it is *prescriptive* regarding the direction of change considered desirable. Much of the writing about sensitivity training is, in fact, normative with respect to outcomes. For example, it is usually considered good for people to become more democratic, bad for them to become more authoritarian. It is good for people to be more open to their own and others' feelings; it is bad for them to reject or suppress their emotionality.

The client's point of view is also generally normative with respect to outcomes. A personnel manager wants to know whether he can expect people he sends to a laboratory in human relations to come back more or less dominant, more or less responsive to the needs and feelings of others, more or less expressive of his own needs and feelings. He is not likely to be satisfied if he is told "it depends on the direction in which the individual needs to change."

Among practitioners there appears to be a historical trend (for example, in the laboratories conducted at Bethel, Maine, by the National Training Laboratories[2]) from a normative approach focused on the development of democratic ideology and its expression in the democratic decision-making group to a concern with *individual growth* as the desired outcome. The individual growth position with respect to outcome would probably focus on the receiving of feedback in the T-group as the basic learning process in laboratory training. The process begins when the individual exposes his characteristic styles of relating to others in the T-group and receives feedback about the reactions of others to his behavior. In general, we would expect that rigidly extreme styles would tend to receive negative feedback at either end of most dimensions of behavior. For example, it is common for both over-talkative and under-participating members to be pressured by the rest of the group to approach the group average in their verbal activity. Similarly, both domineering and very dependent members are likely to receive feedback which, if heeded, would move them toward a more interdependent orientation. The same moderating influence tends to be exerted on both the cold and distant and the overly warm and personal members.

Carried to its extreme, the individual growth point of view would see the T-group as the place where sharp edges are rubbed off people. A more acceptable version of this point of view would be that the T-group is a place where each individual is encouraged to explore and express the latent and underdeveloped aspects of himself. From the standpoint of experimental design, these both come to much the same thing. The Bunker, Miles, and Valiquet

[2] On June 1, 1967, the name of the National Training Laboratories was officially changed to NTL Institute for Applied Behavioral Science, associated with the NEA.

studies referred to above are examples of this approach, and it is noteworthy that there is not, to the author's knowledge, any study which has used this method which has failed to show significant results. The individual growth point of view seems to "fit" the laboratory training process very well.

A third position with respect to outcome has seldom if ever been represented in experimental design, but it is theoretically very important. It is represented by Bennis' 1962 article on the goals of laboratory training. According to this point of view, the objective of laboratory training is neither to teach everyone the same values and behaviors (normative model) nor to improve the adaptation of the individual by changes in values or behavior style which are tailored to his needs. Rather the objective is a *general* improvement in adaptive capability for all members, based on (1) improved accuracy of perception of the self and of one's relationships with others, (2) more complex and accurate cognitive mapping of the realm of interpersonal phenomena, occurring through the development of new concepts which permit the individual to comprehend a wider range of interpersonal phenomena, (3) increases in behavioral range and flexibility, through experimentation with hitherto avoided or unpracticed modes of relating to others, and (4) development of an interest in and a method for continued learning about interpersonal relationships and group phenomena or, as Bennis (1962) puts it, "learning how to learn."

Little progress has been made in measuring the attainment of such goals. Doubtless the Bunker–Miles–Valiquet method gets at these changes as well as others, but only if the describer is himself sophisticated enough to observe and report abstract similarities among behaviors which may seem quite different at the concrete level of description. For example, if the individual has learned to take more risks in trying new interpersonal behavior as part of his "learning how to learn," he may have exhibited this in a wide variety of ways from which the observer would have to abstract the concept, "takes more risks." Consequently, although the highest and most desirable goal of laboratory training in human relations may be this development of the individual's adaptive and learning capacity, it is doubtful that it has yet been a significant object of study, and it probably will not be until a good deal of work is put into the creation of ways of quantifying such changes. I suggest that developing these methods should have a high priority in current research efforts.

Variability in the Training Experience

There are several problems involved in the actual process of working with subjects and gathering data in research on laboratory training. A major one has to do with the difficulty of specifying the nature of the training experience which each participant has. To begin with, there exists a kind of cult of originality among laboratory trainers in which a dominant value is the invention and proliferation of new variations in training design. It thus becomes practically impossible to standardize training design except insofar as the routine inclusion of the T-group experience may be considered standardization. A major difficulty here is that we do not yet have adequate enough theory about the effects of different elements of training design even to permit us to classify laboratories according to design. We may suspect, for example, that there are differences between laboratories in which there is a good deal of formal assistance to the participant in conceptualizing his experience through lectures, discussions, readings, and so on. We do not, however, have clear hypotheses about the relationship between having an experience, having an insight about that experience, and conceptualizing or generalizing the insight to other situations. If I had to select one aspect of training which most needs theoretical formulation and exploratory investigation, I should choose this problem of the relationship between experience, conceptualizing activities, and learning outcome.

A similar but conceptually less murky area has to do with the effects of variations in trainer style on participant learning. Though this area is far from adequately mapped, considerable exploration is going on. For example, Culbert (1966), Peters (1966), and Bolman[3] have all made recent contributions to our understanding. Hopefully, we shall soon have instruments which will permit us to assess trainer style as an independent variable and relate it to kind and extent of outcome.

Our understanding of the effects of group composition is in a similar stage of early exploration. We certainly have consistent and repeated evidence that group composition has a significant effect on the learning of participants, and we know something about the kinds of composition variables which are relevant (for a review of the literature in this area see Harrison, 1965).

[3] Lee Bolman of Yale University constructed an instrument for assessing trainer behavior along several dimensions, rated by participants and by the trainer himself. Personal communication, 1966.

It is a sobering thought indeed that if we take the effects of group composition seriously, we should try to assess the composition of each and every T-group we study. Probably, in studies using a large sample of groups, it is sufficient to randomize assignment of participants to groups and call the groups heterogeneous. It is important to remember, however, that a strong case can be made in favor of the proposition that participants learn better in groups which are intentionally composed to produce conflict between polarized subgroups (Harrison, 1965). So what we do for administrative convenience and simplicity of research design may not result in the best training of which we are capable. As an alternative, it may be worthwhile to explore the routine use of simple instruments and/or observations of participant behavior to compose groups for optimum learning.

The Timing of Data Collection

There are two problems connected with the actual administrative process of data collection which deserve consideration in any research design. One has to do with timing. After considerable experience with the administration of instruments on the opening day of a laboratory, I have come to the conclusion that the anticipatory anxiety which staff and participants alike feel during this period significantly affects the direction and variability of responses to many kinds of instruments. Unlike concerns which arise around events occurring in the process of training, this anticipatory anxiety seems largely irrelevant to any of the concerns of the research. The experience is ubiquitous but transitory, and when the training begins this anxiety is shortly replaced by more realistic concerns.

My current preference is to administer instruments by mail prior to the laboratory, if possible. If not, I sometimes wait a day into the laboratory before collecting "pre-training" data. This introduces problems of interpretation, but I have decided that I can put up with moderate ambiguity of inference in preference to gathering data at a time when most participants are upset and anxious.

Experimenter-Participant Relationships in the Laboratory Setting

Experience has also convinced me that the effects on results of the relationship between experimenter and subjects in research on training are even more significant than we are finding them to be in the academic psychological laboratory. In the latter situation, subjects are usually willing to put up with a lot of actual or suspected manipulation on the part of the experimenter in the interests of the scientific values which are shared by educated adults in our culture. In the training setting, however, we operate according to a norm which holds that the search for truth is a cooperative one which can only proceed successfully if the participants are as open with one another about their experiences, observations, and inferences as it is possible for them to be. An extremely high value is set upon the development and maintenance of trust between staff and participants and among participants themselves.

In this atmosphere, the secrecy of an experimenter toward his subjects and his real or imagined manipulation of the latter are strongly opposed by the dominant values of the laboratory training culture. If he flies in the face of these values, the experimenter runs a very real and substantial risk of being isolated and outlawed and of becoming uninfluential. Furthermore, when the researcher does place himself in this countercultural position, a good deal of the suppressed resentment which has been generated by experiences with behavioral scientists in school or at work comes to the surface. The research is thus affected not only by the relationship between the present researcher and his subjects but also by the latter's past experiences as a subject.

The net result of all this is to produce various kinds and degrees of rebellious behavior on the part of some unknown proportion of the subjects. My guess is that in most research designs this rebellion results in increased variability and unreliability rather than in systematic bias.

Both the timing problem and the experimenter-subject relationship are sources of falsely negative findings. The operation of these factors tends to produce increased error variance so that the relationships which the experimenter is seeking turn out to be in expected directions, but statistically insignificant. This may lead to nonpublication of results and/or the abandonment of a promising avenue of inquiry. I would hypothesize that the heightened sensitivity of laboratory participants to qualities of interpersonal relationships frequently combines with the experimenter's cold and standoffish style to produce such false negatives. Considerable care is required to overcome this source of error. To do so, one must usually run some danger of biased findings. This danger has been the conventional justification for the experimenter to follow his natural inclinations towards nonexposure and low involvement with subjects. I am suggesting a conscious reversal of this practice. This means being open with the subjects about one's intentions, interests, and motives. It means making research data available wherever possible to help the participants in their attempts to learn about themselves. It means making oneself personally available to participants and showing a genuine interest in the personal growth and enhancement which they are seeking in the laboratory.

In my experience, it is possible to move in this direction a considerable way without seriously compromising the canons of experimental design. It is probably not possible to avoid any compromise at all with scientific respectability. One must make a personal choice between his estimate of the dangers of falsely negative results and his trained-in distaste for "messy" designs in which the subjects know too much. It is not possible to avoid making the choice. The respectably sanitary design runs significant risks of being a failure; the design which enlists the subjects as willing participants in the search for truth runs the risk of biasing effects. Ingenuity in design can moderate these effects, but it cannot eliminate them.

Statistical Problems in Training Research

Last, I should like to refer to some statistical problems which are endemic to research involving the measurement of change. These problems have been so well treated in a symposium on change edited by Harris (1963) that I, a nonstatistician, shall do no more than point to them. The chapters by Bereiter and Lord discuss in detail the difficulties in such procedures as measuring the relationship between initial standing on a test or variable and change on that variable, or assessing the relationship between change on a variable and an independent predictor of that change. They also explain the operation of an extremely important phenomenon in measures of change—that of regression toward the mean. Some understanding of these difficulties should be acquired before undertaking research involving measures of change so that the major pitfalls can be avoided or taken into account.

I should like to reiterate that while I believe it is prudent to be concerned about the problems of method which beset our enterprise I believe equally strongly that it is unnecessarily obsessive to be discouraged by them. We should not allow these considerations to dissuade us from conducting research. Nor should we become overly rejecting of the findings of others because they have not overcome all of the obstacles in the way of achieving certainty. The problems to which this paper has been devoted are difficulties; they are not disasters. In spite of them we have already accumulated knowledge through research which is sound enough to lead to significant improvements in practice and increases in understanding. These achievements should encourage us to learn to live with the ambiguities we cannot avoid while working to reduce those which are amenable to improved research design. It is in the service of this goal that the current review is offered.

REFERENCES

Bennis, W. G. Goals and meta-goals of laboratory training. *Human Relations Training News,* 1962, *6* (3), 1–4.

Bunker, D. R. Individual applications of laboratory training. *Journal of Applied Behavioral Science,* 1965, *1* (2), 131–148.

Bunker, D. R., & Knowles, E. S. Comparison of behavioral changes resulting from human relations training laboratories of different lengths. *Journal of Applied Behavioral Science,* 1967, *3,* 505–523.

Byrd, R. E. Training clergy for creative risk taking: A preliminary evaluation. Paper read at the annual meeting of the Society for the Study of Scientific Religion, October 28, 1966, at the Center for Continuing Education, University of Chicago.

Culbert, S. A. Trainer self-disclosure and member growth in a T-group. Unpublished doctoral dissertation, University of California (Los Angeles), 1966.

Harris, C. W. (Ed.) *Problems in measuring change.* Madison: University of Wisconsin Press, 1963.

Harrison, R. Cognitive change and participation in a sensitivity training laboratory. *Journal of Consulting Psychology,* 1966, *30* (3).

Harrison, R. Group composition models for laboratory design. *Journal of Applied Behavioral Science,* 1965, *1* (4), 409–432.

Harrison, R., & Oshry, B. I. The impact of laboratory training on organizational behavior: Methodology and results. Mimeographed technical report. Washington, D.C.: National Training Laboratories, 1967.

Massarik, F. A sensitivity training impact model: Some first (& second) thoughts on the evaluation of sensitivity training. *Explorations in Human Relations Training and Research,* 1965, No. 3. Washington, D.C.: National Training Laboratories.

Miles, M. B. Changes during and following laboratory training: A clinical-experimental study. *Journal of Applied Behavioral Science,* 1965, *1* (3), 215–242.

Peters, D. R. Identification and personal change in laboratory training groups. Unpublished doctoral dissertation, Massachusetts Institute of Technology, 1966.

Schein, E. H., & Bennis, W. G. *Personal and organizational change through group methods: The laboratory approach.* New York: Wiley, 1965.

Valiquet, M. I. Individual change in a management development program. *Journal of Applied Behavioral Science,* 1968, *4,* 313–325.

31 / LABORATORY EDUCATION: RESEARCH RESULTS AND RESEARCH NEEDS

John P. Campbell

In the spirit of the empirical dust bowl, I will attempt to do the following in the next few minutes: (1) Briefly summarize the goals of the laboratory technique and some of the assumptions it seems to be making; (2) reflect the gist of the empirical literature which has tried to demonstrate behavioral effects for the method; (3) suggest some directions that future research might profitably follow. Most of the discussion focuses on the T-group, which I will view as the major component of the more complete program commonly called laboratory education.

I should indicate at this point that I am not a laboratory education practitioner or a T-group trainer and, barring some sort of cataclysm, never will be. Although, this does not imply a *conscious* desire to be negativistic about the enterprise, it is sometimes difficult to speak for one's unconscious.

Objectives of the Method

As gleaned from several sources, the stated goals of the T-group or laboratory method seem to be as follows (Argyris, 1964; Bradford, Gibb & Benne, 1964; Buchanan, 1965; Miles, 1960; Schein & Bennis, 1965; Tannenbaum, Weschler, & Massarik, 1961): (1) Increased self-insight or self-awareness concerning one's own behavior; (2) increased sensitivity to the behavior of others; (3) increased awareness

Unpublished paper presented at the meeting of the Midwestern Psychological Association, Chicago, May 1968. Copyright © 1971 by John P. Campbell. Printed with permission of author.

and understanding of the types of processes that facilitate or inhibit group functioning and/or the interactions between different groups; (4) increased behavioral skills in interpersonal and intergroup situations.

Note that this list of objectives has no direct connection with changes in work role performance. They are stated in general behavioral terms. However, there is the strong implication that achieving these goals will lead to such things as more interdependent and collaborative superior-subordinate relationships and an ability to resolve conflict situations through problem solving, rather than coercion and manipulation; and these in turn will enhance performance in almost any work role.

Technological Elements

What sort of technology does the method use to achieve these goals? Most of you are probably quite familiar already with the general goings-on in a T-group, and there is no need to recount here what is better described elsewhere (e.g., Kuriloff & Atkins, 1966; Klaw, 1961; Weschler & Reisel, 1959). However, it might be wise to mention them briefly.

At the center of things is, of course, the small face-to-face group in which the topic of conversation is each individual's behavior in the group, or the "here and now." Focusing on the here and now is facilitated by the trainer's withdrawal from the leadership role and his lack of reinforcement of previous status symbols and role distinctions.

The resulting vacuum is usually filled by feelings of frustration, anxiety, expressions of hostility concerning what is supposed to be going on, and by eventual attempts of some members to impose structure. It is these behaviors which then become the topic of conversation. They are the raw material with which people are to develop an awareness of their own behavior, the behavior of others, and the nature of group processes.

There are several additional elements which are seen as contributing to the success of the enterprise:

1. Most important is the process of feedback. The participants must be able and willing to inform each other how their behavior is being seen and interpreted and to describe the kinds of feelings they are experiencing.

2. A certain amount of anxiety must be generated at the outset of the training process. It serves the purpose of "unfreezing" the participant (Schein & Bennis, 1965) such that feedback may have its maximum effect and new attitudes and behavior can be reinforced through anxiety reduction.

3. Feedback must also occur in an atmosphere of so-called "psychological safety." The group must act in a supportive way, and each individual must feel that it is safe to expose his feelings and try out new ways of interacting.

4. Finally, the trainer, or his surrogate, is a crucial element in that he serves as a model for the participants to imitate. That is, he provides feedback for others, expresses his own feelings openly and honestly, and is strongly supportive of the expression of feelings in others.

Some Assumptions

The above-mentioned objectives and technology seem to me to imply a number of assumptions that should be made explicit:

1. A substantial number of group members, when confronted with others' behaviors and feelings in an atmosphere of psychological safety, can produce articulate and constructive feedback.

2. A significant number of the group members can agree on the major aspects of a particular individual's behavior. A complete consensus is not to be expected, but neither must the feedback meander off in all directions.

3. Feedback in a T-group is relatively complete and deals with significant aspects of behavior which are representative of the individual's behavior outside the group.

4. Psychological safety can be achieved relatively quickly among either complete strangers or among associates.

5. Almost everyone initially lacks interpersonal competence.

6. Anxiety facilitates new learning.

There is not time to discuss the above list at any length except to comment that if these assumptions reasonably map the true state of affairs, they point up one of the serious difficulties that the T-group method must face. That is, it requires a great deal of skill on the part of the participants. Maslow (1965) suggests that because of the initial skills demanded in this type of learning situation, perhaps only a very small percentage of the population can hope to benefit. Unfortunately, there are no data to enlighten us one way or the other.

Empirical Research Findings

With this much as background, what can we say about the effectiveness of the method for changing the behavior of people in organizations? The following review is based on an extensive survey of the literature through approximately November 1967. To help focus the discussion, consider Figure 1, page 408. This is nothing more than a schematic representation of training effects which attempts to point out classes of variables that deserve consideration.

One of the most important distinctions in the diagram is between external and internal criteria (Martin, 1957). *Internal criteria* are measures linked directly to the content and processes of the learning experience but have no direct linkage to job behavior or the goals of the organization. Examples might include measures of attitude change or measures of performance in simulated problem-solving exercises. To infer that an individual has "learned" a change must be demonstrated on some sort of internal criterion measure. *External criteria* are those linked directly with job behavior. Ratings of technical skill or communication ability are some examples. Neither of these two classes of criteria is more important than the other. The relationship between the two constitutes the basic problem of transfer of training. We must ask first, what is learned in a laboratory, and second, how does what is learned affect job behavior? The discussion of empirical results is organized around this distinction.

We should also preserve the distinction between job behavior and performance outcomes. Although a person's behavior in his work role may change, this may or may not imply a change in the effectiveness with which he contributes to the goals of the organization. For example, communicating more openly with subordinates may not lead to more effective job performance.

An obvious point to note is that attempts to change behavior cannot operate in a vacuum. Properties of the organizational environment may influence the change process at a number of junctures.

In sum, even with this very simple-minded representation of

FIGURE 1
A Schematic Representation of Training Impact

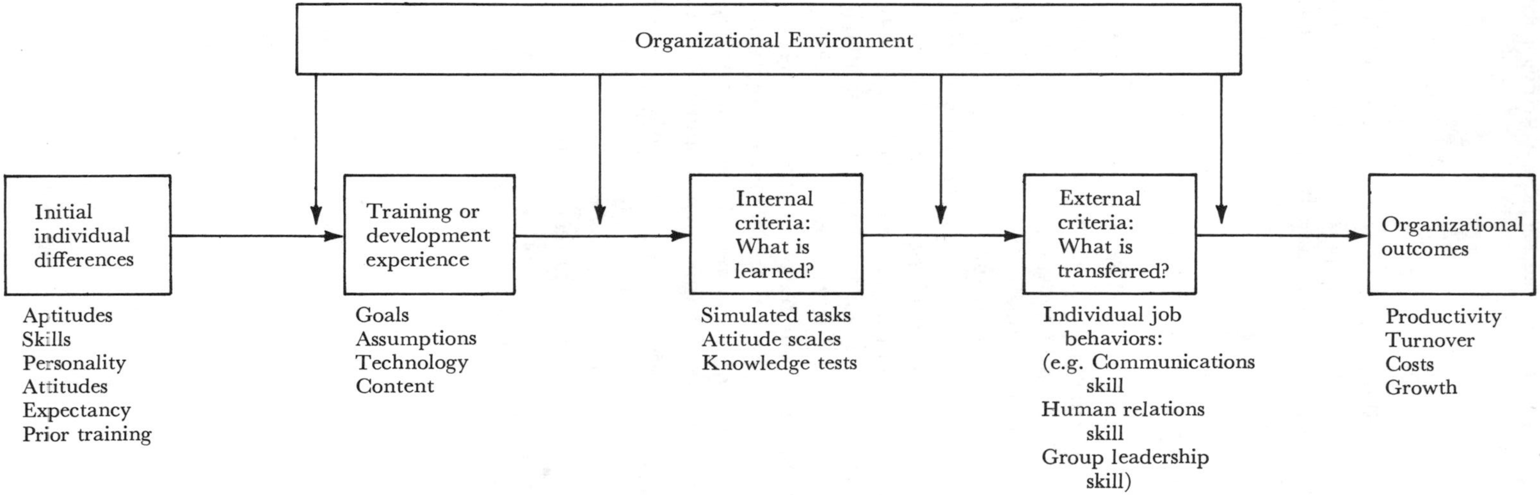

training impact, the overall impression is one of a great deal of complexity and a considerable number of crucial relationships that must be explicated.

External Criteria

Taking a look first at changes on external or job-related changes, the available studies were divided into three categories.

Perceived Change Measure. Five were grouped into the first category because they all employed an open-ended measure of perceived behavior change as the principal criterion (Boyd & Elliss, 1962; Bunker, 1965; Miles, 1965; Underwood, 1965; Valiquet, 1964). That is, several months after conclusion of the training, associates of the subjects were asked to respond to some variant of the following question: "Over a period of time, people may change in the ways they work with other people. Do you believe that the person you are describing has changed his or her behavior in working with people over the past year, as compared with the previous year, in any specific ways? If 'yes,' please describe."

The studies included in this category share a number of other common features. All of them used comparison groups and almost all comparison subjects were chosen via a nomination procedure. That is, the individuals who had been trained were asked to suggest a comparison person who did the same kind of work but who had never been in a T group. Sample sizes approached respectability in two of the studies and were disappointingly small in three. The on-the-job observers of both the trained and untrained subjects were obtained by asking the individuals in the experimental and control groups to suggest several associates who would have an opportunity to observe their job behavior.

Results regarding the open-ended perceived change measure are quite consistent across studies. Between two and three times as many changes were reported for the experimental groups as for the control groups. In absolute terms, about 30 to 40 per cent of the trained individuals were reported as exhibiting some sort of perceptible change. The percentages were somewhat higher in one study (Boyd & Elliss, 1962) where interviews were used to collect data from the observers.

The types of perceived changes that seemed to discriminate best between trained and untrained individuals have to do (in the judgment of the coders) with increased sensitivity, more open communication, and increased flexibility in role behavior.

Obviously, the studies in this category have a number of vulnerable points. For example, the effect of having experimental subjects nominate their own controls is difficult to assess. Perhaps a potentially more serious feature is having subjects nominate their own observers. The observers thus knew who had or had not been through the T-group experience and conceivably could have discussed the whole matter among themselves.

Questionnaire Measures of Perceived Change. Five studies (Beer & Kleisath, 1967; Buchanan & Brunstetter, 1959; Friedlander, 1968; Taylor, 1967; Zand, Steele, & Zalkind, 1967) attempted to assess much the same kind of perceived behavior change as those in the previous category by means of standardized questionnaire measures. The instruments used included the Ohio State Leader Behavior Description Questionnaire (Beer & Kleisath, 1967), a questionnaire designed to measure a manager's orientation toward Theory X and Theory Y, a series of semantic differential scales (Taylor, 1967), a number of items aimed at describing work group interactions (Beer & Kleisath, 1967; Friedlander, 1968), and participants' self-perceptions of their own job behavior. Not every study used all of these measures, but each included an appreciable number of items and subscales.

The studies in this category are also similar in that, with one exception, no control groups were used and the relevant comparisons were between before and after measures. The criterion measures were usually obtained immediately before and ten to twelve months after the completion of the laboratory. In some of the studies data were also obtained immediately after the completion of the program. Another common feature is that the participants in each of the programs were all members of the same organization, and often the training group consisted of almost all the management staff in a particular organizational unit. Also, the particular T-group or laboratory being studied was usually part of a larger and long-range effort at management development.

Results can best be described as mixed. No real consistencies appeared. Probably the most positive results were obtained in the Beer and Kleisath study, where a total of 41 scales yielded 37 changes in the predicted direction; 14 of the 37 were statistically significant. However, the laboratory program under consideration was actually the first phase of the Management Grid, which is a somewhat more structured type of group experience.

Zand et al. (1967) report a rather perplexing finding in that for the items that did show change, there tended to be a decrement in positive perceptions immediately post-training but then a return to original pre-training levels at the time of the one year follow-up. Another disturbing note appeared in the Taylor (1967) study which tended to show significant differences in self-perceptions but not in subordinate descriptions of the trained individuals.

In sum, it is rather difficult to tease out general statements from the studies employing questionnaires. Changes on a number of scales seem to point toward an increase in "employee-centered" behavior, more open communication, and the like; but the results are far from consistent either across studies or within a particular research effort. Contributing to the inconsistency is the fact that questionnaire measures were included in two studies in the previous category which, you recall, showed positive results for the open-ended measure. The questionnaire results were negative.

Global Organizational Criteria. A few studies fall in a third category of external criteria which I have labeled *global organizational measures.* That is, the criterion is a global index reflecting the behavior of the entire organization or organizational subunit. Profit and turnover are examples. The crucial comparison is between estimates of the index obtained before and after the development program.

Results from such research must be interpreted with caution. It is generally impossible to obtain any kind of control or comparison organization, and the Hawthorne effect lurks constantly in the background. Also, the sample size most often is equal to one organization, and zero degrees of freedom preclude an estimate of sampling error. Drawing conclusions from such studies takes a certain amount of courage.

Summing up the findings for studies using external or job-related criteria, the backbone of the evidence seems to reside in the five studies using the open-ended perceived change measure. Results from the other studies are a bit too inconsistent or too open to alternative explanations to allow a great deal of inference.

INTERNAL CRITERIA

Research efforts using internal or training-centered criteria are both more numerous and more diverse in terms of the types of criteria that have been used. It seems most meaningful to carve them up into five classes.

Perception of Self or Self-Awareness. The studies grouped in the first category have attempted to assess changes in individuals' perceptions of themselves over the course of a T-group or laboratory. The results have been quite inconclusive. Three studies (Bennis, Burke, Cutter, Harrington, & Hoffman, 1957; Burke & Bennis, 1961; Gassner, Gold, & Snadowsky, 1964) had subjects use various personality and attitude items to describe their *actual* self and *ideal* self before and after the T-group.

Two of the experiments were done without control groups. One showed significant changes in self-descriptions and one did not. However, the third study showed significant changes for both experimental and control subjects and no difference between the two. In addition, a fourth study (Grater, 1965) which involved a conventional kind of leadership training also produced similar changes in self-description. In sum, based on the empirical evidence, little can be said about how a T-group might change an individual's description of himself.

Interpersonal Sensitivity. In addition to assessing changes in self-perception, a second group of investigators has attempted to measure changes in the accuracy with which subjects perceive characteristics of other individuals or of group processes. Interpersonal sensitivity is perhaps a more common term for this skill.

At least four attempts (Bennis, Burke & Cutter, 1957; Dunnette, 1967; Gage & Exline, 1953; Lohman, Zenger, & Weschler, 1959) have been made to determine if T-group training enhances the accuracy of a subject's prediction of another group member's response on an attitude or personality item. Again, the most common research design was a before-and-after measure without a control group. In the main, results were negative. Only the Dunnette experiment yielded a small difference in the expected direction.

Still within the general category of measuring interpersonal sensitivity, five studies (Bass, 1962; Clark & Culbert, 1965; Harrison, 1962; Harrison, 1966; Oshry & Harrison, 1966) have succeeded in demonstrating that people who have been through a T-group can describe other people and situations in more interpersonal terms. That is, trained individuals tend to use more expressive, interpersonal, and human relations oriented words when describing other people in a T-group, work associates, problem situations, or the behavior of people in a film. However, whether these results actually reflect increases in accuracy and awareness or merely alterations in vocabulary is another question.

Attitude Change. Surprisingly few studies fell into a third group, identified by the use of attitude change as a criterion measure. Schutz's FIRO-B (Fundamental Interpersonal Relations Orientation Behavior) questionnaire was used in three different studies (Baumgartel & Goldstein, 1967; Schutz & Allen, 1966; Smith, 1964) with mixed results. Recall that FIRO-B includes a series of six Guttman scales designed to measure attitudes toward three types of behavior in groups: "control," "inclusion," and "affection." For each type there is a pair of scales designed to assess the respondent's own desire to show the behavior and his desire for others in the group to show it. All three studies used before-and-after measures, and two included appropriate control groups.

Results were clearest for the Smith (1964) study using English managers as subjects. The disparity between one's own behavioral tendencies and that desired in others decreased for the experimental group but not for the control group. Results from the other two studies are not very easily interpreted and cannot be used to argue for or against the ability of T-groups to change attitudes.

Two other studies were unable to demonstrate laboratory produced changes on either the Leadership Opinion Questionnaire or a scale designed to measure "inner" versus "other" directed attitudes. However, the previously mentioned study by Beer and Kleisath did show changes on the LOQ.

Personality Change. A criterion category yielding completely negative results is that having to do with personality change. Two studies using the California Personality Inventory and the F-scale, respectively (Massarik & Carlson, cited in Dunnette, 1962; Kernan, 1964), demonstrated no change as the result of the T-group experience. However, as the authors of these studies are quick to point out, changes in such basic personality attributes may be just too much to expect from such a relatively short experience, even if the T-group is a good one.

Simulations. A fifth criterion which has so far received very little attention but deserves a great deal more is performance on situational tests or tasks designed to simulate job activities or job behavior. Case problems, role playing, business games, and In-basket exercises are examples. Only two studies fall in this category. Argyris (1965) compared experimental and control groups of managers on a case problem discussion. Unfortunately, an elaborate content analysis of the tape recordings yielded few interpretable differences between groups. In the second study, Deep, Bass, and Vaughan (1967) demonstrated that students who played a business game with people from the same T-group lost a considerable amount of money, while teams made up of students from different T-groups made a profit. The results were explained in terms of the intact groups' reluctance to exercise the management control function. However, there was no control group, and any previous group experience might have produced the same effects.

Conclusions

What sorts of general conclusions can be drawn from all of this?

1. The evidence, though limited, does suggest that T-group training produces behavioral changes in the back-home setting for perhaps 25% of the participants. This statement is based primarily on the studies in the first category which used the open-ended perceived change measure as a criterion. However, this conclusion must be regarded with some suspicion because of the way the observers were chosen and the fact that they probably knew who had and had not been trained. Also, it should be kept in mind that no data are available regarding the positive or negative effects of these changes on performance effectiveness.

2. Results with internal, or training-centered, criteria are very inconclusive. We have few empirical clues as to what is actually learned in a T-group. Trying to reconcile the results from these two general kinds of criteria is a bit difficult. It tends to violate the notions I think most of us have that a training or development program is more apt to produce changes on training-centered rather than job-centered measures. There are at least two alternative explanations: (1) The training-centered criteria have not been the appropriate ones and have not yet tapped what T-groups actually teach; (2) the positive results with external criteria are artifactual. Regardless of which of these is true, it is an unsatisfactory state of affairs.

In sum, the assumption that laboratory training has positive utility for organizations must necessarily rest on shaky ground. It has been neither confirmed nor disconfirmed.

Needed Research

Given this generally equivocal state of affairs, it seems proper to ask where T-group research might best divert its energies in the future. Even though more research has been done on the laboratory method than any other technique of individual development in organizations, it is still a paltry amount when the complexity of the behavior at issue is considered.

First, one could make the usual noises about larger samples, more experimental control, more appropriate subject populations, and more awareness of situational variables and individual differences. These things are always desirable, are not to be taken lightly, and are just as lacking for research on other training and development methods as for laboratory education.

Second, the enterprise would benefit a great deal by careful consideration of what Orne (1962) has called the "demand" characteristics of an experiment. That is, if the subjects can discern where the experimental treatment is supposed to lead, they consciously or unconsciously may try to cooperate or not cooperate with the experimenter and insure that his hypothesis is either supported or not supported. In this sense, many of the T-group studies used criterion measures that were relatively transparent and susceptible to a strong response bias. It seems to me that this is a greater problem for T-group research than small samples or a lack of control groups.

However, the problem is not insurmountable. It should be possible to select observers in the organizational setting who are unaware of who was trained and who was not. Perhaps ongoing groups composed of trained and untrained people could be observed in their natural settings by outside observers who are unaware of each individual's prior history. Better still, different types of group activities or standardized role playing sessions could be recorded on video tape. This would allow several types of behavior dimensions to be rated by trained observers who were unaware of which subjects had which kinds of training experience. It would also greatly facilitate investigating the reliability of the criterion observations.

A greater use of simulations such as In-baskets and business games would also help overcome this problem. Such measures have had far too little use so far (almost none, in fact). Simulations could be carried out both with individuals and groups. Thus, interest could be focused on the quality of an individual's performance as well as the nature of his contribution to the group. What I am trying to suggest is a wider use of meaningful internal criteria in a controlled setting. We need to know more about what kinds of behavior change are the direct result of being in a T-group.

Third, one of the chief hang-ups for people wishing to do research on laboratory education is the large number of variations that keep being invented and the large number of possible outcomes that might be expected.

In fact, a possible criticism of a review such as the present one is that trying to draw generalizations is futile since a number of the experimental treatments under study incorporated different approaches. I think this is a lethal point of view, and it should not be allowed to become the law of the enterprise. Someone must specify a basic set of crucial parameters which can be adhered to by an appreciable number of interested parties, and these must become the focal points of a good deal of systematic investigation.

Related to this point is a possible paradox in the T-group technique. On the one hand, the method presents itself as being very unstructured and leaving the responsibility for much of the content up to the participants themselves. Yet the goals and the technology seem to imply a rather sophisticated use of stimulus presentation, feedback, and reinforcement of new responses. Laboratory practitioners may object mightily to any kind of S–R view of things. However, in the absence of any structured approach, it is difficult to talk about what sort of behavioral outcomes to expect. The task of conceptualizing the method is far from finished.

Fourth, the effects of T-group training should be compared more fully with the behavioral effects stemming from other training methods. Perhaps the same behavioral objectives can be realized at less cost to the individual and to the organization by using different methods. We need research results specifying the conditions when T-group training should be used and when other methods should be used.

A corollary to the above is the need to explore the *interaction* of T-group training and other learning experiences. This has immediate relevance because of the frequent practice of combining the T-group with other methods in a laboratory program. The only investigation dealing with such an interaction is Bunker's recent re-analysis of his original data obtained from the 1960 and 1961 Bethel Laboratories (Bunker & Knowles, 1967). Between these two sets of summer programs, the total length of the laboratory was reduced from three weeks to two weeks. However, the total time devoted to T-group sessions remained almost constant, while the cutback was at the expense of theory sessions, lectures, and problem exercises. The two-week group fell about halfway between the three-week group and the control group on the total change index.

Finally, more effort should be directed toward forging the link between training-centered changes and changes in job behavior. So far, the literature offers only one example of an effort to link these two classes of criteria. In a study already cited, Miles (1965) reported that judgments by trainers of the degree of learning shown by participants correlated .55 with the degree of change observed back in their job situations. However, the trainees' own judgments made at the conclusion of the training period were not related to the amount of change their observers reported. Such a finding suggests that self-insight, at least, was not the mediator of the observed behavior changes.

THE TRILOGY

Following the above suggestions will not be easy; it seems obvious that a real, living, breathing organization is a very difficult place in which to do basic research on training effects, even though the ultimate aim is to generalize to organizational behavior. I think it would be more fruitful to view the entire problem in light of Figure 1 and consciously create a division of labor with respect to research sites and populations. I have in mind a trilogy made up of (1) college students, (2) real ongoing organizations, and (3) something I will call a "halfway house." That is, there must be created someplace between the university and the corporation a third type of organization set up to perform a wide variety of training activities for real people but whose principal function is that of research. The administrative and technical staff of such an organization must be rewarded according to how well they can address themselves to meaningful research questions. Such an organization should have a broader base than just the investigation of laboratory education, and ideally it would cover a broad range of methods for changing and enhancing organizational behavior.

Given these three research sites, it would seem profitable to carve up the main effects and interactions in the diagram and assign them to appropriate parts of the tripartite. For example, the first order of business might be to study systematically the interactions between individual differences and training methods with strong situational effects held constant. The basic question is "what is learned" and by whom. The appropriate populations are thus to be found in the university and the halfway house. After some basic questions concerning "what is learned" are answered, emphasis can be switched to the real organization, where relationships between internal and external criteria can be investigated and situational factors allowed to operate. Considerable ingenuity would have to be exercised at this point to identify naturally occurring and relevant situational effects, but at least the researcher would be on firmer ground than if he had spent no time in the halfway house expanding his mind and knowledge.

Relative to this interaction with environmental factors, Frederiksen (1966) and Litwin and Stringer (1964) have shown that it is possible to simulate certain situational variables in an experimental setting. Thus, the situational as well as the task simulation could be given a great deal of attention in the business school and halfway house settings and much of the taxonomic work completed before trying to do follow-ups in the organizational setting.

In sum, without such a division of labor, I do not believe meaningful systematic knowledge on the effects of the laboratory method can ever be gathered. It deserves a better fate.

REFERENCES

Argyris, C. T-groups for organizational effectiveness. *Harvard Business Review*, 1964, *42* (2), 60–74.

Argyris, C. Explorations in interpersonal competence—II. *Journal of Applied Behavioral Science*, 1965, *1*, 255–269.

Bass, B. M. Reactions to *Twelve Angry Men* as a measure of sensitivity training. *Journal of Applied Psychology*, 1962, *46*, 120–124.

Baumgartel, H., & Goldstein, J. W. Need and value shifts in college training groups. *Journal of Applied Behavioral Science*, 1967, *3*, 87–101.

Beer, M., & Kleisath, S. W. The effects of the managerial grid lab on organizational and leadership dimensions. In S. S. Zalkind (Chm.), Research on the impact of using different laboratory methods for interpersonal and organizational change. Symposium presented at the American Psychological Association, Washington, D.C., September 1967.

Bennis, W., Burke, R., Cutter, H., Harrington, H., & Hoffman, J. A note on some problems of measurement and prediction in a training group. *Group Psychotherapy*, 1957, *10*, 328–341.

Boyd, J. B., & Elliss, J. D. Findings of research into senior management seminars. Toronto (Canada): The Hydro-Electric Power Commission of Ontario, 1962.

Bradford, L. P., Gibb, J. R., & Benne, K. D. *T-group theory and laboratory method.* New York: Wiley, 1964.

Buchanan, P. C. Evaluating the effectiveness of laboratory training in industry. *Explorations in Human Relations Training and Research* (No. 1). Washington, D.C.: National Training Laboratories—National Education Association, 1965.

Buchanan, P. C., & Brunstetter, P. H. A research approach to management development: Part II. *Journal of the American Society of Training Directors,* 1959, *13,* 18–27.

Bunker, D. R. Individual applications of laboratory training. *Journal of Applied Behavioral Science,* 1965, *1,* 131–148.

Bunker, D. R., & Knowles, E. S. Comparison of behavioral changes resulting from human relations training laboratories of different lengths. *Journal of Applied Behavioral Science,* 1967, *3,* 505–523.

Burke, H. L., & Bennis, W. G. Changes in perception of self and others during human relations training. *Human Relations,* 1961, *14,* 165–182.

Deep, S. D., Bass, B. M., & Vaughan, J. A. Some effects on business gaming of quasi T-group affiliations. *Journal of Applied Psychology,* 1967, *51,* 426–431.

Dunnette, M. D. People feeling: Joy, more joy, and the slough of despond. Paper presented at the American Psychological Association, Washington, D.C., September 1967.

Dunnette, M. D. Personnel management. In P. R. Farnsworth (Ed). *Annual Review of Psychology.* Palo Alto, Calif.: Annual Reviews, 1962.

Frederiksen, N. Some effects of organizational climates on administrative performance. Paper presented at the American Psychological Association, New York, September 1966.

Friedlander, F. The impact of organizational training laboratories upon the effectiveness and interaction of ongoing work groups. *Personnel Psychology,* 1967, *20,* 289–308.

Gage, N. L., & Exline, R. V. Social perception and effectiveness in discussion groups. *Human Relations,* 1953, *6,* 381–396.

Gassner, Suzanne, Gold, J., & Snadowsky, A. M. Changes in the phenomenal field as a result of human relations training. *Journal of Psychology,* 1964, *58,* 33–41.

Grater, M. Changes in self and other attitudes in a leadership training group. *Personnel and Guidance Journal,* 1959, *37,* 493–496.

Harrison, R. Import of the laboratory on perceptions of others by the experimental group. In C. Argyris, *Interpersonal competence and organizational behavior.* Homewood, Ill.: Richard D. Irwin, 1962, 261–271.

Harrison, R., & Lubin, B. Personal style, group composition, and learning. *Journal of Applied Behavioral Science,* 1965, *1,* 286–301.

Klaw, S. Two weeks in a T-group. *Fortune,* 1961, *64* (8), 114–117.

Kuriloff, A. H., & Atkins, S. T-group for a work team. *Journal of Applied Behavioral Science,* 1966, *2,* 63–94.

Litwin, G., & Stringer, R. The influence of organizational climate on human motivation. Paper presented at Conference on Organizational Climate sponsored by Foundation for Research on Human Behavior, Ann Arbor, Mich., 1966.

Lohman, K., Zenger, J. H., & Weschler, I. R. Some perceptual changes during sensitivity training. *Journal of Educational Research,* 1959, *53,* 28–31.

Martin, H. O. The assessment of training. *Personnel Management,* 1957, *39,* 88–93.

Maslow, A. H. *Eupsychian management: A journal.* Homewood, Ill.: Richard D. Irwin, 1965.

Miles, M. B. Research notes from here and there—human relations training: Processes and outcomes. *Journal of Counseling Psychology,* 1960, *7,* 301–306.

Miles, M. B. Changes during and following laboratory training: A clinical-experimental study. *Journal of Applied Behavioral Science,* 1965, *1,* 215–242.

Orne, M. T. On the social psychology of the psychological experiment: With particular reference to demand characteristics and their implications. *American Psychologist,* 1962, *17,* 776–783.

Oshry, B. I., & Harrison, R. Transfer from here-and-now—to there-and-then: Changes in organizational problem diagnosis stemming from T-group training. *Journal of Applied Behavioral Science,* 1966, *2,* 185–198.

Smith, P. B. Attitude changes associated with training in human relations. *British Journal of Social and Clinical Psychology,* 1964, *3,* 104–113.

Tannenbaum, R., Weschler, I. R., & Massarik, F. *Leadership and organization: A behavioral science approach.* New York: McGraw-Hill, 1961.

Taylor, F. C. Effects of laboratory training upon persons and their work groups. In S. S. Zalkind (Chm.), Research on the impact of using different laboratory methods for interpersonal and organizational change. Symposium presented at the American Psychological Association, Washington, D.C., September, 1967.

Underwood, W. J. Evaluation of laboratory method training. *Training Directors Journal,* 1965, *19* (5), 34–40.

Valiquet, I. M. Contribution to the evaluation of a management development program. Unpublished Master's thesis, Massachusetts Institute of Technology, 1964.

Weschler, I. R., & Reisel, J. Inside a sensitivity training group. Institute of Human Relations, University of California (Los Angeles), 1959.

Zand, D. E., Steele, F. I., & Zalkind, S. S. The impact of an organizational development program on perceptions of interpersonal, group, and organizational functioning. In S. S. Zalkind (Chm.), Research on the impact of using different laboratory methods for interpersonal and organizational change. Symposium presented at the American Psychological Association, Washington, D.C., September 1967.

32 / A COMPREHENSIVE APPRAISAL OF GROUP AND MULTIPLE COUNSELING RESEARCH

George M. Gazda and Mary Juhan Larsen

Definition

The development of group counseling, briefly traced in another publication (Gazda, 1968), was found to have a history of a mere thirty to forty years. Although not immediately accepted, group counseling has evolved as a legitimate form of psychological treatment to a current stage of recognition that is broadly based. No doubt much of this recognition can be related to the current interest in group psychotherapy (its older sister discipline) and other group procedures such as the T-group and sensitivity group.

But what is group and multiple counseling? For purposes of this paper, multiple counseling is used synonymously with group counseling and also as Driver (1962) defined it: i.e., the use of group *plus* individual counseling with a client.

Group counseling is defined as follows:

Group counseling is a dynamic, interpersonal process focusing on conscious thought and behavior and involving the therapy functions of permissiveness, orientation to reality, catharsis, and mutual trust, caring, understanding, acceptance, and support. The therapy functions are created and nurtured in a small group through the sharing of personal concerns with one's peers and the counselor(s). The group counselees are basically

From JOURNAL OF RESEARCH AND DEVELOPMENT IN EDUCATION (*Athens, Georgia*), *1968, Vol. 1, pp. 57–66. Copyright 1968, University of Georgia. Reprinted with permission of authors and publisher. An update of these findings may be found in Ch. 7, "Group Counseling Research," in G. M. Gazda's* Group Counseling: A Developmental Approach. *Boston: Allyn and Bacon, 1971.*

normal individuals with various concerns which are not debilitating to the extent of requiring extensive personality change. The group counselees may utilize the group interaction to increase understanding and acceptance of values and goals and to learn and/or unlearn certain attitudes and behaviors. (Gazda, Duncan, & Meadows, 1967, p. 306)

Group psychotherapy is sometimes used synonymously with group counseling, but frequently it is considered a treatment for the institutionalized individual who is not within the "normal" range of adjustment. Generally, it is performed by medically-oriented therapists: i.e., psychiatrists, clinical psychologists, and psychiatric social workers. The duration of treatment is usually long-term compared to that of group counseling and the intensity is often greater.

Focus of Appraisal

Despite the synonymity, the body of research and literature dealing with group psychotherapy dates back further, is much larger and is somewhat different in clientele treated than that of group counseling. But research in group and multiple counseling is identifiable and the authors have chosen to focus on extant research in a rather comprehensive survey and analysis.

A reason for this more limited focus is the relatively recent introduction of group counseling into the rapidly growing field of group treatments. Such focus presents the opportunity to take stock of the direction of group counseling research as well as to identify its strengths and weaknesses. Since most group counseling takes place in educational settings, a comprehensive review, especially of outcome studies, may be helpful in stimulating adaptations and innovations in group counseling practice and research within educational settings.

The authors attempted an exhaustive search of group counseling research literature, except for masters' theses. While such a goal is never completely attainable, there is reason to believe that the field is well represented. A guide in the selection of literature was the inclusion of the term "group counseling" or "multiple counseling" in the titles. This procedure immediately ruled out most of the research in group psychotherapy, although an occasional article abstracted herein may have better fit the group psychotherapy literature; and, in like manner, some of the research reported under the title of "group psychotherapy" may have better been included with group counseling literature. The task, however, of reviewing all group psychotherapy research for purposes of deciding this issue was prohibitive.

Abstract Method

Richard's (1962) analysis of some twenty-two research studies in group psychotherapy served as a partial guide for topical organization used in the present abstracting of research articles in group counseling.[1] Included are the following topics: experimenter and date, purpose of study, type of group, size of research and control samples, treatment and/or process, criteria or instruments employed, test statistics employed, experimental design, and outcome of study.

Abstracts appear after the foregoing topic-by-topic summary, appraisal and conclusions. For ease in locating, articles are arranged alphabetically by date. All "process" studies are asterisked to distinguish them from "outcome" studies.[2] Complete bibliographic information is in the same order as the abstracts appear.

Topical Summary and Appraisal

Purpose of the Study

Approximately 65 percent of the research studies abstracted were of the outcome variety with a few being combinations of outcome and process. Approximately 15 percent of the studies were process studies.

The fourth area which serves to describe the nature of the studies might be called "comparison." This group of studies, approximately 20 percent of the research reported, included various combinations such as individual versus group counseling, one type of group counseling versus another, group counseling plus some other treatment compared to still another treatment, for example.

[1] The abstracts and complete biographical information which accompanied the original article are not included in this book. See pp. 67–132 of the original article for this material.—Eds.

[2] 10 "process" and 94 "outcome" studies were abstracted, or a total of 104 studies. —Eds.

TYPE OF GROUP

The majority of counseling groups were held in educational settings and with students of these educational institutions. Approximately equal numbers of studies were reported with undergraduate and graduate students as with high school and junior high school students. These studies account for two-thirds of all the studies abstracted. This finding is consistent with an earlier study (Gazda et al., 1967) of the group and multiple counseling literature for the period January 1960–Spring 1965.

The remaining third of the studies abstracted are quite diverse in nature with about five percent being studies of kindergarten and elementary school children, five percent delinquents and prison inmates, five percent parent groups, and the remainder including such groups as hospitalized NP patients, student nurses, and unemployable males.

An analysis of the studies of educational groups revealed that of the college and university groups, the majority (about five-sixths) included freshmen who were, for example, underachievers, potential dropouts, student teachers, or in orientation. Approximately five percent of the college and university groups included graduate students, primarily counselor-education groups.

The junior and senior high school groups were also characterized by almost equally heavy emphasis on underachievers and on behavior problem-type groups including a majority of acting-out individuals and some groups of social isolates. The classes most frequently involved in group counseling were the freshmen and seniors.

The studies of elementary school group counseling included groups of underachievers, slow-learners, and social isolates.

The parent groups were composed of parents of nursery school children, fifth grade underachievers, retarded children, and a group of mothers of secondary school children.

SIZE OF RESEARCH AND CONTROL SAMPLES

Size refers to the N's reported in each study, not the size of the counseling groups. The experimental samples ranged from a process study involving an N of three to an outcome study involving 200 experimental Ss—twelfth-grade graduating boys who received group counseling compared with an equal number who received individual counseling. The average experimental sample was 27. The largest total sample, including both experimentals and controls, was 400.

With 27 as the average experimental group size, it becomes apparent that the outcome studies of group counseling (process studies having even smaller N's) must be viewed with caution. Considering the fact that few of the outcome studies were replicated, even more caution must be observed in interpreting the results. Nevertheless, a beginning has been made (usually by single investigators and frequently doctoral candidates who were doing a dissertation study) but if larger samples are to be obtained and with it, greater credence in outcomes, substantial financial support must be forthcoming.

Approximately 15 percent of the studies abstracted did not report the use of control groups or statistical controls. One might then question the inclusion of these studies in this report of research of group or multiple counseling. They were included because they were read at professional meetings, accepted as dissertation studies and/or were published. Some descriptive studies, such as reported in Driver (1962), were not included in this report. Although descriptive studies have their place in generating research hypotheses, the relatively large number being reported suggests the relative infancy of research in group counseling.

Notwithstanding the above analysis, all is not bleak because the majority of outcome studies reported herein did use controls. Approximately 45 percent reported a "random" assignment of controls, 20 percent "matched" controls, and the remainder of the studies used statistical, or miscellaneous combinations of random and matched designs.

Treatment and/or Process

Since very few authors reported their theoretical orientations and the exact nature of the treatment process utilized in their research, this summary is limited to a brief report of averages and ranges in terms of numbers and hours of group counseling sessions, and process variables for the process studies.

The "treatment" can be described "on the average" as consisting of seventeen group counseling sessions of one hour each week over approximately seventeen weeks. However, the range was extensive: Two sessions of behavioral-type group counseling to one year of group counseling of three-to-five sessions per week represent the range or "intensiveness" of the treatment. One study reported sixty sessions over a period of two years and another fifty sessions over a period of nine months. These represent the most intensive treatment and long-term studies.

The process studies consisted of role analysis, "client growth," topic, referent, and affect classification, counselor-client reinforcement, and phase development. The "client growth" studies utilized various topic or role analysis to appraise or speculate on client change.

The most frequent omissions of the studies abstracted in this report were the lack of a clear statement of the counselor(s) theoretical orientation, a description of the treatment process, and qualifications of the group counselor(s). Until these weaknesses are overcome, little by way of replication studies and comparisons among differing orientations can be accomplished.

One is struck by the wide variation in duration and/or intensity of treatment. Perhaps group counseling will eventually become synonymous with short-term group treatment or merge with group therapy, and length of treatment will not be a differentiating factor of group counseling.

INSTRUMENTS

"Instruments" refers to the means or measures for evaluating process or outcome variables. Since a wide range of evaluative instruments were utilized, only the most frequently employed measures are reported here. Almost all studies reported the use of multiple instruments for measuring outcome and process.

The most popular means for evaluation was the grade-point-average (gpa). Thirty studies reported some use of the gpa for evaluating Ss' change. Twenty-five studies reported the use of judges', teachers', and various supervisors' ratings of Ss. Fourteen studies reported the use of questionnaires, usually the researcher's self-devised instrument. Thirteen studies utilized some variation of the self-report technique aside from self-report standardized personality tests. Interviews were used for evaluation purposes in eleven instances. Q sorts of various types were cited in seven studies and seven studies also cited the use of TAT-type instruments. Six studies utilized the Bills Index of Adjustment and Values. Four studies each used sentence completion items and sociometric tests. Other instruments utilized in at least three studies were the Haggerty-Olson-Wickman Behavior Rating Scale, the Semantic Differential, California Psychological Inventory, and the Allport-Vernon Study of Values.

The "shotgun" method of evaluating the research in group counseling appears to be the rule rather than the exception. In view of the infancy of this area of research this is to be expected as the experimenter attempts to glean as much from his hard-to-obtain data as is possible.

The Cohn (1967) report suggests that the use of multiple measures of group counseling should be encouraged because ". . . multiple measurement of a given concept increases the possibility of reliable measurement" (p. 17). The difference between his report suggestion and what is actually practiced is that his report suggests *several means* of evaluating or measuring a given concept, whereas in actual practice attempts are made to measure several *different variables* or concepts. It is the hope of the authors of this appraisal that the interested researcher will, by careful analysis of the abstracts, find promising instruments to be utilized with specific populations for measuring specific variables.

The instruments for measuring group counseling "process" variables included, for the most part, researcher-devised instruments to classify, for example, client-counselor roles, topics, affect, referents, content, nonverbal behavior. These process scales usually employed some modification of the Bales Interaction Process Analysis instrument and were based on data obtained from on-the-spot group observations, typescripts, audio-tape recordings, and video-tape recordings. Only a beginning has been made in process research in group counseling.

TEST STATISTICS EMPLOYED

Approximately thirty different varieties of test statistics were employed by the authors of studies abstracted in this report. The most popular statistics was the *t*-test of mean differences. It was used in approximately 30 percent of the studies. Analysis of variance was close behind in popularity with approximately 25 percent usage (analysis of covariance was used in 10 percent of the studies). Descriptive statistics of many varieties was third in popularity being utilized in approximately 20 percent of the studies and closely behind it in popularity was the use of Chi square: 17 percent of the studies reported its use. Approximately 15 percent of the authors utilized some form of correlation in their research. The remaining test statistics were used no more than 3 percent of the time in the abstracted studies.

The Cohn (1967) report on research in group counseling recommends multivariate statistical methods as promising for group counseling research because of the many interacting process variables and complexity of goals in group counseling. Especially promising, according to Cohn, is factor analysis. Although multivariate analysis was utilized in almost one half of the studies abstracted in this appraisal, only one was described as factor analysis. Perhaps this represents the lag between what is recommended by the statistician and what the group counseling researcher is now doing, and this may be the reason the Cohn report recommends that the group counselor team up to form an interdisciplinary research team for investigating group counseling.

Experimental Design

Definitions of various designs will be given, then the frequency of their use in the abstracted studies will be cited. In order to categorize the research design of the studies abstracted in this appraisal, the classificatory scheme developed by Campbell and Stanley (1963) was utilized. This scheme presents a summary of models of experimental and quasi-experimental designs most frequently used in educational research.

Campbell and Stanley evaluated and described sixteen designs and variations of these designs according to both internal and external validity threats.

The purpose of following this outline of design models was an operational one. Attempts were made to determine which design most completely described a particular study; "outcome" studies were more readily classifiable by the scheme than were "process" studies. For this reason, process studies were so identified and received no further classification.

The major research design models used were classified as Pre-Experimental Designs, True-Experimental Designs, Quasi-Experimental Designs, and Correlational and Ex-Post Facto Designs (Campbell & Stanley, 1963). The research models applicable to each of these major designs are included under each major design with the number of studies so classified.

For the purposes of this appraisal, the research design models are defined as follows:

Pre-Experimental Designs

One-Shot Case Study. This is a study in which a carefully studied single instance is compared with remembered or observed events. The inferences made are based on general expectations of what the behavior might have been had the treatment not occurred. The total absence of a control group and post-test observations are significant characteristics of this type study. (Two such studies were among those abstracted.)

One-Group Pretest-Posttest Design. This is a design in which both a pre- and a post-observation measure is used in the absence of a control group. (Seven abstracted studies were classified under this model.)

Static-Group Comparison. This design uses only post-treatment observations and the comparison is made between a group which has experienced the treatment and one which has not. Randomization techniques are not employed in group selection. The purpose of the comparison is to establish the effect of the treatment. (Two studies were classified as Static Group Comparison.)

True-Experimental Designs

Pretest-Posttest Control Group Design. This design describes a model in which equivalent groups, as determined by randomization procedures, are used in the experiment. It incorporates many experimental and statistical variations into its model and offers control for all sources of internal validity; and for some but not for all sources of external variation. (Fifty-nine studies were classified under the Pretest-Posttest Control Group Design and its several variations.)

Solomon Four-Group Design. The high rank of this design in the hierarchy of research designs is attributable to its explicit consideration of factors influencing external validity. Since this design did not occur in the studies reviewed, the reader is referred to Campbell and Stanley (1963) for further description.

Posttest-Only Control Group Design. This is a design which employs group randomization and which controls for testing as the main affect but does not yield a measure of these effects. This design is internally valid, offers some external validity and has numerous variations. It is preferable to the Pretest-Posttest Control Group Design when genuine randomness of assignment is assured. However, more powerful statistical tests are available for the Pretest-Posttest Control Group Design. The availability of pretest scores in the Pretest-Posttest Control Group Design allows for the examination of interaction effects and for the more thorough generalization of the results. (Three studies were classified as Posttest-Only Group Design.)

Quasi-Experimental Designs

Equivalent Materials Design. This is a design in which groups which have received equivalent materials (treatments) purported to have enduring effects are compared with groups which have received different content (treatments). The sampling of materials is deemed essential to validity and any degree of proof of the treatment. (One study fits this classification or research model.)

Non-Equivalent Control Group Design. Both experimental and control groups have been administered a pretest and a posttest in this design. The groups of subjects used do not have pre-experimental sampling equivalence, but consist of naturally assembled groups which are available, such as classroom. In this design the treatment is randomly assigned and is under the control of the experimenter. Since many internal and external validity threats are controlled for in this design (Campbell & Stanley, 1963), it is meaningful for use when the employment of True Experimental Designs is impossible. Analysis of covariance is considered to be particularly applicable to this design. (Five studies were classified as fitting this design.)

Separate Sample Pretest-Posttest (No Control) Design. This design is applicable for use in situations where it is impossible to randomly separate subgroups for different experimental treatments and a type of experimental control is exercised by the random assignment of the time which subjects are to be observed. This design affords representative sampling of populations which have been specified prior to the experiments. (Two studies were classified as fitting this model.)

Other Designs

Descriptive-One Group Pretest-Posttest Study. This is a design or study which uses verbal description, rather than statistical procedures, to describe the differences observed between pretest and posttest scores for a single group of subjects. (Three of the abstracted studies were classified as fitting into this design.)

Descriptive-Simple Survey. This type of design or study describes the subject's responses and reactions after his exposure to the treatment. This type study cannot control for the direction of memory bias and the distortions which may have occurred. (Five studies were classified as fitting this model.)

Process Studies

The Process Study. This is a study which attempts to describe and/or explain what is happening in and during the treatment. This "on-going behavior" is the purpose of study. (Thirteen studies were classified as process studies.)

Summary-Experimental Designs

The summary of research or experimental designs is encouraging. Approximately 70 percent of the outcome studies were classified as "True Experimental Designs," which, among other things, means that some form of control groups was employed.

Criteria and Outcomes

Space does not permit an analysis of specific criteria with outcomes; however, each researcher is encouraged to perform this analysis in his area of special interest as he plans his group counseling research.

Examination of the outcome research studies abstracted in this report shows that some positive change or growth was reported in about half of the studies. (That is not to say half of the variables tested show positive change.) The majority of positive changes were reported through descriptive means and hence are not very convincing to the serious researcher. Nevertheless, some objective outcome data show promise for group counseling. For example, about fifty percent of the studies utilizing gpa and/or academic achievement showed significant increases or improvement versus an equal number which showed no significant improvement. Self-concept improvement and related "self" variable changes were reported in approximately 20 percent of the studies. Other significant improvement was reported as decreased anxiety, improved family and peer relations, improved relationships with authority figures, improved behavior in school, improved school attendance, increased acceptance of others, increased educational and occupational information, improved sociometric choices, and improvement in reading.

In the "comparison" studies where individual counseling was compared with the effectiveness of group counseling, the outcomes were about even where one was considered superior to the other. The treatment most likely to produce growth indicated by the abstracted studies is the application of group counseling *and* individual counseling.

A summary of the findings of the process studies is given in the abstract of each study.

Conclusions

The inclusion of approximately one hundred abstracts of research studies in group counseling prohibits intensive analysis of these studies. This decision was deliberate in an attempt to provide the reader and interested researcher with a comprehensive picture of past and current group counseling research. If he is interested in research with a particular population, he can locate all studies abstracted with a similar population and utilize the best of each of these studies as he plans his own research. He perhaps can best do this by looking for the elements of the studies that were most likely responsible for the outcomes. For example, these elements might be the type of group, size, and treatment, or some other combination which can be detected only by a careful analysis of each related study.

The basic conclusion is that group counseling research is inconclusive. This is true for a number of reasons. There is much variation in group size, length and duration or intensity of treatment, type and quality of treatment, sophistication of research designs, instruments of evaluation, and test statistics. The outcome research, however, looks promising because of the number of studies (approximately half) that show some positive changes or growth in the Ss. Since a number of the studies abstracted were doctoral dissertations and one would expect rather careful control over these, it is not surprising that approximately 70 percent of the outcome studies utilized the Pretest-Posttest Control Group Design. This fact should not conceal the other evidence that the most favorable reported results came from simple, uncontrolled (therefore questionable) descriptive "research" reports. Even so, several areas require immediate attention.

One of the more serious problems in need of resolution of outcome research in group counseling is that of defining experimental variables that are common to each group participant. Frequently when data are grouped, gains made by certain Ss are canceled out by other Ss who, to show positive change, may need to and perhaps actually do change in the opposite direction on a given variable.

Because outcome variables suitable for change through group counseling are frequently difficult to specify in advance, more replication studies need to be performed to make possible isolation of these variables. The more heterogeneous the group, the more difficult the problem becomes, and yet, for therapeutic reasons, heterogeneity is frequently preferred.

The use of multiple criterion measures which are factor analyzed may be one means of producing an instrument that is more sensitive to change in behavior than certain instruments used alone. The Cohn (1967) report outlines similar research needs and recommends the use of factoral-analysis-of-variance designs, discriminant functions, and a new model referred to as the Markov Chain. These test statistics would be capable of application to designs controlling for internal and external validity simultaneously.

From another point of view, Carl Rogers (Hall, 1967) suggests that perhaps we should call a moratorium on "rigid scientific research" in the behavioral sciences and go back and do much more naturalistic observation to understand people, behavior, and dynamics. The Cohn report also recommends the use of "clinical judgments" in the evaluation of outcome research; however, it recommends the use of several clinical judgments of the same and differing theoretical orientations to control for observation bias.

Before change variables can be defined and controlled, researchers must become more precise in describing a number of group variables such as age, sex, symptoms of clients, home environment, size of group, nature and goals of treatment, orientation and training of the group counselor, frequency and length of group sessions as well as duration of treatment, and a description of the dynamics and climate of the group. The reader is referred to the Cohn (1967) report and to Goldstein, Heller, and Sechrest (1966) who have drawn upon the group dynamics and social psychological research to generate research hypotheses pertaining to group psychotherapy, namely, but also pertinent to group counseling research.

Insofar as the above variables have been included in the abstracted studies within this paper, the keen observer may begin to piece together more sophisticated research approaches to group counseling. It has been the purpose of this paper to contribute in some small way to improvements in group counseling practice and research.

REFERENCES

Campbell, D. T., & Stanley, J. C. Experimental and quasiexperimental designs for research. In N. L. Gage (Ed.), *Handbook of research on teaching*. Chicago: Rand McNally, 1963. Pp. 171–246.

Cohn, B. (Ed.) *Guidelines for future research on group counseling in the public school setting*. Washington, D.C.: American Personnel and Guidance Association, 1967.

Driver, H. I. *Counseling and learning through small-group discussion*. Madison, Wisc.: Monona, 1962.

Gazda, G. M. (Ed.) *Basic approaches to group psychotherapy and group counseling*. Springfield, Ill.: Charles C Thomas, 1968.

Gazda, G. M., Duncan, J. A., & Meadows, M. E. Group counseling and group procedures—Report of a survey. *Counselor Education and Supervision*, 1967, *6*, 305–310.

Goldstein, A. P., Heller, K., & Sechrest, L. B. *Psychotherapy and the psychology of behavior change*. New York: Wiley, 1966.

Hall, M. H. A conversation with the father of Rogerian therapy. *Psychology Today*, 1967, *1* (7), 19ff.

Moreno, J. L. The third psychiatric revolution and the scope of psychodrama. *Group Psychotherapy*, 1964, *17*, 149ff.

Richard, H. C. Selected group psychotherapy evaluation studies. *Journal of General Psychology*, 1962, *67*, 37–50.

33 / GROUP COUNSELING

Alan R. Anderson

The rapid growth in the professional practice of group counseling has been accompanied by a proliferation of related research studies. Some 240 of the articles reviewed (covering the period from Summer 1965 to Fall 1968) were considered pertinent to this chapter. Among the studies in Gazda and Larsen's (1968) noncritical abstracts of group counseling research studies in the guidance literature, only those which are particularly relevant to the chapter are repeated here. In this chapter, group counseling was considered to include professional attempts to assist non-psychotic clients to examine and modify their values or behavior through small-group interaction. Although many of the studies were well-designed, there were few long-term treatment studies, follow-up studies, or replication studies. Most of Kagan's (1966) evaluative comments are still valid. The spelling out of specific procedures and techniques in sufficient detail to permit replication, although dimly perceptible, is still essentially lacking. Despite the masses of data being collected and analyzed, most studies are relatively unrelated, small-scale efforts which provide only the accumulation of bits of evidence. There is still no body of theoretically related knowledge on which the practice of group counseling can be solidly grounded. The organization of this chapter represents an attempt to systematize these bits of evidence. The chapter sections are arranged to follow the order of the concerns a counselor has in setting up and conducting a counseling group: (1) Client Selection and Preparation, (2) Outcomes, (3)

Alan R. Anderson, "Group Counseling," REVIEW OF EDUCATIONAL RESEARCH, April 1969, Vol. 39, No. 2, pp. 209–226. Copyright by American Educational Research Association.

Group Interaction, (4) Group Development, (5) Leadership Styles and Group Structure, and (6) Innovations and Suggestions for Research. In the final section, Perspective, an attempt is made to identify trends and summarize some of the chapter highlights.

Client Selection and Preparation

In nearly all studies, the basis for client selection was convenience. In most cases, groups were assembled according to a single common factor such as age or a common problem such as low academic achievement. No studies were found in which the composition of counseling or therapy groups was deliberately and systematically manipulated as a primary variable being investigated—although some studies did produce *post hoc* data.

Mezzano (1967) selected, from each of six counseling groups, two members who had shown the highest degree of "investment" (based on the counselee's willingness to explore his own behavior and communicate openly) and two who had shown the least "investment." Among these 24 clients a positive relationship was found between degree of "investment" and academic improvement. Yalom and Rand (1966) found that highly "compatible" (homogeneous in verbal responses to desired interpersonal areas) psychotherapy groups were significantly more cohesive than less compatible groups. Members who were least "compatible" with their group tended to be less satisfied and to leave their group prematurely. An implication of this study, in light of the suggested relationship between attitudinal similarity and interpersonal attraction (Goldstein, Heller, & Sechrest, 1966), is that attitudinally homogeneous groups will generally develop cohesiveness easily and rapidly, but establishing cohesion in heterogeneous groups will require special effort and attention.

Studies of problem-solving groups may be relevant to selecting clients for counseling groups on the basis of personality variables. Goldman, Haberlein and Feder (1965) found that three-member groups of all "conformers" shared ideas and divided work more readily than groups of all "resisters"; the resisters were more hostile and competitive and paid less attention to the ideas of other members. Wallach, Kogan, and Burt (1967), studying the "risky-shift" phenomenon, assigned five-member groups of college students to "discuss a topic to consensus." Groups of field-dependent subjects (affect-oriented) reached consensus more quickly and showed a greater increase in their willingness to take risks than did field-independent subjects (analytically and cognitively oriented). This study has relevance for creating a group climate which encourages members to take such risks as giving negative feedback or disclosing sensitive areas of their own behavior.

Stability of group membership was investigated in two studies. Hall and Williams (1966) compared the decision-making performance of established and ad hoc groups under conflict conditions. They found that established groups were superior in performing under conflict conditions. The established groups tended to resolve differences with increased creativity, but the ad hoc groups tended merely to work out compromises. Goldberg and Maccoby (1965) investigated the effects of stable versus shifting group membership on the behavior of second-grade children in situations which required that the children interact cooperatively to maximize their goals. Children in the stable groups did significantly better, and there was more of a tendency in the shifting groups for high-scoring members to exercise dominance over low-scoring members.

Controversy over optimal group size rages endlessly, but few attempts are made to study the effects of group size on specific process or outcome variables. From their review of research on group size relative to problem-solving groups, Goldstein et al. (1966) observed that as group size increases: (1) the absolute rate of interaction for any given member tends to decrease; (2) the proportion of infrequent contributors to the group interaction increases; (3) more members report feelings of threat and inhibition regarding participation; (4) giving of information and suggestions increases and asking for opinions and showing agreement decreases; and (5) more statements are directed to the leader and the leader addresses more statements to the group as a whole rather than to individual members. Goldstein et al. suggested ending impressionistic speculation and conducting studies of group size related to variables such as nature and rate of verbal interaction and leader interventions.

There were no reports found of studies in which an attempt was made to prepare clients systematically for optimal participation in their group. The procedures designed to prepare a client for his group experience varied from simply sending an invitation to a student to join an academic improvement group to the elaborate steps followed by Bach (1954) which involved extensive testing, several interviews, reading, and trial attendance at a group session. Data obtained from studies of group cohesiveness (Cartwright &

Zander, 1960) suggest the potential productivity of research on the effects of establishing the client's expectations that group experiences will be attractive and valuable or that certain kinds of interaction will be likely to develop among group members. Goldstein et al. (1966) suggested conducting studies which stem from the hypothesis that people tend to "find" more value in experiences in which they have invested considerable energy. Further hypotheses might be formulated relating motivation and expectancies to interaction norms and outcomes; these hypotheses then could form the basis for developing specialized procedures designed to prepare specific clients for participation in specific groups.

Group counseling research reflects little interest in client selection or client preparation as major independent variables. The available data suggest that people who are affectively oriented, flexible, highly motivated to change, and sufficiently well adjusted to interact rationally with others function well in counseling groups. Often, however, if anticipated results are not achieved, it is prematurely concluded that group counseling is not helpful for "this kind of client." Client selection, complex as it is, must be studied in relation to both process and outcome variables. Specifically, composing groups on the basis of predicted compatibility relative to preferred style of interaction appears most promising. Research is needed which will help to predict how a given client will respond under a given set of conditions and with a particular combination of other group members, including the leader. (Additional reference: Thelen & Harris, 1968.)

Outcomes

Although it may be said that all research focuses ultimately on outcomes, this section includes only those studies concerned with achieving specified outcomes through group counseling. Campbell and Dunnette (1968) have suggested three "disarmingly simple" standards for evaluating T-group experiences which, with minor modifications, could be applied to outcome research on counseling groups. The standards are: (1) measures of clients which broadly sample goal-related behavior should be explicitly determined before and after the counseling experience; (2) measured client changes during the time that counseling occurred should be compared with similar, uncounseled persons; and (3) effects of completing the evaluation instruments should be studied. A fourth standard is that the nature of the treatment, the specific procedures used, should be spelled out explicitly in behavioral terms.

Academic Performance

Attempts to improve the grade point averages (gpa) of students were reported in most of the outcome studies. Few studies were found which approached the standards proposed by Campbell and Dunnette. Roth, Mauksch and Peiser (1967) showed that subjects in mandatory counseling groups of 7 to 12 members raised their mean gpa significantly from .94 to 1.74, compared to control subjects whose gpa did not change. The control group, however, was not well matched with the experimentals on either academic aptitude or prior academic achievement. Despite an attempt to account for the regression effect by comparing changes in the gpa of the high- and low-achieving students in both groups, replication with a tightened research design is necessary before definitive conclusions can be drawn. Rationale and treatment procedures are given in sufficient detail that replication is possible. Mezzano (1968) studied the immediate and ten-week effects of group counseling and group-plus-individual counseling on randomly assigned low-achieving high-school students. No differences were found on gpa, study attitudes or self-concept immediately following counseling—but, ten weeks later the counseled groups had significantly higher mean gpas than control groups had.

Dickenson and Truax (1966) suggested that frequent equivocal results of group counseling with underachievers may be a result of lumping together high and low "therapeutic conditions." They matched groups of neurotic, underachieving college freshmen; the freshmen were then counseled under high and moderate therapeutic conditions (accurate empathy, nonpossessive warmth and genuineness offered by the group leader). Significant improvement in mean gpa was found for the subjects who received the high therapeutic conditions, but not found for those in the moderate or control groups.

Although gpa is a socially significant, objectively quantifiable, convenient measure of academic success, it is somewhat inadequate as a single outcome criterion. It is generally acknowledged that many kinds of academic learnings are not reflected in the gpa; this suggests that gpa should only be used as one of several criteria of academic success. In addition, lumping together the various behaviors which contribute to gpa precludes the investigation of the specific behaviors which may be affected by the treatment.

ATTITUDE AND PERSONALITY CHANGE

Three studies in this section approached the standards proposed by Campbell and Dunnette. These three studies used comparable procedures (desensitization) which were operationally defined, were concerned with one independent variable (anxiety), used multiple criteria and had adequate control groups.

Paul and Shannon (1966) provided systematic desensitization of anxiety for two five-member groups of highly anxious students who had been members of a delayed treatment control group in a previous study. The treatment consisted of training the subjects in deep muscle relaxation; constructing a hierarchy of anxiety producing situations; and beginning with the least anxiety-producing situations in the hierarchy, counter-conditioning the anxiety by directing the subjects to "image" the events while in a state of deep muscle relaxation. The images proceeded from least to most threatening items, determined by specific rules of timing. The results indicated that anxiety (as measured by a test battery consisting of anxiety inventories, observer ratings and self-reports) decreased significantly after the group desensitization treatment; the anxiety scores had not changed during the previous semester when no treatment was provided. Subjects in the desensitization groups also had a significantly higher mean GPA at the end of the semester than did the matched control subjects.

Katahn, Strenger, and Cherry (1966) used two groups of six and eight students each to assess the effect of systematic group desensitization combined with group discussion. Anxiety scores, as measured by a modification of Sarason's Test Anxiety Scale, decreased significantly in the two desensitization groups after six weeks; there was no significant decrease of anxiety scores in the control groups, which were composed of similar students whose schedules were such that they were not included in the treatment program. The mean gpa of the therapy groups also increased significantly compared to the control group. The study by Paul and Shannon and the study by Katahn et al. provide rather conclusive evidence that the treatment used was effective in reducing anxiety and improving the academic performance of the highly anxious college students. However, a survey given to the subjects in the latter study indicated that the clients were unanimous in the opinion that it was the informal discussion (also used in the Paul and Shannon study), rather than the desensitization procedures, which was responsible for the results.

Thoresen and Neuman (1968) compared systematic group desensitization (without informal discussion) with group insight counseling in reducing examination anxiety among 54 college undergraduates. Groups of three were led by professonal (Ph.D.'s with clinical experience) or subprofessional (first year, inexperienced graduate students in psychology) counselors for five weekly sessions. The group desensitization treatment was found to reduce anxiety, as measured by three self-report measures of anxiety, significantly more than group insight treament or two control group procedures. Differences were not found between these treatments on an observer checklist; both the group desensitization treatment and the group insight treatment were significantly more effective than control procedures. The subprofessional counselors who administered the treatments were, in general, as effective as the professional counselors. These findings support the efficacy of systematic group desensitization without discussion. However, the investigators found that some subjects in the desensitization groups reduced their anxiety more than others; this was also true for some subjects in the insight groups. Studies are now needed to determine what client characteristics interact with which treatments (or combination of treatments) to produce the most effective, efficient change.

Attempts to evaluate the outcomes of laboratory groups such as T-groups have been conducted in recent years. Space limitations preclude their inclusion here. Campbell and Dunnette (1968) have provided an excellent critical review of research in that field.

CAREER DEVELOPMENT

Despite the appearance of a substantial body of theoretical and research literature on career development (Tennyson, 1968), there have been few recent attempts to facilitate vocational planning through group counseling. Gilliland (1968) randomly assigned Negro high-school students either to all-male and all-female groups for "group-centered" counseling or to a control group. After one year the counseled students showed significant gains in reading ability, English usage, occupational aspiration and vocational development; the control subjects exhibited no significant gains. Treatment procedures were not specified. Jesse and Heimann (1965) tested the effects of group guidance on the vocational maturity of ninth-grade boys. Data from a vocational maturity scale and from interviews indicated no significant change in vocational maturity by the following summer. Specification of treatment procedures, lacking in both of these studies, is necessary for valid conclusions to be drawn.

Stewart and Thoresen (1968) reported two studies with eighth- and eleventh-grade students. Some students in the sessions listened in groups of four to three audio-presented group social models; each presentation was followed by group reinforcement discussion. Other students engaged in reinforcement discussion after completing written materials on topics such as "Possible Interests After High School," "Getting Helpful Information," and "Occupation and Me." Although subjects in the experimental treatments were significantly more engaged, on the average, in information-seeking behaviors than control subjects were, considerable individual variations were found. These findings suggested the need for multivariate studies in which interactions between treatments and subject characteristics are explicitly examined.

Thoresen, Hosford, and Krumboltz (1968) used a multivariate design in four high schools to study interactive effects of social model and subject characteristics on career relevant information-seeking behaviors of 189 male high-school juniors. In one group session, one of nine different audio social models, representing three levels of either academic, social or athletic success, was played to matched groups of seven Ss. Each group was matched on level (high, moderate, low) of academic, athletic or social success. Results were mixed in that the high success athletic model, for example, was significantly more effective with highly and moderately successful athletic subjects in one school, but was ineffective in a second school. Significant interactions were also found among counselors, schools, subjects and treatments; this finding suggested that some counselors using particular model treatments with certain subjects were more effective than other counselors. This study merits replication, but more attention should be given to how group counselor characteristics and increased treatment sessions affect outcomes.

A number of viable career development models have appeared in recent years; they are amenable to implementation through group counseling (Super et al., 1963; Tiedeman & O'Hara, 1963). Specific group procedures attempting to engender behaviors relevant to those theories might be tested on selected groups of clients. More attempts to induce vocational maturity through some generalized form of group counseling are clearly not needed. Vocational maturity and group counseling are not single, clearly understood entities.

What is needed are multivariate projects which utilize multiple outcome criteria and differential treatments. (Additional references: Anderson & Johnson, 1968; Pattison, 1965; Gundlach, 1967; Shapiro & Birk, 1967.)

Group Interaction

Of all the factors which impinge upon a counseling group, none is more pervasive than the interaction among group members. Ultimately, the interactive-communication in a group determines the outcomes. Clear specification of treatment procedures requires systematic identification of the information contained in a unit of communication, the manner in which the information is given, and the effect it has on the relationship between the receiver and sender of the message (Watzlawick, Beavin, & Jackson, 1967). The purpose of group interaction research is to classify systematically and evaluate the communication occurring in a group.

Truax (1968) and Truax and Carkhuff (1967) presented evidence from a number of studies which indicated that changes in group participants usually occurred when a high degree of genuineness, warmth and empathic understanding was being communicated within the group. The evidence also suggested that such changes in group participants were unlikely to occur in the absence of the communication of such relationship qualities. The authors found that the leader's use of these qualities (genuineness, warmth, etc.) to reinforce selectively the self-exploratory statements in counseling groups increased the frequency of subsequent self-exploratory statements. These qualities also influenced outcome criteria such as improved personal and interpersonal adjustment (measured by personality inventories) and the length of time that patients spent outside the mental hospital during the subsequent year. The therapeutic gains in the above studies were attributed primarily to relationship qualities communicated by the group leader.

Working with groups of high-school students, Hansen, Zimpfer, and Easterling (1967) found significant correlations between increased congruence of self-concept and the perceptions which group members had of the relationships offered by other group members. The authors found no correlations between congruence of self-concept and the members' perceptions of relationships offered by the counselor. Unfortunately, these studies have not provided sufficient detail about treatment procedures to allow replication. In addition, it is not possible to attribute specific outcomes to specific kinds of interaction because of the gross description of process and outcomes.

A number of attempts to assess systematically or to classify group interaction have been reported. Mann (1967) developed an interaction scoring system based on psychoanalytic theory and derived from observation of a series of relatively unstructured social psychology classes. Eight of the 16 categories describe members' affective (impulse) responses to the group leader; three categories describe feelings activated by the leader's status in the perceived authority structure; and five categories describe how a member felt about himself in relation to the leader. There were also four levels of relating to the leader, dependent upon the directness of the communication.

The Hill Interaction Matrix (Hill, 1965), developed from observations of psychotherapy groups in a mental hospital, is a two-dimensional system based on Bion's (1959) classification of verbal interaction. The four horizontal categories were derived from the content of the communication; they are *references to topics of general interest, the group, problems and concerns of individual members,* and *relationships of group members to each other in the "here and now."* The five vertical categories are derived from the "work-style," which might also be called the process or relationship dimension. The three "pre-work" categories are *responsive, conventional* and *assertive;* the two "work" categories are *speculative* and *confrontive.* Superimposing the five work-styles over the four content styles creates a twenty-cell matrix into which any statement can be classified according to content and work level.

In a recent study of five-member T-groups composed of college students who volunteered for the study, Dunnette and Campbell (1969) found that after six two-hour sessions there was a significant positive correlation between the level of interpersonal communication, as measured by the Hill Interaction Matrix, and the increase in empathic understanding.

There are a number of constructs in the group dynamics field which, if operationalized, could be fruitfully studied in terms of group interaction. For example, Truax (1961) reported significant relationships between group cohesiveness and degree of patient self-exploration and patient insight. Goldstein et al. (1966) presented evidence from non-therapy groups which showed that group cohesion is a powerful influence on individual member behavior; they proposed a series of testable hypotheses to relate cohesiveness to a number of specific, therapy-related variables. As molar concepts such as norms, cohesiveness, trust, empathy, warmth and congruence are operationalized and quantified within interaction systems, it becomes possible to relate them to counseling outcomes for individual clients in predictable ways. Few studies approach this degree of rigorous specificity. (Additional references: Bonney, 1965; Hoffman, Burke, & Maier, 1965; Ohlsen & Pearson, 1965.)

Group Development

Eight years ago, Hill (1961) listed some 34 "theories" of group development drawn from group dynamics and group psychotherapy literature. Nearly all of the theories were formulated from intuitive observations and couched in the language of each author's theoretical bias. Tuckman (1965), in criticizing group development studies for lack of experimental rigor, suggested a classification scheme based on setting, realm (group structure and task activity) and developmental sequence. Tuckman hoped that this classification scheme would stimulate additional research.

Mann (1967), studying the development of four social psychology classes on group process, suggested a "cyclical" rather than a "phase" model of group development. These groups, rather than moving "ever onward and upward" to maturity, experienced repeated ups and downs. Mann further observed that a shift in the predominant tone of the group was rarely shared by all members equally. The emergence of subgroups appeared to be primarily responsible for the group's cycles, and an attempt was made to identify the issues which created the conditions under which the subgroups emerged, competed and combined, thereby altering the direction of the group's development. Fiebert (1968) observed that leader behavior in a sensitivity group changed from that of a *catalyst* (one who encourages and facilitates) to that of an *orchestrator* (one who directs verbal and non-verbal exercises and deepens explorations of feeling and motives) and then to that of a *participant* (one who takes a member role and blends into the group). Findings by Lubin and Zuckerman (1967) lend some support to Fiebert's observations; they found that the level of anxiety, depression and hostility in a one-week sensitivity training conference rose sharply about halfway through (when the orchestrator was deepening the exploration of feelings) and then declined.

Scott (1965) studied two groups of delinquents assigned to group therapy by the juvenile court. Scott used seven observable characteristics of interaction to identify four discrete phases of group development. Sufficient detail was provided for replication, using differently composed groups or groups meeting under different circumstances. Ahearn (1968) used the Hill Interaction Matrix to study the interaction patterns in a group of ten prospective counselors who held 56 sessions. Ahearn found that the number of statements considered to be of high therapeutic value tended to increase sharply from the first to second quarter; then the number of statements leveled off. Intermediate level interaction decreased in the second quarter and then increased in the last two quarters. This "polarization" is described as a work-flight pattern in which the group alternates between work and tension-release.

Group development is the one area of small-group work in which theoretical models abound but a solid empirical base is lacking. Mann's study illustrates the difficulty and expense of thoroughly studying group development. Each group meeting over a period of time is an n of one. It is likely that the patterns of interaction which develop in a counseling group will depend upon the group composition, leadership style and expected outcomes; however, the precise nature of these variations in relation to those factors is yet to be studied. Such studies are generally feasible only in large institutional settings or through the collaboration of several investigators. (Additional references: Heckel et al., 1967; Foley & Bonney, 1966.)

Leadership Styles and Group Structure

This section contains a review of studies in which two or more "leadership styles" are compared or in which a particular mode of leadership behavior is used as an independent variable. The differences in styles ranged from gross variations such as group-centered versus leader-centered, to very specific variations such as conscious verbal reinforcements of different particular types of interaction.

Thoresen and Krumboltz (1967) examined the relationships between five categories of statements recorded in individual and group sessions and the amount of information-seeking behavior outside the group. They found significant positive correlations of (1) the frequency of counselor verbal reinforcement of client information-seeking responses, (2) the frequency of client information-seeking responses and (3) the number of counselor "cue" responses, with outside information-seeking behaviors. Subjective client rating of the degree of "helpfulness" of the counseling were unrelated to the frequency of information-seeking behavior engaged in by clients.

Truax (1968) demonstrated that mental hospital patients in groups receiving high levels of leader behaviors (described as accurate empathy, nonpossessive warmth, and genuineness) showed significant increases in frequency of self-exploratory responses; the same patients also improved personal adjustment and spent more time out of the hospital during the subsequent year. Truax concluded, as a result of this and related studies, that the "therapeutic-triad" of accurate empathy, nonpossessive warmth, and genuineness could appropriately be construed as reinforcing patient self-exploration and extratherapy improvement.

Culbert (1968) studied the effects of leader self-disclosure in two T-groups of ten college students each; the groups met twice weekly in two-hour sessions for fourteen weeks. One of the weekly sessions was spent in the T-group with two co-trainers; the other session was spent in a dyad pairing with another group member. Culbert found that although an equivalent number of two-person "perceived therapeutic relationships" were formed in each group, subjects in the group with less-disclosing leaders more often entered into relationships with leaders and dyad partners, whereas the subjects with more self-disclosing leaders entered more often into relationships with other group members. Although both groups reached the same level of self-awareness, the group in which the leaders were more self-disclosing reached their peak level sooner.

Salzberg (1967), in a study of the effects of the presence or absence of a leader, examined an open-ended group composed of 35 inpatients of a privileged psychiatric ward; the inpatients participated at various times during a 16 week period. No significant difference in total frequency of statements made was found between sessions attended by the therapist and those sessions which the therapist observed but did not attend. More comments were classified as "spontaneous" when the therapist was absent, but fewer comments were classified as "relevant"; this result suggests that the group members worked harder on individual problems when the leader was present. Seligman's (1968) study produced similar results. Leaderless groups in Seligman's study spent significantly more time on "low-level" interaction (measured by the Hill Interaction Matrix) than leader-led groups spent; the reverse finding was true for "high-level" interaction.

The amount of structure optimally provided by the leader is a subject of considerable controversy in group counseling—despite evidence from group dynamics which suggests that the need for structure in a group depends upon the situation. Gilbreath (1967) found that leader-structured groups were more effective in increasing the ego strength and gpa of freshmen and sophomore male underachievers than were non-directive or group-structured groups. Gilbreath also found that the subjects with high dependency needs (measured by a second order factor of the Sterns Activity Index) tended to raise their gpa when they participated in leader-structured groups; dependent subjects participating in non-directive groups did not tend to raise their gpa. In contrast, independent subjects improved their gpa in the non-directive groups, but showed no improvement in gpa in the leader-structured groups.

The weakness of most of these studies lies in the researchers' vagueness about the specific procedures involved in the various treatments. The strength of these studies lies in the researchers' attempt to test the differential effects of a given process variable on different kinds of clients. (Additional references: Bates, 1968; Delaney & Heimann, 1966; French, Sherwood, & Bradford, 1966; Shaw & Blum, 1966.)

Innovations and Trends

Presenting a section on innovations involves the risk of being perceived either as "behind the times" or as "faddish" and unscientific. Nevertheless, exciting things are happening in group work, and many of them will have great impact on future practice and research. Human-encounter groups of various kinds and labels are becoming popular in churches, neighborhoods, schools, hospitals and businesses. "Self-help" groups, encouraged by the success of Alcoholics Anonymous, were given a kind of scientific respectability by Mowrer's *The New Group Therapy* (1964) and by the Integrity Therapy movement. Groups such as Alanon for families of alcoholics and Alateens for children of alcoholics are becoming common throughout the country. There are also many half-way houses for alcoholics. Synanon, a half-way house organization for narcotics users; Recovery, Inc., for former mental patients and excessively nervous people; and TOPS, for weight-watchers, are examples of self-help groups which use a variety of group procedures.

Esalen (Murphy, 1967) represents the focal point of a relatively new movement attempting to "expand the mind of man" through encounter groups and non-verbal individual and group experiences.

Esalen attracts both the "hippies" and the elite; it has been extolled by some and condemned by others. Nonetheless, Esalen appears destined to have a substantial impact on counseling and therapy—particularly in group settings. *Sense Relaxation* (Gunther, 1968) and *Joy* (Schutz, 1967) deal with concepts and experiences designed to stimulate man to a greater sense of his own existence in relation to that of others. These works presage what appears to be the major thrust in *Humanistic Psychology*.

One of the more conventional innovations in group counseling and therapy is the *marathon,* in which groups meet either continuously or with short breaks for 12 to 72 hours. These groups may be composed of people looking for relief from conflict and loneliness or of people who are essentially happy but are seeking new ways to enrich their interpersonal encounters and their own self-awareness. Bach (1967, p. 995) has described marathon groups as the "most direct, the most efficient, and the most economical antidote to alienation, meaninglessness, fragmentation and other hazards of mental health in our time."

Gazda (1968) has compiled a number of accounts of innovative approaches to group therapy; he has included marathons, videotape feedback, the TORI process and others. Otto (1967) has presented a theory and program for developing human potential through specified group activities; Boocock and Schild (1968) have collected a series of simulated games for use in a variety of groups. Bessell (1968) is organizing a Human Development Program in which personal confidence and desired classroom behaviors are learned through modeling and rehearsal of these behaviors in brief, small-group sessions held daily in the classroom.

The evidence regarding the precise nature and impact of these innovations is either lacking or is based on intuitive observation. Hopefully, each innovation will be investigated with sufficient rigor that it can be systematically defined and then either refined or discarded. These innovations represent one of the frontiers of knowledge in group counseling. In one sense, they differ from many of the "tried and true" ways only because they are new, but not because there is any less evidence regarding their efficacy. In another sense, they differ radically from standard approaches. These innovations are not bound by the standard constructs which place heavy emphasis on verbal communication. Man is viewed more comprehensively, as a biological-psycho-social system, and non-verbal activities such as music, dance, color and games are utilized to induce imagery, fantasy, bodily contact, introspection and experimentation—which appear to influence behavior more dramatically than talk strategies.

The changes that result from such non-verbal activities (dance, music, etc.) are often referred to as experiential learnings. Can such learnings be isolated and related to specific kinds of stimuli? Do they last, or do they simply serve as temporary facilitators of more permanent learnings? Do these learnings tend to generalize and transfer to normal life situations or are they existential? Do these learnings interfere with defense mechanisms in a psychologically dangerous manner, or is it possible to predict the impact of a particular experience on a given client and thus to construct experiential programs which will teach the desired behaviors? Does the very act of asking such questions inhibit the existential impact of the experience? Hopefully, such questions will be answered through rigorous inquiry and experimentation. It is relatively unexplored territory for the group researcher. (Additional reference: Lazarus & Bienlein, 1967.)

A Perspective

Counseling is increasingly viewed as an influence process, and counselors are exploring more active ways of helpfully intervening in the lives of their clients. There are indications that the field of group counseling is maturing. The amount of research activity is increasing rapidly, and there is liberal dissemination of information through professional journals. The series of desensitization studies is encouraging because it represents a successful effort to replicate procedures and tighten research design. In the desensitization studies, the treatment procedures and the nature of the clientele and the outcomes were precisely specified. This specificity is also evident in the operant conditioning studies. Solid evidence is accumulating that operant conditioning; desensitization procedures; and the presence of accurate empathy nonpossessive warmth and genuineness in a relationship tend to produce consistent, predictable outcomes with selected clients.

Despite Gundlach's (1967, p. 205) conclusion that "there is no simple, universal patient; there is no universal treatment named group therapy; and there is no simple, wonderful, universal outcome measure," many studies still seem to be searching for "the truth." Much of what is published is inconsequential because it contributes little or nothing to the pool of knowledge about group counseling. In most studies, researchers used gross, non-operational descriptions of treatment procedures (or none at all) and single criteria such as a gpa. There was a common failure in most studies to specify why the treatment that was used should be expected to produce the predicted outcomes with the particular clientele studied. Efforts were seldom made to study the differential effects of treatment procedures on different clients.

Group counseling needs studies that specify concrete, measurable goals for individual clients, detailed analysis of verbal and non-verbal communication which constituted the treatment, and a variety of appropriate criteria. The formulation of general principles about group counseling still awaits the use of identical treatment procedures in different settings with different clientele, as well as multivariate approaches which compare several treatment procedures in similar settings with similar clientele (Cohn, 1967). Immediate and long-term treatment effects must also be studied.

Theoretical models, broad enough to span both counseling theory and group dynamics (and perhaps the humanities), need to be formulated; broadly conceived research methodology must be developed to test these models. Gazda's (1968) compilation of basic approaches to group counseling may provide a beginning. However, it is doubtful that sufficient experimental rigor can always be provided in natural settings. Experiments on "quasi-counseling" groups are needed as interim steps to provide necessary controls and to reduce the risk to clients. Institutional or collaborative research that is based on these theoretical models and within which small coordinated studies can be conducted appears to hold the most promise for the future.

REFERENCES

Ahearn, T. R. An interaction process analysis of extended group counseling with prospective counselors. Unpublished doctoral dissertation, University of Georgia, 1968.

Bach, G. R. *Intensive group psychotherapy.* New York: Ronald Press, 1954.

Bach, G. R. Marathon group dynamics. *Psychological Reports,* 1967, *20,* 995–999.

Bessel, H. The content is the medium: The confidence is the message. *Psychology Today,* January 1968, *1,* 32–35, 61.

Bion, W. R. *Experiences in groups.* New York: Basic Books, 1959.

Boocock, S. S., & Schild, E. O. *Simulation games in learning.* Beverly Hills, Calif.: Sage, 1968.

Campbell, J., & Dunnette, M. D. Effectiveness of T-group experiences in managerial training and development. *Psychological Bulletin,* 1968, *79,* 73–104.

Cartwright, D., & Zander, A. *Group dynamics: Research the theory.* Evanston, Ill.: Row, Peterson, 1960.

Culbert, S. A. Trainer self-disclosure and member growth in two T-groups. *Journal of Applied Behavioral Science,* 1968, *4,* 47–73.

Cohn, B. (Ed.). *Guidelines for future research on group counseling in the public school setting.* Washington, D.C.: American Personnel and Guidance Association, 1967.

Dickenson, W. A., & Truax, C. B. Group counseling with underachievers. *Personnel and Guidance Journal,* 1966, *45,* 243–247.

Dunnette, M. D. People feeling: Joy, more joy, and the slough of despond. *Journal of Applied Behavioral Science,* 1969, *5,* 25–44.

Fiebert, M. S. Sensitivity training: An analysis of trainer intervention and group process. *Psychological Reports,* 1968, *22,* 829–838.

Gazda, G. M. (Ed.). *Basic approaches to group psychotherapy and group counseling.* Springfield, Ill.: Charles C Thomas, 1968.

Gazda, G. M. (Ed.). *Innovations to group psychotherapy.* Springfield, Ill.: Charles C Thomas, 1968.

Gazda, G. M., & Larsen, M. J. A comprehensive appraisal of group and multiple counseling research. *Journal of Research and Development in Education,* 1968, *1,* 57–132.

Gilbreath, S. H. Group counseling, dependence, and college male underachievement. *Journal of Counseling Psychology,* 1967, *14,* 449–453.

Gilliland, B. E. Small group counseling with Negro adolescents in a public high school. *Journal of Counseling Psychology,* 1968, *15,* 147–153.

Goldberg, M. H., & Maccoby, E. E. Children's acquisition of skill in performing a group task under two conditions of group formation. *Journal of Personality and Social Psychology,* 1965, *2,* 898–902.

Goldman, M., Haberlein, B. J., & Feder, G. J. Conformity and resistance to group pressure. *Sociometry,* 1965, *28,* 220–226.

Goldstein, A. P., Heller, K., & Sechrest, L. B. *Psychotherapy and the psychology of behavior change.* New York: Wiley, 1966.

Gundlach, R. H. Outcome studies in group psychotherapy. *International Journal of Group Psychotherapy,* 1967, *17,* 196–210.

Gunther, B. *Sense relaxation: Below your mind.* New York: Macmillan, 1968.

Hall, J. S., & Williams, M. S. A comparison of decision making performance in established and ad hoc groups. *Journal of Personality and Social Psychology*, 1966, *3*, 214–222.

Hansen, J. C., Zimpfer, D. G., & Easterling, R. E. A study of the relationships in multiple counseling. *Journal of Educational Research*, 1967, *60*, 461–463.

Hill, W. F. Group development. *Group psychotherapy: Collected papers in practice, theory and research*. Provo: Utah State Hospital Press, 1961.

Hill, W. F. *Hill Interaction Matrix*. Los Angeles: University of Southern California Press, 1965.

Jesse, B. A., & Heimann, R. A. Effects of individual and group counseling on vocational maturity of ninth grade boys. *Journal of Educational Research*, 1965, *59*, 68–73.

Kagan, N. Group procedures. *Review of Educational Research*, 1966, *36*, 274–287.

Katahn, M., Strenger, S., & Cherry, N. Group counseling and behavior therapy with test anxious college students. *Journal of Consulting Psychology*, 1966, *30*, 544–549.

Lubin, B., & Zuckerman, M. Affective and perceptual-cognitive patterns in sensitivity training groups. *Psychological Reports*, 1967, *21*, 363–376.

Mann, R. D. *Interpersonal styles and group development: An analysis of the member-leader relationship*. New York: Wiley, 1967.

Mezzano, J. A consideration for group counselors: Degree of counselee investment. *The School Counselor*, 1967, *14*, 167–169.

Mezzano, J. Group counseling with low-motivated male high school students—Comparative effects of two uses of counselor time. *Journal of Educational Research*, 1968, *61*, 223–224.

Mowrer, O. H. *The new group therapy*. Princeton, N.J.: Van Nostrand, 1964.

Murphy, M. Esalen: Where it's at. *Psychology Today*, December 1967, *1*, 34–39.

Otto, H. A. *Guide to developing your potential*. New York: Scribner's, 1967.

Paul, G. L., & Shannon, D. T. The treatment of anxiety through systematic desensitization in therapy groups. *Journal of Abnormal Psychology*, 1966, *71*, 124–135.

Roth, R. M., Mauksch, H. O., & Peiser, K. The non-achievement syndrome, group therapy, and achievement change. *Personnel and Guidance Journal*, 1967, *46*, 393–398.

Salzberg, H. C. Verbal behavior in group psychotherapy with and without a therapist. *Journal of Counseling Psychology*, 1967, *14*, 24–27.

Schutz, W. C. *Joy.* New York: Grove Press, 1967.

Scott, M. Group development: An exploratory study of small group growth patterns. Unpublished Master's thesis, Brigham Young University, 1965.

Seligman, M. Verbal behavior in therapist-led, leaderless and alternating group psychotherapy sessions. Unpublished doctoral dissertation, University of Oregon, 1968.

Stewart, N. R., & Thoresen, C. E. Behavioral group counseling for career development. Symposium presented at American Personnel and Guidance Association Convention, Detroit, 1968.

Super, Donald E., et al. *Career development: Self concept theory.* New York: College Entrance Examination Board, 1963.

Tennyson, W. W. Career development. *Review of Educational Research,* 1968, *38,* 346–366.

Thoresen, C. E., & Krumboltz, J. D. Relationship of counselor reinforcement of selected responses to external behavior. *Journal of Counseling Psychology,* 1967, *14,* 140–144.

Thoresen, C. E., & Neuman, D. R. Professional and subprofessional counselors using group desensitization and insight procedures to reduce examination anxiety. Unpublished manuscript, School of Education, Stanford University, 1968.

Thoresen, C. E., Hosford, R. E., & Krumboltz, J. D. Determining effective models for counseling clients of varying competencies. Unpublished manuscript, School of Education, Stanford University, 1968.

Tiedeman, D. V., & O'Hara, R. P. *Career development: Choice and adjustment.* New York: College Entrance Examination Board, 1963.

Truax, C. B. The process of group psychotherapy: Relationships between hypothesized therapeutic conditions and intrapersonal exploration. *Psychological Monographs,* 1961, *75* (7, Whole No. 505).

Truax, C. B. Therapist interpersonal reinforcement of client self-exploration and therapeutic outcome in group psychotherapy. *Journal of Counseling Psychology,* 1968, *15,* 225–231.

Truax, C. B., & Carkhuff, R. R. *Toward effective counseling and psychotherapy: Training and practice.* Chicago: Aldine, 1967.

Tuckman, B. W. Developmental sequence in small groups. *Psychological Bulletin,* 1965, *63,* 384–399.

Wallach, M. A., Kogan, N., & Burt, R. B. Group risk taking and field dependence-independence of group members. *Sociometry,* 1967, *30,* 323–338.

Watzlawick, P., Beavin, J. H., & Jackson, D. D. *Pragmatics of human communication.* New York: Norton, 1967.

Yalom, I. D., & Rand, K. Compatibility and cohesiveness in therapy groups. *Archives of general psychiatry,* 1966, *15,* 267–275.

ADDITIONAL REFERENCES

Anderson, A. R., & Johnson, D. L. Using group procedures to improve human relations in the school system. *School Counselor*, 1968, *15*, 334–342.

Bates, M. A test of group counseling. *Personnel and Guidance Journal*, 1968, *46*, 749–753.

Bonney, W. C. Pressures toward conformity in group counseling. *Personnel and Guidance Journal*, 1965, *43*, 970–973.

Delaney, D. J., & Heimann, R. A. Effectiveness of sensitivity training on the perception of non-verbal communications. *Journal of Counseling Psychology*, 1966, *13*, 436–440.

Foley, W. J., & Bonney, W. C. A developmental model for counseling groups. *Personnel and Guidance Journal*, 1966, *44*, 576–590.

French, J. R. P., Jr., Sherwood, J. J., & Bradford, D. L. Change in self-identity in a management training conference. *Journal of Applied Behavioral Science*, 1966, *2*, 210–218.

Gundlach, R. H. Outcome studies in group psychotherapy. *International Journal of Group Psychotherapy*, 1967, *17*, 196–210.

Heckel, R. V., et al. Emergence of distinct verbal phases in group therapy. *Psychological Reports*, 1967, *21*, 630–632.

Hoffman, L. R., Burke, R. J., & Maier, N. R. F. Participation, influence, and satisfaction among members of problem-solving groups. *Psychological Reports*, 1965, *16*, 661–667.

Lazarus, H. R., & Bienlein, D. K. Soap opera therapy. *International Journal of Group Psychotherapy*, 1967, *17*, 252–256.

Ohlsen, M. M., & Pearson, R. D. A method for the classification of group interaction and its use to explore the influence of individual and role factors in group counseling. *Journal of Clinical Psychology*, 1965, *21*, 436–441.

Pattison, E. M. Evaluation studies of group psychotherapy. *International Journal of Group Psychotherapy*, 1965, *15*, 382–397.

Shapiro, D., & Birk, L. Group therapy and experimental perspective. *International Journal of Group Psychotherapy*, 1967, *17*, 211–224.

Shaw, M. E., & Blum, J. M. Effects of leadership style upon group performance as a function of task structure. *Journal of Personality and Social Psychology*, 1966, *3*, 238–242.

Thelen, M. H., & Harris, C. J. Personality of college underachievers who improve with group psychotherapy. *Personnel and Guidance Journal*, 1968, *46*, 561–566.

Part Five

ETHICS:
ISSUES, QUESTIONS,
AND RECOMMENDATIONS

Many counselors have regarded the emergence of group procedures
as a panacea for therapy and growth. The group experience is
thought by many to be a viable means for accomplishing all the
worthwhile goals beyond the scope of individual counseling. However, recent literature in the field suggests that a number of group
counselors—perhaps no less enthusiastic than their colleagues about
the potential of the group experience—have encountered a morass
of professional and ethical issues.

The quantity of articles dealing with ethics and professional issues suggests that the group phenomenon has only recently achieved
sufficient prominence to allow—and simultaneously demand—careful examination. Counselors who use the new group methods have
tended to practice rather than to conceptualize and evaluate,
which has been true of applied behavioral science in general. Consequently, the sudden growth and excitement of the group experience have added to the conflict of interests among group counselors.
Until recently the attitude seems to have been that although out-

comes are attainable and worthwhile, they are not to be predetermined nor accounted for once achieved!

Many important questions in the field of group counseling need to be answered: How are counselor and client responsibilities defined in the group experience? Is the group movement anti-intellectual in nature? What training is necessary for group work? Who should be authorized to conduct group experiences? What are the standards for training and practice? What is the rationale for a given group experience? Are the processes of feedback, confrontation, and "authenticity" effective, or are they just mental gymnastics?

The amount of attention these questions have received in the field may be taken as evidence that the group phenomenon is finally "coming of age." Like the adolescent, the group movement is full grown, lively, strong, and impetuous but still lacking in some of the essential characteristics of maturity.

The application of sensitivity methods and human relations training has revitalized group programs of growth and therapy. The development of sensitivity training as a form of group experience separate from both counseling and therapy has raised several professional issues. As described by Lakin (1969) these issues are important to all counselors who use the methodology, regardless of purpose or setting. The fact that the NTL Institute for Applied Behavioral Science published, in 1970, a set of training standards a full twenty-three years after its organization emphasizes the dilemma in group counseling arising from the absence of theoretical concepts and ethical guidelines. To date, neither the American Personnel and Guidance Association nor the American Psychological Association has published an outline of preparational sequences or a code of ethics for group counseling, despite the great number of their members who practice it.

The article by Lakin on ethical standards, "Some Ethical Issues in Sensitivity Training" (1969), and the NTL "Standards for the Use of Laboratory Method" (1970) are welcome additions to the literature on groups. Both the novice and the experienced counselor will find these parameters useful for determining what constitutes professional behavior and practice.

Shostrom, in "Group Therapy: Let the Buyer Beware" (1969), deals specifically with the matter of competence. As a variety of group experiences have become increasingly available to anyone with the price of admission, the problem of professional qualification has been severely aggravated. There is no consensus within the major professional organizations as to what extent formal preparation is required, and it is unlikely that local boards, agencies, or certification programs will take independent action in the near future. As Shostrom points out, the person who seeks group therapy —or any kind of group experience—must make his own evaluation of competent group leaders. Definitions of the group process are not specific, and evaluative criteria for staff members are limited and arbitrary. In view of the number of people who have had an unfortunate group experience, Shostrom's warning to the potential group member to proceed with caution should be heeded.

In "Confrontation Groups: Hula Hoops?" (1969), Beymer poses several questions related to philosophical and theoretical bases, counselor responsibility, techniques, and outcomes. The coverage is comprehensive, and the author's thoughtful discussion establishes the relevance of each question. His suggestion that the group experience is anti-intellectual in nature, for example, contains a number of implications for counselor education programs: Should the primary goal of preparation programs be personal authenticity, or cognitively acquired skills? Is there a desirable balance which can be achieved? Unlike other authors who have been merely critical, Beymer offers some concrete recommendations for systematic inquiry and action geared toward resolving some of the main professional and ethical issues.

Gazda, Duncan, and Sisson, in "Professional Issues in Group Work" (1971), describe the explosion of activity in group work, with the resultant lag in developing standards for training and practice and in forming a code of ethics. The authors draw conclusions from questionnaire data on ethics and professional issues in group work. In addition, they provide recommendations for solving the problem of ethics in group practice.

In "Innovative Group Techniques: Handle with Care" (1970), Dreyfus and Kremenliev direct their attention to another problem in the current group movement—the haphazard use of demonstrations which require audience participation. The practice of demonstrating group methods at professional conferences has played an important role in disseminating innovations in methodology. This contribution to the increased use of appropriate and effective group procedures, however, potentially could be diminished by a few practitioners who seek glory for themselves. In order to preserve the appropriate use of laboratory demonstrations, Dreyfus and Kremenliev outline some safeguards for the concerned and responsible group leader.

Rosenbaum, in "The Responsibility of the Group Psychotherapy Practitioner for a Therapeutic Rationale" (1969), calls for philosophical and theoretical accountability. Openly critical of the emphasis on experience and emotion for their own sake, he observes that they may be more valuable within a conceptual framework. He asserts that feeling good is simply not enough and, like Beymer, identifies the directions in which steps must be taken to establish a rationale for the use of group methods in psychotherapy.

The NTL Institute for Applied Behavioral Science has developed its own system for training leaders and conducting programs. This organization, however, is neither closed nor self-contained. Except for a small cadre of professional staff members, those who participate in activities of the NTL Institute are employed in a variety of fields including education, psychology, religion, business, and industry. As a result, the laboratory method has had widespread use in our society. Structured activities, exercises, T-groups and other forms of experiential learning—all variations of the laboratory method—are widely used in counselor preparation and practice. The NTL's "Standards for the Use of Laboratory Method" (1970) are applicable to all settings and purposes and represent the only clearly articulated guidelines in print at the present time.

Our purpose in Part Five is to identify and review some of the significant ethical issues for the practicing group leader. We also wish to remind the reader that groups are neither a cure-all nor a curse. The group experience is an approach which, in many cases, can help people to deal with their concerns and to become more fully aware of their humanity. The judgments in the selected readings are of great value in considering the critical responsibilities one assumes when working professionally with people in groups. The proposals, recommendations, and standards which follow clearly document the potential impact of a group experience. The selections in Part Five make it clear that it is the responsibility of the group practitioner to be fully aware of both the uses and the abuses of group processes.

34 / SOME ETHICAL ISSUES
IN SENSITIVITY TRAINING [1]

Martin Lakin

Sensitivity training, in its various forms, has evolved over the past two decades. It is a powerful form of experiential learning that includes self, interactional, and organizational understanding. It has its origins in the study of change and conflict resolution through attention to underlying as well as overt interactional processes. It has been widely used to reexamine managerial, pedagogic, and "helping relationships" from the factory to the classroom, from the community to the home. Typically, small groups of participants under the guidance of a "trainer" use the data of their own spontaneous interactions, and reactions to one another. The trainer functions to facilitate communication, to indicate underlying problems of relating, and to model constructive feedback. He keeps the group moving and productively learning about processes and persons and helps to avoid counterproductive conflict or unnecessary damage to participants. With the evolution of mutant forms of

[1] This paper was presented at the meeting of the Southeastern Psychological Association, New Orleans, February 1969.

EDITOR'S NOTE (October 1969): The Committee on Scientific and Professional Ethics and Conduct has formed an ad hoc committee to consider if the "Ethical Standards of Psychologists" require modification in areas related to professional psychology. Starke Hathaway will chair the committee. Also, a Task Force of Divisions 12 and 29 will soon begin work on developing a set of standards for innovative services. Finally, at the Ethics Committee convention workshop, a meeting of individuals who have been studying ethical issues in group procedures was held.

training, particularly over the past few years, and their growing popularity, examination of latent ethical questions has become urgent. This article is presented not to censure an obviously significant and often helpful growth in American psychology, but rather to open for discussion and scrutiny elements of it that affect public welfare and reflect on professional standards.

The number of persons who have experienced some form of training is rapidly growing. However named (training, encounter, human relations), the experience invariably involves emotional confrontations and even an implicit injunction to reconsider if not actually to change personal behavior patterns. Since participants are not self-avowed psychotherapy patients but "normal" persons, and because the trainers are presumably not concerned with reparative but with learning or personal enhancement, it is difficult to draw a firm line between it and other psychotherapeutic forms. Indeed, comparison inevitably forces itself upon us and suggests strongly what many of us realize so well, that a distinction between "normal" and "pathological" behavior is hazy at best. However, the comparison also compels one to consider ethical implications of the differences between the contractual relationships between participant and trainer, on the one hand, and those between patient and therapist, on the other. Concerns about the contractual implications have been only partially met by statements of differences in the goals of training from those of therapy and by the difference in self-definition of a participant from that of a patient, as well as by the avowed educational objectives of trainers. Also, formerly it could be argued that the trainer had little therapeutic responsibility because he initiated little; that interactions of the group were the resultant of collective interchange and give-and-take, and did not occur at his instance; that is, a participant "discloses" intimate details of his life or "changes" behavior patterns as a result of a personal commitment or a collective experience rather than because a trainer directs him to do so. Training groups evolved from a tradition of concern with *democratic* processes and *democratic* change. The generally accepted hypothesis was that the best psychological protection against unwarranted influence was individual and collective awareness that could forestall insidious manipulation by dominant leaders or conformist tyranny by a group.

Many people currently involved in the various forms of training are not as psychologically sophisticated or able to evaluate its processes as were the mainly professional participants of some years ago. The motivation of many present participants is cathartic rather than intellectual (e.g., seeking an emotional experience rather than an understanding). Particularly because training is increasingly used as a vehicle for achieving social change, it is necessary to explore its ethical implications—notwithstanding our as yet incomplete understanding of its special processes. There are ethically relevant problems in setting up a group experience, in conducting the group, and following its termination.

Pregroup Concerns

A psychotherapeutic intention is clear by contrast with the training intention. Sophisticated therapists know that this clarity is not absolute; complex issues of values and commitment to specific procedures cannot really be shared with patients, despite the best intentions of a therapist to be candid. Nevertheless, the therapist's mandate is relatively clear   to provide a corrective experience for someone who presents himself as psychologically impaired. By contrast, participant expectancies and fantasies about training vary much more widely. By comparison with the therapist, the trainer's mandate is relatively ambiguous. For example, some trainers view the group experience primarily as a vehicle to produce increased awareness of interactional processes to be employed in social or organizational settings. However, currently, some others dismiss this goal as trivial in favor of an expressive or "existential" experience. Both approaches are similar in that they require a participant-observer role for the trainee. Yet, the emphasis upon rational and emotional elements differs in these approaches, and this difference makes for divergent experiences. The problem is that there is no way for a participant to know in advance, much less to appraise, intentions of trainers, processes of groups, or their consequences for him. It is not feasible to explain these because training, like psychotherapy, depends upon events that counter the participant's accustomed expectations in order to have maximum impacts. Since it is inimical to training to preprogram participant or process, the nature of the training experience depends more than anything upon the particular translations, intentions, and interventions the trainer makes. This makes it imperative for the trainer to be first of all clear about his own intentions and goals.

Training has begun to attract the participation of more psychologically disturbed persons in recent years—a higher proportion of more frustrated individuals seeking personal release or solutions.

Correspondingly, there is a larger supply of inadequately prepared persons who do training. To my knowledge, only the National Training Laboratories—Institute of Applied Behavioral Science has given systematic consideration to the training of leaders, but even its accredited trainers are not all prepared to deal with the range of expectations and pathologies currently exhibited by some participants. Some people who are inadequately prepared are suggesting to other people what they feel, how to express their feelings, and interpreting how others respond to them. Some, equally poorly prepared persons, are engaged in applying training to social action and to institutions. Recently, it has come to my attention that there are inadequately prepared trainers who lead student groups on college campuses without supervision. Several eye-witness accounts of these groups suggest that highest value is placed upon intensity of emotionality and on dramatic confrontations. Screening of participants is virtually unknown and follow-up investigation of the effects of these groups is unheard of. Their leaders are usually individuals who have participated in only one or two experiences themselves. Most disturbing of all, there is no sign that these leaders are aware of or concerned about their professional limitations. I think it must be recognized that it will be difficult to restrain poorly prepared individuals from practicing training in the absence of a clear statement of standards of training, trainer preparation, and the publication of a code of training ethics. (An antiprofessional bias is very popular just now, as we all know, and training fits nicely the image of "participative decision making.") Unfortunately, accredited and competent trainers have done little to deter the belief that training requires little preparation and is universally applicable. I do not exempt the National Training Laboratories from responsibility in this regard.

"Adequate preparation" should be spelled out. One would wish to avoid jurisdictional protectionism, although a degree in a recognized educative or therapeutic discipline is certainly one index of responsible preparation. For work with the public, trainers should have had, in addition to a recognized advanced degree in one of the "helping professions," background preparation in personality dynamics, a knowledge of psychopathology as well as preparation in group dynamics, social psychology, and sociology. They should also have had an internship and extensive supervised experience.

It should be recognized that it is difficult, if not impossible, to do effective screening in order to prevent the participation of persons for whom training is inappropriate. One reason is that it is almost impossible to prevent false assertions about one's mental status on application forms. It is also true that it is difficult to assess the precise effects of training upon a particular individual. It could be argued that short-range discomfort might be followed by long-range benefits. Probably the most important step that could be taken immediately would be the elimination of promotional literature that suggests by implication that training is, indeed, "psychotherapy," and that it can promise immediate results. Why has such a step not been taken until now? I suggest that one reason is that currently many trainers do indeed view training as a form of therapy even though they do not explicitly invite psychologically troubled applicants. They do not wish to screen out those who do seek psychotherapy. But this reluctance to exclude such persons makes it almost certain that psychologically impaired individuals will be attracted in large numbers to training as a therapy.

More serious is the fact that there is little evidence on which to base a therapeutic effectiveness claim. To me it seems indefensible that advertising for training should be as seductive as it is in offering hope for in-depth changes of personality or solutions to marital problems in the light of present inadequate evidence that such changes or solutions do occur. Greater candor is necessary about the needs that are being addressed by the newer training forms. A legitimate case could perhaps be made for the temporary alleviation of loneliness that is unfortunately so widespread in contemporary urban and industrial life, but the training experience as a palliative is neither learning about group processes nor is it profound personal change. Such candor is obviously a first requisite in face of the fact that some training brochures used in promotion literally trumpet claims of various enduring benefits. I suggest that immediate steps need to be taken to investigate these claims, to reconsider the implementation of screening procedures, set up and publicize accreditation standards, and monitor promotional methods in order to safeguard the public's interest and professional integrity.

Ethical Questions Related to the Processes of Training Groups

Being a trainer is an exciting role and function. Being looked to for leadership of one kind or another and being depended upon for guidance is a very "heady" thing as every psychotherapist knows. On the other hand, training, in its beginnings, was based on the idea that participation and involvement on the part of all the members of the group would lead to the development of a democratic society in which personal autonomy and group responsibility were important goals. The trainer had only to facilitate this evolution. Personal exertion of power and influence, overt or covert, was naturally a significant issue for study and learning in group after group. Evaluation of the trainer's influence attempts was crucial for learning about one's responses to authority. The trainer was indeed an influence, but the generally accepted commitment to objectification of his function made his behavior accessible to inquiry and even to modification. Correspondingly, experienced trainers have almost always been aware that the degree of influence they wield is disproportionately large; therefore they, themselves, tried to help the group understand the need for continual assessment of this factor. Awareness of this "transference" element has stimulated trainers in the past to emphasize group processes that would reveal its operations and effects.

However, with the advent of a more active and directing training function that includes trainer-based pressures upon participants to behave in specific ways, but without provision for monitoring of trainer practices, the "democratic" nature of the group interaction is subverted. More important is the fact that there is less possibility for participants to overtly evaluate the influences exerted upon them by the trainer. In some groups that emphasize emotional expressiveness, some trainers purposefully elicit aggressive and/or affectionate behaviors by modeling them and then by inviting imitation. Some even insist that members engage one another in physically aggressive or affectionate acts. Still others provide music to create an emotional experience. Such leadership intends to create certain emotional effects. It does so, however, without sufficient opportunity to work them through. Moreover, analytic or critical evaluation of such experiences would almost certainly be viewed as subversive of their aims.

It will be argued that participants willingly agree to these practices. The fact that the consumer seeks or agrees to these experiences does not justify them as ethically defensible or psychologically sound. It should be remembered that "the contract" is not between persons who have an equal understanding of the processes involved. It cannot be assumed that the participant really knows what he is letting himself in for. At the request of the trainer, and under pressure of group approval, some aggressive displays (e.g., slappings) or affectional displays (e.g., hugging) have occurred that some participants later came to view as indignities.

The question of group acquiescence involves a related point. A crucial element in the history of training was its stress upon genuine consensus. This emphasis was a deterrent to the domination of any single power figure or to the establishment of arbitrary group norms. Action and "decision" were painstakingly arrived at out of group interaction, consisting of increasingly candid exchanges. Influence could be exerted only under continuing group scrutiny and evaluation. Some trainers who are impelled to elicit expressiveness as a primary goal are also committed to democratic values; however, owing to their primary commitment to the significance of emotional expressiveness, they may employ their sensitivities and skills to achieving it in ways that are relatively subtle or even covert. When the participant is encouraged to experience and express strong emotions, the trainer's function in promoting these is often obscured. What is often *his* decision or initiative is presented as *group* initiative. In his recent book, Kelman (1968) has suggested that a group leader has the responsibility of making group members aware of his own operations and values. I find no fault with that suggestion; however, it is very difficult to accomplish this. It is made even more difficult, if I am correct, because some trainers may even have an interest in the group remaining *unaware* of their particular manipulations because they wish to sustain the illusion that it is the group's rather than their own personal decision that results in a particular emotional process. The intention may not be to deceive consciously. It is difficult for trainers to practice complete candor with their participants and yet to facilitate the processes of train ing for reasons I suggested above. Nevertheless, in the light of these questions, trainers should reexamine their own activities. It might be that aroused concern will lead established trainers to take the necessary steps to educate aspirants for professional status to a new sensitivity to these issues.

Learning and Experiential Focuses

There are genuine differences in point of view and in emphasis between trainers. Some regard the emotional-experiential as the primary value in training. Others uphold a more cognitive emphasis, while recognizing that a high degree of emotional engagement is a vital part of training. For their part, participants are, more often than not, so emotionally involved as to be confused about just what it is that they are doing, feeling, or thinking at a given point in time. We know that participants slide back and forth between cognitive and affective experiencing of training. The participant must partially depend upon external sources for confirmation or disconfirmation. He looks to other members, but most of all to the trainer himself, for clarification. Surely, dependency plays a huge role, but it will not be destroyed by fiat. It is the responsibility of the trainer to make as clear as he can his own activities, his own view of what is significant, and to encourage exchanges of views among participants so that all can have the possibility of differential self-definition and orientation during the training process. This would help prevent a situation where inchoate and inarticulated pressures push individual participants beyond their comprehension.

In training, as in any other society, there are pressures of majority upon minority, of the many upon the one. Scapegoating, where recognized, would be objected to as demeaning whether it occurs as a means of inducing conformity or to build self-esteem. When the focus is upon group processes, it is often brought into the open, discussed, and countered. Where, however, the emphasis is purely on personal expressiveness, the same phenomenon may be used as a pressure rather than exposed. The implicit demand for emotionality and emphasis upon nonverbal communication even makes it more difficult to identify scapegoating when it occurs in such groups.

Ethical Issues and Evaluations

Participants sometimes come to training under "threat" of evaluation. The implications of a refusal to participate by an employee, a subordinate, or a student have not been sufficiently studied. I recall one instance where an employee of a highly sensitive security agency was sent for training. His anxious, conflicted, and disturbed response to training norms of "trust" and "openness" were not only understandable but, in retrospect, predictable. True, the commitment to maintain confidentiality was honored; nevertheless, should his participation have been solicited or even permitted? Evaluation as a participant concern is unavoidable, despite protestations and reassurances to the contrary. Training of trainers should emphasize the professional's ethical responsibility in these matters, but it will not obviate these concerns. The increase in unaccredited and marginally prepared trainers must increase them. It is difficult for most people to monitor their own tendencies to gossip or inform. Especially if the trainer is also an evaluator of participants, he cannot really compartmentalize the impressions he gets of behavior in training, from other data that he has about the participants. Perhaps it would help to make everyone aware of this fact. At least the "risk" then becomes explicit from everyone's point of view.

A diminution of risk was thought to be one of the major advantages of "stranger" groups where time-limited contact was thought to encourage a degree of candor and interpersonal experiment that was nominally proscribed. Obviously, this cannot be the case in groups where participants are related, classmates, or involved in the same company or agency. It should be recognized that it is almost impossible to assure confidentiality under such circumstances or to prevent "out of school" reports. Trainers need to be especially sensitive to this in preparing other trainers. For example, where graduate students are involved in training groups and have social or other connections with one another, or with those they observe, numerous possibilities for teaching the importance of professional detachment present themselves. Trainees should learn how important it is to avoid irresponsible behavior in order to maintain the confidence of participants, how vital it is to inhibit a desire for personal contact when they have a professional role to play. Essentially, they have the same problem that faces the fledgling psychotherapist in inhibiting his own curiosity and social impulse in order to fulfill a professional function. The necessary detachment emphasized here is yet another significant and ethically relevant area that emotional expressiveness as an end in itself does not articulate. Responsibility is taught and modeled. It should be as consciously done in training as in any other helping relationship.

Posttraining Ethical Issues

A strongly positive reaction to training more frequently than not impels the gratified participant to seek further training experiences. Unfortunately, almost as frequently he seeks to do training himself. After all, it appears relatively easy. The apparent power and emotional gratifications of the trainer seem very attractive. If steps in professional preparation in becoming a trainer are not better articulated, and closely wedded to the traditional helping professions, we shall soon have vast numbers of inadequate trainers who practice their newly discovered insights on others, in the naive conviction that they have all but mastered the skills involved in group processes and application to personal and social problems.

A final issue to which I wish to call your attention is that of post-training contact with the participant. Participants are often dramatically affected by training. In some cases, trainer and group are mutually reluctant to end the group. In a recent case that came to my attention, my view is that the trainer was seduced, as it were, by the group's responsiveness to him. In turn, the participants were delighted by the trainer's continuing interest. Trainers must be aware of the powerful desire to sustain a relationship with them. Therefore, they must be clear at the outset what limits they propose for training. It is as important to be determinate about the termination point of training as about any other aspect of its conduct. Under the conditions of ambiguity and ambivalence of an "indeterminate" relationship, participants appear to be caught, as it were, midstream, uncertain as to the definition or possibilities of a relationship with this presumed expert upon whom they naturally depend for guidance and limit setting.

The questions that I have raised do not admit of a quick solution. They are ethical dilemmas. Steps to eliminate or ameliorate the grossest of them can be taken through awareness and self-monitoring. One practical step that I propose is the immediate creation of a commission by our professional organization to investigate training practices, standards of training preparation, and to recommend a code of ethics for accredited trainers. Research may help, but I doubt that it can come quickly enough to affect the increasing danger of the current and potentially still greater excesses in this area.

Sensitivity training is one of the most compelling and significant psychological experiences and vehicles for learning as well as a promising laboratory for the study of human relationships, dyadic, and group. It may be a superior device for personal and social change, even for amelioration or resolution of social conflict. However, it may also be abused or subverted into an instrument of unwarranted influence and ill-considered, even harmful, practices. The immediate attention of the profession is necessary to maintain its positive potential and correspondingly respectable standards of practice.

REFERENCE

Kelman, H. C. *A time to speak—On human values and social research?* San Francisco: Jossey-Bass, 1968.

35 / GROUP THERAPY:
LET THE BUYER BEWARE

Everett L. Shostrom

Joan was a fine scholar and teacher. She was fat and difficult, and had a grotesque limp, but true students loved her. She had made brilliant contributions to the High Minoan period, and her colleagues trembled as they waited to see what or whom she would demolish next. Joan was also pathologically sensitive about certain episodes of her adolescence. In a moment of distraction—she had been gleefully rebuked for a serious bibliographical error—Joan responded to an ad in the local underground paper; this ad promised an "encounter" group, and Joan was eager to encounter something. To her surprise she found that two of the three other participants, including the leader, were university people whom she knew. Uncharacteristically, Joan said what the hell, and plunged into those interactions she had heard about. She found herself under cruel attack by the other participants, all of them therapeutically sophisticated; they quickly located and probed into the most painful segments of her life.

Initially, Joan felt herself rather better for the experience. In the weeks that followed, however, she thought she heard allusions to her deeply classified torments, even at the most superficial of faculty gatherings. Soon she began to suspect her most valued students of noninnocent, nonprofessional slyness—a quizzical smile here, a cool "Don't you think" there, a chuckle running through the lecture hall. . . . Three weeks later, on a bright afternoon, Joan drove her

Reprinted from PSYCHOLOGY TODAY *Magazine, May, 1969. Copyright* © *Communications/Research/Machines, Inc.*

dusty and heretofore slugglish sedan into a bridge abutment, at 80 miles an hour.

Doug worked in personnel, and his corporate star was rising. His people—applicants he had recommended—were turning out very well in the jobs he had selected them for. Doug was, however, bored and uneasy about his job—he felt that his "gift" his superiors were always talking about was overvalued. Doug went to an "attack-in" organized by his church; he was encouraged to give vent to his hostilities and critical scorn, and he did. It was great fun, and Doug carried the techniques back to his job. He got into a number of violent shouting matches with applicants and superiors, and was suddenly, and violently, fired.

Mr. and Mrs. Wassail had been married 23 years; they had done a commendable job of raising their children; they maintained respect for each other; and they had intelligent friends, eclectic but solid. On the advice of one of these close and trusted friends, they went to a sensory-awareness seminar. They arrived at a spectacular estate where very quickly they and some other persons very much like them abandoned themselves to systematic depravity. Mr. and Mrs. Wassail enjoyed themselves for a while but found that they were literally unable to face each other or their children. After a few months, they separated, with a great deal of oblique bitterness.

Bill was a slender, handsome young man who had been fighting clearsightedly what he had identified—correctly, but on principle and without professional help—as homosexual panic. Bill read a newspaper ad that promised awareness and self-expansion. He signed up for sessions and was told—or rather shown—that everybody was really homosexual. Bill promptly, and with great relief, became a screaming queen. He alienated his parents and friends and found himself committed to a world in which he was by breeding, interests and insight, truly and hopelessly alien.

Carl Rogers has said that the encounter group may be the most important social invention of the century, and he is probably right. The group experience has invaded every setting—industry, the church, universities, prisons, resorts. Corporation presidents have become group members, along with students, delinquents, married couples, dropouts, criminals, nurses, educators.

The demand for group experience—whether in the form of actualization groups, as I call them, or T-Groups, Synanonlike attack-ins, sensitivity-training groups, or marathons, nude and otherwise—has grown so tremendously that there are not now enough trained psychologists, psychiatrists or social workers to meet it directly. As a result, groups organized by lay leaders have proliferated. While some of these lay groups have honestly and efficiently fulfilled their almost miraculous promises, others have been useless, stupid, dangerous, corrupt, and even fatal. I shall make it clear later that I am not arguing against lay leadership, but rather for lay leadership that has been trained in such a way that the public will be protected. What I'd like to do at this point is suggest a few practical guidelines for choosing an encounter group, and then later take up a few general why's, maybe's, and what-to-do's

Each of the four examples with which I began this article contains elements that may be taken as fairly strict no's:

1. Never respond to a newspaper ad. Groups run by trained professionals, or honestly supervised by them, are forbidden by ethical considerations to advertise directly. Modest and tasteful informational brochures are circulated among professionals in relevant disciplines, and referral by a reputable and well-informed counselor is one of the surest safeguards. Cheap mimeographed flyers promising marvels, especially erotic ones, are danger signals, as are donations or fees of less than $5.00. A good group is backed by a lot of labor and experience, which are today in very short supply

2. Never participate in a group of fewer than a half-dozen members. The necessary and valuable candor generated by an effective group cannot be dissipated, shared and examined by too small a group, and scapegoating or purely vicious ganging-up can develop. Conversely, a group with more than 16 members generally cannot effectively be monitored by anyone, however well-trained or well-assisted.

3. Never join an encounter group on impulse—as a fling, binge or surrender to the unplanned. Any important crisis in your life has been a long time in preparation and deserves reflection. If you are sanely suspicious of your grasp on reality, be doubly cautious. The intense, sometimes apocalyptic experience of the group can be most unsettling, particularly for persons who feel that they are close to what one layman calls "controlled schizophrenia." A trained person responsible for a meaningful session would not throw precariously balanced persons into a good encounter group. Nor would he allow persons who are diabolically experienced in the ways of group dynamics to form a group. If you find

yourself in a group in which everybody talks jargon, simply walk out.

4. Never participate in a group encounter with close associates, persons with whom you have professional or competitive social relations. Be worldly wise, or healthily paranoid, about this. As a corollary, never join a group that fails to make clear and insistent distinctions between the special environment of the group and the equally special environment of society. You should be told crisply, that everything occurring within the group must be considered vitally privileged communication. You should always feel that the warm, vigorous disalienation that flowers in a good group is to a certain extent designed to suggest the richness of possibilities—in terms of self-knowing and other-knowing—and does not by any means imply a rigid code of behavior. In these matters, consult your common sense—it probably is one of the worst enemies you have, but it still is an entirely internalized enemy, hence deserving of notice.

5. Never be overly impressed by beautiful or otherwise class-signaled surroundings or participants. Good group sessions can be held in ghetto classrooms, and all good sessions will include persons and life-styles with which you do not identify intimately or on a day-to-day basis. Social or intellectual homogeneity in a group usually suggests an unimaginative, exploitative hostess mentality. A good group session should, I think, eventually unfold itself to every member as a kind of externalization or dramatization of himself —himself as fawner and snob, weakling and bully, villain and victim, poet and bureaucrat, critic and nice guy—himself as a small but complex galaxy of contraries. If you have a strong feeling that, as Huck Finn said, you've "been there before," you most probably have.

6. Never stay with a group that has a behavioral ax to grind—a group that seems to insist that everybody be a Renaissance *mensch,* or a devotee of *cinema verité*—or a rightist or leftist, or a cultural, intellectual or sexual specialist. This is narrow destructive missionary zeal, or avocational education, and it has nothing to do with your self, your sweetest goals or your fullest life as a self-knowing, self-integrating human being.

7. Never participate in a group that lacks formal connection with a professional on whom you can check. Any reputable professional has a vital stake in any group he runs or in any group whose leader he has trained and continues to advise and con-

sult. Such a professional may be a psychiatrist (M.D.), a psychologist (M.A. or Ph.D. in psychology), a social worker (Mrs. W.), or a marriage counselor (Ph.D.). One of the most significant questions to ask is, *Are you, or is your professional consultant, licensed to practice in this state?* If he has a Ph.D. and is not licensed, find out why not. Most reputable professionals are members of local, usually county, professional organizations; such organizations in many instances determine who may be listed where and how in your local Yellow Pages. If you can't find your group leader or the group's adviser in the Yellow Pages, check with the professional organization to find out why. It must be said at this point that all the training and accreditation in the world will not guarantee that every man in every place will be a good, efficient, worthy or honest practitioner. Everyone knows that, but I am after all talking about rules-of-thumb and rules and thumbs will take us just so far.

Any encounter group that uses the words *psychologist, psychiatrist, psychotherapy, psychotherapist, psychology* or *therapy* in describing itself is usually subject to regulation by state laws and by the American Psychological Association, the American Psychiatric Association, or the National Association of Social Workers. In the past decade or so, however, humanistic psychology has explicitly and implicitly de-emphasized therapy, at least in the sense of curing or treating people who are, on the analogy with physical medicine, mentally sick. Humanistic psychology, from whose passionate forehead the encounter group has sprung, tends to talk about *emotional growth, fulfillment of one's potential, feeling, contact* and the participative *experiencing* of oneself and others with *honesty, awareness, freedom* and *trust*. It has dealt usually with persons who are performing within socially acceptable parameters of legality, productivity, and success. It speaks usually to those who are not sick but rather normal—normally depressed, normally dissatisfied with the quality of their lives, normally tormented by irrelevance, meaninglessness, waste, loneliness, fear and barrenness. Anyone can appropriate this humanistic vocabulary, set up shop as a lay encounter leader and evade all professional and legal regulation by omitting psychological, psychiatric and therapeutic terms from his descriptive catalogue or notice.

There are dangers in all group encounters—groups are crucibles of intense emotional and intellectual reaction, and one can never say exactly what will happen. It can be said generally, however, that well-trained people are equipped to recognize and deal with problems (and successes) before, while and after they happen, and that ill-trained or untrained people often are not. Yet training—in the sense of specialized, formally accredited education—will not guarantee that a man or woman will be a helpful or successful group leader. Indeed, such researchers as Margaret Rioch have shown that natural group leaders with almost no training can facilitate precisely the kind of ideal, joyful, alive, tender and altogether marvelous self-learning that the most highly trained leaders strive for. Since there are not enough trained professionals to go around, the problem is to get good group leaders—to develop a set of standards that will allow us to enroll good people, teach them the necessary skills, and send them out with some formal approval that will give the public a fair chance to stay out of trouble.

Such well-selected, well-trained leaders should have a title and a certificate of some sort indicating that they have met certain nationally accepted standards. They would stand in some fairly well-defined relationship to professionals and to other licensed counselors. The analogy that most quickly, and perhaps most unhappily, comes to mind is the relationship of registered nurses to physicians.

A good model for the kind of nationwide programmatic training I have in mind should be developed by such groups as the national psychological and psychiatric associations. (The California State Psychological Association is considering legislation that would permit nonlicensed persons to practice group leadership only when they are supervised by trained psychologists.) Research is badly needed to evaluate and measure competence and codify standards. In the meantime, there is a pilot program that can serve as an example at the National Center for the Exploration of the Human Potential in La Jolla, California, which sponsors a one-year course for adults who want to be encounter-group leaders. The center is advised by Abraham Maslow, Jack Gibb, Gardner Murphy, and Herbert Otto, among others.

Applicants for this training must have, among other things, a bachelor's degree. They must have some leadership experience (as a teacher, or administrator, for example), and extensive encounter group experience. They also must be evaluated by a psychologist or a psychiatrist. Then they are trained intensively and intelligently.

I'd like to propose that persons with such training call themselves facilitators and refer to their work in such a way that they distinguish themselves from certified counselors who work in institutional settings, and from licensed psychotherapists in professional practice.

The National Center program is just an example, and it appears that many similar programs are developing. I think that the public is entitled to some ready means for distinguishing a rigorously selected and coached facilitator from, for instance, a member of Esalen Association. (Anyone may become a *member* of Esalen Association by paying annual dues; this indicates no other connection with Esalen Institute.)

Encounter groups in all their forms are far too valuable—and the demand for such groups is far too clamorous and desperate—for us to let ignorance, psychosocial greed, or false prophecy tarnish them.

36 / CONFRONTATION GROUPS: HULA HOOPS?

Lawrence Beymer

Counselor educators and supervisors must come to grips with the implications and applications of group process techniques which are literally sweeping the country. It should be apparent from recent television programs, from articles in popular magazines, and from the newspapers that all kinds of activities are occurring in groups which claim to be oriented toward bringing about desirable behavior changes in the participants. The 1969 Las Vegas APGA Convention Program listed at least sixteen sessions which referred to one type of group process or another.

Twenty-five years ago the Committee on Community Interrelations of the American Jewish Congress called together a distinguished committee of social scientists to seek out the underlying causes of prejudice. Three years later the first National Training Laboratory in Group Development was conducted. From these rather recent beginnings the growth of the group movement has been phenomenal. Today many bizarre things are going on under the general heading of confrontation groups.

One commercial television station broadcasts 45-minute segments of videotaped group sessions, complete with tears, confessions, and accusations. Fourteen college students caused a furor on their campus by turning an experimental class into a nude "sensory awareness" session. (The university public affairs director said the students "apparently did not have sexual relations.") In Washington,

From COUNSELOR EDUCATION AND SUPERVISION, *1970, Vol. 9, pp. 75–86. Copyright 1969, American Personnel and Guidance Association. Reprinted with permission of author and publisher.*

D.C. one can gain admission to a psychodrama theater by walking in off the street and buying a $2.75 ticket. The *Wall Street Journal* reported that one evening the leader "deftly involved nearly all of the 35 or 40 people present." Nude marathon sessions are not uncommon, some taking place at nudist camps. Some have been video-taped. Other approaches involve dancing to rock-and-roll music and rolling about over others in the grass.

It may very well be, as Carl Rogers (1967) has suggested, that "there is no sharp dividing line between the cutting edge in psychology and the too-far-out hogwash." It is not the contention of this paper that confrontation groups are "hogwash." It is the thesis of this paper that confrontation groups, at their present state of development, have become psychology's hula hoop—a widespread fad. Unlike usual fads, this one is not necessarily harmless.

Everyone likes to be a critic, but nobody wants to be criticized. It is also quite likely that the term "constructive criticism" is the term assigned by the critic to his comments, but a term rarely applied to these comments by the one being criticized. Two varieties of non-constructive criticism of group processes can be identified. One is overkill directed at "far-out hogwash" activities such as those referred to above. It is not fair to claim that silly isolated examples represent the great bulk of group activities taking place today. One must make allowances for the distorting tendencies of the modern press, which repeatedly attempts to create the impression that an isolated incident is a random sample and an indication of the wave of the future. To flail away at these fat targets of aberrations, exaggerations, and exhibitionisms needs not be done here. It is likely that they bring more than a little embarrassment to those who are deeply involved in gaining more understanding of group phenomena, and of phenomena appearing in individuals or groups. These targets are too fat and too indefensible, and shooting at them is poor sportsmanship. The other type of unwarranted, unnecessary, and unconstructive criticism is typified by hysterical accusations that group process activities are communist threats, and akin to brain-washing (Hindman, 1957; Dieckmann, 1968).

But the criticism can be constructive, and progress is made by alternating innovation with assessment and evaluation. The attitude that proponents of group processes are somehow immune to criticism because they have good intentions or because they are experimenting must be rejected. No one wants to keep responsible professionals from experimenting with methods designed to develop more effective methods of understanding people and helping them, whether those individuals are contacted on a one-to-one basis or in groups. Advocates of group approaches are seeking and obtaining a lot of attention, they are promising much, and they are involving many. It is now time for us to check if the emperor is downtown in his underwear again. To do so is dangerous, for the gentle practitioners of the helping professions are often vicious when challenged. Question the tenets of psychoanalysis, and you will receive in return an interpretation of your basic hostility and aggression. Protest and it will be reflected as defensive. Eysenck reported that when he was compiling his data on the effects of psychotherapy many of those he contacted reacted as if asking such a question was slightly blasphemous, as if he were attempting a statistical test of the effectiveness of prayer.

Four Criticisms of Present Day Confrontation Group Practices

1. *Confrontation groups are excessively anti-intellectual.* This is evidenced in two ways: (a) the consistent rank-ordering of feeling above knowing, and (b) the implication that techniques can be learned quickly by almost anyone, making intensive and carefully-supervised training unnecessary.

This value structure which holds emotions so highly has been explained in the following manner by Huff:[1]

. . . I think there is a growing recognition of the lack of deep human relationships in people's lives. Hence, they are searching for ways of gaining such relationships. The current "fad" is to regard the group encounter as a quick answer to the question of the above-mentioned void. Whether it is or not remains an unanswered question . . . What we are seeing now is a strong reaction against a growing disregard of human feelings as manifest in our growingly mechanized society. This reaction is characterized by an anti-intellectual quality which finds expression in living experiments such as Esalen where "feeling is god" rather than thought—where sensing keenly is more valued than intellectualizing.

Dreyfus (1967) suggests that young people outwardly express a need for closeness, contact, and relatedness, but also fear such intimacy should the opportunity for it occur. He suggests that:

Manifestations of this search and conflict can be seen in the various movements which adolescents engage in: free sex, occultism, Zen, pot

[1] Personal communication to the author, 1968.—Eds.

parties, and LSD seances. . . . The extent of this feeling . . . is further reflected in the large numbers of students who participate in sensitivity training and other group therapeutic experiences where they are searching for meaning, dialogue, and a sense of community and fellowship.

He refers to a "flight into intimacy," which he defines as "an overwhelming urgency which leads to premature, hence, superficial familiarity."

Perhaps we're passing through a stage of pendulum swing which will be followed by a better balance between feeling and knowing. But at the present time, many of the publishing and practicing group encounter advocates are behaving like white-collar hippies.

This anti-intellectual perspective is most dangerous when it appears in the form of overt disregard for the necessity of careful training and supervised practice.

A licensed psychologist who is also a college professor makes the following statement in an article which advocates T-group experiences for parochial schools:

At first, it might be best if a few teachers and students had an opportunity to attend a laboratory experience before attempting to establish any program within a school or school system.

If that isn't possible, he makes the following suggestion: ". . . It is possible to bring trainers to a region or institution to conduct human relations institutes for leaders which last from one day to one month" (Harris, 1966). One would hope that nobody ever initiates an encounter group with the benefit of only one day or a few days' contact with a visiting fireman of the group process persuasion!

Even for those who do advocate trained therapists, problems arise in filling such positions. For instance, although *Time* magazine reports that "All the professionals who have participated agree that nude marathons are worth further trials, provided they are conducted by a trained leader" (*Time*, 1968). One wonders where such training is available.

Other sources are not so direct in stating their faith in the competence of almost anybody who has played the game, but the implication is usually there. This is especially dangerous when one contemplates the possible consequences to individuals within such groups. It is not unlike advocating that the techniques of hypnosis be taught to anyone who is interested, who, in turn, is thereby ready to be sent out into the world to practice his newly attained skills.

2. *Encounter group advocates seem to neglect the fact that any psychological experience can cause the participants to be better OR worse adjusted.* Carkhuff and Truax (1966), in their review of counseling literature, and Bergin (1966), in his survey of psychotherapy research findings, demonstrate conclusively that while few significant average differences are found in the outcomes between treatment and·control groups, there is a pronounced trend toward significantly greater variability in post-treatment change indices of treatment groups when compared with control groups. Interpersonal encounters can hurt or help; they can be for better or worse; they have simultaneous potential for constructive or deteriorative consequences.

You won't find much acknowledgement of this in the literature of confrontation groups. Almost routinely, accounts of encounter groups include claims of near-universal satisfaction and positive effects upon participants. Encounter group advocates seem to have adopted Hugh Hefner's "Playboy Philosophy" model, in which consenting participants interact in a simple, un-complicated, easily-managed relationship. Hefner overlooks the fact that casual sex can hurt as well as heal, and that afterwards the participants can be, and often are, less happy than they had expected to be, and be perhaps even worse off than before. The analogy holds for confrontation groups. Hard-sell encounter group advocates are like small boys who, having discovered the hammer, find that everything needs to be pounded. Does everybody stand to benefit from participation in encounter groups? If not, then what criteria should be applied? How many participants develop negative reactions? What are the symptoms? How should such situations be handled?

3. *Too many encounter group practitioners advertise one service but deliver another; they label what they do as group dynamics, but make conscious and deliberate attempts to move the groups they work with in the direction of group therapy.* This is especially ironic when it is noted that some who are doing this are the same individuals who, just a few years ago, were slashing out at operant conditioning as immoral because the consent of the individual wasn't obtained before the change process was begun.

Certainly we can differentiate between group dynamics and therapy groups, just as we can differentiate between counseling and psychotherapy and neurosis from psychosis. As Stefflre (1965) has observed,

Just as first aid may shade into the practice of medicine so counseling may shade into psychotherapy, but no one thinks that it is impossible to distinguish the application of a bandaid from brain surgery.

Goldman (1964) has offered another relevant analogy:

True, there are times around dusk, when one is uncertain about turning on the lights. . . . Do these borderline decisions mean that there is no value in differentiating between day and night?

Space limitations here prohibit a detailed comparison between training groups and therapy groups, but excellent comparisons can be found in Horwitz (1964) and Thelen (1963).

Groups provide settings for many kinds of learning, and choices are always made concerning the kinds of experiences which will be pursued and developed. Practitioners at a major West-coast university have written that:

Gradually we have moved from a strong emphasis on group variables to a relatively greater attention on individual dynamics and the unfolding of a more fully functioning personality . . . Our discussions in early training groups often dealt, at a rather superficial level, with there-and-then matters; but as time has passed there has been increasing involvement in "gut level" here-and-now events. Whereas before, much effort was devoted to working on the specific, immediate, on-the-job problems of participants, now only minor emphasis on such matters remains. Rather, much attention is centered on broader, pervasive concerns of the group members, such as their central life values and their rarely faced feelings about themselves and others. . . . For us (and no doubt, for many others) sensitivity training is no longer primarily a technique for the improvement of group functioning, the development of interpersonal skills, the intellectual discussion of human relations problems, or the more surface discussion of neurotic manifestations (Weschler, Massarik, & Tannenbaum, 1962).

It is obvious that this is not "group dynamics," as defined by one pioneer, Cartwright (1951):

. . . the forces operating in groups . . . a study of these forces, what gives rise to them, what conditions modify them, what consequences they have, etc. The practical application . . . consists of the utilization of knowledge about these forces for the achievement of some purpose.

This brings us back to a previously-mentioned problem: that of vocabulary and variables and goals and techniques. In the Alice-in-

Wonderland world of group processes today, each practitioner seems comfortable in defining and using words just as he pleases, allowing them to represent what he wants them to represent, no less, and no more.

We are not quibbling with semantics here: we are dealing with truth in packaging. We are dealing with the moral and ethical responsibilities which every professional has: to make it clear to his patrons just what kind of services he is offering. Admittedly, no individual entering counseling or therapy ever really does know what he's getting into at the beginning. But this is different from the situation in which an individual enters a training group under the implicit assumption that the focus will be upon group dynamics, and then finding that he is trapped in a therapy-type situation where group pressures are exerted to keep him there.

The group leader or trainer is chiefly responsible for determining the direction of emphasis of a group's concern and activity. As Weschler et al. (1962) have observed:

In the early life of almost any sensitivity training group . . . the members begin to react in characteristic ways to the lack of both structure and overt direction. When this occurs, the trainer can move in at least two directions. He can help the group to analyze and discuss the role of structure in effective group functioning and can assist it to find a pattern appropriate for its purposes, or he can help the members of the group to become aware of and try to understand the nature of their feelings as they have responded to the lack of structure. In our judgment, the former intervention (and subsequent ones like it) will lead to a concern with group variables; whereas the latter intervention (together with subsequent ones of like kind) will move the group in a direction of concern with individual variables.

Leaders should make it clear to their groups at the very beginning just what the course of the experience is likely to be, and what the leader's preferred goals are. It is time that those who do go in for the therapeutic approach stop sniping at those who prefer the group process perspective. I refer to the suggestions that such leaders are unable to face themselves emotionally, and are frightened of intense emotional encounters which involve expressions of hostility, anger, love, fear, etc. It is suggested that perhaps they are unable to share their own feelings with others, and are, in fact, using the defense mechanism of intellectualization. Perhaps this is true for some, but I would suspect that it is just as true that some who prefer the therapeutic model do so on highly neurotic grounds. In such an atmosphere one can work through unresolved problems. If one is somewhat personally alienated, such experiences can provide an opportunity to experience close and intense interpersonal encounters which do not exist in one's personal life.

Gertz (1967), writing in NTL's *Human Relations Training News,* takes the following position:

What criteria can we use to distinguish when a T-Group is truly a sensitivity training model as distinct from a psychotherapy model? Are there specific events in the history of the group that can determine which direction the group will take? What clues from group members and what feelings that are evoked within the trainer can serve as a signal to indicate a critical point in the life of the T-Group? I am not sure that I have all the answers to my own questions. I immediately think of such variables as focusing on here-and-now behavior, decentralizing authority, sharing responsibility for the group work with T-Group members, and continually reinforcing in one way or another the notion that the purpose of our T-Group is to take the frame of reference. What is it about our behavior that helps make this group tick? In contrast to the model of What makes you tick? I suspect that what is most needed is an explicit statement by a trainer of the underlying strategy that is used to guide the learning process in a T-Group.

A most reasonable suggestion.

4. *Confrontation group leaders are unusually reluctant to accept reasonable responsibility for the consequences of their own actions and inactions.* The responsibility for determining the course of group activity ought to carry with it some degree of responsibility for the consequences of the course of action which is chosen. Unfortunately, there appears to be almost shocking nonchalance among confrontation group advocates about the responsibility of the leader for managing the forces he sets into motion. For example, one advocate of marathon groups contends that people are capable of coping with undiluted, intense experience and do not require carefully measured exposure to therapy. This practitioner writes that:

The importance of avoiding labels is shown by the experience of a young bachelor, who was urged by myself and other group members to stop frittering away his time at the YMCA when he should be involved in the heterosexual world. By the last day of the marathon he walked like a tiger—his growth was impressive. Then I discovered that he was a former mental patient (Stoller, 1967).

Two pertinent incidents are known personally to the author. During a summer institute at a midwestern university, one participant was precipitated into psychosis by involvement in a confrontation group where the leader was skilled in removing defenses but either unable or unwilling to deal with what was exposed by this process. He rejected any personal responsibility for this tragedy. The second case involves a group leader who has lost three of his group participants to suicide during the last year or so. He is reported to have replied in answer to an inquiry that, "People do what they have to do."

In counselor education, one of the first tasks is to teach the novice not to expose the client to more pain than he can bear, not to allow sociodrama to drift into psychodrama, not to take away defense without being in a position to replace them with strengths. By the very definition of the technique, the group has many individuals, and each has unique reactions. The group leader needs to recognize that he has no more, but certainly no less responsibility than a counselor working individually with clients one at a time.

These criticisms should not be taken as blanket condemnation and rejection of group work. The majority of the typical school counselor's day is spent not with individuals, but with groups of individuals ranging from a few to a roomful—administrators, teachers, parents, and students. We can no longer justify counselor education programs which focus exclusively upon dealing with people one at a time.

No realist can be convinced that within the foreseeable future will we ever have enough competent professionals to furnish every individual in need with a psychological adjustment tutor in the form of a counselor. We must seek ways and devise methods to multiply our influence in order to reach more people more effectively than we are doing now. People *can* learn and *can* come to modify their behavior as a result of common experiences with others in group settings.

How Does a Promising Idea Become Distorted?

How does an idea like group dynamics become so diverse, so complicated, and so burdened by extreme modifications? Perhaps it will be easier for us to salvage the sound and useful aspects of group work if we consider the present confusing state of the art as merely an early developmental stage of any new and revolutionary idea.

Every new opinion, at the beginning, is a minority of one. As it becomes known, the number of sympathetic supporters grows. And then a curious phenomenon takes place: Individuals on the periphery of the idea, who possess only partial and/or superficial knowledge and understanding, rush in like jackals and seize whatever parts of the idea they find most palatable and most useful for their purposes. This happened to Jesus Christ, to Freud, to Darwin, to John Dewey, to Carl Rogers, to Sartre, to A. S. Neill, and to many others. According to the *New York Times* (de Gramont, 1968), it is happening now to Claude Levi-Strauss, a French ethnologist who has spent over 30 years studying the behavior of North and South American Indian tribes. He calls the method he uses to study the social organization of these tribes "structuralism." Now, to his horror, he finds his terminology and methodology being applied indiscriminately to areas for which he never intended them, including political science, art, and poetry. The author of the *Times* article on Levi-Strauss and structuralism makes this pertinent observation:

There is an endemic French illness in which the works of serious thinkers mysteriously spread beyond the small circle of initiates for whom they are intended and become the object of a cult. The thinker is afflicted with disciples he never wanted, preaching a gospel he never taught. He is hailed by worshippers who never read a line of his work. He spends his time denying the paternity of deformed offspring bearing his name. If the movement persists, he must finally imitate Marx, who denied being a Marxist.

Marx is not the only thinker who found it necessary to make statements in order to try to correct what is perceived to be using names and ideas in vain. John Dewey wrote *Experience and Education* in an attempt to correct exaggerated distortions of his ideas on the proper nature of education and schooling. Carl Rogers has stated repeatedly that his methods are not "non-directive." A. S. Neill wrote *Summerhill,* and a few years later felt it necessary to publicly disassociate himself from all American private schools using its names and claiming his methods. In 1966 he published a paperback book titled *Freedom—Not License!* in order to clarify what he did advocate in *Summerhill* and what he did not advocate in *Summerhill.*

Clearly we stand in need of such a reappraisal of group processes today, but it is difficult to make a specific request for clarification and revision because no single individual or small number of individuals is responsible for these ideas. But somehow this pruning process must occur. The areas which need clarification are numerous.

Eight Recommendations for Future Practice

1. *Let's move toward some standardization of terminology and vocabulary.* Just what are the differences and similarities between "encounter groups," "confrontation groups," "training groups," "sensitivity groups," and "psychodrama"? Can we not agree upon such variables as goals, techniques, role of the leader, role of participants, etc.? If it is found that much overlapping exists, then let that become clear, along with the fact that undefined aspects remain. Communication is difficult under ideal circumstances, but the present state of the literature of group work is a semantic disaster area. If it becomes impossible to agree upon such definitions, then let every writer and advocate present his own definitions every time he writes for others, with understanding as his goal.

2. *Let us bring some semblance of balance into the basic anti-intellectualism of group work by first making it very clear that this is no business for well-intentioned amateurs.* We must emphasize that a competent group leader must have understanding that ranges beyond techniques to the possible consequences of using techniques. Potential leaders must understand from the beginning that these understandings cannot be attained quickly or easily, and that if knowing without feeling is unacceptable, then feeling without knowing is intolerable. If the techniques of hypnotism were being taught and advocated with the same passion as group therapy techniques, we would have a massive and justifiable negative reaction.

The intellectual credentials of the movement would be greatly strengthened if some progress would be undertaken to build a model of the technique, if not a full-blown theory. Many would be interested in seeing how an individual is supposed to become more sensitive as a result of a group experience in which he has been attacked and has attacked others, and what merit is supposed to come out of being "torn apart," or of losing self-respect or the respect of others.

3. *Since such experiences can have negative as well as positive consequences, let us see an increased interest in screening participants, in the study of those who drop out, and in follow-up of those who*

seem to have been harmed by the experience. It would also be refreshing to hear more qualified claims for outcomes from those rabid enthusiasts who are now so gushingly enthusiastic about any and all activities which take place in groups.

4. *Let us insist upon complete, accurate, and honest labeling of group activities.* We should insist that each leader make it very clear to potential participants his perception of the nature of the experience, and what is likely to happen. We must put an end to the psychological seduction of participants. We should insist that whenever an individual finds the climate of the group unsatisfactory, he should be allowed to withdraw without penalty. To do otherwise is to ask the group to assume responsibilities the leader will not assume, even though he is better prepared to bear them. To do otherwise is likely to be interpreted as holding back until someone else takes the first steps, of holding back until one is able to take the role he prefers.

5. *Let us make it very clear to our colleagues who function as group leaders that they cannot dismiss their professional responsibility when opening Pandora's Box, and that they must conduct themselves accordingly.* If a group leader does not know what he is doing and cannot predict with some reasonable degree of confidence what will occur as a result of some action on his part, then he should not do that act. Group participants should have an opportunity to request and obtain individual counseling concurrent with their group experience.

6. *Perhaps instead of attempting to construct a brand-new behavioral science area we might take more time to learn and apply those we already have.* The area of sociology contains an abundant supply of theories, techniques, and models which counseling has barely noticed. And sociologists have been working with groups for years.

7. *In our quest for more knowledge about groups, let us make it very clear that at the present time our efforts are suitable only for consenting adults who have volunteered themselves.* We must not allow the impression to develop that we are training school counselors in techniques which they are to supply in schools with young people. If our counselors were adequately trained, if the schools understood these techniques and requested them, and if the needs

of the so-called "normal" students were being met, there might be some justification. But not now.

8. *Finally, let us heed the advice of Kagan, who suggested that we focus less upon techniques and more upon the outcomes we are striving to attain.* Every helping person has, in his mind's eye, some conception of goals for those with whom he is working. Perhaps we should have more debate on destinations before we spend too much time arguing about methods of traveling.

As counselor educators, we need to make the same who-what-where-when-why decisions about group process activities as we do about all other aspects of counselor education curricula. We need to make individual, institutional, and profession-wide decisions as to the proper and defensible role that such activities have in our counselor preparation programs. It is hoped that this article will serve as a stimulus to such activities.

REFERENCES

A conversation with Carl Rogers, the father of Rogerian therapy. *Psychology Today*, December 1967, *19–21*, 62–66.

Bergin, A. E. Some implications of psychotherapy research for therapeutic practice. *Journal of Abnormal Psychology*, 1966, *71* (9), 235–246.

Carkhuff, R. R., & Truax, C. B. Toward explaining success and failure in interpersonal learning experiences. *Personnel and Guidance Journal*, March 1966, *45*, 723–728.

Cartwright, D. Achieving change in people: Some applications of group dynamics theory. *Human Relations*, November 1951, *4*, 381–392.

de Gramont, S. There are no superior societies. *New York Times Magazine*, January 28, 1968, 28–40.

Dieckmann, E. Sensitivity training—exposed and opposed. *American Mercury*, Spring 1968, *104* (488), 7–12.

Dreyfus, E. A. The search for intimacy. *Adolescence*, Spring 1967, *2* (5), 25–40.

Gertz, B. Trainer role versus therapist role. *Human Relations Training News*, 1967, *2* (3), 6–7.

Goldman, L. Another log. *American Psychologist*, June 1964, *19*, 418–419.

Harris, P. R. Human relations training in Christian education. *Catholic School Journal*, March 1966, *66* (3), 37–39.

Hindman, J. A leftist trap. *American Mercury,* August 1957, *85* (403), 29–36.

Horwitz, L. Transference in training groups and therapy groups. *International Journal of Group Psychotherapy,* April 1964, *14,* 202–211.

Psychodrama therapy: Group sessions blend fiction with reality. *The Wall Street Journal,* August 28, 1967, 1.

Steffire, B. *Theories of counseling.* New York: McGraw-Hill, 1965.

Stoller, F. The long weekend. *Psychology Today,* December 1967, *1,* 28–33.

Thelen, H. A. Purpose and process in groups: Editorial. *Educational Leadership,* December 1963, *21* (3).

Time, February 23, 1968, 68.

Weschler, F. M., & Tannenbaum, R. The self in process: A sensitivity training emphasis. *Issues in Training,* National Education Association, 1962. Selected reading series 5, edited by Weschler and Scheon.

37 / PROFESSIONAL ISSUES
IN GROUP WORK [1]

G. M. Gazda, J. A. Duncan, and P. J. Sisson

Whenever interest and practice in a particular treatment mode
exceeds a theoretically based rationale and research support, a
backlash against the mode or movement can be predicted. Perhaps
because the time was right—i.e., there was a gradual but perceptible
alienation among such groups as the young and old, black and
white, rich and poor, and various others—the 1960's saw an explosion of interest in and application of small group procedures as
a mode of treatment and training in interpersonal relations. By
the end of the 1960's the backlash had already begun to set in.
With man's experiencing alienation and seeking more intimacy
with his fellow man, the small group appeared to offer the ideal
medium through which he could achieve this closeness. In addition
to the demand for intimate, small group encounters, many individuals assumed group leadership roles for which they were un-
prepared by a sound theoretical foundation, research, and experience.

Many practitioners consider intimacy through encountering others to be a key ingredient of psychotherapy. Like any potent medicine, it can help or harm the recipient. Unfortunately, many group

[1] The topic of this article has been dealt with in Gazda's "Ethics and Professional
Issues," Chapter 8 of *Group Counseling: A Developmental Approach* (Boston:
Allyn and Bacon, 1971).—Eds.

From PERSONNEL AND GUIDANCE JOURNAL, *April 1971, Vol. 49, pp. 637–643. Copyright 1971, American Personnel and Guidance Association. Reprinted with permission of authors and publisher.*

workers view the achievement of intimacy or honesty with oneself and others as *the* goal, and they have failed to realize that the *method* of achieving it must somehow be relevant to everyday living if there is to be a transfer of learning from the laboratory group to "real" life. When these fundamental facts were obscured, along with the fact that durable intimacy and honesty is not achieved without a significant amount of empirical testing, many group leaders found that they were providing regular kicks for group bums, similar to those provided by drugs for drug addicts and alcohol for alcoholics. In effect, they were providing an opportunity to escape from reality rather than a means of preparing one to face and deal with reality. Also, the neurotic need of many leaders to view themselves as significant helpers of others often made it impossible for them to be objective about whose needs were actually being met.

Over 10 years ago, J. L. and Z. T. Moreno (1960) recognized these dangers facing the group movement and recommended a set of professional standards which would be sufficiently broad in scope to include both medical and nonmedical content and expertise. And again in 1962, J. L. Moreno stated that "two great problems are waiting for a solution: (1) the definition of professional standards of performance and skill and (2) a code of professional ethics" (1962a, pp. 263–264). Also in 1962, J. L. Moreno wrote a "Code of Ethics for Group Psychotherapy and Psychodrama" (1962b).

Since the general public has begun to attack many group practices, the various professional associations whose membership engage in group procedures as both treatment and training have begun to study the accusations brought against them. The American Personnel and Guidance Association, the American Psychological Association, the American Psychiatric Association, the National Training Laboratory Institute, among others, have responded by appointing various commissions, task forces, and ad hoc committees to investigate the problems of group practices and make recommendations for remediating them.

As concerned group practitioners, my colleagues and I were interested in surveying members of an APGA Interest Group on Group Procedures regarding the extent of problems of ethical practice in group work, according to their perceptions, and also to investigate other related problems. We developed a questionnaire, taking into account some points that Merle Ohlsen, then president of APGA, considered relevant. This article contains a summary of our findings from the survey and our interpretations of the data[2] as well as some general recommendations.

In the fall of 1969 the questionnaire was sent to 1,000 members of the APGA Interest Group, and 164 people, or approximately 16 percent, returned usable questionnaires. This small percentage return is consistent with the findings of Golann (1969) which shows an average of 15 percent return of questionnaires requesting reports of actual incidents involving potential unethical practice or behavior.

Violations of Ethical Behavior

The *basic* purpose of the questionnaire was to attempt to establish the extent of unethical practice/behavior in the broad field of group work. Each respondent was asked to report any violation of this nature that he had witnessed or had heard about from reliable sources.

There were, however, several additional purposes for the questionnaire. First, we attempted to obtain information about the respondents so that they could be adequately described. Secondly, we asked the respondents whether or not one should try to differentiate among group procedures, i.e., group guidance, group counseling, group psychotherapy, T-groups, sensitivity groups, and encounter groups. Thirdly, we asked them to describe the purpose of each of these six group procedures and the persons served most appropriately by them. And they were also asked to specify the training or education required for the leader of each procedure. We also included several other miscellaneous questions.

NATURE OF RESPONDENTS

The typical respondent was a 42-year-old male with a doctoral degree who worked in a university setting. He was most likely a member of APGA and was not extensively trained in group work. (In this age of group work, few people are *extensively* trained.)

---

[2] Space did not permit the inclusion of tables that summarized the questionnaire data. These tables may be obtained from the senior author.

Illustrative Reported Violations

Of the 164 respondents, there were only 20 reported violations of ethical practice or behavior. The following brief descriptions are illustrative of the types reported:

1. A university professor who teaches introductory counseling courses was conducting encounter groups which students in these courses were required to attend. Several became upset but felt they had no recourse.

2. A group leader was reported to be encouraging the use of drugs by participants.

3. Nude encounter groups with sexual experimentations were held for beginning teachers in a particular school system.

4. Under the pretense of a group marathon, a group leader permitted participants to be inflicted with abuse, which created a situation resulting in psychotic decompensation of a participant.

5. Sensitivity training involving encounter experiences were conducted without safeguards for support or follow-up.

6. A medical doctor (general practitioner) untrained in group work was reported to be serving as a psychologist-hypnotist doing family group therapy.

Without a careful investigation of the incidents reported, there is no way, of course, to be sure that these 6 examples or the 14 others all represent unethical practice or behavior. Nevertheless, several *appear* to represent violations of ethics.

Twenty reported incidents from 164 respondents do not appear to be a large number of violations, but it is not so much the number of violations as it is the harm done to the participants as well as the damage done to the helping professions as a result of the "bad press." At the time of this writing, in 1970, the backlash against the group movement appears to be gaining momentum to the point that practitioners have been reluctant in certain areas to speak of doing sensitivity training or basic encounter group work. Paradoxically, however, there are more people seeking these kinds of small group encounters. The college student population and young and middle-aged adults constitute the bulk of group participants in growth centers, and most of these individuals come from the middle and upper classes (American Psychiatric Association, 1970).

GROUP PROCEDURES

Since the data obtained for this section of the questionnaire essentially support the position taken by Kirby, Mahler, Gordon and Liberman, and Eddy and Lubin—all authors in this issue[3]—and since space required omitting some of the questionnaire findings, this section has been cut from the report. However, the results may be obtained from the senior author upon request.

PROFESSIONAL PREPARATION

The question asked in this area was: "What are the essential professional preparation requirements for practicing group guidance, group counseling, group psychotherapy, T-groups, sensitivity groups, and encounter groups?" Insofar as highest academic-degree level of education is concerned, group psychotherapy was assigned the greatest frequency at the doctoral level (Ph.D.'s and M.D.'s); group guidance appears to have the lowest frequency of doctoral-level training recommended, and group counseling the next lowest. T-groups, sensitivity groups, and encounter groups were about equal in the emphasis of doctoral-level and post-master's training recommended, and they ranked next to group psychotherapy. The recommendations of doctoral-level and post-master's training for these groups could, of course, be a reaction to the recent criticism—perhaps an overreaction.

Aside from degree-level training recommended, the emphasis on internships and supervised practice or practicum experience requires some comment. Once again group psychotherapy was singled out as the one group procedure, of the six investigated, for which recommended internship and practicum experiences combined ranked first; group guidance was the group procedure for which they ranked last. There was little difference among the remaining four groups in terms of the rankings of the recommendations of supervised experience or practicum. Experience and practice combined ranked among the top recommendations for the professional preparation of group leaders in these four areas. The essential similarity of the training recommended for group counseling, T, sensitivity, and encounter group leaders as well as the high degree of similarity in perceived purpose and clientele best served suggest

[3] The issue referred to here is the April 1971 issue of the *Personnel and Guidance Journal*. This special issue of the *Journal* carried the subtitle "Groups in Guidance" and was devoted entirely to the "group scene."—Eds.

the need for clarifying the unique contributions made by these group leaders.

GUIDELINES FOR DEFINING ETHICAL BEHAVIOR OR PRACTICE

When asked to "define ethical behavior/practice for those who serve as leaders for the types of groups cited (guidance, counseling, psychotherapy, sensitivity, T, and encounter) by citing or listing your guidelines," the largest number (40) of those responding chose to focus *only* on the client's or group member's welfare. However, 21 additional respondents listed guidelines which focused on the group member's welfare through the personal and professional qualifications of the group leader. A total of 26 responses was devoted to the description of professional and personal qualities which the leader should possess to provide group leadership which is "ethical."

There were very few responses which focused on the combined leadership qualities and client needs. This significant omission cannot be ignored. Perhaps it is only illustrative of the overall problem —that too little consideration has been given to the problem of defining ethical behavior for group workers. This hypothesis appears to receive additional support from the fact that 62 questionnaire respondents failed to respond to this item, suggesting their unpreparedness or their unwillingness to attempt such an endeavor via the questionnaire medium.

POLICING GROUP PRACTITIONERS

Each respondent was asked to reply to the question, "Who is responsible for punishing those whose practices and/or behavior in group procedures is unethical?" Two distinct statistics evolved. First, almost all the respondents expressed their opinion that some kind of professional organization should punish persons for their violations. Secondly, approximately one-half of the questionnaire respondents did not reply to this question. This phenomenon may indicate that a large number of group practitioners have not decided how the field should be policed. This observation is further strengthened by the responses to another questionnaire item: "Is new legislation needed to govern practitioners of group work? If 'Yes,' what type?"

The majority of respondents answered "No" to this question (76 answered "No," while 55 answered "Yes," and 33 did not respond). Of those who answered "Yes," 31 listed the type of new legislation needed. Licensing and certification, respectively, were each recommended by seven respondents. National and state laws was a recommendation given by six, professional organizations was a recommendation by five, and miscellaneous recommendations were given by six others. There is obviously no clear directive in these recommendations for new legislation to govern practitioners of group work.

A related question illuminates the issue a little further. In reply to the question, "What is your view for rectifying problems facing those practicing in the group procedures areas?," the most frequent recommendation appears to include more and better training programs for group practitioners. Also high on the list was a recommendation to establish some type of certifying or accrediting agency that would be able to provide a list of certified group practitioners. A third area ranking high in the recommendations was informing the public of pros and cons of various group procedures.

A NEW DIVISION?

A final question concerned with professionalization within the field of group work was asked: "Would you affiliate with a new division of the American Personnel and Guidance Association or the American Psychological Association if it were developed for professionals active in various types of group work?" There were 94 "Yes" responses for affiliation with APGA and 38 "No" responses. (This finding is the reverse of a similar poll taken by Gazda, Duncan, & Meadows, 1967, five years earlier.) Seventy-eight said "Yes," and 44 said "No" regarding their willingness to affiliate with APA. Thirty-six persons did not respond to the question, and some showed a desire to join a new division of one or both professional groups.

Recommendations

It would be ideal if associations such as APA, APGA, the NTL Institute, the American Group Psychotherapy Association, the American Society of Group Psychotherapy and Psychodrama, and the American Psychiatric Association could send representatives to a national conference for the purpose of reaching some consensus on definitions of group practices, on subsequent setting of goals, training or competencies required, and clientele to be served by each one, and on similar criteria which would lead to some mutual understandings among professionals of related disciplines and would provide some guidelines for practitioners. If this kind of national conclave is not possible, each of the professional associations whose membership includes practitioners of group procedures should define these practices and set up standards and ethics for group practitioners within their own membership. Until such time as these standards and code of ethics can be developed on a multi-disciplinary level, each professional association is obligated to provide interim guidelines for its membership. If necessary—and certain unique features of group treatment or practice suggest that it is—current standards and ethical codes should be revised to incorporate those aspects particularly relevant to group procedures. Some of the features which are unique to group practices and therefore should receive special attention in any set of standards or code of ethics include the following:

1. Perhaps the most unique feature of group work is the fact that the group includes the clients or members who themselves serve as co-therapists, co-trainers, co-helpers, etc., but who often are not professionals and are not guided by a professional code of ethics. This creates unique problems in dealing with confidentiality and privileged communication.

2. Working in a helping relationship with several individuals simultaneously requires, in our estimation, a special kind of security in the leader, a special understanding of small group processes, and a high level of sensitivity necessary to maintain some type of direction or control which can be used for the benefit of each individual in the group. Thus, standards for leaders must be set for the different levels of group work.

3. Nonverbal techniques of many varieties have been developed for use in group settings, yet little research evidence is available to validate their use or to tell us when they may be most appropriately employed. Some direction must be given to protect the group participant from some potentially harmful nonverbal methods and physical contacts, e.g., Attack Therapy.

4. Special consideration must be given to methods of grouping individuals for training and treatment. For example, the degree of risk involved in working with close associates such as superiors and subordinates may preclude the potential benefits of such a group if adequate safeguards are not established.

5. On a one-to-one basis, the professional helper has fewer problems of deciding when his assistance should terminate; however,

members in group training or treatment progress at different rates. Therefore, when closed groups are set up, the professional helper or trainer must assume responsibility for those group members who need further assistance even though a termination date has been previously agreed upon. Even when the professional helper or leader can safely terminate the group at a predetermined date, there is frequently a need for follow-up contacts of group participants individually or as a group. Frequently this responsibility has not been assumed by the trainer or leader. The ethical responsibilities here must be clarified.

6. Further examination needs to be done in the area of *required* group counseling, group therapy, encounter group, and related group experiences for students or trainees. Especially questionable is the practice of placing students or trainees with classmates in a group led by the instructor for that course.

7. The group is potentially capable of exerting extreme pressures on a given member or the leader to conform to its norm. This facet of a group is potentially helpful and equally as potentially harmful. Group leaders must be capable of resisting group pressures for the welfare and protection of the individuality of a given participant. The use of the group norm as a pressure tactic must be clarified since it affects the autonomy of a given group member.

The NTL Institute has published *Standards for the Use of Laboratory Method* (1969) which provides general guidelines for its trainers. Although it represents a commendable first step, the standards used should be more specific than a simple endorsement of *Ethical Standards of Psychologists* as guidelines for NTL members. The American Psychiatric Association (1970) task force report also draws some implications for psychiatrists regarding encounter groups. Hurewitz (1970) discusses ethical considerations in leading therapeutic and quasi-therapeutic groups, and Lakin (1969) raises several ethical issues in the area of sensitivity training. These groups and individuals have discussed many of the issues which we have also highlighted in the foregoing seven points. We believe that these points—as well as many others that could probably be discussed—represent some of the issues to which NTL, APA, APGA as well as other professional associations must soon address themselves. We hope that this report of the questionnaire survey and the issues raised will result in some positive action.

REFERENCES

American Psychiatric Association. *Task force report 1: Encounter groups and psychiatry.* Washington, D.C.: American Psychiatric Association, 1970.

Gazda, G. M., Duncan, J. A., & Meadows, M. E. Group counseling and group procedures—Report of a survey. *Counselor Education and Supervision,* 1967, *6,* 305–310.

Golann, S. E. Emerging areas of ethical concern. *American Psychologist,* 1969, *24,* 454–459.

Hurewitz, P. Ethical considerations in leading therapeutic and quasi-therapeutic groups: Encounter and sensitivity groups. *Group Psychotherapy and Psychodrama,* 1970, *23,* 17–20.

Lakin, M. Some ethical issues in sensitivity training. *American Psychologist,* 1969, *24,* 923–928.

Moreno, J. L. Code of ethics for group psychotherapy and psychodrama. *Psychodrama and Group Psychotherapy Monographs,* No. 31. Beacon, N.Y.: Beacon House, 1962. (a)

Moreno, J. L. Common ground for all group psychotherapists: What is a group psychotherapist? *Group Psychotherapy,* 1962, *15,* 263–264. (b)

Moreno, J. L., & Moreno, Z. T. An objective analysis of the group psychotherapy movement. *Group Psychotherapy,* 1960, *13,* 233–237.

National Training Laboratory Institute. *Standards for the use of laboratory method.* Washington, D.C.: National Training Laboratories, 1969.

38 / INNOVATIVE GROUP TECHNIQUES: HANDLE WITH CARE

Edward A. Dreyfus and Elva Kremenliev

Innovative approaches to group process are as volatile as they are effective; their enormous potential for opening people up to new growth is accompanied by the ominous possibility of opening them up to new disaster. While T-groups—or encounter groups, sensitivity groups, or whatever they may be called—do constitute an inspiring break in the conservatism of counseling and psychotherapeutic attacks on personal problems, they can become lethal weapons in the hands of self-proclaimed facilitators or inexperienced professionals. One sensitivity session and the most enraptured poring over such popular "how-to" books as those by Schutz (1967) and Gunther (1968) do not prepare anyone to lead a group.

Several psychologists (Bindrim, 1969; Perls, 1969; Shostrom, 1969) have commented on their concerns regarding the group therapy phenomenon and the fad-like quality of the movement currently sweeping the U.S. Their concern has been primarily with the effects groups have on the participants when in the hands of inexperienced group leaders. Perls (1969), for instance, says of the group movement:

. . . we are now entering a new and more dangerous phase. We are entering the phase of turner-oners; turn on to instant cure, instant joy, instant sensory awareness. We are entering the phase of the quacks and the con-men, who think if you get some breakthrough, you are cured—

From PERSONNEL AND GUIDANCE JOURNAL, *1970, Vol. 49, pp. 279–283. Copyright 1970, American Personnel and Guidance Association. Reprinted with permission of authors and publisher.*

disregarding any growth requirements, disregarding any of the real potential. . . . (p. 1)

Workshops and Demonstrations

The impact that a "workshop on group encounter" or an "encounter group demonstration" has on professionals (educators, psychologists, social workers, etc.) who participate has received less attention, although this part of the problem is more accessible to solution than is the case with the lay participant. Furthermore, in workshops or demonstrations in which audience involvement is required or urged with the thrust of group pressure, the effects that a single experience has on participants are multiplied when the audience is made up of potential group leaders. In these situations particularly is when our professional duty must be to exercise extreme caution.

We live in a society that fosters alienation, anomie, disenfranchisement, dissociation, loneliness, and schizoid coolness (May, 1969). People wish for and fear intimacy (Dreyfus, 1967). The proponents of humanistic approaches to counseling and psychotherapy (Gunther, 1968; Maslow, 1967; Otto, 1966; Perls, 1969; Rogers, 1967; and Shutz, 1967, to name a few) have developed a wide variety of powerful techniques and methods for facilitating human growth, self-discovery, and interpersonal relatedness. The effectiveness of these approaches in cutting through resistances, breaking down defenses, releasing creative forces, and promoting the healing process has been amply demonstrated.

The methods themselves seem innocuous, reminiscent of games we played as children; in and of themselves these games can be fun. Most of them are rather simple: getting to know a person by looking him in the eyes without words, holding hands with a sharing of the feelings involved, touching people and things while blindfolded, falling backwards into a group, cradling one person in the arms of all those around him, and inundating all the senses by simultaneously stimulating them (Gunther, 1968; Shutz, 1967). These methods have potent effects, however, when we consider the context of the alienating society in which we live and when we know the needs of the people who seek help in psychologists' offices and in the newly developing "growth centers" such as Esalen Institute, Kairos, and Topanga Center for Human Development. Where the methods are applied effectively people will certainly get stirred up, frightened, and turned on, and they may be filled with feelings and needs difficult to integrate into their daily lives. The responsibility for contending with such effects extends not only to the patients and clients of those in the helping professions but to workshop participants as well. Any technique as powerful as the group phenomenon must be handled with care.

When we invite someone to relinquish repressed feelings, we must be willing to stay with him as he tries to master his new awareness. The leader who "packs up his bag of tricks and splits" may, as Truax and Carkhuff (1967) have pointed out, be offering an experience which is psychonoxious rather than psychotherapeutic. Willy-nilly use of new methods is like morphine in the hands of an adolescent: A quick turn-on now may lead to later disaster. The more active, dynamic, innovative interventions may be more powerful than traditional methods, but they may also be proportionately more noxious. We must therefore set up greater precautions against misuse. For openers, I suggest that participants in workshops should have the opportunity for a follow-up meeting with the demonstrator, who can then spot any potential ill effects of the experience.

The Structure of Workshops

At our professional conventions, the main purposes of the workshop should be to inform colleagues of new approaches and to obtain critical appraisal of methods by soliciting feedback. As leaders, we ought to eschew proselytizing or bandwagon appeals. Further, and more importantly, we must apprise the audience of the potential dangers of such volatile methodology, so that viewers do not go off to use indiscriminately methods they only partially understand, as has sometimes happened. The innovators themselves have been the first to caution that their methods are only as effective as the facilitator who uses them.

However, many practitioners who give demonstrations of their approaches get caught up in the beauty of the experience and want to share it with others on a large scale, sometimes with a loss of professional responsibility. To become apostles of humanness is not bad in and of itself; however, many people aren't ready for such an experience. Both practitioner and client alike have to be slowly introduced to group methods, learning to integrate the potent *affect* and energy which may be released.

One simple first step might be to limit the participants in a workshop or demonstration to a number with whom the facilitator can establish direct contact. When as many as 300 people are sitting on the floor "experiencing," the whole scene is reminiscent of Holy Roller revival meetings instead of a close, person-to-person interaction session.

Just as television demonstrations of hypnosis have been forbidden because of the danger of viewers being hypnotized long-distance, so do large-scale demonstrations of these potent methods cry out for stricter professional guidelines. Even the micro-lab method with non-participating audiences can be fraught with danger. Nor is it safer to assume that professionals are immune: Can we say that no professional counselors are hung up on problems of intimacy? Or that all such professionals, at all times, possess sufficient ego strength to withstand the bombardment of explosive new techniques? Moreover, demonstrations draw a certain percentage of professional groupers seeking free therapy, a sexual experience, or a quick emotional turn-on. They believe (and evidence bears them out) that the "hold-me, feel-me, touch-me" people are eminently seducible. Even where sexual freedom may be a desirable goal, professionals must question the patterns of certain people that keep repeating themselves.

Many people who pick up some of these methods at demonstrations merely emulate those others who use and are successful with the new approaches. The copiers don't have the faintest idea of the underlying theoretical rationale and don't know how to deal with the variety of possible outcomes. Those who are disseminating these methods have a responsibility to suggest adequate safeguards and attempt to dissuade those who are less skilled from using them without supervision. Many students, lay people, and even professionals who are trying these methods are unable or unwilling to cope with the effects they instigate.

Furthermore, in this era of group encounters, many professionals feel pressured to utilize these "in" approaches even when they themselves do not feel wholly competent with them. Thus many unqualified persons pick up a bag of techniques and interpersonal games and apply them indiscriminately to all comers. Very few cautions are offered to workshop participants, and many persons use techniques to hide behind rather than using them to engage clients in real relationships (Dreyfus, 1968). By attending these workshops, and even some professional encounter groups, people can learn a new language behind which to hide new modes of inauthentic behavior. That is, they learn to sound like genuine *human* beings (Dreyfus & Mackler, 1964) and to look like authenticating self-actualizers; but these overt manifestations merely serve to cover the underlying fear of closeness, warmth, and intimacy. Group behavior can become a new form of phoniness; it looks and sounds real but lacks genuineness, depth, and commitment.

A Suggested Model

A model for workshops and demonstrations to follow might help avoid some of their more blatant misuses:

1. Where possible, demonstrations should be limited in size to a number of people which would permit the leader to keep in contact with each participant.
2. It should be remembered that demonstrations are for the purpose of education and not for treatment or proselytizing.
3. Workshops should be limited to persons who can best profit from the intended and expressed purpose of the workshop.
4. There should be provision for follow-up on each of the workshop participants and on all those who partake of invited or impromptu audience participation groups.
5. For large-scale demonstrations with potentially volatile innovations, we suggest that professional actors be used in lieu of audience participation. Or skilled professional leaders, fully conversant with the methods, might offer a microlab in which they role-play typical participant response. In this way the methods can be studied, questioned, and vicariously experienced as in good theater.

Such a format may deter the voyeur, the exhibitionist, the seeker of the instant turn-on, and the psychopath from participating since these types could not remain invisible. The ensuing discussion of methods would give the audience the opportunity to question and integrate the entire sequence and subsequently reflect on it. The entertainment effects of an audience participation, Holy Roller-type meeting would be avoided, and critical appraisal of the methods permitted. The audience would discover the rationale for the method and realize that the method is not as easy to apply as it first might seem.

Participatory experience without cognitive integration permits neither retention nor generalization. It is difficult if not impossible for participants in a group experience to learn what went on without some assistance in the cognitive process. Participants become so wrapped up in their own experiencing that concentration on group process and method is at best minimal. Only through the cognitive integration occurring through dialogue can learning occur. *Both* the experiential *and* the cognitive integration are necessary for effective learning.

One of the problems in large-scale demonstrations, in addition to the absence of control of the effects, is the enormous pressure from the group for all to participate. It is possible to whip a group into a frenzy, the effects of which continue for some time afterward. If they are positive effects, and they often are, all is well and good; if they are negative effects, that's something else. Our concern must be not with the relative proportion of positive to negative effects, but only with the negative, however limited. People who visit a demonstration enter in good faith; we have a responsibility to them. It does not take much to move from an intimate experience to a frenetic holocaust when dealing with large numbers of people. More stringent safeguards taken with workshop and demonstration participants than with regular group sessions seem merely a matter of professional responsibility—a requirement to police ourselves. Individuals in the helping professions are going to go back out into the world trying these methods, often without sufficient information and/or experience. Furthermore, innovators must accept a responsibility not only to the participants in any given demonstration but also to the public who eagerly pick up an apparently simple innovation. When techniques turn into parlor games, the phenomenon is out of control. Our present concern should be first for containment and next for accelerated—but responsible—and supervised training of leaders.

REFERENCES

Bindrim, P. Nudity as a quick grab for intimacy in group therapy. *Psychology Today*, 1969, *3*, 24–29.

Dreyfus, E. A. The search for intimacy. *Adolescence*, 1967, *2* (5), 25–40.

Dreyfus, E. A. Humanness and psychotherapy: A confirmation. *Journal of Individual Psychology*, 1968, *24* (1), 82–85.

Dreyfus, E. A., & Mackler, B. On being human. *Journal of Existentialism*, 1964, *17*, 67–76.

Gunther, B. *Sense relaxation.* New York: Collier Books, 1968.

Maslow, A. Self-actualization and beyond. In J. F. T. Bugental (Ed.), *Challenges of humanistic psychology.* New York: McGraw-Hill, 1967.

May, R. Love and will. *Psychology Today,* 1969, *3,* 17–64.

Otto, H. *Explorations in human potentialities.* Springfield, Ill.: Charles C Thomas, 1966.

Perls, F. *Gestalt therapy verbatim.* LaFayette, Calif.: Real People Press, 1969.

Rogers, C. Process of the basic encounter group. In J. F. T. Bugental (Ed.), *Challenges of humanistic psychology.* New York: McGraw-Hill, 1967.

Shostrom, E. Group therapy: Let the buyer beware. *Psychology Today,* 1969, *2,* 12, 36–40.

Schutz, W. *Joy.* New York: Grove Press, 1967.

Truax, C. B., & Carkhuff, R. R. *Toward effective counseling and psychotherapy.* Chicago: Aldine, 1967.

39 / THE RESPONSIBILITY OF THE GROUP PSYCHOTHERAPY PRACTITIONER FOR A THERAPEUTIC RATIONALE

Max Rosenbaum

Since the end of World War II, the field of group psychotherapy has grown enormously. A technique which was once used because of the shortage of trained psychotherapists was found to have an essential validity of its own (Mullan & Rosenbaum, 1962). Today, a cursory examination of the literature in the field of group psychotherapy indicates a geometric progression in the amount of articles published each year (Rosenbaum, 1965). From the vantage point of over twenty years of practice in the field of psychoanalytic group psychotherapy, and before this the practice of group psychotherapy based on a variety of theories, the articles seem to be long on the exposition of clinical practice and quite barren with reference to the exposition of theory. Perhaps this is related to American pragmatism or perhaps it is related to the unwillingness of practitioners to face their own responsibility to the science of human behavior.

This is understandable. All too often advocates of dynamic psychotherapy are unreal in their expectation of psychotherapy results and become defensive. They forget that Freud himself did not hold out elaborate promises for the techniques of psychoanalysis and was primarily interested in the research implications of his work. The tedious process of psychoanalytic exploration is often frustrating to psychotherapists. It was probably just as frustrating for Freud. After all, he was essentially interested in research and became a practitioner to earn a living. He was a poor boy and throughout his professional lifetime he was plagued with anxiety about finances.

From JOURNAL OF GROUP PSYCHOANALYSIS AND PROCESS, *1969, Vol. 2, pp. 5–17. Copyright 1969, Association for Group Psychoanalysis and Process, Inc. Reprinted with permission of author and publisher.*

After the ruinous inflation of post World War I, where all of his savings were wiped out, he became particularly concerned about money. He used to communicate with his favorite students and caution them about the economics of life as a private practitioner. He could not look forward to research grants and in Vienna his findings were referred to as "Jewish pornography." Consequently, he does not seem to have been deeply concerned about the problems of the illiterate or the disenfranchised. None of this is meant in a pejorative sense. Freud reflected the culture in which he lived as well as the social strata from which he derived his income. He did not treat Austrian peasants. His colleague, Alfred Adler, was quite another story. Adler was what we would call today a social activist. He was politically sophisticated and gathered around him a group of people who were committed to socialism and the problems of the working class. Adler, rather unkempt in his personal appearance, would finish work and enjoy a coffee at one of the Viennese coffee houses. If he met a patient there he might invite him to his table to speak or break bread. Freud meanwhile was busy at home compiling clinical material and writing papers. Contrast then the fastidious Freud, basically a researcher, with the gregarious Adler, sitting in a coffee house, like as not, with cigar ashes on his clothing, socializing with patients, politically aware and active. The personality clash was bound to obscure the relevance of Adler's contributions and particularly Adler's concern with the community applications of psychoanalytic findings. These historical comments are made to remind the reader that the early advocates of psychodynamic psychotherapy were not naive or unaware. The history of early psychoanalysis is replete with instances of people trying out new and innovative techniques: Groddeck, referred to as the "wild analyst" (1961, 1965); Sandor Ferenczi radically experimenting with technique using prohibitions, commands, and active interference (1933, 1934); Hitschmann (1956) with his biting wit and studies of great men; Pfister (1917) the pastor and educator who introduced psychoanalysis into education and religion; Jones (1959) the adventuresome Welshman who was cruelly maligned in the early years of psychoanalysis and defamed by the charges of two young women in London so that he chose a voluntary exile in Canada for some years; Aichorn (1935) the courageous educator who treated incorrigible youths—working even when Vienna was occupied by Nazis —and so many more innovators. One may ask what relevance this has to current problems of psychotherapy. It has every relevance. For none of these courageous pioneers avoided a basic responsibility of the scientific practitioner. They set down in some coherent form their experiences so that those who followed would be able to compare and test and hopefully form some body of theory. Consider Adler who decided that sitting behind a patient who was reclining on a couch did not promote parity. So he faced the patient and described his method as free discussion and not free association. It is only speculative but was Harry Stack Sullivan aware of Adler's innovative methods? Or was Trigant Burrow (1958) one of the first American psychoanalysts, who also sat in a face to face relationship with patients and who later complained that Sullivan had never acknowledged his indebtedness to Burrow's theoretic constructs? No matter. For all of these men set down a body of information. It is not relevant to set down the order of discovery.

What do we find today? Freud's earlier pessimism about what would happen to psychoanalysis in the USA seems confirmed. He cautioned Theodor Reik about working in the USA and stated that every effort would be made by the American public to make psychoanalysis more palatable. He was concerned about the gimmick quality of America and the way in which pragmatism was invoked to mask sloppy thinking. It is worth noting that Freud was constantly inquiring, honest and creative. He searched but there was a direction to his thinking. This writer has been collecting the literature of group psychotherapy since the end of World War II. Again and again one reads articles that are repetitions of earlier work. Is this merely the information explosion or the problem of information retrieval? Or is this merely the unwillingness of the practitioner to sit down in the library and do the hard and tedious work of studying the literature? It is almost as if every generation of therapists rediscovers the wheel. My first reaction was one of amusement. Was it possible that someone who kissed a patient was unaware of the transference implications? Could all this be written off as spontaneity, warmth and unconditional regard? Did all recent converts to active psychotherapy and community psychotherapy believe that the former generation of psychotherapists were all hiding behind desks or couches? Long before the rage of *Games People Play* (1968) the warm August Aichorn would introduce a young patient with the comment: "Is this one a scamp. If he keeps it up he's going to become a pimp." And the young man replied warmly to Aichorn: "I am a pimp." Or Aichorn would use the terms "adolescent impostor" or "con man." He would celebrate Christmas with his most disturbed young delinquents, give them presents, set up a tree and generally set up an ego model as a loving father. But rather than just set down reminiscences, Aichorn organized his material and discussed the meaning of his work in terms of the transference relationship. In short, he attempted to codify a theoretic structure. Years later, Johnson and Szurek (1948) in their work on anti-social behavior, were able to expand on Aichorn's elaboration of the parental super-ego and its meaning as well as the pressure of transference reactions to modify behavior. We need no new descriptions of working in deprived communities. Aichorn did it. He remained in Austria during the Nazi occupation and ardently pursued his work. After all, he knew the psyche of "criminals" and delinquents and he could cope with the Nazis. Now we need elaboration of the theoretic problems we face as we work in Watts, Harlem, Appalachia and an Indian Reservation.

For this writer there is a thin but definite line that is obscured by the "swinging" practitioners. In the effort to combat the over-emphasis on the "head," they over-emphasize the "gut." There is a precedent as well in the history of psychoanalysis. Wilhelm Reich, a second generation psychoanalyst of the 1920's, broke with Freud as Reich began to espouse more and more concepts which while satisfying to Reich's political conscience, appeared at least to Freud, to vitiate the main thread of Freud's theories and metapsychology. Like many of today's therapists Reich became impatient and uneasy about the effectiveness of a "talking cure," with the emphasis on ideas and information. Finally he developed a method of character analysis with a strong reliance on posture, style of speech, muscular rigidity and so forth. He ultimately gave up the talking cure since he believed that neurotics suffer from unsatisfactory sexual orgasms. He described the energy of the orgasm as "orgone energy" and called this a basic life force. So far so good. It's a concept as good as any. After all, no one has ever seen electricity yet we work with the concept. It was when Reich stated that the "orgone energy" could be trapped in a box he devised and that this energy could be used to treat a variety of physical ills including cancer, that his troubles began with the U.S. Federal Food and Drug Administration. He was accused of peddling a fraud, his orgone energy accumulator. Since Reich was always the defiant one he did not answer the complaint and finally ended up in the federal penitentiary at Lewisburg. He died there in 1957 of a heart attack. So much then for the historic precedent of people who questioned the "talking cure." After all is said and done the head is necessary. Even Wilhelm Reich (1949) stated that a human being is both more retarded in bodily development and consequently more sexually precocious than any other animal.

The purpose of this paper is not to castigate but to enlighten; not to admonish but to inform. The point is that group therapists need to operate on established principles that have been found to be therapeutic through repeated application. Practitioners should be concerned about too much random interaction, and especially the use of techniques that are based on the pathological needs of the group therapist. Infrequently, all too infrequently, more experienced therapists discuss the implications of the therapist touching the patient's body. Frequently they digress from an *ad verbum* approach to an *ad hominem* approach. Thus, Burton and Kantor (1964) while apparently aware of the enormous transference implications of body contact between patient and therapist, generalize with the concept that psychotherapists who do not encourage this contact dislike their bodies at the unconscious level. It only takes a short hop, skip and a jump for these advocates of the theory to conclude that therapists who do not respond physically to patients are bound by their own neurotic problems. But this becomes a kind of playing with words. To illustrate: Psychopharmacologists cannot bear interpersonal relationships and hide behind drugs; interpersonal psychotherapists need human companionship; advocates of video-tape in psychotherapy have unresolved problems of voyeurism; and so on. It appears that the values of humanism that Burton and Kantor espouse, have beclouded their capacity to think through the substantive issues involved. This is the problem with much of what *passes* for group therapy—whether it be labeled as T-group, encounter group, marathon group, sensitivity training or multiple impact therapy. People who either practice or become involved in sensitivity training are confused as to their goals or the problems they attempt to cope with. Any experienced group therapist will note that people who attend sensitivity group meetings expect psychotherapy. Yet as recently as June 1969, the National Training Laboratory Institute News and Reports Newsletter declared flatly in answer to the question: What is the difference between sensitivity training and group therapy? *Sensitivity training is not intended or practiced as a means for correcting significant psychological deficiencies, and persons needing or seeking psychotherapy are discouraged from participating.* This statement, by the responsible organization which promotes sensitivity training does not withstand close examination because in countless educational settings, sensitivity groups are promoted as a form of psychotherapy. And why not? The same NTL Institute describes sensitivity training program as "varying in length from roughly two days to two weeks." Further, it is stated: "The length of a program cannot be considered separately from its goals. Longer programs typically offer broader, deeper and more detailed learnings and practice." It appears to this writer that the wish for "magical aid" helps to becloud theoretic issues that are present when we work with groups. The therapist becomes caught up in the band wagon. The result is theoretic chaos. The focus for many therapists has shifted away from the private and introspective and toward the social and communicative. The premium is on "interpersonal openness," where individuals convey personal feelings and impressions and this is called "growth" and "insight." No amount of touching, inspiration, sub-cultures (see the Esalen fad) can obviate the responsibility for the therapist to have an idea of what he is doing. The idea of "winging it" applies to entertainers but not to serious practitioners of psychotherapy. A further danger arises when therapists who are not too sure of what they are doing, and sureness does not imply inflexibility, become panicked by the mass exodus of patients who have discovered a new panacea for suffering. Intensive psychotherapy was never intended to relieve the world of suffering. Essentially it was intended that the unhappy patient become able to live in a world of grief and despair without faltering in his resolution to face life. There are no easy solutions and therapists deceive themselves as well as their patients when they espouse a clinical technique devoid of a theoretic rationale. After all, what essentially was Freud's great contribution? Quite succinctly, he wrote down what he observed in his clinical practice and tried to make some order and sense out of his clinical observations. Of course he started with an edge, the fact that he was research oriented and essentially interested in research. Practically speaking he does not appear to have been a particularly gifted psychotherapist but this is of little import when one evaluates his genius. But what of his early followers and students? Most of them were astute clinicians but more important they always attempted to codify the clinical material they obtained.

It is a matter of concern for this writer to observe colleagues who espouse concepts they believe to be revolutionary and which are to be found in a cursory reading of the group therapy literature. Enthusiasm is no substitute for thought. Cody Marsh, a minister who became a psychiatrist, has described with great *joie de vivre* his work in the later 1920's and early 1930's (Rosenbaum & Berger,

1962). Through sheer "total push" he managed to involve patients in a variety of activities, extending from readings to tap dancing. He incorporated all conceivable recreational activities in his therapy program, replete with body contact (dancing). His enthusiasm was no substitute for sound theory. How many of the readers have ever heard of Cody Marsh? In this writer's opinion he was another "activist" who didn't conceptualize.

The therapists, busy practicing, claim they are too burdened to conceptualize. They have abdicated responsibility. But why should current research material come from the research of academicians who use samples of college students or industry executives? The abstract answer for some is that study of encounter groups is "not confined to the sick," or so says Burton (1969) who has edited a book on the theory and practice of encounter groups. Further he states that in encounter groups, "the responsibility for growth is actually returned to the individual as his own responsibility." The implication is that psychotherapy in depth does not place responsibility upon the patient. This is certainly a theoretic statement that is easily answered empirically. This writer's conclusion is that afficionados of the encounter group are at best naive if they do not understand the ultimate meaning of a psychotherapy conducted in depth. Further, statements that an encounter group does not deal with "sick" people merely denies the fantasies that bring people to these encounter groups. It is after all, the rare college student who comes to general psychology to study the science of human behavior. In the main he comes to obtain clarification about problems that are "bugging" him. This can easily be validated by college instructors who attempt to give a comprehensive course in general psychology only to find that the students desire to spend the semester or academic year in discussions of personality and clinical material —preferably their own cases. However we "cut the mustard" in the main, encounter group participants see themselves in psychotherapy.

It is only when psychotherapists are informed about their goals and the issues involved that group psychotherapy can be carried out effectively and honestly. No amount of technique gimmickry and quick appeals to the immediate experience will serve as a substitute for a theoretic rationale. There are real research problems. Rotter (1967) in a study of ethnic groups and sensitivity training, found that Jewish students express more interpersonal trust than Protestants and Catholics. What does this say about the ethnic composition of psychotherapy groups? (See Fischer & Winer, 1969.) Argyris (1969) in surveying his research as well as others suggests that in the social psychology of interpersonal relations the infrequent deviant behavior may be the component of "healthy" behavior. Further, students of sensitivity and T-groups note that this may become the new method of manipulating behavior, with little or no awareness of the value systems and normative assumptions involved.

This is probably the crux of the problem. As noted earlier, Freud was always suspicious of the USA taking his depth psychology and making it more palatable—sort of cutting out the guts of it all. Group experiencing without any theoretic structure that just speaks of a "here and now" is palatable treatment. Granted that Freud was chained with his psychoanalytic theory to the biological and physical framework of the early 1900's. This writer has discussed this in detail in other settings (Rosenbaum, 1969). But psychoanalysis was never intended as a cure-all for the problems of human behavior but a presentation of a set of discoveries to help understand human behavior. The problem of immediate "cure" which occupies the time of those who attack depth psychotherapy as well as those who defend it is quite irrelevant to the larger issues of depth therapy which are the re-evaluation of one's own life. Those therapists who look for the cause-effect and cure relationship simply miss the essence of a depth approach to human behavior which emphasizes discoveries. Rogers (1967) senses some of this but treats it too casually when he states: "If a theory is to be held at all, it seems to me it should be held tentatively, lightly, flexibly, in a way which is freely open to change, and should be laid aside in the moment of encounter itself." This is where confusion ensues. A theory cannot be held so lightly that it is floating all over the place, like some oil that has escaped into the ocean from a sea-going tanker. Therapists who are faced with the discouragement that touches all of us who work in depth may find easy solace in the writings of a Jay Haley (1969) who angrily attacks straw men in psychotherapy and speaks of the real work that therapists avoid—namely helping people solve their problems. He stresses efficient and economical approaches in an age of "efficiency." But we can only find solace in such diatribes if we avoid our responsibility to define theoretic structure in our work. If we deeply believe that we are out to relieve symptoms, we must leave a depth psychotherapy and turn to behavior modification techniques. And there too, we shall have to work within a theory. Pavlov did not "wing it." If we want to be known as students of behavior, we have to be something more than proprietors of tea-leaf reading salons. For this writer, only the detailed attention to "why are you here" will answer this question. The emphasis on "what are you feeling" does not preclude our responsibility as practitioners of psychotherapy for helping to continue the map-making as we define human behavior. You can't make up maps without latitude, longitude and points of the compass. Otherwise, we all end up drifting around in a great big ocean.

There are points to be made positively about encounter groups. The advocates of encounter groups force group psychotherapists to think through the scientific underpinnings of psychotherapy. But this does not relieve encounter group enthusiasts from responsibility for defining the "underpinning" of the method. It is refreshing that psychotherapists be challenged. It helps them to fight the complacency and smugness that we may all fall prey to. But it is difficult to evaluate the content and assertions of encounter groups since platitudes while they are palatable are no substitute for specific statements of intent. Some encounter group practitioners perceive participants as essentially "very tough" and people who can be confronted. If this point is spelled out it *may* be put to some clinical test and evaluated by concerned researchers.

What is involved here are value assumptions about human behavior. What are the goals of encounter groups or forms of psychotherapy? Historically, Rank, Ferenczi and Stekel attempted to abbreviate therapy. But they specified what they were doing.

Are we dealing with a type of mass phenomenon when we direct attention to the content and assertions of encounter, sensitivity or marathon groups? Is there a secret, non-verbal agenda in encounter groups? Is this an effort to promote a pseudo-intimacy? Group experiences are very powerful in their impact. What type of impacts are participants experiencing in encounter groups or sensitivity groups and what lessons can psychotherapists learn from observations of these groups? After all psychotherapy is a discipline. For many of us who have been practicing group psychotherapy for some years, the psychoanalytic background is the best map as we practice.

For this writer, let me state that I will accept the technical tools and contributions of advocates of encounter, sensitivity and marathon groups, but will the advocates accept the responsibility to define the system?

Finally, the question is encounter for what? Is this a new religion or a substitute for people who resist exploring value systems? In the spirit of dialogue we must all confront these questions.

REFERENCES

Aichorn, A. *Wayward youth*. New York: Viking Press, 1935.

Argyris, C. The incompleteness of social psychological theory. *American Psychologist*, 1969, *24*, 893–908.

Balint, M. Sandor Ferenczi, obituary, 1933. *International Journal of Psychoanalysis*, 1949, *30*, 215–219.

Berne, E. *Games People Play*. New York: Grove Press, 1968.

Bottome, P. *Alfred Adler: A portrait from life*. New York: Vantage Press, 1957.

Burrow, T. *A search for man's sanity: The selected letters of Trigant Burrow*. New York: Oxford University Press, 1958.

Burton, A. (Ed.) *Encounter: Theory and practice of encounter groups*. San Francisco: Jossey-Bass, 1969.

Burton, A., & Kantor, R. E. The touching of the body. *Psychoanalytic Review*, 1964, *51*, 122–134.

Fischer, E. H., & Winer, D. Participation in psychological research. *Journal of Consulting and Clinical Psychology*, 1969, *33*, 610–613.

Groddeck, G. *The book of the It*. New York: Random House, 1961.

Grossman, C. M., & Grossman, S. *The wild analyst: The life and work of George Groddeck*. New York: George Braziller, 1965.

Haley, J. *The power tactics of Jesus Christ and other essays*. New York: Grossman, 1969.

Hitschmann, E. *Great men*. New York: International Universities Press, 1956.

Johnson, A. M. Sanctions for super-ego lacunae of adolescents. In K. R. Eissler (Ed.), *Searchlights on delinquency*. New York: International Universities Press, 1948.

Jones, E. *Free associations: Memoirs of a psychoanalyst*. London: Hogarth Press, 1959.

Lorand, S. Sandor Ferenczi, obituary. *Journal of Nervous and Mental Diseases*, 1934, *79*, 372–374.

Mullan, H., & Rosenbaum, M. *Group psychotherapy*. New York: The Free Press, 1962.

Pfister, O. *The psychoanalytic method*. New York: Moffat, Yard, 1917.

Reich, W. *Character analysis*. New York: Noonday Press, 1949.

Rogers, C., Stevens, B. et al. *Person to person: The problem of being human*. Walnut Creek, Calif.: Real People Press, 1967.

Rosenbaum, M., & Berger, M. *Group psychotherapy and group function*. New York: Basic Books, 1962.

Rosenbaum, M. Group psychotherapy and psychodrama. In B. Wolman (Ed.), *Handbook of clinical psychology*. New York: McGraw-Hill, 1965.

Rosenbaum, M. Current controversies in psychoanalytic group psychotherapy and what they mask. In L. D. Eron & R. Callahan (Eds.), *The relation of theory to practice in psychotherapy*. Chicago: Aldine, 1969.

Rotter, J. B. A new scale for the measurement of interpersonal trust. *Journal of Personality*, 1967, *35*, 651–665.

The educational method widely known as sensitivity training was introduced in the late 1940's by a group of social scientists who were seeking ways to translate theory and knowledge about human social behavior into more effective individual and group action. These scientists and their associates, for the most part leaders in adult education, systematically observed and reacted to their own behaviors, primarily in small face-to-face groups called training groups, or T Groups. The process came to be called "laboratory method."

In the laboratory method, individuals learn from studying their own behavior and the interaction of members of the group. This includes time spent in the following activities:

1. Members of the group behave and interact in relation to a task or in the development of a more effective group.

2. Data produced by that interaction, including feelings, and reactions of members, are analyzed and related to theory.

3. Members of the group are encouraged to experiment with new kinds of behavior, including taking a variety of different roles.

4. Consideration is given to the relationship of events in the group to the members' everyday life settings.

The behavioral scientists working to develop laboratory method and to apply the emerging theories and techniques in the world of social action organized the NTL Institute in 1947 as the focal agency of their work. The group of scientists, most of them in positions at universities across the country, became known as the "NTL Network."

Today, NTL Institute is one of many organizations providing services based on laboratory method, and elected members of the Institute network now represent only a fraction of those offering to perform these services. Programs based on laboratory method are found in a variety of forms and contexts and under several names. "Sensitivity training" has become the most commonly used generic term for the method.

The rising popularity of laboratory training and the apparent relevance of laboratory method to the solution of human relationship problems in a wide range of social contexts has greatly increased the demand for individuals who can apply the method. In turn, that demand has increased the need for guidelines to protect both prospective clients and the developing profession of applied behavioral science. NTL Institute has therefore undertaken to formulate this statement of standards for its programs and its members.

The Institute believes that the standards presented here are applicable to any program or service based on laboratory method and to any person conducting such a program. However, because the NTL Institute network embraces a wide range of personal styles and interests in a developing field, new questions related to standards continually arise. An annual review of this statement is anticipated.

1. Purpose

The overriding purpose of NTL Institute is constructive societal change. Its programs focus on the development of individual and organizational dynamics to help create organizations that continually promote both personal and social growth. The Institute conducts programs of training, consultation, research, and dissemination. The consultation and training programs, to which these standards are addressed, have the following aims:

To help individuals acquire the experience, knowledge, and skills to increase their creativity in relationships with others.

To help leaders in all walks of life enhance their ability to lead others toward greater individual and social improvement.

To help organizations diagnose human issues and build structures and processes that satisfy both organizational and individual needs.

To help individuals and organizations understand and cope with forces of change and initiate desirable social change using democratic methods.

2. Values

NTL Institute places high value on the following:

The utilization of scientific method and the application of behavioral science knowledge to social problems.

The individual's dignity, his potential for creative living, and his right of choice.

Authenticity in relationships, openness of communication, wide participation in group affairs, development of interpersonal competence, confrontation of issues leading to effective problem solving, and democratic decision making.

3. Program Standards

1. The Institute believes that "laboratory training must operate on the basis of a system of values which emphasizes inquiry, not ideology" and that the appropriate aim of laboratory training is "to enhance the range and validity of alternatives and to improve the processes of choice" (Schein & Bennis, 1965).

2. Institute programs should be directed to the specific purposes and needs of the client group as they are agreed upon by consultant and client. They should be designed to include only those processes and techniques appropriate to the agreed-upon purposes and needs.

3. Both verbal and nonverbal communication techniques are appropriate in laboratory training to the extent that they meet the requirements in (2) above.

4. A central concept of laboratory method is that feelings are relevant to and may either enhance or inhibit learning. It is therefore expected that Institute programs will evoke, recognize, and focus on the emotional reactions of participants as this emphasis is relevant to the specific program goals.

5. Insofar as it is possible to distinguish between education and psychotherapy, NTL Institute programs are applied for educational, not psychotherapeutic purposes. The Institute does not design or conduct programs to cure or alleviate pathological, mental or emotional conditions.

6. All Institute programs should include specific provision for recognizing and dealing with possible participant emotional difficulties. In longer-term residential programs, those provisions should include (a) the designation of a qualified staff member as counselor and (b) a relationship with a local physician for consultation and referral.

7. Recognizing the importance of experimentation to the development of knowledge, NTL Institute approves of experimental approaches in laboratory training to the extent that they are consistent with the standards presented in this paper and in *Ethical Standards of Psychologists*, a publication of the American Psychological Association. (See Appendix for especially relevant passages.)

8. NTL Institute recognizes the importance of furthering participants' application of what they have learned through the laboratory. Participants should be helped to—

   conceptualize their learning

   clarify the extent to which approaches and techniques appropriate to the laboratory setting are also appropriate to daily life

   relate laboratory learning to their daily lives

   recognize the difference between participation in and preparation to conduct training laboratories (See also note, Section 5, item 6.)

9. Because the success of a training or consultation program is highly related to staff effectiveness, Institute programs should have (a) staff members who accept the defined purposes and needs of the client group and the goals of the program and who can be expected to work together effectively; (b) ample opportunities to develop common staff understandings and to resolve differences which may emerge during the program.

10. NTL Institute program announcements should be guided by the standards presented in this paper and the ethical principles on misrepresentation and advertising in the *Ethical Standards of Psychologists*.

4. Selection of Trainees

1. Programs using laboratory method are deemed appropriate for persons of any age, occupation, or educational level, provided they are designed and conducted in keeping with the standards presented in this paper.
2. A person undergoing psychotherapy or intensive counseling should consult his therapist before enrolling in a laboratory training program.
3. Persons in the following categories should not ordinarily participate in a laboratory training program:

   Those whose participation is based primarily on the wishes or demands of another, e.g., an employer, rather than on any degree of personal motivation.

   Those whose goal in participating would be to cure or alleviate a severe mental or emotional disturbance.

   Those with a significant history of incapacitating response to interpersonal stress.

To the limited extent that personal difficulties are predictable and screening procedures make it possible, prospective participants should be screened for these conditions.

5. Standards for Trainers and Consultants

1. NTL Institute endorses the *Ethical Standards of Psychologists* of the American Psychological Association and urges its members to guide their conduct accordingly.
2. In relationships with individual clients and client groups, persons representing NTL Institute are expected to discuss candidly and fully goals, risks, limitations, and anticipated outcomes of any program under consideration.
3. NTL Institute trainers and consultants are expected to endorse the purposes and values and adhere to the standards presented in this paper.
4. NTL Institute trainers and consultants are expected to have mastered the following skills:

   Ability to conduct a small group and to provide individual consultation using the theory and techniques of laboratory method.

Ability to articulate theory and to direct a variety of learning experiences for small and large groups and for organizations.

Ability to recognize their own behavior styles and personal needs and to deal with them productively in the performance of their professional roles.

Ability to recognize symptoms of serious psychological stress and to make responsible decisions when such problems arise.

5. NTL Institute trainers and consultants are expected to have a strong theoretical foundation. This ordinarily implies graduate work in a behavioral science discipline or equivalent experience in the field.

6. NTL Institute trainers and consultants are expected to complete the following training experiences:

Participation in at least one NTL Institute basic Human Relations laboratory.

Supervised co-training with senior staff members.

Participation on laboratory staff with experienced trainers in programs for a variety of client groups.

Participation in an NTL Institute or university program specifically designed to train trainers.

NOTE: Basic human relations laboratories, executive development programs, and similar beginning-level programs are designed to help participants be more effective in personal and job roles, not to become trainers. No capabilities as a T-Group trainer or consultant should be assumed as a result of participation in one or more basic laboratories or other short-term experiences.

7. NTL Institute trainers and consultants are expected to continually evaluate their own work, to seek individual growth experiences, and to contribute to the evaluation and development of the art and science of training and consultation.

6. Guidelines for Evaluating Competence

The following questions are suggested as an approach to evaluating groups or individuals offering services using laboratory method and its derivatives:

How do the education and training of staff members compare with the standards listed in this paper?

Are the services and programs regularly evaluated, and is evidence of such evaluations available?

What controls and standards does the group utilize to assure adherence to ethics?

Is the staff able and willing to articulate the rationale for the approaches and design elements it utilizes?

Does the group have experience in working with similar clients?

REFERENCE

Schein, E. H., & Bennis, W. G. *Personal and Organizational Change Through Group Methods.* New York: Wiley, 1965.

ADDITIONAL REFERENCES

Batchelder, R. L., & Hardy, J. M. *Using sensitivity training and the laboratory method.* New York: Association Press, 1968.

Bradford, L. P., Gibb, J. R., & Benne, K. D. *T-group theory and laboratory method: Innovation in reeducation.* New York: Wiley, 1964.

Nylen, D. J., Mitchell, J. R., & Stout, A. *Handbook of staff development and human relations training: Material developed for use in Africa.* Washington, D.C.: National Training Laboratories, 1967.

Wechsler, I. R., & Schein, E. H. *Issues in training.* Washington, D.C.: National Training Laboratories, 1962.

Appendix

A list of principles from the *Ethical Standards of Psychologists* of the American Psychological Association considered relevant to NTL Institute trainers and consultants.

PRINCIPLE 2B. COMPETENCE

The psychologist recognizes the boundaries of his competence and the limitations of his techniques and does not offer services or use techniques that fail to meet professional standards established by recognized specialists in particular fields. The psychologist who engages in practice assists his client in obtaining professional help for all important aspects of his problem that fall outside the boundaries of his own competence. This principle requires that provision be made for the diagnosis and treatment of relevant medical problems.

Principle 3. Moral and Legal Standards

The psychologist in the practice of his profession shows sensible regard for the social codes and moral expectations of the community in which he works, recognizing that violations of accepted moral and legal standards on his part may involve his clients, students, or colleagues in damaging personal conflicts, and impugn his own name and the reputation of his profession.

Principle 4a. Misrepresentation

A psychologist does not claim either directly or by implication professional qualifications that exceed his actual qualifications, nor does he misrepresent his affiliation with any institution, organization, or individual, nor lead others to assume he has affiliations that he does not have. The psychologist is responsible for correcting others who misrepresent his professional qualifications or affiliations.

Principle 7. Client Welfare

The psychologist respects the integrity and protects the welfare of the person or group with whom he is working.

Principle 10. Advertising

A psychologist who advertises or makes public announcement of his services, describes them with accuracy and dignity, adhering to professional rather than to commercial standards.

Principle 11. Interprofessional Relationship

A psychologist does not normally offer professional services to a person who is receiving psychological assistance from another professional worker except by agreement with the other worker or after the termination of the client's relationship with the other professional worker.

Index